Home Office of the Company, 346 & 348 Broadway, New York.

SEMI-CENTENNIAL HISTORY

OF THE

NEW-YORK LIFE INSURANCE COMPANY

1845–1895

By

JAMES M. HUDNUT

NEW YORK
PUBLISHED BY THE COMPANY
1895

TO

THE AGENTS OF THE COMPANY—
LIVING AND DEAD—WHOSE
LABORS CONSTITUTE A
HISTORY TOO VOLU-
MINOUS TO BE
WRITTEN,

THIS VOLUME IS RESPECTFULLY
INSCRIBED.

PREFACE.

WHILE I have endeavored to set forth in their order the dominant facts pertaining to the history of the NEW-YORK LIFE INSURANCE COMPANY, as seen from the Home Office, I am conscious that the greater part of the work involved in the upbuilding of such an organization, and the greater part of the benefits conferred on the community by its operations, are beyond the power of my pen to describe. The history of a great army can only give an outline of its organization, campaigns, victories and losses; it cannot take account of the toils, the sufferings, the hopes and the fears of the hundred thousand individuals of which the army is composed. The labors of a large corps of faithful agents during half a century; the motives that have induced the application for over six hundred thousand policies of insurance, each one of which had in view certain benefits to others in the event of the applicant's death while the policy was in force; the benefits actually received by reason of payments aggregating nearly two hundred million dollars, over half of which was paid in death-claims and endowments;—these are the things that can never be described by mortal man, and yet they all belong to the history of the NEW-YORK LIFE INSURANCE COMPANY.

Every great corporation is the product of two forces—the one internal, the other external—the management, and the times in which it has its existence. It did not seem possible, therefore, to write a history of the NEW-YORK LIFE INSURANCE COMPANY without making copious references to the history of Life Insurance during the last half century and to the conditions by which its growth has been affected. The log-book of a ship makes mention of the weather, as well as of the distance sailed, and sometimes the best of seamanship avails but little save to keep the vessel to her course. The life companies of fifty years' standing have sailed over stormy seas, and it is not a little to the credit of their managers to have brought their precious cargoes safely into port. They have shown themselves skillful seamen, not only in breasting financial storms, but also in taking advantage of fair weather. The references to contemporaneous history have added considerably to the size of this work, and I trust will add something to the interest of those who may be its readers.

Acknowledgments are due, for information furnished, to Hon. Carroll D. Wright, Commissioner of Labor, in charge of the Eleventh Census; Hon. James H. Eckels, Comptroller of the Currency; Hon. W. J. Harris, United States Commissioner of Education; Hon. Charles Preston, Superintendent Banking Department, State of New York; Daniel O'Dell, Esq., formerly the Company's Superintendent of Agencies; and to the Editors of the "World Almanac" and of the "Iron Age"; also to the Librarian of Columbia College, for courtesies extended; and to the Equitable Life Assurance Society, for free access to the "Walford Library."

J. M. H.

New York, November, 1895.

CONTENTS.

CHAPTER I.

Charter and Organization.

PAGE.
Acts of May 21, 1841, and April 18, 1843 1
Election of the first Board of Trustees 2
Election of Officers and issue of first Policy 2
Name changed by Act of April 5, 1849 3
General powers under the Charter 3
Amended Charter of 1893 3
Subscription Notes—list of—how used 4
Dividends—how to be made and redeemed 5
Advertisement of the Company, August 14, 1845 6

CHAPTER II.

Life Insurance in 1845.

Life companies doing business in the United States in 1845 7
Early history of life companies in Philadelphia 7
Companies in Massachusetts and in the South 8–9
The New York Life and Trust Company 9
Report of President Bard on Mutual Insurance 10
The *Magna Charta* of Life Insurance 11
Organization of the Mutual Life 11
English life companies in 1845 12

CHAPTER III.

The United States in 1845.

Constituency and population of the Union 13
Political questions of the time 13
Men prominent in public life 14
Means of communication 17
Postal and telegraphic systems 17
An agricultural people 18
Growth in elements of civilization 18
Increase of the humane spirit 19
Relation of changes to Life Insurance 19

CHAPTER IV.

The First Thousand Policies.

PAGE.

First office at 58 Wall Street 20
First Policy and Application forms 20
Policy conditions and limit of risk 21
Extra premiums charged 22
Slave policies—first death-claim 22
Schuyler Colfax appointed agent 23
Business of first year—first dividend 24
Premium notes authorized to be taken 25
Tabular history of first 1,000 policies 25
Early policies in force in 1894 26
Portraits of two policy-holders insured in 1845 26–8

CHAPTER V.

The First Million Dollars.

1845–1855.

Mr. Merchant elected President 29
Mr. Franklin succeeds Mr. Merchant as President 29
Notable men brought into the Company's service 29
Efforts to increase the business 30
Interest paid on dividends 30
Office removed to 68 Wall Street 30
Traveling agents appointed 32
Changes in the Vice-Presidency 32
Business year made from January 1 to December 31 32
Prevalence of cholera in 1849 32
Company's action re cholera, and deaths from 32
Special Agency Committee and appointments 33
California risks 34
Yellow fever and rates in Southern sea-ports 35
Suicide clause eliminated from policy 35
Subscription notes canceled 35
Removal to 106 Broadway 35
Premium notes exchanged for dividends on lapsed policies 36
Re-insurance of the Phœnix Insurance Company of St. Louis 37
Deposit law of April 8, 1851 37
Massachusetts law of 1852 38
General decline of life insurance business 38
Reports required of life companies under laws of 1849 and 1851 39
New-York Life's report criticised 39
First valuation of policies 40
Comptroller certifies to Company's solvency 40
Yellow fever in 1853; yellow fever losses 41

PAGE.
Life Insurance promoted by higher elements of character 43
Yellow fever at Norfolk and Portsmouth, Va., in 1855 43
Extra rates on Southern risks 43
Eleventh annual report shows assets $1,059,008.65 44

CHAPTER VI.

Non-Forfeiting Policies and the Redemption of Dividends.

1856–1860.

Laws governing life insurance companies, 1855–60 46
Financial crisis of 1857 49
Purchase of property 112 and 114 Broadway 49
Distribution of business and losses 50
Canadian agency opened and closed 50
Redemption of dividends discussed and postponed 51
Report of Examining Board on Mutual Life's dividends 51
Attempts at fraud on the Company 53
Pike's Peak risks and hand-bill 53
American Life Underwriters' Convention 53
California agency and rates 57
Comparison of Northern and Southern business 58
Second meeting of Life Underwriters' Convention 58
Discussion on non-forfeiting policies 59
Customs of the companies 60
The New-York Life issues a non-forfeiting policy 63
An Epoch in Life Insurance 63
Subscriptions for Post Office and Captain Wilson 63
Question of war risks raised and postponed 64
Plan for redemption of dividends adopted 65
Table of life insurance business for 1860 66

CHAPTER VII.

Period of the Civil War.

1861–1865.

Perplexities of the life companies 68
Fidelity of Southern agents 68
Business continued until forbidden 69
Inquiries of Southern policy-holders 70
A prophetic letter 70
An inquiry from Fort Sumter 71
The companies decide to issue war permits 73
Status of Southern policies 74
Business interrupted by war preparations 76
"Home Guard" permits granted free 77
Effect of secession on the Company's policies 79

PAGE.
Effect of proclamations and court decisions 81
Mails to seceded States discontinued 82
Exchange on New York at a high premium 83
The "American Letter Express" 84
Commercial intercourse with the South forbidden 85
Hard times at the North 86
Liberal measures of the Company 87
Subscription for Sanitary Commission 88
First investment in Treasury Notes 89
Annual report for 1861 90
Taxation of life companies by Congress 91
Resumption of business in Norfolk 92
Resumption of business in New Orleans 94
Dr. Copes' retrospect in 1879 95
An inquiry from Mobile *via* Havana 96
"Home Guard" permits for Baltimore policy-holders 98, 104–6
Colonel Donnelly's war permit 99
Business in Norfolk 100
Annual report for 1862 101
Death of General Agents; war losses 102
Liability for "scrip dividends" 103
Claim paid under Mobile policy 104
Policy heading used in 1863 105
Resignation of Actuary Freeman 107
Annual report for 1863 107
Construing the non-forfeiture clause 108
Mr. Beers elected Actuary 108
Increasing competition for business and agents 109
"Home Guard" permits issued in 1864 110
War losses paid in 1864 111
Annual report for 1864 113
First letters from Savannah and Richmond 114
First letters from Mobile and other Southern cities 116
Re-instatement of Southern policies 117
War losses paid in 1865 118
Review of the Company's war experience 119
Business of all companies in 1865 120

CHAPTER VIII.

From Peace to the Panic.

1866–1873.

Industrial and commercial activity 121
Extension of the Company's business **122**
Agents and taxes in the South 122–3

PAGE.
Commissions and extra rates 123
Distribution of the Company's business 125
Copy of application attached to policy 126
Plans for building at 346 and 348 Broadway 126
Contribution plan of distributing surplus adopted 127
Flood and yellow fever in Louisiana 129
Issue of a "Return-Premium Endowment Policy" 130
Annual report for 1867 131
Increase in the executive staff 131
Volume I., Number 1, "New-York News-Letter" 132
Letter from Bishop Green, of Mississippi 133
The "Southern Department" established 134
The Company enters Canada 134
Death of Mr. George I. Richardson 135
A competitive circular of the time 136
Annual report for 1868 138
Redemption of dividends completed 138
Re-insurance of Southern Life Assurance and Trust Co. 140
Extension of the Company's business westward 140
"Black Friday" and profits on gold 141
Notable claims paid in 1869 143
Business extended to Pacific coast and to Europe 144
The Home Office moves to 346 and 348 Broadway 145
Competition in the South 146
Payment of General Thomas' policy 149
Surplus by three different standards 149
First death-claim paid in England 150
Issue of the "Ten-Year Dividend Policy" 150
Life companies' suggestions to Insurance Commissioners 151
Death of Mr. Henry A. Dyer 152
Contribution to Chicago fire sufferers 153
Letter of Rev. Edward Everett Hale 154
Issue of the "Tontine Investment Policy" 155
The cash surrender value feature 156
Approval of eminent actuaries 158
The Mutual Life proposes to reduce premium rates 159
Opposition of eighteen other companies 160
The Colvocoresses case 161
Disasters of 1873 on sea and land 162
Southern coast mortality and rates 164
Laws governing the purchase of wives' policies 165
Financial panic of 1873 166
Business of all companies in 1873 166
Agencies returning over $100,000 in 1870 and 1873 167

CHAPTER IX.

EFFECT OF THE PANIC ON LIFE INSURANCE.

1874–1879.

PAGE.
Commercial and financial failures 168
A "Life Insurance Tree" ..... following page 168
Life Insurance failures 169
Public hostility to Life Insurance 170
The "Chamber of Life Insurance" 171
Cartoon ridiculing the companies 172
Examinations by Insurance Department 173
Abuses of receiverships 174
Business of the companies 175
Effect on the NEW-YORK LIFE 176
Withdrawal from California 177
Frauds in Ireland 177
Spanish-American Department established 178
The Custer massacre and death-claims 178
Attempt to blackmail the Company 180
A forged check 182
A legislative inquiry 183
A bogus interview printed in the "Herald" 184
Superintendent's report on the Company 185
The Company withdraws from Canada 187
The Company re-enters California 187
Notable policies paid 188
Enlargement of the Home Office 190
Belated and insufficient legislation 190
Business of all companies in 1879 192

CHAPTER X.

TEN YEARS OF RAPID GROWTH.

1880–1889.

A period of industrial and commercial prosperity 193
Prosperity of Life Insurance 195
Results under old, and new, policies 197
Important bills fail of passage 197
A policy-holder's letter 198
Results under Ten-Year Dividend Policies 200
Notable claims paid in 1881 202
Letter from Mrs. Garfield 203
Results under 10-year Tontine policies 206
Purchase of an office building in Paris 209

	PAGE.
Other office buildings in Europe	210
Business of the Paris office 1876–1882	210
The Company's Paris Building	211
A false report contradicted	212
Contested claims in 1882	212
The Company's Amsterdam Building	213
The Company's Berlin Building	215
The Company's Vienna Building	217
Attacks on the Tontine plan of insurance	217
The Company's Budapest Building	219
Death of Dr. Charles Wright	221
Dr. Henry Tuck elected Second Vice-President	221
Issue of the "Non-Forfeiting Limited-Tontine Policy"	222
An old farce re-enacted	223
Death of Trustee William Barton	223
The limit of risk increased to $100,000	224
Property saved from tax sale	224
An anti-Tontine crusade	225
Investigation by the New York Assembly	226
Investigation by the Ohio Senate	227
Report of the Ohio Senate Committee	228
Issue of a "Five-Year Dividend Policy"	231
Death of President Franklin	231
Mr. Beers elected President	233
Issue of the "Non-Forfeiting Tontine Limited-Endowment"	233
Superintendent McCall investigates Tontine accounts	234
Notable claims paid in 1886	235
Office Buildings erected in the West	237
The Company's Kansas City Building	238
The Company's Omaha Building	239
The Company's St. Paul Building	240
The Company's Montreal Building	241
The Company's Minneapolis Building	242
Repeal of the law taxing income of life companies	243
Fifteen-year Tontine policies mature	244
Charges of mismanagement	245
Report of Investigating Committee	246
Issue of the "Insurance Bond with Guaranteed Interest"	247
Issue of the "Non-Forfeiting Free Tontine Policy"	248
Notable claims paid in 1888	248
An "incontestable clause" authorized	249
Anti-rebate law passed	250
The Johnstown disaster	251
A relic of the Johnstown flood	252
Issue of the "Distribution Policy"	253

PAGE.
Exhibits sent to the Paris Exposition 254
A Silver Medal awarded the Company 256
Notable claims paid in 1889.... 256
Paris Exhibits in miniature....257-9-61-3-5
Death of Mr. H. S. Homans.... 260
The Company's assets exceed $104,000,000.... 262
A ten years' review.... 266
Business of 1889.... 267

CHAPTER XI.

A Period of Change.

1890–1895.

Controversy over the Distribution Policy.... 269
Copy of the Policy 272
The Budapest Building authorized 273
Notable claims paid in 1890 273
The Merzbacher defalcation 276
An official examination requested 277
A five years' review 278
Results under 20-year Tontine policies.... 280
Report of the Superintendent of Insurance 280
Action of the Trustees on the report.... 283
Review of the report by Mr. Beers 284
Mr. Beers resigns 285
Hon. John A. McCall elected President 289
Mr. McCall's address to the Trustees and Agents 292
Address to the policy-holders.... 295
Reörganization of the executive staff.... 297
President McCall meets the Western agents.... 298
Reörganization of the Board of Trustees 299
Reörganization of Home Office 300
Death of Mr. J. Fisher Smith 301
Montreal Convention 301
Mr. Beers' contract referred to the courts 302
Issue of the "Accumulation Policy" 303
Services of agents recognized 306
"Certificate of Merit and Appreciation".... 307
A "Surprise Party".... 308
The "Principle of Steady Production" 310
"A Christmas Greeting" to agents 311
Changes in method of making annual report 313
Enlargement of the Home Office.... 315
President's address to Western agents 316
Convention of agents in London 318

PAGE.
President McCall's address before Columbian Insurance Congress.............. 320
NEW-YORK LIFE'S Columbian Convention 321
Action of the Convention on rebates 322
President McCall's address on form of report 323
President McCall's letter on rebates 325
The Company's Columbian Exhibit.. 328
Awards at Chicago and San Francisco 335
Death of Mr. Beers 338
President McCall's "Special Bulletin" 339
Action of the Board of Trustees.. 342
The Roach law and the Missouri Insurance Department....................... 343
Reviewing the work of 1893.. 346
The new methods vindicated 350
"A campaign of education" 351
The "Seven States' Examination" 351
Methods of the Agency Department 355
Distribution of the Company's business.................................... 356
President McCall on the expense question 357
Commissioners' Certificate 359
Death of Auditor James A. Brown 360
Mr. John C. Whitney appointed Auditor 361
The Vice-President visits foreign agencies 361
The Company's report for 1894... 361
Issue of the "Registered Bond Policy"..................................... 363
Death of Associate Actuary Horace C. Richardson........................... 364
The "Golden Policy," *fac-simile*...............................following page 364
Classification of extra-hazardous risks................................... 365
Fiftieth anniversary of organization...................................... 366
Registered Bond, *fac-simile* ....following page 366
President McCall's address on fiftieth anniversary........................ 368
First annual report... 370
Resumé of receipts and expenditures, 1845-1894........................... 371
Commemorative lines 372
Business of the Company, 1890-1894 373
Business of all life companies in New York, 1894.......................... 374

CHAPTER XII.

RETROSPECT—PROSPECT.

The changes of fifty years, character of................................. 375
The reserve fund, nature and treatment of................................. 375
Growth of non-forfeiture customs.. 376
Loans on policies 376
Application of theories of mortality...................................... 377

PAGE.
Application of investment theories........ 379
Conditions of future progress........ 380
Two prominent elements of Life Insurance........ 380
Moral laws underlying Life Insurance........ 381

APPENDIX.

Statistical notes........ 383
Tables of Income and Disbursements........ 387
Tables of Insurance, Assets, Surplus, etc........ 389
First premium table used by the Company........ 390
Classification of deaths........ 391
Trustees of the Company, 1845-1894........ 392
Currency of the United States in 1845, by James De P. Ogden........ 395

LIFE INSURANCE

Makes scientific adjustment between the possibilities and probabilities, the accidents and averages of life. It enables the individual to merge his constant liability to death in the average longevity of the race, and to share in the productiveness of life in general, whatever may be his own fate. It discounts probability and gives certainty.

In its adaptations to practical life and finance, Life Insurance enlists the cumulative power of small investments through long periods of time, and utilizes the far-off interest of prudence for present needs. It applies scientific method to those impulses of generosity which would otherwise encourage improvidence, and provides for the needs of all through the love of each for his own. It gives affection a place to stand and a lever with which to work. It transforms forethought and good-will into practical helpfulness and well-being. It enables us to realize for our loved ones the hopes we cherish for their future, which might otherwise be blighted by death.

To the husband and father Life Insurance is duty, opportunity, partnership with vast and indestructible forces, guaranty of average success in a field where individual failures are sure to be many and disastrous. Under all Accumulation and Endowment forms, it is protection for loved ones during a term of years, and benefit to the insured in case of survival; it is manhood and middle age relieved from anxiety, and old age relieved from want. To the wife and mother it is protection, security, the fulfillment of marriage vows, the assurance of love stronger than life and over which death has no power. It bridges over the abyss of poverty that may at any time open for herself and her children, the fear of which causes many an anxious hour. To children it is guardianship, the pledge of support and of the continuance of educational and social advantages, until they are prepared to take up the burdens of life with adequate preparation and strength.

Founded in the nature and needs of man, allied to the most persistent forces in the business world, adapted to circumstances the most common, ministering to ends the most dear, approved by the wisest, and patronized by the best, of men—Life Insurance fulfills a mission without parallel in the financial world.

PRESIDENT NEW-YORK LIFE INSURANCE COMPANY, APRIL 12, 1845—APRIL 19, 1847.

SEMI-CENTENNIAL HISTORY

OF THE

NEW-YORK LIFE INSURANCE COMPANY.

I.

CHARTER AND ORGANIZATION.

UNTIL the adoption of the State Constitution of 1846, all charters for insurance companies were granted by special Acts of the Legislature. The initial enactment, out of which the NEW-YORK LIFE INSURANCE COMPANY finally grew, was an Act passed May 21, 1841, authorizing the establishment in the City of New York of an insurance company for marine, inland navigation and transportation, and fire risks, to be called the "NAUTILUS INSURANCE COMPANY." Messrs. Addison Dougherty, J. B. Nones, D. A. Cushman, H. W. Childs, Caleb S. Woodhull and William V. Brady were named in the Act commissioners to receive subscriptions to the capital stock of the Company, which was fixed for purposes of organization at two hundred thousand dollars. Two years were allowed for organization. Just before the two years expired (April 18, 1843) the original Act was so amended as to allow the Company, "in addition to their chartered rights, the privilege of organizing and doing business under the plan of mutual insurance, and for that purpose to have and enjoy a charter similar in every respect to that of the New York Mutual Insurance Company," a corporation authorized by an Act passed April 12, 1842, with power to do life, fire and marine insurance. The commissioners named in the Act of May 21, 1841, were continued, and they were authorized to organize the Company when applications for insurance amounting to $300,000 had been received. Two years from the date of the amended Act were allowed for organization. The records of the Company show that on April 10, 1845, a meeting of Commissioners Woodhull, Brady, Childs and Nones was held at the office of John N. Taylor, Esq., No. 3 Nassau Street, and it was voted that, "applications in excess of the amount required having been received and approved, and notice for the election of twenty trustees and three inspectors to preside at the next annual election having been duly published," the poll be opened for such election. Upon closing the poll the commissioners certified to the election of the following persons:

TRUSTEES.

JAMES BROWN,	JOHN CRYDER,	EDWARD C. CENTER,
WM. H. ASPINWALL,	SCHUYLER LIVINGSTON,	EDWARD F. SANDERSON,
HENRY W. HICKS,	SPENCER S. BENEDICT,	PROSPER M. WETMORE,
THOMAS W. LUDLOW,	DAVID A. COMSTOCK,	RICHARD IRVIN,
LEONARD SUAREZ,	ALMER REED,	JAMES REYBURN,
ADAM NORRIE,	ALBERT WOODHULL,	ROBERT L. TAYLOR,
THOMAS B. RICHARDS,		LORING ANDREWS.

INSPECTORS.

WILLIAM W. HOWLAND,	JAMES MAIRS,	ADAM M. FREEMAN.

At a meeting of the Trustees, held April twelfth, at the office of the Contributionship Insurance Co., 57 Wall Street, James De Peyster Ogden was elected President, A. M. Merchant Vice-President, and Lewis Benton was appointed Secretary. The Board adjourned, to meet on the sixteenth, at 15 Wall Street, the office of the President, at which time Pliny Freeman was appointed Actuary, to take charge of the Life Insurance Department. On the seventeenth, Policy No. 1 for $5,000 on the life of Lewis Benton and Policy No. 2 for $5,000 on the life of Pliny Freeman, were issued, and thus the long and glorious record began. Two fire risks were also taken for one year from April sixteenth, one for $5,000 at fifty cents per $100, on merchandise in stores at 219 Greenwich Street and 71 Barclay Street, and one for $500 at thirty-five cents per $100, on furniture in residence at 27 Hudson Street; but the By-Laws reported by a Committee appointed

June second restricted the business of the Company to "insurance on life and all and every insurance pertaining to life," and the two fire risks were re-insured in the Alliance Mutual Fire Insurance Company.

By an Act of the Legislature, passed April 5, 1849, the name of the Company was changed to "NEW-YORK LIFE INSURANCE COMPANY," and the scope of its authority was enlarged to include the power to "make and execute trusts," thus giving it all the privileges of a trust company, which it still retains and exercises, as occasion demands, in the interest of its policy-holders. Under this provision money is received by the Company as Trustee, whether from insurance under a policy or otherwise, and paid to beneficiaries as designated. Money thus deposited with the Company is protected by the laws applying to trust funds.

The Acts of May 21, 1841, and of April 12, 1842, authorized the establishment of a corporation "to continue thirty years," and the Legislature might at any time alter or repeal the charter thereby granted; but, by Section 20, Chapter 463, of the Laws of 1853, it was provided that, every charter created by or under the laws of this State for the purposes of life, health, or casualty insurance should continue until repealed. By the "Insurance Law" of 1892, and the amendments thereto, approved May 18, 1893, any domestic corporation then existing was allowed to amend its charter, or to adopt in whole or in part a new charter in accordance with the statute, with the approval of the Superintendent of Insurance; and upon such adoption and consent, and upon filing a copy of the new or amended charter with the record of adoption and consent in the office of the Superintendent of Insurance, such corporation was authorized to enjoy the same perpetually, and declared to be a continuation of the corporation which existed prior to such re-incorporation. In accordance with these provisions of law the Board of Trustees adopted a new charter July 12, 1893, embodying in a single document the authority necessary to carry on the business of the Company. This charter was certified by the Attorney-General of the State to be in accordance with the law, on July 26, 1893, and received the consent of the Superintendent of Insurance on the same day, upon being filed in the Insurance Department.

The original charter of the Company provided that, for the better security of its policy-holders, it might receive notes for premiums in advance, of persons intending to receive its policies, and might negotiate such notes for the purpose of paying claims or otherwise in the course of its business; and that upon such portion of said notes as should exceed the amount of premiums paid by the respective signers thereof, a compensation not to exceed five per cent. per annum might be allowed and paid from time to time. The total amount of the original subscription notes was $55,815.25.*

These notes were to be given up and canceled when the accumulations of the Company reached two hundred thousand dollars. Of the fifty-six original subscribers forty-six took policies in the Company, and

---

*SUBSCRIPTION NOTES RECEIVED "IN ANTICIPATION OF PREMIUMS AND TO CONSTITUTE A CAPITAL."

Name	Amount	Name	Amount
A. M. Merchant,	$2,500.00	George Whitaker,	$500.00
R. E. Purdy,	3,000.00	William Storie,	500.00
Lewis Benedict & Co.,	3,000.00	Joseph Nelson,	500.00
David A. Comstock,	2,500.00	Joseph Chamberlain,	500.00
John M. Flint,	1,000.00	R. C. Root & Co.,	500.00
Alfred Freeman, M. D.,	5,000.00	Edward Pierce,	500.00
Truman Roberts,	1,000.00	George Cox,	500.00
A. M. Freeman & Co.,	1,000.00	A. B. Tripler,	500.00
John T. Gilchrist,	250.00	R. H. Brinckerhoff,	500.00
John Rice,	300.00	Lewis Benton,	500.00
Edward Kellogg,	500.00	James P. Wallace,	500.00
Lord, Warren, Salters & Co.,	500.00	John J. Bryant,	500.00
Orsamus Bushnell,	1,000.00	John McMichael,	250.00
George H. Ellery,	350.00	H. A. Hughson,	250.00
John V. Richardson,	500.00	James B. Douglass,	1,250.00
Samuel S. Hill,	5,000.00	Nathan W. Easton,	500.00
William Salisbury,	2,000.00	Edgar Van Kleeck,	500.00
John Mairs,	5,000.00	H. F. Colesworthy,	300.00
John W. Martin,	2,000.00	James Lawson,	300.00
I. N. Taylor,	1,000.00	John J. Storm,	250.00
Caspar W. Wever,	1,000.00	Henry A. Nelson,	500.00
G. Pitt Stevenson,	500.00	Jeremiah M. Wardwell,	250.00
P. M. Wetmore,	500.00	J. B. Nones,	500.00
N. Carroll,	500.00	Thos. N. Ayers,	1,200.00
W. H. Townsend,	500.00	C. Henry Edwards,	250.00
G. H. Tracy,	1,000.00	Conrad Teese,	250.00
O. S. Fowler,	1,000.00	Joseph Hollingsworth,	250.00
Franklin Whiting,	500.00	Elias T. Aldrich,	115.25
			$55,815.25

on June second the Board of Trustees fixed the amount of the notes to be held at $50,000. The notes were to mature in one year, and at the end of the year settlement was made of the premiums chargeable against them and new notes were given. Notes which, through changes of business standing, became unnegotiable, were returned to the makers and others secured in their place. No compensation was made to the signers until December, 1847, when it was voted to pay them five per cent. per annum, in accordance with the charter. This was continued until November 30, 1850, when, the cash assets of the Company being in excess of $200,000, the notes were given up and canceled.

The makers of these subscription notes acquired no special rights in the Company which, from its inception was made a purely mutual organization. By the amended charter of 1843 "every person having taken a policy during the preceding year, and every person holding in his own name certificates of dividends declared" to the amount of one hundred dollars, was to be deemed a member of the Company and entitled to vote in person or by proxy at all elections. This feature was re-affirmed in the amendatory act of 1849, and was extended to cover running policies, by the provision that "each insured member for any sum paid in or secured as a premium of insurance to said Company during the year preceding such election shall have one vote either in person or by proxy," and certificate holders were allowed one vote for each hundred dollars in certificates held.

Dividends were to be made annually from premiums earned, after deducting losses and expenses, and certificates were to be issued for the same for amounts of ten dollars and multiples thereof. Dividends for smaller amounts were credited on the books of the Company. While outstanding these certificates might, at the discretion of the Trustees, bear interest at a rate not exceeding six per cent. per annum, and were to be liable for losses until redeemed. The Trustees were authorized to begin their redemption, in the order of issue, when the sum outstanding should exceed $500,000, and were required to do so when the sum outstanding should exceed $1,000,000. An advertisement of the Company published in the "Evening Mirror" of August 14th, 1845, says: "This Company, recently organized upon the improved and deservedly popular plan of Mutual Assurance, commences with a capital of $50,000, which will be continually augmenting as its business increases. One of the peculiar advantages attending insurance with this Company is that, all the assured share annually in its profits and are interested in its success. The earned premiums or profits will be safely invested by the Company, constituting a permanent fund annually augmenting for the benefit and security of all parties interested."

However sanguine may have been the hopes of the promoters of the infant Company, we may be sure none of them dreamed that its fiftieth year would show over forty-five million dollars paid in dividends, and accumulations "for the benefit and security of all interested" of one hundred and sixty-two millions more!

II.

LIFE INSURANCE IN 1845.

THE "NAUTILUS (MUTUAL LIFE) INSURANCE COMPANY"—as the early title ran—being now fairly launched, let us look about a little and consider upon what sort of sea it is to sail. When the NAUTILUS issued its first policy, there were in the United States eleven American companies and one English company doing a general life insurance business, and two corporations which issued insurances and granted annuities for the benefit of the families of clergymen. Eight of these organizations were trust companies, as well, and four of them still survive as such, having ceased to take life risks. The three companies which confined their operations to life insurance had all been organized during the preceding two and a-half years.

The earliest life policies issued in this country were written by fire insurance companies and by individual underwriters. The earliest life companies were stock companies, and usually combined with their life business either a trust business or a fire insurance business. Life policies were mostly for short periods, the early premium tables providing for one year policies, seven-year policies, and whole life policies. The first company organized to do a general life insurance business was the Pennsylvania Company for Insurance on Lives and Granting Annuities, which was incorporated by the Legislature of Pennsylvania in 1812. The Girard Life Insurance, Annuity and Trust Company, organized in Philadelphia in 1836, issued 248 policies during the first ten months of its existence, and seems to have done most of the life business in Philadelphia thereafter until after 1845. It was the first life company in this country to share profits with policy-holders, and declared its first dividend December 27, 1844, in the form of reversionary insurance payable with the policy. On January 1, 1845, the Pennsylvania Company announced that thereafter all premiums for one or more years would entitle the policy-holder to a credit of one-half the profits; certificates of profits to be issued every five years, or oftener, and to bear interest at six per cent. until redeemed. The first dividend, declared five years later, was paid in cash. This was the beginning of reversionary, and cash, dividends in American life insurance.

The Massachusetts Hospital Life Insurance Company (1818–23) was required by its charter to pay the Massachusetts Hospital one-third of the net profits on its life business, after deducting legal interest on its paid-up

THE FOLLOWING TABLE GIVES, AS NEARLY AS CAN BE ASCERTAINED, THE BUSINESS OF ALL THE COMPANIES DURING THE YEAR NEXT PRECEDING APRIL, 1845:

Incorporated.	NAME OF ORGANIZATION.	POLICIES ISSUED.		POLICIES IN FORCE.		Premiums Received.	REMARKS.
		No.	Amount.	No.	Amount.		
1759	(1) Presbyterian Ministers' Fund, Pa.	2	$214.24	1	$1,000*	$56.62	Annuities.
1769	(2) Protestant Episcopal Corporation, Pa.......	No	record.				
1812	(3) Pennsylvania Co. for Ins. and Annuities, Pa.	No	record.				
1818	(4) Massachusetts Hospital Life Ins. Co., Mass.	25	44,150	142	238,125	$6,212	Year 1845.
1830	(5) New York Life Ins. & Trust Co., N. Y......	No	record.				
1830	(6) Baltimore Life Insurance Co., Md.	No	record.				
1835	(7) New England Mutual Life Ins. Co., Mass...	343	948,110	340	946,110	23,499	
1836	(8) Girard Life and Trust Co., Pa.	199	445,175	389	1,015,275	20,670	Year 1845.
1838	(9) Globe Life and Trust Co., Pa...............	No	record.				
1840	(10) Ohio Life and Trust Co., Cincinnati, O.	No	record.				
1840	(11) Odd Fellows Life and Trust Co., Pa.	No	record.				
1842	(12) Mutual Life Insurance Co., N. Y.	616	1,968,922	908	2,960,083	83,233	
1845	(13) Mutual Benefit Life Insurance Co., N. J.....	Be	gan busi	ness	April, 18	45.	
1837	(14) National Loan Fund, London †	50	125,000	100	250,000	4,000	

* Also 53 Family Annuities for $5,677.72, and 2 Deferred Annuities fcr $200.
† Estimated Business in U. S.

(1) Chartered January 1, 1759, as an annuity company for Presbyterian ministers; authorized to do a general life insurance business in 1875. (2) Chartered February 7, 1769, as an annuity company for Episcopal ministers; began life insurance in 1833; business small—less than 250 lives insured during first 100 years. (3) Incorporated March 10, 1812, with authorized capital of $500,000; began business in 1813 with $100,000 capital paid in; authorized to do trust business in 1836; ceased to take new life risks about 1870; still in business as a trust company; January 1, 1894, had 46 life policies in force, insuring $181,700. (4) Chartered in 1818 as a life and trust company; began business in 1823 with capital of $500,000; life business always small, last risk matured in 1793; still in business as a trust company. (5) Chartered 1830 as a life and trust company with $1,000,000 capital; ceased to take new life risks in 1875; still in business as a trust company; January 1, 1895, had 21 life policies in force insuring $60,500. (6) Organized 1830 with $50,000 capital stock, which was increased to $100,000 in

capital, and the same requirement was to be imposed upon any other life company that should be chartered. The result of this was two-fold—the company did very little life business, and no other life companies were organized in Massachusetts for twenty years. The New England Mutual, chartered in 1835, did not begin business until December, 1843, and then with a guarantee capital that was to be retired at the end of ten years.

In the South there had been several attempts to establish life insurance in connection with the trust business and marine insurance, but the only Southern company doing a life business in 1845, was the Baltimore Life. This company was essentially a banking company, doing but little life insurance and that on a very conservative basis, all premiums received being reserved for the payment of its policies. In transferring its risks to the Equitable in 1867, it exacted for them more favorable conditions than they enjoyed by the terms of their contracts, and three or four that refused to be transferred were kept on its own books until they expired. Its former building, at 11 South Street, still bears its name cut in the marble.

The New York Life Insurance and Trust Company, chartered in 1830, issued during the first nine years of its existence 1,821 life policies, of which 694 were in force, insuring $2,451,958, on January 1, 1840. At the end of this period the profits on its life business, as estimated by its President and Actuary, Mr. William Bard, and confirmed by the London Actuary, Mr. Finlaison, amounted to $189,000. This result was reached,

---

1836; in 1838 authorized to do a trust business and to have a capital of $2,000,000; life business small; re-insured risks, 99 in number, with Equitable of New York in 1867. (7) Incorporated April 1, 1835; began business December 1, 1843, with a guarantee capital of $100,000 redeemable at the end of ten years. (8) Began business in 1836 as a life and trust company with $250,000 capital; had the largest life business of any of the early companies; ceased to take new life risks in 1888; still in business as a trust company; January 1, 1894, had 318 policies in force insuring $809,934.40. (9) Began life business in 1838; did but little; closed in 1857. (10) Chartered 1840 with $100,000 capital to do life and trust business; banking business large, life business small; risks re-insured in 1856 in Jefferson Life Insurance Company of Cincinnati; both failed in 1857. (11) Chartered 1840 with $50,000 capital to do fire and life business; name changed in 1857 to City Insurance Company, and business confined to fire insurance. (12) Incorporated as a purely mutual company April, 1842; began business February 1, 1843. (13) Incorporated January 31, 1845, as a purely mutual company; began business April, 1845. (14) Began business in London in 1837; had board of directors in New York in 1845 and issued 32 policies through New York office; name changed to International in 1855; excluded from Massachusetts in 1859; did little new business in United States after 1860; re-insured later in the Hercules, which became insolvent. The figures of the Presbyterian Ministers' Fund, of the Massachusetts Hospital Life, and of the Girard Life and Trust, were kindly furnished by these organizations for this table.

however, by compounding premiums semi-annually at six per cent., charging the business with no other expense than commissions and death-losses and with the reserve necessary to re-insure outstanding policies. From the surplus thus earned the company resolved to pay a dividend of two per cent. per annum upon its capital, but was soon obliged to use the gross amount to make good an embezzlement of funds by its secretary. In February, 1844, the company had in force 711 policies, of which 126 were life policies, and the remainder for shorter terms.

The success of the mutual principle as applied to fire and marine insurance, as well as the surplus earnings of life insurance companies, led the board of trustees to inquire of the president whether it would not be for the interest of the company to adopt the mutual principle, or whether they would not be forced by competition to do so. In a special report dated February 6, 1844, Mr. Bard reviewed the history of the Equitable, of London—the oldest and most successful English life company—and the experience of his own company, and after considering the probable profits of life insurance in this country, he gave it as his opinion that the mutual principle offered no advantage to the insured that should lead the board to apprehend its influence on the business of the company, or which should induce them to alter its charter from a stock, to a mutual, company.

It is interesting, in the light of subsequent events, to look back to this report and consider how much depended on it; since if the company had adopted the mutual principle and had made diligent efforts to increase its life business, there seems no reason to doubt that, with its established position, its large capital, and the high repute of its officers and directors, it might have become the leading life insurance company of the country. Mr. Bard's underestimate of the volume of business available, and his conclusion that most men would take policies for short terms, were natural enough under the circumstances; but his estimate of the amount of surplus that could be divided among policy-holders contained an error that should not have escaped notice, since he assumed that surplus in hand at the end of five years would not be available to the policy-holder except in case of death, and would, therefore, only have a present value in proportion to a man's chances of death.* If only the dying received any part of the surplus, their share would be greatly increased, both by forfeitures and by expiring term policies, and the amount arising from each maturing life policy would be increased by interest until maturity.

April 1, 1840, New York placed upon her statute books a law which has proved the *Magna Charta* of life insurance, viz., the law authorizing a married woman to insure her husband's life for her own benefit, free from the claims of her husband's creditors. This beneficent statute has been very generally adopted by other States, and where it was lacking the companies of the period sometimes introduced its provisions in their charters. The era of mutuality was now at hand, and its most notable exponent was the Mutual Life Insurance Company of New York, which was incorporated April 12, 1842, and began business February 1, 1843. During this interval of eight months applications were secured for over $700,000 insurance, and the issues of the first year were 470 policies, insuring $1,640,718. At the end of nineteen months (September, 1844) 796 policies had been issued, of which 419 were for whole life, 287 for seven years, and the balance for shorter terms.

Life insurance in the United States had passed the experimental stage. The conservatism and high financial standing of most of the early life and trust companies undoubtedly did much to establish confidence in the safety of life insurance. The early tables of premium rates had been based upon English experience, modified by such data as had been collected in this country and which showed a higher death-rate than in Europe. The mortality experience of the companies thus far had been less than the assumptions, and rates had been gradually reduced until, in 1845, the English Carlisle Table was generally accepted as the standard.† The Actuaries' Table, based upon the experience of seventeen English life companies, and published in 1843, had not yet displaced the Carlisle, either in England or America.

---

* Report to the Board of Trustees of the New York Life Insurance and Trust Company, on Mutual Insurance, by William Bard. New York, 1844.

† McCulloch's Dictionary of Commerce.

In England the social and financial conditions had been more favorable to the growth of life insurance, and in 1845 there were 115 English companies in existence, with an estimated premium income of nearly $25,000,000 per year, under policies approximating $675,000,000.* The English companies were also adopting the mutual system, only 8 of the 115 being classed as proprietary, while 20 were purely mutual, and 87 mixed.† In a pamphlet of the time,‡ written in the interest of the older companies, it was said that 25 new companies were organized in 1845, and 71 more projected; and that the mixed companies were striving to outbid each other in the proportion of profits offered policy-holders, from one-half in the "Guardian" to nine-tenths in the "Star." It was estimated that in order to give each company an income of £150,000 per year—which was not so much as some of the older companies were receiving—would require an amount equal to twelve per cent. of all the incomes in Great Britain and Ireland above £150 per year. A heavy mortality in companies was predicted, which came to pass in due time.

The business of American life companies in 1845 was still small, but the principle was well-established, and under the stimulus of the mutual principle and the energy of the life insurance solicitor, who was soon to appear upon the field, the system was destined to take its place among the great financial interests of the country, and to claim pre-eminence among the beneficent forces of the time.

---

*Theory and Practice of Life Assurance, by W. E. Hillman, Actuary of the Star Assurance Office. London, 1847.

†Life Insurance Offices, by George Isabel Soper. London, 1846.

‡Life Insurance Offices, New and Speculative. London, 1846.

III.

THE UNITED STATES IN 1845.

THE conditions under which the NAUTILUS INSURANCE COMPANY began its career in 1845 can hardly be appreciated by the present generation without a glance at the political, industrial and social conditions of half a century ago. In April, 1845, there were twenty-seven States and three Territories in the Union, and the total population was about twenty millions. Florida had been admitted during the month preceding, and the same Act had made provision for the admission of Iowa upon her acceptance of certain boundaries prescribed. The other two Territories were Wisconsin and Minnesota. The only States west of the Mississippi River were Louisiana, Arkansas and Missouri; Kansas and Nebraska, Montana and the two Dakotas, Colorado, Wyoming and Oklahoma were as yet unorganized and unsettled. The only territory west of the Rocky Mountains to which the United States laid claim was known as the "Oregon country," and comprised the present States of Oregon, Washington and Idaho. Its title to this, by virtue of discovery and original occupation, had been acknowledged by Spain under the treaty of 1819; but it had been jointly occupied by the United States and Great Britain, without prejudice to the rights of either, since the treaty of 1818, which fixed the northern boundary of the United States, from the Lake of the Woods to the "Stony Mountains," at the 49th parallel of north latitude. The vast domain which now includes the States of Texas, California and Nevada, and the Territories of Utah, Arizona and New Mexico, was yet to be acquired.

James K. Polk had just been inaugurated President, having been elected over Henry Clay on a platform that declared for the annexation of Texas, and the occupation of Oregon as far north as 54° 40′—one of the war-cries of the presidential campaign having been "fifty-four forty or fight." Texas was admitted to the Union in December after Mr. Polk's

CITY HALL PARK, NEW YORK, 1845.

From a Steel Engraving in the possession of William Abbatt, Esq.

[The building on the right, showing the large flag, is the Park Theatre; the church beyond is the old Brick Presbyterian, where Dr. Gardiner Spring preached; its site is now occupied by the "Potter," and "N. Y. Times," buildings. Beyond it, and beyond the trees, is seen Tammany Hall, where the "Sun" building now stands. The engraving was made shortly before the large fountain, at the southern end of the Park (now many years gone) was erected; otherwise, the scene is exactly correct as in 1845.]

inauguration, and this brought on the Mexican War, in May, 1846. The Oregon boundary dispute was settled under the treaty of June 15, 1846, which provided that the 49th parallel of latitude should be the line from the Lake of the Woods to the Pacific Ocean.* Many of the most notable men the country has produced were then living and in public life. John

* President Polk announced as the four great measures of his administration—a reduction of the tariff, the independent Treasury, a settlement of the Oregon boundary question, and the acquisition of California; and he carried them all to successful completion.—*Schouler's History of U. S.*, vol. iv., p. 498.

C. Calhoun had just left the office of Secretary of State where, by his zeal for the annexation of Texas, he had regained—what he was never again to lose—his place in the affections of the southern people. Andrew Jackson, from his retirement at the Hermitage, was looking with gratification upon the political changes that had brought his old opponent, Calhoun, again into favor, and defeated the political aspirations of his "heir apparent," Martin Van Buren,—because these changes had also compassed the defeat of his later opponent, Henry Clay. Mr. Clay was not in the Senate at this time, but five years later was to come forth from his retirement to lead the great compromise debate, with which his name will always be inseparably connected. Mr. Webster had just been returned to that body, in which he had won his great fame, after valuable but inconspicuous service in the Cabinets of Presidents Harrison and Tyler. John Quincy Adams, "the old man eloquent," who had seen

THE SOCIETY LIBRARY BUILDING, AT 346 & 348 BROADWAY, IN 1845.

[From a lithograph in the possession of the Society Library. Copied by permission.]

thirty-one years of public service in various offices, including the highest, before he entered the House of Representatives, was now completing his fourteenth year in that body, where he had gained his greatest renown as champion of "the right of petition."

Besides these great names there were others little less conspicuous, the mere mention of which recalls much of the history of their time. Among the older of these men were Thomas H. Benton, Lewis Cass, John J. Crittenden and Thomas Corwin, in the Senate, Joseph Story, of the Supreme Court, Richard Rush, Minister to France, Sam Houston, ex-President of Texas, and Silas Wright, Governor of New York—who were then at the zenith of their fame; while others, like James Buchanan, Secretary of State, Robert J. Walker,* Secretary of the Treasury, George Bancroft, Secretary of the Navy, Edward Everett, Minister to England, Hannibal Hamlin, John P. Hale, Joshua R. Giddings, Stephen A. Douglas, David Wilmot, Andrew Johnson and Alexander H. Stephens, in Congress, and Millard Fillmore,† William H. Seward, Thaddeus Stevens, Samuel J. Tilden, Charles Francis Adams, Charles Sumner and Abraham Lincoln, outside of it, were the rising young men of the time. In literature the great names were Cooper and Irving, Bryant and Emerson; Longfellow and Poe, Lowell and Whittier, Hawthorne and Prescott, Bancroft, Holmes and Willis were men of brilliant promise; Francis Wayland, Eliphalet Nott, Lyman Beecher and Horace Mann were the foremost educators. Looking backward from 1845, the last war with Great Britain was no farther in the past than the Civil War is to the observer of to-day; General Scott, who had won his first laurels and his first star at Lundy's Lane, was commander-in-chief of the army, and destined to win still greater renown upon the plains of Mexico in the war then impending. A retrospect of fifty years at that time brought one to the first administration of Thomas Jefferson; and the elderly men of 1845 were the sons and the familiars of the founders of the Republic.

---

*Mr. Walker, who was author of the "Walker tariff" of 1846, insured in the NAUTILUS, April 10, 1847, under Policy No. 1,072, for the term of one year. In consideration of an extra of $12.09 per $1,000, all restrictions and all conditions of the policy, except the payment of premiums, were waived.

†In 1859 Mrs. Fillmore sold her life interest in the Schuyler Mansion in Albany, N. Y., which she inherited from her first husband, to Mr. John Tracey, for the sum of $6,000. In order to protect himself in case of her early death, Mr. Tracey took a policy of insurance on Mrs. Fillmore's life for the same amount. This policy, No. 12,877, was issued by the NEW-YORK LIFE, February 1, 1859, and upon Mrs. Fillmore's death, in 1881, was paid to the son and executor of Mr. Tracey.

Perhaps nothing marks the difference between 1845 and 1895 more distinctly than the difference in means of communication. In 1845 the world was just upon the threshold of that wonderful development in the use of steam and electricity that has revolutionized methods of production and distribution. Steamboats were in common use on our lakes and rivers in 1845, but of railroads there were only 4,633 miles in the whole country. Only one railroad—the Harlem—entered New York City, and the first all-rail *route* to Albany was not yet completed. Before the opening of the Erie Canal it cost one hundred dollars to transport a ton of freight from Buffalo to New York; hence any considerable commerce between distant points not connected by water-ways or the few railroads that then existed was practically impossible. Mr. Edward Atkinson estimates that to do the present freight work of our railways would require fourteen million horses. The first line of telegraph had been put up between Baltimore and Washington in 1844, and Mr. Morse's offer to sell his invention to the Government for a small sum had been refused on the ground that it was of no practical importance.* Letter postage was from six to twenty-five cents, according to distance, for each single sheet of paper. On July 1, 1845, it was reduced to five cents per sheet for three hundred miles or less, and to ten cents for over three hundred miles. The total revenue of the Post-Office Department was only about one-eighteenth as much as at the present time. The material civilization of the present day may be said to rest practically upon coal and iron; in 1845 the coal mined was only about one-eightieth, and the iron manufactured about one-one hundred and eightieth, of the present annual output.† For illuminating purposes whale oil and tallow were then the chief reliance; petro-

* The first number of "Fisher's National Magazine," published in June, 1845, contains an article on Electro-Magnetic Telegraphs, by F. O. J. Smith, of Maine, afterwards prominent in the business, reviewing the progress made, and closing as follows: "Who is fool-hardy and blind enough to doubt that the time has come when these structures [telegraphic lines] will start into being and action all over our country, and that the business and calculations of our merchants and men of enterprise should be shaped with reference to such a new condition of their relations?"

† The early railroads used a wooden rail with an iron strap. The first iron T rail used in this country was laid on the Erie road in 1845. The Erie was then complete from Piermont to Middletown, 53 miles. The price of wrought iron was then about $80 per ton; the present price of steel rails is about $22 per ton. Wood was generally used for fuel until about 1860.

leum, of which the present annual product is over thirty-five million barrels, was first obtained by boring during that year, but it was not generally used until about twelve or fifteen years later.

In 1840 about seventy per cent. of the total population were engaged in agriculture, and about fifteen per cent. in manufactures and trades; in 1890 the percentages were about forty-eight, and twenty-four, respectively. In 1840 there were twenty-two cities with a population of over fifteen thousand each, and 8.52 per cent. of the total population dwelt in cities;* in 1890 there were two hundred and sixteen cities with a population of over fifteen thousand each; and 29.12 per cent. of the total population dwelt in cities. In 1840 the population was a little more than one-fourth (27.1 per cent.) as great as in 1890, but the value of manufactures was only about one-thirtieth as great, imports and exports about one-seventh as much, the money† in circulation about one-eleventh as much, the deposits in savings banks about one-hundredth as large, the children in common schools about one-seventh as many, and the newspapers about one-twelfth as many.

Of the almost numberless labor-saving machines of the present day, the sewing-machine, the rotary printing-press, the mower and reaper, the steam elevator, and the type-writer are the most common,—yet not one of these was in practical use in 1845. The result of their introduction has been to increase very largely the productive capacity of mankind, and so

---

* The "National Magazine" for October, 1845, contains an article on Chicago, by D. D. Griswold, giving its population by the census of 1844 at 10,864, and estimating its population in 1845 at "nearly 13,000." It contains the following pen-picture of its business: "Wheat, the great staple of northern Illinois, is brought into the city in wagons, not unfrequently from a distance of 250 miles. Long trains, reminding one of the caravans of the East, are seen crossing the prairies and approaching the city, heralded by clouds of dust, in all directions. The business streets are rendered almost impassible by the number of wheat wagons and fine strings of oxen attached to them. Those employed in the warehouses are constantly and actively engaged in the reception of this grain; runners are eagerly and noisily competing with each other in the purchase of it; you run against a load of wheat or a wheat buyer at every turn. During a portion of the winter the pork trade is carried on under almost equally brisk and lively circumstances." The article concludes in this hopeful strain: "We have good reason for the confident belief that the business interests and prosperity of Chicago are as firmly based as those of any town in the Western States."

† The "National Magazine," already quoted, contains an article by the first President of the Company, Mr. Ogden, on the Currency of the "United States," which is re-printed in full in the appendix. The figures for 1845, upon which the above comparison is based, are taken from "Twenty Years in Congress," vol. i., p. 643.

to enable men to secure more of the comforts and luxuries of life. Mr. Edward Atkinson has shown by elaborate statistics that, while the hours of labor were greatly reduced between 1850 and 1890, the wages of men of special skill and those of the average mechanic will now purchase about twice as much of the ordinary articles of food and clothing as in 1850. The census of 1850 showed the average wealth *per capita* to be $308; the census of 1890 showed it to be $1,039.

In addition to the marked changes in the material conditions of our civilization since 1845, there has been a marked increase in the humane spirit, which will not tolerate organized injustice or oppression, and which seeks to alleviate human suffering of every kind. This spirit has found expression in the abolition of slavery and of dueling; in the reform of laws relating to married women and to the employment of children; in the temperance and prison reforms; and in the rapid increase of industrial schools, orphan asylums and other institutions for the care of the unfortunate.

The bearing of all these changes upon the possibilities of life insurance is obvious. Easier communication between all parts of the country, a greater average intelligence, more leisure to read and to think, more money to spend, and an increase of the humane spirit, have supplied the conditions and motives necessary to a rapid growth of the system.

THE CAPITOL AT WASHINGTON IN 1845.

IV.

THE FIRST THOUSAND POLICIES.

THE offices of the Company were first established at No. 58 Wall Street, and the first policies were dated there. We give on the following pages *fac-simile* illustrations, slightly reduced, of the first application and policy forms. The policy selected is No. 5, issued May 17, 1845, on the life of John Rice, one of the signers of subscription notes which constituted the first financial basis of the Company. Mr. Rice afterward took two other policies in the Company and kept them all in force until his death, which occurred in 1856. The application shows the numbers and amounts of all his policies, and the approval of the Loss Committee when they became claims, also an extract from the law under which such insurances might be made for the sole benefit of married women and their children. The law was construed literally in those days—the application was signed by the wife, her name appeared on the books as the owner of the policy, and she frequently conducted the correspondence in paying the premiums. Medical Examiners of the Company were not appointed until June second, and policies issued prior thereto were issued by the officers of the Company, on the statements of the applicant, the family physician of the person insured, and the certificate of an intimate friend. This application bears the signatures of Mrs. Rice, Dr. A. Sidney Doane, and Ammi Dows.

The first policy form differs in its terms but slightly from the form in use by the Girard Life and Trust Company of Philadelphia as far back as 1837, but the difference, such as it is, gives larger liberty to the policy-holder, namely, permission to travel in the United States south of Virginia and Kentucky between November first and June first. The only benefit and of the annual prem

One Hundred & Sixty Five — dollars and — Fifty — cents, to be paid on or b

Seventeenth — day of — May — in every year during the continuanc

s Policy, **Do Assure** the Life of John Rice — commission merch

the City of New York — in the County of — New York — S

New York, for the sole use of the said Sarah H Rice —

the amount of Five Thousand — dol

the term of his natural Life —

And the said Company do hereby **Promise and Agree,** to and with the said assured, her execu

ministrators, and assigns, well and truly to pay, or cause to be paid, the said sum insured, to the

ured, her executors, administrators, or assigns, for her sole use, within sixty days after due notice,

of of the death of the said — John Rice — And in cas

death of the said Sarah H Rice — before the decease of

d John Rice — the amount of the said insurance shall be pay

er her death to her children, for their use, or to their guardian, if under age, within sixty days a

notice and proof of the death of the said John Rice — as aforesaid.

Provided always, and it is hereby declared to be the true intent and meaning of this Policy,

same is accepted by the assured upon these express conditions, that in case the said —

— John Rice —

all die upon the seas, or shall, without the consent of this Company previously obtained, and endorsed u

s Policy, pass beyond the settled limits of the United States, (excepting into the settled limits of

British Provinces of the two Canadas, Nova-Scotia, or New-Brunswick,) or shall, without such pre

nsent thus endorsed, visit those parts of the United States, which lie south of the southern boundaries o

tates of Virginia and Kentucky, between the first of July and the first of November, or shall, wi

h previous consent thus endorsed, enter into any military or naval service whatsoever, (the militia n

tual service excepted;) or in case he shall die by his own hand, in, or in consequence of a duel, or by

nds of justice, or in the known violation of any law of these States, or of the United States, or of

id Provinces, this Policy shall be void, null, and of no effect.

And it is also Understood and Agreed, to be the true intent and meaning hereof, that if the declar

ade by the said Sarah H Rice —

d bearing date the thirteenth — day of — May — 1845 — and upon

ith of which this agreement is made, shall be found in any respect untrue, then, and in such case, this P

all be null and void: or in case the said Sarah H Rice —

— shall not pay the said annual premiums on or befor

veral days herein before mentioned for the payment thereof, then and in every such case, the said Comp

all not be liable to the payment of the sum insured, or any part thereof: and this Policy shall cease

termine.

And it is further agreed, that in every case where this Policy shall cease, or become or be null or

l previous Payments made thereon shall be forfeited to the said Company.

N. B. If Assigned, notice to be given the Company.

provided under the policy was the insurance payable at death, while it became null and void, and all payments thereon were forfeited to the Company, from any of the following causes:

(1) The non-payment of any premium; (2) death by the insured's own

First Engraved Policy Heading Used.

[Policy No. 19 was issued May 30, 1845, on the life of Edward Pierce, a boatman, of Kingston, N. Y. Mr. Pierce died early in 1850, and the policy bears the receipt of Mrs. Gertrude Pierce, dated March 5, 1850, in payment of the claim.]

hand; (3) any untrue statement in the application; (4) death upon the high seas; (5) death in consequence of a duel; (6) death by the hands of Justice; (7) death in the known violation of any law of the United States, or of any State or Province wherein residence and travel were permitted; (8) residence or travel south of the southern boundaries of Virginia and Kentucky, between July first and November first, or at any time beyond the settled limits of the United States and the British Provinces of Canada, Nova Scotia and New Brunswick; (9) military or naval service, the militia not in actual service excepted.

The limit of risk upon one life was placed at $5,000. Among the first 1,000 policies there were six for $10,000 each; all others were for $5,000 or less. In the case of the six $10,000 policies, the excess was re-insured in the National Loan Fund, the Mutual Life, and the Mutual Benefit of N. J. The premium rates were based on the Carlisle Table of Mortality with interest at four per cent. There seems to have been no discrimination made between northern and southern risks upon persons who were thoroughly acclimated, but liberty of residence and travel was very much restricted in the South, even to residents. Under the first 1,000 policies twenty-six persons residing in the cities of New Orleans, Mobile, Natchez, Little Rock and Augusta, paid extra premiums of from one-half to one per cent. on the amount insured, to travel or reside in any part of their respective States. Northern policy-holders were charged one-half of one per cent. for permission to travel or reside in any part of the Union (except New Orleans and Mobile) between July first and November fifteenth. Passengers by sea to southern ports, to Havana, and to Europe, were charged one-half of one per cent.; a sea captain was charged one per cent., with many restrictions as to the ports he might enter. One per cent. extra was charged for permission to go to California and return, and three per cent. extra for permanent residence there. A surgeon of the United States Army paid five per cent. extra to accompany the army to Mexico, the permit not to cover the risk of death in battle or from wounds received.

Beginning with May, 1845, the business of the Company averaged about 20 policies per month during the remainder of the year; in January, 1846, there were 36, and in February 119. This sudden increase was due to the enterprise of a few southern agents who persuaded the Company to accept risks on the lives of slaves. During these two months 86 slave policies were issued, and of the first 1,000 policies 339 were on the lives of slaves. The amounts were usually less than $500, and the term one year; occasionally one policy covered several lives. Policy No. 799 was issued on the lives of three slaves, and Policy No. 268 was issued on the lives of ten slaves and one white man. The first death-claim paid by the Company was under a slave policy, the entry in the Journal, under date of November 2, 1846, reading as follows: "Paid F. Alonzo Clarke [of Richmond, Va.,] the amount insured on his slave, Philip Swan, per Policy No. 228 [died August, 28, 1846], $225." There were three death-claims under slave policies in the period under review, the total amount

THE NAUTILUS (MUTUAL LIFE) INSURANCE COMPANY OF NEW YORK,

OFFICE 58 WALL STREET.

Particulars required from Persons proposing to effect Assurances on Lives in this Company.

The Thirteenth day of May 1845

No. 1. Name, Residence, and Occupation of the Party, on whose behalf the Assurance is proposed.	Sarah H Rice — wife of John Rice — New York city
2. Name, Residence, and Occupation of the Party whose life is proposed to be assured. (If a married female or a widow, state also her maiden name).	John Rice — city of New York commission merchant
3. Place and date of Birth.	Geneva New York — 5th August 1804
4. Age next Birthday.	Forty One Years —
5. Is the Party, whose life is to be Assured, Married or Single? (and what are the Party's habits of Life?)	Married — habits active & temperate —
6. Has the Party resided abroad, and if so, where, when, and for what period; (and did the health suffer from such residence?)	No
7. Has the Party been, or is he, employed in the Military or Naval Service, or in a Seafaring Life?	No
8. Has the Party had the Small Pox, or the Cow Pox?	has been Vaccinated —
9. Has the Party's Family been afflicted with Pulmonary Complaints, or any other Disease that tends to shorten Life?	not to my knowledge his mother is alive aged about 75
10. Has the Party been afflicted, since his childhood, with Rupture, Fits or Convulsions, Dropsy, Asthma, Liver Complaint, Gout, Consumption, Spitting of Blood, or Insanity, and if so, which?	No —
11. Has the Party an habitual Cough, or any Disease or Symptom of Disease?	No
12. Has the Party been afflicted with Disease of the Heart, or Disease of any of the Vital organs, and which?	No
13. Has the Party been afflicted, during the last seven years, with any severe or constitutional disease, and what?	None
14. Is the Party now afflicted with any disease or disorder, and what?	no
15. Has the Party ever met with any accidental or serious personal injury, if so, of what nature?	no
16 Name and Residence of the Party's usual Medical Attendant, (or if he have none) of some other Medical person to be referred to for information as to his health.	A Sydney Doane —
17. Name and Residence of an intimate Friend, to be referred to for similar information.	Ami Dows New York city
18. Is there any other circumstance or information, touching the past or present state of health, or habits of life, with which the Directors ought to be made acquainted?	none that I know of
19. Sum to be assured, $5000 —	Five Thousand dollars —
20. Term for which the assurance is required.	whole term of life —
21. Is the Party aware that any untrue or fraudulent allegation, made in effecting the proposed Assurance, will render the Policy void, and that all Payments of Premium, made thereon, will be forfeited.	Yes —

Signed, Sarah H Rice

Witness,
Ammi Dows

The two first questions will have the same answer when the applicant Assures his own life—different answers if he Assures the life of another person.
N. B. Persons proposing an Assurance, are desired to answer all the questions; to fill up one of the declarations, and to affix their Signatures in the presence of a witness, previous to transmission to this office.

[TO FOLLOW PAGE 22.]

paid being $1,050. The issue of such policies was discontinued by direction of the Trustees, April 19, 1848.

Among the letters in the Actuary's letter-book of this period is one dated November 25, 1845, and addressed to "Schuyler Colfax, Esq., South Bend., Ind.," acknowledging the receipt of a copy of the "St. Joseph

Valley Register," with Mr. Colfax's name as "editor and agent of a fire and marine insurance company, both marked for notice," from which it was inferred that he would accept the agency of a life company. Mr. Colfax replied under date of December tenth, offering to accept the agency

or to recommend some suitable person if the Company preferred another.* He was appointed, but under date of April 15, 1846, wrote that his other business had increased to such proportions that he had no time for life insurance, and recommended as agent in his room, Mr. Charles M. Heaton. Thus a good life insurance agent was spoiled to make a Vice-President of the United States.

1846. UPON closing the books for the first year it was found that 449 policies had been issued, insuring $929,038, of which 359 policies, insuring $799,000, remained in force. The premium income had been $22,602.71, interest receipts $33.60, and the total expenses $5,140.76. No death-losses had been reported. The "net earned premiums," calculated according to the time the policies had run, were found to be $10,311.92, of which expenses had consumed about one-half. The committee appointed to examine the accounts recommended that "a dividend of 50% on the net earned premiums of the past year should be declared to the policy-holders." It is difficult to understand how any one with a spark of actuarial knowledge, or with any conception of the function of a reserve fund, could have recommended or approved this action. The management of the early companies was strong on the practical or business side, but weak on the theoretical or scientific side.† Life insur-

* "In the past year the prejudices formerly existing against life insurance have been weakening and becoming eradicated. Its benefits—so important and undeniable—are becoming appreciated; and it has been recently a subject of favorable consideration with many of our citizens. Requests made by several of them to me to procure an agency from a company doing that business prompted the sending of the marked paper to which you allude. The business which an agency would do might be limited at first—but, I feel well-convinced, would be a steadily increasing one. If you feel disposed, therefore, in view of the facts I have stated, to appoint an agent here, I will either accept the appointment myself and do all I can for the interests of the Company, or will recommend some suitable person if you would prefer another. I have been written to by Mr. J. Leander Starr, agent of the mammoth English company, to accept a sub-agency of his company here. I replied to him as I have to you—still, on reflection, I think the western anti-British feeling would operate against an English company, and of course favorably to yours. However, I bring this to your consideration, that you may weigh it in deciding whether to establish an agency here. For my own part, I am impressed with the conviction that the more numerous are life insurance companies and agencies (within the bounds of reason and discretion) the heavier and larger will be the business of them all. Causing discussion and examination, the certain result is increased and more numerous insurings. * * * Accompanying this I send you a recent number of my paper with an article on Life Insurance marked."

† The first dividend declared by this Company was in February, 1848. This dividend was fifty-two per cent. on the premiums paid; payable with each policy at death only. An error in this dividend was brought to the notice of the Trustees by Edmund Blunt, Esq., of the U. S. Coast Survey. Mr. Gill [Actuary of the Mutual Life in 1858] examined the principles upon which the dividend was based, and declared that the dividend actually earned was less than thirty-three per cent. This dividend has since been adjusted upon sound principles.—*Mutual Life Report, 1858.*

THE NAUTILUS (MUTUAL LIFE) INSURANCE COMPANY OF NEW YORK.

OWN LIFE

Declaration to be made and signed by a Person proposing to make an Assurance on his own Life.

Sum Assured

$

I,
of in the County of
in the State of the Person described on the other side, being desirous of effecting an ASSURANCE with THE NAUTILUS (MUTUAL LIFE) INSURANCE CO. OF NEW YORK, in the sum of Dollars, upon my own Life, during the*

DO HEREBY DECLARE, that my Age, next Birth-day, will be years: That I have had the Small Pox: that I have been Vaccinated: That I have had the Gout: That I have not been afflicted with Rupture, Fits, Dropsy, Asthma, or Spitting of Blood; and that I am not now afflicted with any Disorder that tends to the shortening of Life. And I hereby agree, that this Declaration shall be the basis of the Contract between myself and the said Company: And if any untrue or fraudulent allegation is contained in this Declaration, all Moneys which shall have been paid to the Company on account of the Assurance to be made in consequence thereof, shall be forfeited for the benefit of the said Company. AND I DO HEREBY FURTHER DECLARE, that of my Medical Referee, and of my private Friend, are, in my belief, fully competent to give information as to my present and general state of health.

Witness to the Signing hereof

Dated this day of in the year of our Lord one thousand eight hundred and forty-

SIGNED,

The first Declaration is to be signed where the applicant assures his own life.—The second where he assures the life of another.

LIFE OF ANOTHER.

Declaration to be made and signed by a Person proposing to make an Assurance on the Life of Another.

PAGE 2 OF APPLICATION.

I, Sarah H Rice
of the City of New York — in the County of New York —
in the State of — New York — one of the Persons named on the other side, being desirous of effecting an ASSURANCE with THE NAUTILUS (MUTUAL LIFE) INSURANCE CO. OF NEW YORK, in the sum of Five Thousand Dollars, upon the Life of John Rice of the City of New York — in the County of New York — in the State of — New York — the other person described on the other side, during the* whole Continuance thereof — DO HEREBY DECLARE, that the Age of the said John Rice next Birth-day, will be Forty One — Years: That he has not had the Small Pox. That he has — been Vaccinated. That he has — not — had the Gout: And that he has not been afflicted with Rupture, Fits, Dropsy, Asthma, or Spitting of Blood; and that he is not now afflicted with any Disorder which tends to the shortening of life. And that I have an interest in the Life of the said John Rice to the full amount of the said Sum of Five Thousand Dollars. And I hereby agree, that this Declaration shall be the basis of the Contract between myself and the said Company: And if any untrue or fraudulent allegation is contained in this Declaration, all Moneys which shall have been paid to the said Company, on account of the Assurance made in consequence thereof, shall be forfeited for the benefit of the Company. AND I DO HEREBY FURTHER DECLARE, that of the Medical Referee, and Ami Dows — of New York city — are, in my belief, fully competent to give information as to the present and general state of health of the said John Rice

Dated this Thirteenth — day of May — in the year of our Lord one thousand eight hundred and forty-five —

Witness to the Signing hereof

Ami Dows

SIGNED, Sarah H Rice

* Whole continuance thereof, Or term of Years.

ance was largely for short periods only. Of the 449 policies issued by the NAUTILUS during its first year, only 127 were for the whole term of life; the remainder were mostly for one year or for seven years. As by the terms of the charter dividends were not to be paid at once and were to be liable for losses until paid, they answered all the purposes of a reserve fund. This was the first life insurance dividend declared to policy-holders in this country, except that of the Girard Life and Trust Company, already referred to, which was declared in reversion.

During the first year all premiums were required to be paid in cash, except in the case of persons giving subscription notes; but the business of the year did not equal the anticipation of the officers and trustees, and on May 16, 1846, it was voted to allow policy-holders the option of giving notes for forty per cent. of the premium.

Policy No. 1,000 was issued March 16, 1847. To reach this point had required twenty-three months. During the year 1894, over 81,000 policies were issued—an average of nearly 7,000 per month. The measure of the Company's service to the public is therefore about 160 times as great now as it was in 1845–6. The following table shows the distribution of the first 1,000 policies, according to the periods for which they were written, the modes of their termination, and the domicile of policy-holders:

TABULAR HISTORY OF THE FIRST 1,000 POLICIES ISSUED BY THE NEW-YORK LIFE INSURANCE COMPANY, TO JUNE 24, 1894.

DISTRIBUTION BY RESIDENCE.				Term.	No. Issued.	Not Taken.	Lapsed	Surrendered.	Expired.	Death-Claims.	In Force.
				Life	342	34	178	26	....	97	7
				15 Years.	1	....	1	....	....	....	....
Me.	1	S. C.	44	14 "	12	2	10	....	....	....	....
N. H.	4	Ga.	30	7 "	224	6	153	....	55	10	....
Vt.	2	Ala.	10	6 "	1	....	....	....	1	....	....
Mass.	6	La.	12	5 "	7	1	4	....	1	1	....
R. I.	14	Ark.	7	4 "	1	....	1	....	....	....	....
Conn.	12	Cuba	1	3 "	1	1	....	....	....	....	....
N. Y.	382	Ohio	9	2 "	2	....	2	....	....	....	....
N. J.	18	Mich. ...	6	1½ "	2	....	1	....	1	....	....
Pa.	13	Ind.	1	1 "	374	3	4	....	364	3	....
Md.	24	Ill.	7	6 mos...	27	....	....	....	27	....	....
Va.	179	Wis.	5	4 " ..	2	....	1	....	1	....	....
Ky.	114	Iowa	3	2 " ..	2	...	....	....	2	....	....
N. C.	96			1 " ..	2	....	....	....	2	....	....
	865		135	TOTALS.	1,000	47	355	26	454	111	7

Among these policies was one joint-life policy, issued upon the lives of husband and wife, and fourteen other policies upon the lives of women, in addition to many policies on the lives of female slaves. Of the 342 whole life policies ten per cent. were not taken, fifty-two per cent. lapsed, eight per cent. were surrendered, and thirty per cent. have become claims or are still in force. The names of the seven policy-holders whose policies are in force at this writing (July 25, 1894) are as follows: James P. Wallace, Brooklyn, N.Y.; John R. Lee, Hamburg, N. Y.; William H. Sweet, East Saginaw, Mich.; Morris E. Fuller, Schuyler, Neb.; Joseph Lee, Brooklyn, N. Y.; Daniel W. Ingersoll, St. Paul, Minn.; John Hinde, New York City. Of these seven policy-holders, two, Messrs. James P. Wallace and John R. Lee, insured in 1845, and have both paid their fiftieth premium. Their record entitles them to the foremost place among the policy-holders of the Company, and their portraits are given herewith.

Wishing you continued prosperity. I am as ever Sincerely Yours James P. Wallace July 13/94

Mr. Wallace was born April 3, 1816. His policy is No. 15, and was issued May 24, 1845. In reply to the Company's congratulations and its request for his photograph, Mr. Wallace wrote under date of July 13, 1894:

I accept with pleasure your congratulations that I have reached the age of seventy-eight years, and that I hold the earliest policy of your Company now in force. I was one of the original subscribers in getting up your Company, and have a pride in its suc-

THE NAUTILUS (MUTUAL LIFE) INSURANCE COMPANY OF NEW YORK.

Questions to be answered by the **Physician** *of the* **Party** *applying for Insurance.*

1. How long have you known John Rice. Have you been in the habit of seeing him frequently, and giving him Medical attendance, and for what diseases?	Eight years. A very poor customer. Has been troubled once or twice with Dyspepsia
2. Has the party's family, to your knowledge, been afflicted with Pulmonary Complaints, or any other disease that tends to shorten life?	Father died at 65 years of age Mother living now at the age of 75.
3. Has he at any time, to your knowledge, been afflicted with Insanity, Gout, Dropsy, Palsy, Disease of the Heart, Aneurism, Rupture, Spitting of Blood, Affection of the Lungs, or other Viscera, or with any organic Disease?	No
4. Do you believe that he is now in good health?	Yes
5. Is he sober and temperate?	Yes
6. Is he accustomed to much exercise, or is he sedentary?	Takes active exercise freely
7. Do you believe that he possesses a healthy constitution?	Yes
8. Are you aware of any particular circumstances tending to shorten his life?	No

Signed, A. Sidney Doane A.M. M.D.

Dated, May 17 1845.

THE NAUTILUS (MUTUAL LIFE) INSURANCE COMPANY OF NEW YORK.

Questions to be answered by the **Friend** *of the* **Party** *applying for Insurance.*

1. How long have you known John Rice	Ten years and upwards
2. Are his general habits of life temperate or otherwise?	Temperate
3. Is he accustomed to much exercise, or is he sedentary?	Accustomed to considerable Exercise in a business way
4. Has the party's family, to your knowledge, been afflicted with Pulmonary Complaints or any other disease that tends to shorten life?	I have no knowledge in respect to this except I have heard that his elder brother Stephen, who died about five years ago, was troubled with Dyspepsy
5. Has he been afflicted with any serious disease?	Not to my knowledge
6. Has he been afflicted with any mental derangement?	Not to my knowledge
7. Do you esteem him a healthy man, and free from any circumstances tending to shorten life?	I do
8. Do you believe him to be now in perfect health?	I do
9. Do you think his life safely insurable?	Yes

Signed, Amni Doss

Dated, New York May 16th 1845.

[To follow page 26.]

John Rice 531

No. 5 — insured 5000
476 — " 2500
477 " — 1500

Sarah H Rice $ 9000

477 — Elizabeth Rice 1000

Total. 10,000

All cash —
certificates all issued
interest all paid

THE NAUTILUS
(MUTUAL LIFE) INSURANCE COMPANY.
OF NEW YORK.

No. OF POLICY. 5

Dated 17th day of May 1845
Proposer Sarah H Rice
Life of John Rice
Age 41.
Sum assured $ 5000
Term of Life
Premium . . $ 165 50
Policy . . . $ 1

$ 166.50

Recd. October 6. 1850

Approved by
Wm Coxe Dusenbury
John S Bussing
Comm. Committee

AN ACT

In respect to Insurances on Lives for the benefit of Married Women.

Passed April 1st, 1840.

The People of the State of New York, represented in Senate and Assembly, do enact as follows:

§ 1. It shall be lawful for any married woman, by herself, and in her name, or in the name of any third person, with his assent, as her trustee, to cause to be insured, for her sole use, the life of her husband for any definite period, or for the term of his natural life; and in case of her surviving her husband, the sum or net amount of the insurance becoming due and payable by the terms of the insurance shall be payable to her, to and for her own use, free from the claims of the representatives of her husband, or of any of his creditors; but such exemption shall not apply where the amount of premium annually paid shall exceed three hundred dollars.

§ 2. In case of the death of the wife, before the decease of her husband, the amount of the insurance may be made payable after death to her children for their use, and to their guardian, if under age.

Page 4 of Application, with Endorsements.

cess. I cordially congratulate you on its long and successful and eminently honorable career, and assure you that my policy has been a comfort to myself and family during every year of its existence; especially was it so in my younger days when I had little else to leave them in case of my death. * * * * * * * *

Mr. John R. Lee was born July 6, 1809. He was appointed agent of the Company at Buffalo, N. Y., in July, 1845, and continued to act as such for several years. His letters and reports, in those early days, before the methods of the Company had been systematized, were models of brevity, promptness and accuracy. Mr. Lee was a banker at that time, and was afterward Secretary and Treasurer of the Buffalo, Bradford and Pittsburg Railroad Company. He replied to the Company's letter of congratulation, on his last birthday, closing his letter as follows:

John Randolph Lee
November 20, 1894
In his 86th year

> The one word, "weariness," tells the story of old age; but notwithstanding that, I will hope and desire to live to see the document you propose to issue, setting forth the colossal condition of the NEW-YORK LIFE INSURANCE COMPANY after an experience of fifty years.*

The business of the second year showed a marked increase over that of the first. The net earned premiums were about double all expenditures, and a second scrip dividend of fifty per cent. was declared to policy-holders, and it was voted to pay six per cent. interest on the dividends outstanding.

---

* Mr. Lee died March 31, 1895.

PRESIDENT NEW-YORK LIFE INSURANCE COMPANY, APRIL 19, 1847—DECEMBER 22, 1848.

V.

THE FIRST MILLION DOLLARS.

1847. AT the annual election, April 19, 1847, Mr. A. M. Merchant, the former Vice-President, was elected President, and Mr. Robert B. Coleman succeeded him as Vice-President. Mr. Benton had retired from the secretaryship in February preceding, and the work of the Secretary was devolved upon the Actuary. The period upon which we have now entered brought into the Company's service four men who were to be, during many years, conspicuously identified with its management and growth. Hon. Morris Franklin, who had been State Senator, and was then President of the New York Board of Aldermen, was elected a Trustee at the second annual meeting, and in December, 1848, upon the resignation of Mr. Merchant, he was elected President—a position to which he was re-elected at each annual meeting following until his death in 1885. On December 1, 1851, Mr. William H. Beers entered the office of the Company as accountant, and thus began a forty years' service, during which time he did more than any other one man to make the Company one of the foremost financial institutions of the world. On June 13, 1849, Mr. William Barton was elected a Trustee, and remained an active member of the Board until his death in 1884, being for many years Chairman of the Finance Committee and devoting all his time to the service of the Company. On June 9, 1852, Mr. William H. Appleton was elected a Trustee, and after forty-three years' service, during which he has seen the Company's assets grow from half a million dollars to one hundred and sixty millions, still remains a member of the Board and deeply interested in the Company's prosperity. Mr. Appleton has been Chairman of the Finance Committee since Mr. Barton's death.

In May, 1847, the office of the Company was removed to No. 29 Wall Street.

The early life companies, with their large capital stock and their trust and annuity business, had other sources of income than life insurance, and employed no agents to secure such business; but with the advent of mutual companies devoted exclusively to life insurance, and relying for capital upon their accumulations from insurance premiums, came the life insurance solicitor and the agency system. During the first two years of the NAUTILUS about forty agents were appointed, and agencies were established in the principal cities of the South and West. A twenty per cent. tax on premiums imposed by Act of April 23, 1829, barred other State companies from Pennsylvania until January, 1849,* and the few agencies established by the Company in New England did very little business.

The records of the Board of Trustees at this period contain frequent references to efforts made to increase the Company's business. Commissions were first fixed at five per cent. on each premium, but towards the close of 1845 the allowance on the first premium was increased to ten per cent., and in May, 1847, the commission on renewals was limited to a term of five years. In the revised By-Laws adopted December, 1847, No. XX. made it the duty of the officers and trustees "to impress upon each other and upon all agents of the Company the propriety and importance of severally insuring their lives in this Company and so becoming directly interested therein." The business of the Company for the third year showed a fair increase over that of the second, and the usual dividend of fifty per cent. of the net earned premiums was declared at the meeting of the Trustees in April, 1848, and it was also voted to pay six per cent. interest in cash on dividends outstanding.

In May, 1848, the office of the Company was removed to No. 68 Wall Street.

---

*Fowler's History of Insurance in Philadelphia, pp. 653, 672.

ALL COMMUNICATIONS ARE STRICTLY CONFIDENTIAL.

TARIFF OF PRICES

From New York to	NUMBER OF WORDS.																	
	15	20	25	30	35	40	45	50	55	60	65	70	75	80	85	90	95	100
Poughkeepsie, Hudson, ...	$.25	.35	.45	.55	.65	.75	.85	.95	1.05	1.15	1.25	1.35	1.45	1.55	1.65	1.75	1.85	1.95
Albany, ... Troy, ... Utica, ... Rome, ...	.35	.50	.65	.80	.95	1.10	1.25	1.40	1.55	1.70	1.85	2.00	2.15	2.30	2.45	2.60	2.75	2.90
Syracuse, ... Auburn, ... Geneva, ... Rochester, ... Buffalo, ...	.50	.70	.90	1.10	1.30	1.50	1.70	1.90	2.10	2.30	2.50	2.70	2.90	3.10	3.30	3.50	3.70	3.90
Ithaca, ... Oswego, ... Lockport, ...	.75	1.05	1.35	1.65	1.95	2.25	2.55	2.85	3.15	3.45	3.75	4.05	4.35	4.65	4.95	5.25	5.55	5.85

From the Office of the New-York, Albany, & Buffalo Telegraph Co.
POST'S BUILDINGS, EXCHANGE PLACE.

No.

Hour. Minute.

New-York, Oct 17 1848 day,

By Telegraph from Utica

For Raney Sherman

29 Wall

Please Telegraph in rel-
-ation to Fire agency as sev-
-eral policies expire this week

H. W. Backus

37

Answer paid

THE FIRST TELEGRAM IN THE COMPANY'S RECORDS.

1848. In 1848 two travelling agents were appointed, with authority to establish local agencies, and in December of this year the limit of risk on one life was increased to $10,000. The business of the year was nearly double that of any preceding year, although there was dissension in the Board of Trustees over the resignation of Mr. Merchant as President which, in February, 1849, led to the resignation of the Vice-President and three Trustees. The new Vice-President was Mr. Spencer S. Benedict, who filled the office acceptably until February 12, 1851, when he retired from office, and, in April following, from the Board, to the great regret of his associates. Mr. Benedict was one of the original members of the Board and is the only survivor. The office of Vice-President—which was an honorary one—remained vacant until the annual election in April, when the Board elected Mr. Isaac C. Kendall, who held the position for twelve years. By Act of the Legislature, April 5, 1849, the name of the Company was changed and its business year was made to correspond to the calendar year. The date of the annual election was not changed. The dividend declared at the end of the fourth year's business was forty per cent. in scrip and six per cent. in cash on former dividends.

1849. In 1849 there were 31,506 deaths in the United States from cholera, of which number 5,071 occurred in New York City. The disease had been brought from Havre to both New York and New Orleans in December of the preceding year, and from these points it gradually spread over the country, following lines of travel. Over 1,000 emigrants died on the overland *route* to California. The first case of the year in New York occurred May fifteenth, and the number of deaths rapidly increased from 35 in May to 2,625 in July. It then began to abate, the deaths in August being 1,452 and in September 161. On June thirteenth the Board of Trustees voted "that during the prevalence of the cholera the Company will issue no policies except at the regularly established *life* rates, upon the lives of persons residing in the cities of New York and Brooklyn, and that in reference to other localities the propriety of issuing policies for a term of years at present rates of premium

PRESIDENT NEW-YORK LIFE INSURANCE COMPANY, DECEMBER 22, 1848—OCTOBER 22, 1885.

be referred to the Committee on Applications, together with the President and Actuary, with power." This resolution remained in force until August eighth, when it was rescinded.*

Strenuous efforts were made during the latter part of this year to increase the Company's agency force. A Special Committee was appointed to act with the regular Committee on Agencies, and $10,000 was appropriated for their work. The general agency system, under which one man was given control of a certain territory with authority to appoint local agents, was adopted. "A suitable lecture designed to illustrate the principles of life insurance, to be delivered or otherwise disposed of," was prepared for the use of agents. This was the beginning of the system of Company publications, which has been a valuable means of educating the public to an appreciation of life insurance. An agency was established in Philadelphia late in this year, and the Boston agency, which had been discontinued in September, 1847, was revived. The Joint Committee reported, on January 13, 1850, that 97 agencies had been established; that there had been issued to new agents up to that time C5 policies with premiums amounting to $4,193.12; and that the total expenditures of the Committee had been only $948.66. The work had been so well done that the Joint Committee was made permanent. Among the agents appointed in Indiana at this time appear three names that have since become known to fame—Hugh McCulloch, Lew Wallace and Thomas A. Hendricks. The first of these afterward became Secretary of the United States Treasury, the second a distinguished soldier and author, and the third, Vice-President of the United States.†

---

* The following table shows the Company's mortality experience from cholera from 1845 to 1892:

Year.	No.	Year.	No.	Year.	No.	Year.	No.
1849,	7	1863,	1	1873,	8	1888,	2
1850,	25	1865,	1	1875,	1	1889,	2
1851,	3	1866,	18	1876,	1	1890,	2
1852,	3	1867,	2	1878,	2	1891,	1
1853,	5	1870,	1	1886,	1	1892,	4
1854,	4	1872,	1	1887,	5	TOTAL,	100

† INDIANAPOLIS, Jan. 14, 1850.

Dear Sir: You would oblige me, and forward the interest of the Company very much, by sending me a list of persons to whom losses have been paid within a month or two past. I'll have to "puff" here considerably. Two other companies have agencies of older date and larger run, and so far they have the advantage of me. I'll have to work up with them, as it were, "hand over hand."

Yours most respectfully, LEW. WALLACE.

The discovery of gold at Sutter's Mill, in the town of Coloma, Upper California, in February, 1848, was the signal for an immigration of gold-hunters and the building of a prosperous commonwealth that are without parallel in the history of civilization. Previous to this time the Company had taken occasional risks on the lives of traders and ship-masters visiting the Pacific Coast, at varying rates. In February, 1849, a uniform rate of three per cent. extra on the amount insured was adopted, the policies being written on the seven-year table, to run three years only.*

The extra rate was reduced to two and one-half per cent. in March, 1852; to two per cent. in February, 1853; to one per cent. in 1858; and in 1859 it was taken off entirely for persons residing in San Francisco.

The *routes* first prescribed were *via* Cape Horn or the Isthmus of Panama, but in March, 1850, "the overland *route* through Missouri" was added.†

1850. THE fifth annual report, comprising the business of about eight and a-half months (April 16 to December 31, 1849), showed proportionally a slight falling off in new business and a slight increase in premiums. A dividend of forty per cent. on earned premiums was declared in scrip, and four per cent. interest on dividends outstanding.

---

* "HUDSON, N. Y., Feb. 7, 1849.

Please find enclosed application of Hugh H. & Levi Bain for an assurance of $500 for three years on the life of Milton Bain. He expects to go to California in the Hudson Company. This company go out provisioned and provided with everything to take care of one another, intending to engage in trading and mining. Mr. Bain is the very picture of health—a stout, active young man. I inclose a copy of the By-Laws of the Company. S. L. MAGOUN, Agent."

The By-Laws provided that the company should consist of fifty men or more, each of whom should pay to Barnard Curtiss & Co., of Hudson—who were designated as receivers—the sum of $500, to be used in fitting out a vessel and for other purposes of the expedition. Other articles provided for the government and management of the company, and for a division of the profits. The Hudson "Weekly Record" of September 29, 1894, published in response to an inquiry a complete list of the company, and the statement that they sailed from New York on the bark "Monsam," March 8, 1849. The officers were Henry Waldo, Captain; Stephen J. Coffin, 1st Mate; H. Burr Carey, 2d Mate; J. W. Burrough, Physician.

† "VERMONT, COOPER CO., MO., Dec. 24, 1853.

I am here with from $20,000 to $25,000 worth of horses, cattle and sheep wintering and preparing to cross the plains to California next summer. I expect to leave here from the middle of May to the first of June, and shall want a California permit. I have the most complete outfit ever started—have about 25 men well-mounted and armed, and have no kind of fear from Indians or sickness. I have two partners; our names are Lathrop, Fish and Rawson. Write me if you still charge two and a-half per cent. for California risks, and I will send with my next semi-annual pay a year's extra.

H. B. LATHROP, Policy No. 4,225."

In October, previous, it had been voted to pay no dividends on policies issued after January 1, 1850, for any period less than whole life.

The presence of yellow fever in the sea-ports of the Southern States had always been considered an additional risk to policy-holders residing therein, and early in 1850 careful inquiries were made of resident physicians, and the following rules adopted respecting the issue of policies: Persons who had recovered from yellow fever, or who had resided continuously in a southern sea-port for five years in one of which yellow fever had prevailed, were to be insured at the usual rates; persons who resided in such ports in winter, and in healthful portions of the interior in summer, were to be charged an extra of one-half of one per cent. on the amount insured; persons who had resided in such ports continuously for two years, and who continued so to reside, were to be charged one per cent. extra. Persons not falling in one of the above classes were not to be insured.

This year witnessed a change in the policy-form, which was the precursor of other changes which have since taken place, and which culminated in 1892 in the issue of the Accumulation Policy, without any restrictions whatever. On November 13, 1850, a Committee of the Trustees—consisting of Orsamus Bushnell, Attorney of the Company; Isaac C. Kendall, Vice-President; and Henry A. Nelson—recommended "that the words, 'shall die upon the seas,' and the words, 'shall die by his own hand, whether sane or insane,' be omitted in the policies; and that the words, 'that lie east of the Rocky Mountains,' and the words, 'or in case his death shall be caused by intoxicating drinks or opium,' be inserted in said policies."

The business of 1850 was more than double that of the partial year 1849, and the accumulated funds of the Company being now in excess of two hundred thousand dollars, as required by the charter, the unused portions of the subscription notes were given up and canceled at the end of November. A scrip dividend of fifty per cent. was declared in January, 1851, and interest at six per cent. in cash paid on dividends outstanding.

In July, 1850, the Company's office was removed to 106 Broadway.

1851. THE Company had now been in existence six years, and during the last five years had been declaring dividends, for which scrip had been issued to policy-holders who paid their premiums in cash, and credits given on the books to such as gave notes for a part of the pre-

FIRST OFFICE ON BROADWAY—1850.

[The American Surety Company has recently erected a twenty-story marble building on this site.]

mium. All policies were forfeitable for non-payment of premium, and lapsed policies had no surrender value, either in cash or paid-up insurance. The scrip dividends issued on such policies, however, were a contingent liability of the Company, and the Company held on many lapsed policies notes for forty per cent. of the premiums. The dividends slightly exceeded the notes, and on March 12, 1851, the officers of the Company were authorized to exchange premium notes for dividends on discontinued policies, dollar for dollar. Discontinuing policy-holders fared much better therefore in the NEW-YORK LIFE, previous to the issue of non-forfeiting policies, than in an all-cash company, as their insurance only cost them sixty per cent. of the table rates.* The all-cash plan was favorable to the policy-holders who kept up their policies, because they shared in the surplus which was created by the forfeiture of reserves; it enabled the companies practicing it to make large dividends, because in the absence of non-forfeiture provisions their policies were practically Tontines, with whole life periods.

On April 8, 1851, the New York Legislature passed a law requiring all life companies doing business in the State to deposit $100,000 in securities with the Comptroller during the next ten months, and to make full annual reports to that officer. The NEW-YORK LIFE'S deposit was authorized by the Trustees July twenty-third and made September nineteenth. During this year the risks of the Phœnix Insurance Company of St. Louis, 856 in number, insuring $1,146,715, with annual premiums of $32,763, were transferred to the NEW-YORK LIFE, to date from June fourteenth. Of the policies thus re-insured 161 were whole life policies, and the remainder were for short terms; 535 were California policies, of which number 488 expired within the year. At the meeting of the Trustees, held in January, 1852, a scrip dividend of forty per cent. was declared and six per cent. ordered paid in cash on former dividends.

The law of April 8, 1851, in requiring other-State companies to deposit $100,000 in New York, and to pay taxes on this amount in the county where their chief office was situated, caused great dissatisfaction on the part of such companies, twelve of which withdrew from the State. It also provoked retaliatory legislation on the part of other States, in consequence of which the NEW-YORK LIFE ceased to do new business in Connecticut in April, 1852, and in Massachusetts in September, 1852. In June, 1853, the New York law was so modified as to permit the re-

*The cause of the Massachusetts non-forfeiture act of 1861 was to prevent all-cash payers from being treated worse in case of a discontinuance of the policy than those who had paid part by note.—*Elizur Wright, in North American Review, July, 1886.*

quired deposit to be made with the chief financial officer of the State by which the company was incorporated. Modifications of the laws in Massachusetts and Connecticut followed, and the NEW-YORK LIFE re-entered the former in October, 1854, and the latter in June, 1855. The business of the Company in the New England States was, however, insignificant at this time. Its Boston Agent, Mr. Samuel Jenks, was appointed State Actuary, under the Massachusetts law of 1852.* His successor did but little business and the agency was again abolished. Whether by reason of a hostile public feeling of which such legislation was the outcome, or from more general causes, the business of life insurance seems to have entered a period of decline early in the fifties. Nearly all the life companies show either a falling-off or only small gains. The eight companies whose figures are accessible show $14,233,193 of new insurance issued in 1850, which proved high-water mark for nine years.† The business of the NEW-YORK LIFE shared in the general decline.

---

*The Massachusetts law of 1852 is historically important, as being the first attempt to compel a showing by the life companies that should indicate their real financial standing. By its terms the returns of the companies were to include the present value of existing policies, the present value of premiums receivable on the same, and a statement showing amount of assets, how invested, etc. No mortality table and no rate of interest were prescribed, and each company chose its own. There was a curious misunderstanding on the part of some companies of the phrase "present value of existing policies." The author of the law evidently meant the aggregate of the single premiums required to insure all the policy-holders for amounts equal to existing policies, else there was no significance in requiring the present value of premiums receivable. Four Connecticut companies made their returns on this basis, while three companies from New York and one each from New Jersey, Pennsylvania and Maine gave as the "present value of existing policies" their reserve funds, regarded as the difference between the present value of the insurance and the present value of future net premiums. Nevertheless, the companies that misunderstood the law made the more reasonable showing; for the others computed their premiums receivable in gross, and so showed a surplus in excess of their assets. The criticisms of Hon. Elizur Wright on the law, and those of Harvey G. Tuckett, Editor of "Tuckett's Monthly Insurance Journal," on the returns made under it, seem to have grown out of a like misunderstanding of its terms. See "Insurance Blue Book," Centennial Edition, page 45; Tuckett's "Journal" of May 14, 1853; and for the returns themselves, the "Journal" of March 15, 1853.

†The following table comprises the new business and total premiums received of the Mutual Benefit of N. J., Mutual Life of New York, National Life of Vt., New England Mutual, NEW-YORK LIFE, State Mutual of Mass., and Union Mutual of Me.:

	No. of Pols. issued.	New Insurance.	Total Prems. for Ins.		No. of Pols. issued.	New Insurance.	Total Prems. for Ins.
1850, . .	6,856	$14,233,193	$1,405,599	1855, . .	3,767	$11,099,261	$1,827,965
1851, . .	6,246	12,925,555	1,542,436	1856, . .	4,638	13,246,806	2,292,360
1852, . .	5,564	10,175,878	1,634,324	1857, . .	4,355	13,323,339	2,274,651
1853, . .	4,241	9,642,146	1,716,557	1858, . .	4,813	14,659,820	2,515,984
1854, . .	3,882	10,139,704	1,832,148				

1852. UNDER the general insurance law of 1849 life insurance companies not incorporated by special Act of the Legislature were required to make annual reports to the Comptroller of the State, and under the law of April 8, 1851, this requirement was made general. The NEW-YORK LIFE—which had heretofore published annual reports in accordance with its charter—made its first report under the new law in June, 1852. This report gave in detail the securities of the Company, the amount of dividend for each year, and the number and amount of policies then in force according to year of issue. The latter table showed that the proportion of whole life policies then issued was much greater than in the earlier years of the Company. The blanks sent out by the Comptroller contained over forty questions relative to the management of the business. No fault seems to have been found with the returns of the companies until about the time for sending out blanks for the next reports, when Mr. Edmund Blunt, who had been appointed by the Governor a commissioner to examine into the condition of life companies doing business in the State, wrote hurriedly from Brooklyn to the Comptroller, that some of the answers were "insufficient." "Perhaps," he said, "the officers of the companies do not understand the questions, and it may be necessary to explain them; I should hope it were so, were not some of the answers in an evasive form, which, I am sorry to say, forbids it."* On December twentieth Mr. Blunt wrote again, saying the NEW-

* From a letter of Mr. Blunt, afterward published in the "Courier and Enquirer," it is evident the NEW-YORK LIFE was here referred to. Mr. Blunt therein gives as "a specimen of evasion," question 19 and answer, as follows: "*Question.*—State the method by which the amount of surplus was determined. *Answer.*—By deducting the dividends from the assets." Instead of being an evasion this was the literal truth, as may be seen by a reference to the Company's printed report for January 1, 1850, from which the following is an exact transcript:

"Amount of accumulated capital,		$211,829.50
Deduct amount formerly appropriated for dividends and interest,		74,540.60
Surplus, 1st January, 1850,		$137,288.90
Of which is appropriated as a Reserved Fund,	$85,322.15	
" " " Dividend of 1st Jan., 1850, 40 per cent.,	49,078.75	
" " as Interest on former Dividends, 4 per cent.	2,888.00	
		$137,288.90."

The difficulty arose from a misunderstanding of terms, and it shows how loosely terms were then used, which have since come to have a fixed and definite meaning. Quite likely they had then to Mr. Blunt, who was attached to the United States Coast Survey and was presumably a man of scientific attainments.

YORK LIFE'S losses, expenses and dividends in 1851 were more than its premium receipts, and that it should be prevented from declaring a dividend for 1852.

1853. THE Trustees, however, seem to have been earlier in the field than Mr. Blunt, and to have begun a thorough investigation of the Company's affairs before he examined its report, as the annual report issued in February, 1853,* contained the following statement:

> During the last year a competent mathematician has been engaged in valuing each outstanding policy upon the principle adopted by the "Equitable" of London—the mammoth company of the world—in order to ascertain the propriety of making, or dispensing with, the usual scrip dividend at the present time. The result of such calculations has satisfied the officers and the Board that the assets of the Company are amply sufficient to re-insure all their risks, and pay all the dividends heretofore declared, in cash, leaving a surplus [$25,313.90], but that such surplus would not now justify a further scrip dividend. * * * Under these circumstances the Finance Committee recommended, and the Board unanimously agreed, that although upon the principle previously adopted, the usual average dividend could have been made, leaving a large available surplus, yet, as stability, rather than great profits, should be the aim of life insurance companies in an especial manner, they believed that the interests of the policy-holders would be best promoted by passing the dividend for the present year, but that six per cent. interest be paid, in cash, upon all dividends heretofore declared.

Notwithstanding this prompt and wise action of the Trustees, a determined effort seems to have been made to discredit the Company before the public. The Company finally addressed the Comptroller on the subject, asking "whether from the statements on file in his office, or in his possession, or from information upon which he relied, he believed the Company to be in a sound and healthy condition." The Comptroller replied, under date of April 6, 1853, that the Company's last report had been "submitted to a gentleman of high character and integrity from a neighboring State," "an officer of one of the best-conducted and soundest companies in that State," who gave his opinion, "derived from an examination of this return, and other means of accurate knowledge, your

---

* This report is interesting in that it includes a statement of the various kinds and amounts of policies then in force, as follows: 2,364 life policies insuring $2,358,883.90, 80 paid-up policies insuring $209,050, California policies insuring $678,315, short-term policies insuring $1,060,800, 4 joint life policies, 1 endowment policy and 1 annuity. The amount of dividends outstanding was $303,484, of which $19,945 were upon canceled policies. The premium notes on these policies were $17,662.39.

Company is entirely sound and able to re-insure all its outstanding risks in a well-conducted company, and pay for the same out of their cash assets, and then have left in cash an amount very nearly, if not quite, equal to that now necessary for the organization of a new company." As the amount necessary to establish a new company was $100,000, the Company's estimate of its surplus was very conservative. This seems to have ended the controversy, and with the Comptroller's letter certifying to its solvency, and the commendation of the best insurance authorities of the time for its courage in passing a dividend as soon as the new system of valuing policies showed it to be necessary, the Company went on its way paying its claims and so fulfilling its mission. (See next page.)

During the year 1853 the yellow fever was epidemic in various southern sea-ports and along the Mississippi River. It was especially virulent in New Orleans, the number of deaths there being 7,970. The highest number in any preceding year was 2,259 in 1847, and in any subsequent year 3,889 in 1858.* On August tenth the Board of Trustees appropriated $250 to be expended among the sick and destitute of that city, and on October twelfth $150 was appropriated for the same purpose in Mobile.

At the meeting of the Trustees held in January, 1854, a scrip dividend of 30 per cent. of the premiums on policies one year in force was declared, and six per cent. interest in cash was ordered paid on dividends outstanding.

1854. In the years 1854 and 1855 the new business of the Company reached its lowest ebb; the new policies were less than 500, and the new insurance less than $1,500,000 in each year—figures which, in the later years of the Company's history, have frequently been surpassed

---

* The losses of the Company from yellow fever, from 1845 to 1892, have been as follows:

Year.	No.	Year.	No.	Year.	No.	Year.	No.
1853,	7	1867,	5	1881,	1	1888,	9
1854,	3	1870,	4	1883,	5	1889,	4
1855,	12	1873,	19	1884,	3	1890,	3
1862,	1	1876,	1	1885,	5	1891,	6
1864,	1	1878,	26	1886,	1	1892,	18
1866,	1	1879,	1	1887,	2	TOTAL,	138

Baltimore 407 W Lombard St.
24th November 1852

* *

If I could I would desire [to in]crease the amount of Insurance to the [u]tmost limit. – Small as is the sum it [co]sts much self-denial to spare it — but [wh]at is self-denial to the Mother of two [n]oble boys whom even this sum may [a]id to educate?

With great respect
Mary Bradford

[B]altimore 15 July 1853 Received of New York [Li]fe Insurance Company their Check on Metropolitan [B]ank for Eleven Hundred & thirty nine dollars Eighty [o]ne cents in full for Policy No 7784.

For Mary Bradford
Hugh Sanders

by the record of a single day. It would seem that life insurance is not stimulated to any great extent by fear, but rather by the higher elements of human character.* The year 1849 was the worst cholera year, and the year 1853 was the worst yellow fever year, this country has ever known; yet the first immediately preceded, and the second occurred in the midst of, a period marked by the greatest apathy toward life insurance. In 1854 and 1855 both cholera and yellow fever† prevailed to a considerable extent, and the latter was epidemic at Norfolk and Portsmouth, Va., in 1855. On September twenty-fifth of the latter year the Company contributed $250 toward a fund raised in New York for the sufferers in these cities. The Company had eight losses in Norfolk, including its Medical Examiner.‡

Late in the year 1854 a circular letter was sent to agents asking their views respecting the effect on the business of a change to the all-cash system. The replies were, upon the whole, adverse to a change from the custom of receiving forty per cent. of the premiums in notes, when desired by the policy-holder. Late in December of this year the Company decided to make an extra charge of one-half of one per cent. on whole life policies issued to residents of Southern States, and of one per

---

* "January 25, 1854.

Accompanying this note please find my life policy No. 7,350, which I send to you for obvious reasons. At the time I took the above policy it was made, as you will observe, 'for the benefit of my two sisters,' being then, as I am yet, unmarried, but how long I may continue so, time will determine. I also at that time learned that I could have it transferred to any other person (or persons) whenever I might choose, and now, in accordance with those conditions, I feel warranted in requesting that you will transfer said benefit from my sisters therein mentioned, to my esteemed friend (Miss) C—— E—— H——."

Whether or not the course of true love failed to run smoothly, we do not know, but the new policy was not issued at this time. Cupid, however, had his way at last, for in 1877 a policy was issued on this life in favor of C—— E——, "wife" of the insured.

† Deaths from yellow fever in New Orleans in 1854, 2,423; in 1855, 2,670.

‡ PORTSMOUTH, VA., Nov. 30, 1855.

The late terrible affairs in our stricken town have caused me to be absent for some time, having had to remove the wreck of my family to North Carolina. My sufferings are truly great, but I am now home again, and next week will remit to you my account and balance due up to the end of this month. On my return I was sick and sent to the hospital, but am now, thank God, convalescent. The death of my wife, sister, eldest son, and two dear friends, I trust will be sufficient excuse for my late remissness. * * * * * * * * * *

MATT. W. AYLWIN, *Agent.*

cent. on short term policies. These rates were for acclimated persons; rates for unacclimated persons were left to be determined when the insurance was applied for.

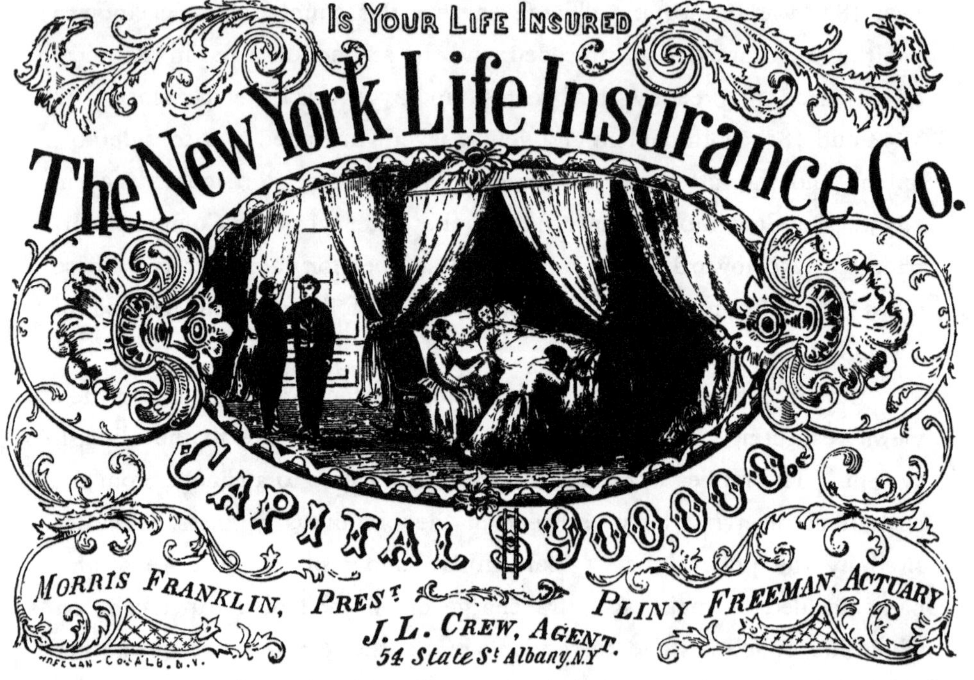

FROM A CIRCULAR USED IN 1854.

1855. AT the meeting of the Trustees held in January, 1855, the Finance Committee reported that the present value of outstanding policies had been carefully made by Mr. Beers and that the surplus of the Company was $117,682.59. A dividend of thirty per cent. upon the premiums of policies one year in force was declared, and interest at six per cent. in cash ordered paid on dividends outstanding.

The eleventh annual report was presented to the Trustees January 26, 1856, and showed the assets of the Company to be $1,059,008.65. Of this amount $392,288.21 was in premium notes, $573,652.63 in other

July 3, 1855, application received from J. C. Lewis, agent at Washington, D. C., for $500 insurance on life of Mary Hawkins, colored, in favor of Thomas Bates, as security for money advanced to purchase her freedom.

interest-bearing securities, $42,560.11 in cash, and $50,507.70 in accrued interest, deferred premiums and agents' balances. There was over a clean million dollars, therefore, in cash and invested securities; and the Finance Committee reported that, after making provision for the re-insurance of all existing policies, all dividends previously declared, together with interest due and all other claims, there remained a surplus of $148,718.23. The dividend declared was the same as that of the previous year.

Nearly eleven years had passed since the Company began business, and, although its officers were inexperienced and its early methods were crude, it had paid to policy-holders $1,027,202.64, and had on hand $1,059,008.65 as security for policies in force amounting to $10,277,101. It was now on solid ground as respects liability and reserve under its policies, and was prepared henceforth to conduct its operations intelligently and effectively.

DESIGN USED ON ENVELOPES IN 1855–6.

VI.

NON-FORFEITING POLICIES AND THE REDEMPTION OF DIVIDENDS.

1856–1860.

DURING the year 1855 the NEW-YORK LIFE paid taxes, licenses and fees in twelve different States to the amount of $3,015.44, and made certified statements concerning its organization, business and financial condition to the officials of five States.* At the close of the period now under review twenty of the thirty-three States of the Union had enacted laws for the regulation of the business of life companies, and in most of them annual statements were required.† These statements were of all degrees of fullness, from a simple return of premiums received, for taxation, which in some States was made by the chief agency, as in Maryland, to the full statement demanded by the Insurance Department of Massachusetts, which had been created in 1855. The requirements of the laws were new both to officers of the States and to company officials, and it was not always easy to present acceptable evidence of the condition of a company.‡

---

*New York, Ohio, Illinois, Kentucky and Tennessee. The statement for Rhode Island was prepared but not filed, as no new business was done there in 1855.

†The Company filed its statement for 1860 in ten States—New York, Ohio, Illinois, Kentucky, Tennessee, Rhode Island, Wisconsin, South Carolina, Pennsylvania and Michigan. The Michigan statement was returned to have the acknowledgment taken before a Commissioner of Deeds instead of a Notary. The South Carolina statement has the following note: "Forwarded to James H. Taylor, Charleston, Feb. 11, 1861; Feb. 18th, received back with a string of objections."

‡Office of PENN MUTUAL LIFE INSURANCE CO.,
N. E. cor. of Third and Dock Sts.

MORRIS FRANKLIN, Esq., President, PHILADELPHIA, June 13, 1856.
NEW-YORK LIFE INS. CO., New York, N. Y.

Dear Sir:— * * * * * * * We have not decided yet to comply with the new Kentucky Law regarding Foreign Insurance Companies. I should like to know what you are going to do, and whether in your opinion the second paragraph of section 8 of the law applies to life companies, and what you intend to give the Auditor as liabilities. I am very much at a loss on these points and shall be very glad to have your views to assist me in deciding. Very respectfully,

JNO. W. HORNOR, *Secretary.*

1856. A LONG correspondence was had with the Auditor of Illinois in 1856, in order to satisfy him that the Company was duly incorporated and that it was possessed of securities to the amount of $100,000, as required by the law of his State. The evidence required was such that, under date of February fifteenth, the President of the Company wrote somewhat despairingly: "We are desirous to comply with your law if it can be done, but we are now altogether at a loss, with assets amounting to $1,000,000, what evidence will enable us to do so." It was not until November eleventh that the Company's agent at Springfield wrote: "The papers forwarded me for Auditor are satisfactory. Certificates have been issued and mailed to agents."

The legislation which was increasing every year had behind it three motives: First, the protection of the people from insolvent corporations; second, the collection of taxes; and third, local jealousy of other-State companies. The influence last named came first in the order of time. The early laws of Pennsylvania (1829–1849) and New York (1828–1837) taxing the premiums of other-State companies twenty, and ten per cent., respectively, had been practically prohibitive of such companies, and were intended so to be. The great fire of 1835 taught New York that insurance should not be made a local matter, and Pennsylvania learned the same lesson when she saw the insurance sceptre—which she held prior to 1845—depart from her borders. The New York deposit law of 1851 was a step backward, but it was soon retraced. The highest tax imposed on premiums during this period was three* per cent., and the highest price demanded for a county license was $300;† the latter was practically prohibitive except in large cities. In New York no tax was imposed on the premiums of life companies, but home companies were assessed on personal property to nearly the full amount of their assets, under the law

---

* In Pennsylvania, Maryland and Rhode Island; reduced to two per cent. in the latter State in 1857.

† In Missouri; reduced to $40 in 1859.

taxing the capital of corporations.* The law of April 10, 1849, had provided that no life insurance company should be formed thereafter without at least $100,000 capital; the Act of June 29, 1853, provided that any mutual life insurance company incorporated previous to the law of 1849 should be subject to taxation in the same manner as if it were incorporated under the law of 1849 with a capital of $100,000; while the law of March 4, 1855, declared that any such company should be subject to taxation on $100,000 for personal property, and no more, and that such was the intention and true construction of the Act of 1853. The life companies contended for the construction of the law given by the Act of 1855, and in 1857 the Court of Appeals decided that they were right only with respect to assessments made subsequent to the passage of the law, —that it had no retroactive application.†

It was soon perceived by those who had the public welfare at heart that the possession of a certain amount of assets was no guarantee of a life company's solvency, unless the liabilities under its policies were ascertained in a scientific manner, and a balance struck between the two sides of the account. The crude attempt made under the Massachusetts law of 1852 was supplemented under the law of 1858 by requiring the life companies to furnish the Insurance Commissioners with the data necessary to make an annual valuation of their policies. No table of mortality or rate of interest was prescribed by the law, but the Commissioners adopted the Actuaries' Table of Mortality with four per cent. interest. The first returns were made under this law as of November 1, 1858. The system of supervision by an Insurance Department, and the requirements of an annual net valuation of outstanding policies, thus begun, have since been established in nearly every State in the Union.

---

* TAX COMMISSIONERS' OFFICE,
NEW YORK, May 17, 1856.

The President, etc., of the NEW-YORK LIFE INSURANCE CO. are hereby notified that said Company are assessed for the year 1856 at $1,000,000, the same as last year. The Tax Commissioners cannot allow the Company's construction of the law and its amendments, which regulate the assessment of said Company, until the same is so settled and disposed of by the Court of Appeals, to which the question has been carried.

Respectfully, etc.,

J. W. ALLEN, W. J. PECK, A. J. WILLIAMSON, *Tax Commissioners.*

† People *ex. rel.* The Mutual Life Insurance Company *vs.* Board of Supervisors County of New York.

At the meeting of the Trustees, held January 31, 1857, the usual dividend of thirty per cent. was declared, and six per cent. interest on dividends outstanding. The reserve value of policies in force was $598,816.54; dividends outstanding were $457,027; leaving an unappropriated balance of $135,702.05. The dividend declared required $82,058, and interest $27,421.62.

1857. THE year 1857 was marked by a severe financial crisis. The failures were nearly five thousand in number, with aggregate liabilities of nearly three hundred million dollars. The failure of the Ohio Life and Trust Company was the beginning of the crisis, but it had previously ceased to do a life insurance business. The other life companies stood firm and did about the same amount of business as in '56; the NEW-YORK LIFE'S business showed an increase. Among the prominent failures in New York City was that of the dry goods house of Bowen, McNamee & Co., at 112 & 114 Broadway. In November a Committee of the Trustees, appointed in 1856 on a permanent location for the Company, reported that the premises then occupied by this firm could

OFFICE AT 112 & 114 BROADWAY.
[Occupied May, 1857.]

be bought for $110,000. After having the premises examined by an architect, the Board voted, on November nineteenth, to make the purchase. The second floor of the building was at once put in order for the accommodation of the Company, the remainder being arranged for rental. When the Company took possession of its new offices in May following, the rents from tenants were equal to over six per cent. on the purchase price and the cost of improvements.

At the meeting of the Trustees, held January 29, 1858, the Finance Committee reported that, notwithstanding the financial crisis of the previous year, the Company had sustained no losses on its investments. The annual report showed a decrease in the number of term policies in force, and upon this it was remarked: "The officers believe such a result rather desirable than otherwise. Experience demonstrates that the present rates of premium are not sufficient for the risks incurred, most of which are of an extra hazardous character, and such as were not contemplated in the establishment of the rates." The number of short-term policies issued during the year was 62, insuring $169,000, and the number in force was 276, insuring $785,000.

About ten per cent. of the applications received during the year were rejected. The results under "Phœnix" policies and California risks were shown to be favorable. The general agency from which most business had been received up to this time was that in Baltimore.* The usual dividend of thirty per cent. of the premiums on whole life policies one year in force, and interest at six per cent. on former dividends, were voted.

1858. In February, 1858, a Canadian agency was established at Toronto, with Mr. J. Leander Starr as General Agent. The agency was discontinued in January, 1860, on account of the excessive cost of business procured.

*The new business and losses at the Home Office and principal agencies to July 1, 1857, were reported as follows:

Home Office	Policies,	2,127	Premiums,	$672,080	Losses,	$216,212
Mobile	"	266	"	124,163	"	94,700
New Orleans	"	386	"	184,438	"	83,170
Baltimore	"	786	"	254,309	"	101,174
Buffalo	"	364	"	84,211	"	29,350
Cincinnati	"	121	"	42,633	"	13,000
St. Louis	"	292	"	113,616	"	21,750

In July, 1858, a Committee of the Trustees was appointed to consider the question of beginning the redemption of dividends. The Committee reported adversely in December. The charter permitted such redemption after the dividends reached the sum of $500,000, and required it after they reached the sum of $1,000,000; but the amendment of 1849 forbade the declaration and payment of any dividend "that would impair the capital or accumulation of the Company." The total dividends now outstanding were $593,234, of which $59,740 were declared prior to 1850. The language of the Act of 1849 was obscure, and it was thought that additional authority would be required to redeem the scrip issued subsequent to 1850, and that to begin redemption without a comprehensive plan, and full authority to continue, would be unwise. A further reason for postponing the subject as long as possible was found in the fact that the dividends were really funded surplus which was held subject to the liabilities of the Company, and that until redeemed they constituted an additional resource which greatly strengthened its position in case of financial disaster or a mortality in excess of the tables. Up to this time no considerable tabulation of American mortality had been made, and whether English experience would prove trustworthy at the older policy ages was still an open question.*

In this position the Trustees were confirmed by the report of a Board of Examiners appointed by the Mutual Life Insurance Company in 1856. The dividends of the Mutual Life had up to this time been declared every five years, and were in the form of reversionary additions to the policies and payable with them. In 1853 the insured were allowed the option of converting the dividends into annuities for permanent reduction of the premiums on the policies. The principle underlying dividends in life in-

*The most important contribution made to mortality upon insured lives in the United States that had been made public at this time was the experience of the Mutual Benefit Life Insurance Company, published in 1857. The data covered eleven years and the equivalent of 45,000 lives for one year. The number of deaths was 510 as compared with 578 expected deaths by the Carlisle Table, and 538 by the Actuaries' Table. The Mutual Life of New York published in the same year a brief table showing 315 actual losses as against 387 losses expected during the preceding four years, to which was added this comment: "It must be borne in mind that life insurance is only in its infancy in this country, and that full thirty years must elapse before we can calculate results with any degree of certainty." (*Mutual Life's Fourteenth Annual Report.*)

surance is that the policy-holder has paid more than was necessary; but this was the very point that was not yet considered settled by actual experience, and the Examiners did not approve the relinquishment of any part of the premiums, and expressed the opinion that funding the surplus, after the manner of the NEW-YORK LIFE, was the safer method.*

At the meeting of the Trustees, held January 26, 1859, it was found that the assets exceeded one and one-half million dollars, and that the surplus, after the usual dividend of thirty per cent. on premiums and six per cent. interest on outstanding scrip, was $100,296.73. The short term policies had decreased to 237, insuring $654,900.

AN OLD LETTER HEADING.

*The Examining Board consisted of Hon. Luther Bradish, Hon. William Kent and Professor Henry James Anderson, L.L.D., and its report was in part as follows: "A reduction of these future premiums as a concession for the waiver of claims, avowedly subject to numberless contingencies, may hereafter under a less skillful administration than the present, surrender prematurely and irrevocably funds to which the company has an uncontested right, and which should be retained under the control of the Trustees until the last moment allowed by the charter. And the Examiners cannot refrain from approving the disposition which they understand prevails with the Trustees to watch with increasing vigilance the real object of remitting positive and secured future income in exchange for a release from contingent and secondary obligations. So much do the Examiners commend this view of the matter, that they cannot withhold the expression of their hope that the company will prefer to see their reversionary additions assume a more durable, rather than a less durable form. This might be effected, within the limits of the charter, by offering as the equivalent they present for the additions to the sums insured, not an extinction of a part of their future assets, but the conversion of the present, or reversionary value of each distributive share which exceeds a small fixed amount, into shares of proprietary stock [*i.e.*, scrip like the NEW-YORK LIFE'S dividends] bearing a suitable interest, negotiable under the usual conditions, and subject, in the legal order of liabilities, to respond in case of failure of earlier resources. A surplus thus funded would obviate the only sound objection to the mutual principle, and would not be open to the complaint so often urged against proprietary companies, that the stockholders reap the fruits of others' savings than their own."

The report recited several cases of attempted fraud upon the Company. In one case a conspiracy was entered into by the insured and several other persons. All went fishing; the insured fell overboard and "was not seen to rise." Some time afterward a body in an advanced state of decomposition was found, and upon it clothing and a finger ring belonging to the insured. When the scheme seemed about to succeed the conspirators quarrelled among themselves, the plot was exposed, and the insurance was not claimed. Another case was cited to show the prejudice of courts and juries against corporations. An itinerant Methodist minister in Kentucky disappeared and it was claimed that he had been murdered, and suit was brought against the Company for the amount of his policy. Witnesses were produced by the Company who testified that they had seen him alive subsequent to the time of his alleged demise; one of them had been married by him. Upon the first two trials the jury disagreed; upon the third a verdict was found against the Company. The Court of Appeals refused to interfere on the ground that it was a question of fact for the jury, and not of law for the court. Meanwhile an attachment was issued against the property of the insured on the ground that he was an absconding debtor; it was resisted on the ground that he was dead, but the attachment was sustained. By these two decisions the insured was judicially dead with respect to the Company, but judicially alive with respect to his creditors.

1859. GOLD was discovered near the base of Pike's Peak, Colorado, in 1858, and early in 1859 the Company, after a careful consideration of its experience on California risks, issued a circular to agents announcing that it would accept risks upon emigrants to the new gold regions at an extra of one and one-half per cent. A circular of the time, reduced about one-half, is shown on the following page.

In May, 1859, the NEW-YORK LIFE united with thirteen other American, and two English, companies in the American Life Underwriters' Convention.* The first suggestion of such a gathering seems to

---

* Aetna, American Mutual of New Haven, American Temperance, Berkshire, Charter Oak, Connecticut Mutual, Knickerbocker, Manhattan, Massachusetts Mutual, Mutual Life, Penn Mutual, Union Mutual, United States, Eagle and Albion of London, Royal of Liverpool.

PIKE'S PEAK
GOLD REGIONS!

LIFE INSURANCE!

Policies granted by
THE NEW-YORK LIFE INSURANCE CO.
112 & 114 Broadway, N.Y.

ACCUMULATED CAPITAL
ONE MILLION, SIX HUNDRED THOUSAND DOLLARS

In view of the extensive emigration to the Gold Regions, the above well-known Company of 14 years standing, are now prepared to issue policies for that locality. Parties can thus secure to their families or friends some resource in case of accidents, and creditors protect themselves from loss for advances. For full particulars, as of Rates, &c., apply to

______________________ **Agent, at** ______________________

have come from Mr. Gilbert E. Currie, Editor of the "United States Insurance Gazette," who, by correspondence and personal solicitation, induced the principal companies to promise representation, and who acted as Secretary until the Convention was organized. Mr. Franklin, of the NEW-YORK LIFE, was made temporary Chairman, and Vice-President of the permanent organization. Mr. Winston, of the Mutual Life, was made President. The sessions were held at the Astor House. The following subjects were reported upon by committees and discussed by the Convention: Extra rates; mortality in the various geographical divisions of this continent, and the collection of vital statistics; the renewal of lapsed policies; and State legislation. It was voted that the companies be requested to contribute the data from which the combined mortality experience of American life companies could be deduced, according to residence, occupation and term of insurance.* On the subject of lapsed policies, informal conversation between members of the Convention was recommended. The report on legislation set forth the difficulties under which the companies labored in complying with the laws of the various States,† and recom-

THE FIRST EAGLE USED BY THE COMPANY, IN 1859.

* At the session of the Convention held in May, 1860, the Committee on Vital Statistics, of which Mr. Sheppard Homans, then Actuary of the Mutual Life, was Chairman, reported that returns had been promised by twenty-two companies and already received from thirteen. These statistics were afterward made the basis of the "American Table of Mortality," constructed by Mr. Homans.

† The laws of the States which relate to life insurance and their agencies are found to be very dissimilar, and in many instances not only conflicting, but retaliatory, in their origin and character. [During the debate it was stated by Mr. E. A. Bulkeley, then President of the Aetna Life of Hartford, that in one State "a law had been passed which expelled every company that had complied with the law of a neighboring State."] * * * The frequent modification of these laws, and the severe enactments which are added, and the complications that grow out of the various forms for making returns adopted by the officers which these laws create, have so far confused the public mind and embarrassed the business of life insurance, that relief should be afforded. The uniform law-abiding spirit which is interwoven into the management of life insurance companies induces on their part a strenuous effort to comply with all laws and evade none; but they are met constantly by new laws and new requirements

mended that a committee be appointed to draft a general law relating to life insurance companies incorporated in other States and in foreign countries.

The Convention adjourned, after a very harmonious session, to meet at the call of the President, on request of any three companies represented. President Winston in his closing address dwelt upon the zeal, intelligence and harmony that had marked the proceedings and upon the value of their combined experience with respect to mortality and the investment of funds. He urged the companies to unite in collecting, arranging and perfecting such a system as would be useful to themselves, and reflect credit on the Convention.

The sessions of the Convention were followed by a dinner at the Astor House, at which Vice-President Franklin presided. In his opening address Mr. Franklin dwelt upon the blessings of life insurance in protecting the family from distress, saying there was no act of his life which he performed with greater satisfaction than the payment to widows and orphans of the funds which their husbands and fathers had provided for them. Other addresses were made by Hon. Daniel F. Tieman, Mayor of the City, and members of the Convention.*

---

which, by undertaking to comply with, literally established for them results in different States which conflict with each other, and again add to the difficulty above alluded to. Your Committee are not the advocates of no law; on the contrary, in their opinion it is eminently wise and just, on the part of every State, to enact laws relating to life insurance companies and their agencies. And they recognize the right of every State to hold the companies which are organized under their own laws to a strict accountability. * * * Each company should be required to exhibit its condition in a proper manner, so that the public may know the amount of its capital, accumulations and surplus, how the same are invested, and such other facts as are necessary to a proper understanding of the condition of the company.—*From the Committee's Report.*

At the session of the Convention held in 1860, the Committee appointed to draft a general law made a verbal report favoring the principles of the Massachusetts law, but questioning the advisability of the Convention endeavoring to secure such legislation in other States.

* The following extracts will serve to indicate the growth both of the city and of life insurance:

By Mayor TIEMAN: "I do not know that I can say anything to our friends from abroad, except that I am happy to meet them. I welcome them as the father of the city, though I am not a very old father. Perhaps it would not be amiss to tell our friends from abroad how old I am. I am so old, gentlemen, that I remember the market gardens on the other side of Chambers Street, opposite the City Hall. I remember when they used to raise cabbages, salads and radishes on the. ground where Stewart's store is. [Then at the corner of Chambers Street and Broadway.] I was mentioning to the President what seemed to astonish him—that I was born in New York, have never lived outside of New York, and never lived in a house adjoining another. When I was about three years old my father

In view of the heavy losses sustained in Mobile, Ala., it was decided August tenth to add two per cent. on the amount insured to the rates then charged upon policies issued at this agency.

On the same day the Trustees voted to establish an agency in San Francisco, Cal. Mr. William F. Herrick was appointed agent. A local Board of Trustees was organized and, owing to the great distance from New York, authority was given to issue temporary policies good for ninety days, until applications could be passed upon at the Home Office. The extra rates fixed upon were one-half of one per cent. for San Francisco and one per cent. for the whole State. The protests against any extra charge became so numerous that the Company collected all the obtainable data on the mortality of the State, including a report of the State Register, and in November recommended to the Trustees that thenceforth residents of San Francisco be required to pay, in lieu of an extra, the fee for medical examination, and the exchange on New York in transmitting premiums. The recommendation concluded as follows:

> This we have reason to believe would satisfy applicants, as the objection does not appear to be so much the price for insurance as the, to them, apparently humiliating fact that the increase is called and charged an "extra," thereby alleging, at least by implication, that the climate of California is inferior to our own.*

---

moved to Twenty-third Street and Fourth Avenue, where he now lives on the same ground. There our friends would come from the city to see us one day and go back the next. It was too far into the country to go and come the same day. I can remember distinctly that when they wanted to come to the city they got ready the day before. * * * At the time of which I speak, New York extended only up to Chambers Street, and when people used to go to see the stone bridge which was at Canal Street, they had to get a hack!"

By J. GREEN PEARSON: "I suppose I am indebted for this call to an unfortunate remark I made this morning to my friend, Mr. Dennison, in relation to a circumstance connected with a marine insurance company, more than twenty year ago. [The company was the Union Marine, chartered in 1818.] The company set apart a fund of $100,000 for life insurance. Professor Renwick Lee, of Columbia College, was appointed actuary, and after a protracted effort and by bringing to bear the influence of the directors, embracing some of the most influential men of the city, they succeeded in about two years, I believe, in obtaining twelve policies. The majority of these were from the officers and members of the company. They found it was utterly impossible to induce people to effect insurance upon their lives, and the community at that time was somewhat like the old lady who objected to traveling in steamboats, because she considered it wicked to go against wind and tide. After making these efforts for two or three years, they determined to abandon the business, and the policies were all canceled."

*"DOWNIEVILLE, LIMA CO., CAL., December 21, 1859.

Your Company ought to allow me two per cent. for residing in the heathiest country on the American Continent.

C. A. JOHNSON,
Insured under Policy No. 8,984."

In response to a resolution of the Trustees, the officers of the Company submitted in December, 1859, a report showing the premiums received and the losses incurred at Northern and Southern agencies, respectively, as follows: Premiums received on Northern business $2,556,929, Northern losses $904,941, being 35.5 per cent. of the premiums; premiums received on Southern business $580,225, Southern losses $309,870, being 53.5 per cent. of the premiums. The estimate of total insurance carried one year in the South was $18,000,000, from which it was concluded that an addition of three-fifths of one per cent. to the extras then charged was necessary to place the business of the two sections on an equal basis. It was recommended, however, that no action be taken until further investigation could be made.*

At the meeting of the Trustees, held January 24, 1860, it was noted that the income for 1859 exceeded half a million dollars, and that the amount of insurance written was larger than in any previous year since 1851. Of the new insurance written $2,914,825 was upon Northern, and $177,700 upon Southern, lives. The number of term policies in force showed a slight decrease, and the number and amount of applications declined showed an increase.† The surplus of the Company, after providing for a dividend of thirty per cent. on premiums and six per cent. interest on dividends outstanding, was $51,529. It was voted that the officers have prepared a more attractive policy heading.

1860. AT the second meeting of the Life Underwriters' Convention, held May 23–24, 1860, the subject of the non-forfeiture of policies was discussed at considerable length. Hon. Elizur Wright, senior Insurance Commissioner of Massachusetts, and Hon. William Barnes, the newly-appointed Superintendent of the New York Insurance Department, were

* The mortality experience of the Mutual Life, 1843–1857, published in 1860, contains a table showing the extra that should be charged, according to the company's experience, to equalize the risks of the various sections; and a statement of the extras then charged. The latter (in 1858) were slightly below the former (for the whole period) and were as follows: Southern Atlantic States, one-half of one per cent.; Gulf States, two per cent.; California, one per cent. The last corresponded very nearly to the California risk subsequent to 1853; prior to that date the risk had averaged over five per cent. above that of the Eastern, Middle and Western States combined.

† Number declined in 1858, 66, amount $234,300; number declined in 1859, 96, amount $359,750.

present as honorary members and participated in the discussion.* Mr. Wright was the author of the system of net valuations adopted in Massachusetts, and in his reports of 1858 and 1859 had urged the passage of a

SECOND ENGRAVED POLICY HEADING, FIRST USED JUNE 17, 1861.

non-forfeiture law. In March, 1859, he had submitted the draft of such a law to the Joint Standing Committee on Mercantile Affairs and Insurance of the Legislature of Massachusetts, but no action was taken.† Mr. Wright had urged with great pertinacity and force that forfeitures were unjust, because the policy-holder did not receive what he had paid for; impolitic, because the fear of forfeiture prevented many from insuring on the whole life plan, which was the most advantageous plan for the com-

---

* The law establishing the New York Insurance Department was passed April 15, 1859. It simply created the Department and enacted that all insurance companies should report thereto instead of to the Comptroller, as under previous laws. William Barnes was appointed Superintendent, January 12, 1860.

† The original draft of the Massachusetts Non-forfeiture Law provided that four-fifths of the net value of the policy, according to the Actuaries' Table of Mortality with four per cent. interest, should be applied as a single net premium to the purchase of temporary insurance according to the age of the insured at the time of lapse. The law as finally approved, April 10, 1861, provided that any indebtedness on the policy should be first deducted from the net value, and that in case of the death of the insured during the term of extended insurance the Company should have the right to deduct from the amount insured the amount of premiums foreborne at the time of death, with interest at six per cent. per annum.

panies, as it secured the best risks; and that it enabled the worst-managed companies to keep up their financial standing with the best by a greater profit on forfeitures. He showed by tables of policies lapsed in 1859 and not restored in 1860 that the profits on such policies, after deducting premium notes, amounted to about $144,000, and that this profit was very unequally distributed among the companies, being eighty times as great in proportion to income in one company as in another. He also constructed tables by which the term of extended insurance under the proposed law could be easily ascertained.

The discussion in the Convention elicited the fact that every life company in the United States, save one, paid surrender values for policies, either in cash or paid-up insurance, after about the fifth year, provided they were surrendered before lapse, and in some cases after lapse, but there was no common rule or practice, and none of the companies agreed in the policy to pay such values. The companies had already, therefore, admitted, by their practice, that some concessions were due to policy-holders which were not expressed in the contract. The argument for such expression was thus concisely stated by Superintendent Barnes:

All the suggestion with which I will trouble the Convention is, whether it may not be desirable for companies to incorporate this idea in their policies to a greater extent than at the present time, so that I, or any other person, can have a certainty by the contract that, if we fail to pay at a certain time, for any reason, we can have a whole life policy, or term policy for a period regulated by the amount we have paid, according to the practice of the "Eagle and Albion," or something of that kind. The greatest objection to life insurance is in relation to these forfeitures. It is well to say that the companies do not enforce this; but, gentlemen, you should go further. If it is just, you should incorporate it in the policy, as a part of the original contract. If you anticipate legislation [*i. e.*, by putting non-forfeiture conditions in the policy], undoubtedly no legislation would be had in this State—the various officers can anticipate,—you can get at the true value of a lapsed policy a great dealer better than any Legislature can do it; and, in this way, by securing the parties on the face of the contract, you show to the community that you do not require insurers to come into your offices and beg of you, as a matter of favor, that which you are bound to give them. I simply suggest that, whatever the real value is, the assured should have it, under the circumstances, so that when the assured person comes into your office to ask for the value of his policy, he can come with boldness and ask for his rights, and not for a charity or gratuity on the part of the company.

The objections of the companies to a hard and fast law on the subject, which could not be varied according to their mortality and financial experience, were thus set forth by Mr. Winston:

First. It alters the contract in the policy, which is, that as long as the premium is paid the policy is in force—no longer; whereas this proposal says to the policy-holder, your policy is in force whether you pay or not. *Second.* It interferes with the law of average—so necessary to our safety—for the sound lives are those who decline to pay, and finally give up their policies, after having exhausted their dividends. The unsound and the feeble keep up their policies to an early end.* *Third.* It is dangerous to the Company. We have no American experience and can have none, which will be entirely reliable, as to mortality among assured lives, for years to come; therefore we do not know what it costs us to insure lives in this country. The rate we shall receive for interest on our accumulations in coming years is quite uncertain, and may be much lower than in our past history. There is a disposition in this country to tax life insurance, though it is not taxed elsewhere, and as we cannot raise our rates for insurance in competition with foreign companies, which are not taxed on their capital, taxation here would greatly reduce the financial ability of our companies, if it left them enough to pay their liabilities. *Fourth.* It would make policy-holders careless of life insurance, and lead them to undervalue and neglect it, and thus would be an injury to them and not a benefit. I cannot therefore believe that justice, sound policy or the good of policy-holders, as a whole, would be promoted by the proposition of the Commissioner of Massachusetts upon this subject.

The Officers of the NEW-YORK LIFE took no part in the discussion of the question;† but on June thirteenth, following, they submitted the following proposition to the Board of Trustees:

---

* Mr. Wright had answered this objection in advance, as follows: "In actual practice, the presumption that only the sounder lives will wish to surrender is not considered as a good reason for withholding more than one-quarter or one-third of the value of the policy. From sixty-six to seventy-five per cent. of the value is paid to the healthiest, if the application to surrender is made while the policy is in force. Yet it has been the uniform practice in this country, and till very lately in Great Britain, to make the whole value of the policy, as well as the right to further insurance [*i. e.*, renewal], the forfeit of a failure to pay the annual premium on a specified day. Failure to pay premiums may arise not only from confidence of long life, but from misfortune, imbecility of mind, preoccupation or unavoidable detention. Hence the class of lapsed policies may embrace cases below as well as above the average vitality of the company, and consequently there is less reason to justify the company in withholding the whole or a part of the value from the holders of lapsed policies, than from the holders of policies in force who wish to surrender. But when we carefully consider how the *sense* of vitality fails to correspond to the actual fact, and how much more likely the subjects of some of the most destructive maladies are to indulge in visions of longevity than the tenants of sounder constitutions, we can hardly believe that the average vitality of the holders of lapsed policies ever has been or ever will be appreciably above the average of those who remain.—*Mass. Report for 1859.*

The experience of the companies on this point, so far as published, has shown that the loss of average vitality by surrenders does not exceed two and one-half per cent. of the whole.—*Adverse selection by Withdrawal, by Howell W. St. John, Proceedings Actuarial Society of America, 1889–90, No. 3, page 18.*"

† August 14, 1860.

Hon. WILLIAM BARNES, Albany, N. Y.

Dear Sir: You may remember that at the late meeting of our Convention considerable discussion was had in reference to the valuation of lapsed policies and the duty of companies in relation thereto.

The officers represent for the sanction of the Board that they have prepared with great care a table of rates by which persons may purchase policies by ten annual payments, which will be forever thereafter exempted from forfeiture. Objections are not infrequently made to the present system that in the event of inability promptly to meet the annual premiums, the money previously paid becomes a total loss to the assured. By the proposed plan we design that after the payment of two or more premiums, and either from want of ability, or from any other cause, the payments are discontinued, the policy does not become forfeited, but that in lieu thereof a new one will be issued to the original policy-holder if living, for an equitable proportion of the money paid, or if deceased, a similar amount will be paid to his family or legal representatives. The officers are satisfied after a careful examination of the proposed system that it is not only strictly equitable, as between man and man, but is calculated when fairly understood to commend itself to the judgment of all who may investigate the same, and become a very popular and profitable measure to the Company.

The Superintendent referred in his next annual report to the forfeiture of policies, as having "long been a serious obstacle to the increase of life insurance," and said: "I cannot but regard it, therefore, as a matter of public congratulation that the NEW-YORK LIFE INSURANCE COMPANY has issued a table of rates of premium for life policies, expressly stipulating that after the receipt of two or more annual premiums, if further payments are discontinued, a new policy will be issued to the original holder, if living, for a specified proportion of the sum insured; or, if deceased, an equitable sum will be paid to his family or legal representatives."

The plan and rates were adopted, and thus the principle of non-forfeiture, as a right, was first officially recognized by an American life insurance company doing a general business.* The rates first adopted were calculated on the Carlisle Table of Mortality with five per cent. interest, and with fifteen per cent. loading for expenses. The paid-up insur-

---

We have acted upon the suggestions then made and have prepared a table predicated upon the purchase of a policy by ten annual payments, and providing for carrying out the original design of the assured if from any cause he should be unable [to continue], or desire to discontinue the regular payment of premiums. We beg leave to inclose you a copy, together with our circular explanatory thereof, and remain with great respect, Your obed't serv't, MORRIS FRANKLIN, *President.*

* In 1852 the Presbyterian Corporation, which began about this time to do a life insurance business within the Presbyterian ministry, adopted a rule whereby the net value of a policy, less five per cent., might be used as a single premium for the purchase of insurance due at death. The first policy of which this rule was made a part by reference was issued August 30, 1852, and the first policy in which the clause was incorporated was issued September 3, 1856. This information was furnished by Robert P. Field, Esq., Actuary, for an address by Hon. John A. McCall on the "History of American Life Insurance," read before the Life and Accident Insurance Congress, Auxiliary of the World's Columbian Exposition, Chicago, 1893.

THE NEW YORK LIFE INSURANCE COMPANY.

This Policy of Insurance

WITNESSETH, THAT

THE NEW YORK LIFE INSURANCE COMPANY,

ANNUAL PREMIUM.
$54.47
for ten years

in consideration of the sum of Fifty four dollars and forty seven cents to them in hand paid by Julia H. Sigourney wife of William Harrison Sigourney and of the annual premium for nine of Fifty four dollars and forty seven cents, to be paid on the Thirteenth day of August of the years 1861, 1862, 1863, 1864, 1865, 1866, 1867, 1868, 1869 ~~in every year during the continuance of this Policy~~, Do Assure the Life of William H. Sigourney Post Master of Watertown in the County of Jefferson State of New York for the sole use of the said Julia H. Sigourney in the amount of One Thousand dollars for the term of his Natural Life commencing on the Thirteenth day of August 1860 at noon.

Age 45 years.

SUM INSURED.
$1000.

Premium payable
Aug 13. 1860 $54.47
" 1861 – 54.47
" 1862 – 54.47
" 1863 – 54.47
" 1864 – 54.47
" 1865 – 54.47
" 1866 – 54.47
" 1867 – 54.47
" 1868 – 54.47
" 1869 – 54.47

And the said Company do hereby Promise and Agree, to and with the said assured, his executors, administrators and assigns, well and truly to pay, or cause to be paid, the said sum insured, to the said Julia H. Sigourney or her legal representatives, within sixty days after due notice and proof of the death of the said William H. Sigourney

And in case of the death of the said Julia H. Sigourney before the decease of the said William H. Sigourney the amount of the said insurance shall be payable after her death to her children, for their use, or to their guardian, if under age, within sixty days after due notice and proof of the death of the aforesaid William H. Sigourney as aforesaid, ~~deducting therefrom all Notes for Premiums on this Policy unpaid at that time.~~ — Without profits.

Provided always, and it is hereby declared to be the true intent and meaning of this Policy, and the same is accepted by the assured upon these express conditions, that in case the said William H. Sigourney shall, without the consent of this Company previously obtained, and endorsed upon this Policy, pass beyond the settled limits of the United States that lie east of the Rocky Mountains, (excepting into the settled limits of the British Provinces of the two Canadas, Nova Scotia, or New Brunswick,) or shall, without such previous consent thus endorsed, visit or reside in those parts of the United States which lie south of the southern boundaries of the States of Virginia and Kentucky, between the first of July and the first of November, or shall, without such previous consent thus endorsed, enter into any military or naval service whatever, (the militia not in actual service excepted,) or in case he shall die in, or in consequence of a duel, or by the hands of justice, or in the known violation of any law of the United States, or of any state or country, or in case his death shall be caused by intoxicating drink or opium, this Policy shall be null and void.

And it is also Understood and Agreed, to be the true intent and meaning hereof, that if the declaration made by the said Julia H. Sigourney and bearing date the Sixth day of August 1860 and upon the faith of which this agreement is made, shall be found in any respect untrue, then and in such case, this Policy shall be null and void: or in case the said Julia H. Sigourney shall not pay the said premiums on or before the several days herein before mentioned for the payment thereof, then and in every such case, the said Company shall not be liable to the payment of the sum insured, or any part thereof; and this Policy shall cease and determine.

N. B. If Assigned, notice to be given the Company.

In Witness whereof, the said NEW YORK LIFE INSURANCE COMPANY, have, by their President and Actuary, signed and delivered this Contract, this Thirteenth day of August one thousand eight hundred and sixty. —

[signature] President

Pliny Freeman Actuary.

After receipt of two or more annual premiums, if the party desires to discontinue the insurance, he can exchange this Policy for a new one, for the full value thereof, without further payment.

All Receipts for Premiums paid at Agencies are to be signed by the President or Actuary.

Exam'd C. H. E.

[To follow page 62.]

The First Non-forfeiting Policy Issued by any Life Company Doing a General Business.

ance due at the end of the various years being found to be very nearly equal to one-tenth of the original policy for each premium paid after the first, new and slightly higher rates were adopted July eleventh in order that the paid-up policy promised might follow the simple rule of proportional parts. On August eighth a form of policy was adopted, and on the thirteenth of the same month the first policy containing the new guarantee was issued.* It marked an epoch in life insurance. It preceded the enactment of the Massachusetts law on the subject by about eight months, and competition proved as powerful as law, for the other New York companies speedily adopted the plan of the NEW-YORK LIFE, although there was no statute on the subject in this State until 1879. The objections which were urged against the non-forfeiture principle have proved unfounded, and the fears of conservative managers have been dispelled by the practical results of over thirty years. The elimination of this feature in a special class of policies (Tontine) during a limited period, with special benefits to survivors who kept their policies in force, attracted custom for awhile, but proved repugnant to the moral sense of insurers, and was abandoned for a more liberal system than that of companies which had opposed it.

In June of this year the Trustees authorized a subscription of $500 toward the fund then being raised to secure the permanent location of the city Post Office at Nassau, Cedar and Liberty Streets. The price asked for the ground by the trustees of the Dutch Church was $250,000, and the Post Office Department had been authorized to expend $200,000 for a site; business men and institutions interested in the value of property in that part of the city subscribed the balance. In November of the same year the Company subscribed $200 to a fund raised by the life insurance companies of the city, for the purpose of settling "an annuity for his benefit, and that of his wife if surviving, on the life of Captain Wilson of the Brig 'Minnie Schiffer,' for his heroic conduct in rescuing from the burn-

* Attention is called to the date given above, inasmuch as an earlier date has been given in some of the printed documents of the Company, under the impression that the first ten-payment life policy issued was non-forfeitable. Policy No. 14,415, of which a *fac simile* is given, is believed to be the first policy issued with the non-forfeiture clause. As is usually the case, the makers of history left but scant records of their action. There is one ten-payment policy issued previous to 14,415 and now in force, upon a policy-holder whose present address is not known. There is nothing in the Company's records indicating that it contains a non-forfeiture clause.

ing steamer 'Connaught' more than six hundred human beings." The amount of the annuity proposed by the committee in charge is not mentioned in the minutes of the Trustees, but it is recorded that the subject "was referred to the officers with power, in accordance with the views of the Board, if acceptable to the other companies, to *increase* the proposed annuity to two hundred and fifty dollars."

On the sixth day of November, Abraham Lincoln was elected President of the United States; on the seventh the Legislature of South Carolina issued its call for a convention to meet in the city of Columbia on December seventeenth; on December twentieth the ordinance of secession was passed, and the closing days of the year were darkened by the ominous clouds of civil war. The Company soon began to receive letters from its Southern policy-holders, asking what would be the effect upon their policies of a dissolution of the Union, or of the holders engaging in war. The officers of the Company, in accordance with the prevailing opinion at the North, believed there would be no bloodshed, and on December twelfth "the subject of the Company assuming risks upon the lives of persons engaged in war having been introduced, the Board [of Trustees] concluded to postpone indefinitely the consideration thereof." To all inquirers on the subject the answer was returned that the mere fact of secession would not impair the validity of their contracts, but that if death should ensue in consequence of actual engagement in war the Company would not consider itself liable—as was expressly declared in the policy.*

---

* PETERSBURG, Dec. 22, 1860.

My policy-holders are asking every day if their insurance will be jeopardized by the dissolution of the Union; to which I reply that, in my opinion, it will not. Am I right? If not, what will be the policy of the Company?

A. B. GARLAND, *Agent.*

A. B. GARLAND, Esq., Petersburg, Va. NEW YORK, December 24, 1860.

Dear Sir: * * * Nothing but the insolvency of the Company can have any effect upon their policies; the entire dissolution of the Union could not alter our contract. Under any and all circumstances of a political character, they are unquestionably good. * * * In the earnest hope that our political relations may not be disturbed, I remain,

Yours, with great respect, MORRIS FRANKLIN, *President.*

R. M. CARY, Esq., Hampton, Va. December 31, 1860.

Dear Sir: We have your favor of the twenty-eighth inst. The subject therein referred to has received the attention of our Trustees, and they are unanimously of the opinion that the Company is not warranted in assuring the risk of death occasioned by an unfortunate hostile collision between persons residing in different States of the Union. With an earnest prayer that such may never occur, I am with great respect, Your obedient servant, MORRIS FRANKLIN, *President.*

The annual report for 1860 showed 1,024 policies issued of which 932 were life policies, 79 were term policies, and 13 were endowments. It was noted that 28 of the life policies were issued on the non-forfeiture plan; also, that "an unusual number of policies had been surrendered in consequence of the unfortunate condition of the political relations between the Northern, and Southern, States." The report was accompanied by a table showing the mortality experience of the Company during the previous fourteen years, as compared with the expected mortality by the Carlisle Table; the actual deaths had been 302, as compared with 329 deaths expected.

The report of the Finance Committee showed that the dividends outstanding amounted to $735,444, upon which the Company was paying six per cent. interest. Nevertheless there was much dissatisfaction among policy-holders, and the certificates were selling at about fifty cents on the dollar. The Committee presented a plan for the redemption of all outstanding dividends during the next six years. There being some doubt as to the authority of the Trustees in the premises, without an amendment to the charter,* the legal question was referred to Judge John W. Edmonds (of Edmonds, Bushnell & Hamilton), and the plan itself to a special committee. Judge Edmonds gave his opinion that the Trustees had full power over the dividends of the Company without further legislation, and this opinion was concurred in by the Superintendent of the Insurance Department. The special committee recommended a scrip dividend of thirty per cent. for the year; that the payment of interest on outstanding dividends be discontinued; and the payment in cash, during 1861, of all declared prior to 1850, and of twenty per cent. of all declared between 1850 and 1860. The plan was adopted, with the understanding that the remaining dividends then outstanding should be redeemed in equal annual installments in the years 1862, 1863, 1864 and 1865. It was expected that after 1865 the Company would redeem one dividend each year, pay-

* A bill giving the Company specific authority in the premises was introduced in the Legislature, but failed to pass. The gentleman in charge of it, Hon. Wm. H. Bogert, said it was an evidence of prosperity that the only legislation asked for was authority to pay *dividends*.

ing each dividend five years after it was declared; but it did better. In 1865 the last installment of dividends declared prior to 1861 was paid, and in addition the dividends declared in 1861 and 1862; in 1866 the dividends declared in 1863 and 1864 were paid; in 1867 the dividend declared in 1865 was paid; in 1868 the dividend declared in 1866 was paid and also the dividend of 1868 which was declared on the contribution plan; in 1869 the dividend declared in 1867 was paid in addition to the dividend declared in 1869 on the contribution plan. All outstanding dividends being thus redeemed, the NEW-YORK LIFE thenceforth took its place in the front rank of companies paying annual cash dividends, available in settlement of the second and subsequent annual premiums.

TABLE SHOWING THE CONDITION OF THE LIFE COMPANIES DOING BUSINESS IN NEW YORK, DECEMBER 31, 1860, THEIR BUSINESS FOR THE YEAR, THE SAME ITEMS FOR THE NEW-YORK LIFE, AND THE NEW-YORK LIFE'S SHARE OF ALL:

ITEMS.	SEVENTEEN COMPANIES.	NEW-YORK LIFE.	N.-Y. L'S SHARE.
Assets	$24,115,687	$2,004,858*	8.3
Premium Notes and Loans in Assets	4,285,706	756,058	17.7
Surplus	6,955,814	134,457*	1.9
Liabilities	17,159,873	1,870,411*	10.8
Surplus to Liabilities, Per cent.	40.5	7.2	....
Insurance in Force	163,703,455	16,396,709	10.0
New Insurance Written, 1860	35,589,934	3,023,275	8.5
Total Income, 1860	5,998,144	599,606	10.0
Premium Notes and Loans in Income	1,197,864	129,771	10.5
Death-Claims Paid	1,375,216	204,007	14.8
Death-Claims per $1,000 Insured	$9.00	$12.88	....
Total Paid Policy-holders	2,130,199	274,155	12.9
Expenses and Taxes	807,134	96,960	12.0
Per cent. to Income	13.5	16.2	....

*These figures differ somewhat from those furnished the Insurance Department, which required that all dividends declared be included at their face value, although a large proportion was not redeemable until further action by the Trustees, and bore no interest. The valuation of policies for the Department was made on the Carlisle Table of Mortality with four per cent. interest—a new requirement—no valuations having previously been made for New York Reports, and the Company's own valuation being made at six per cent. interest.

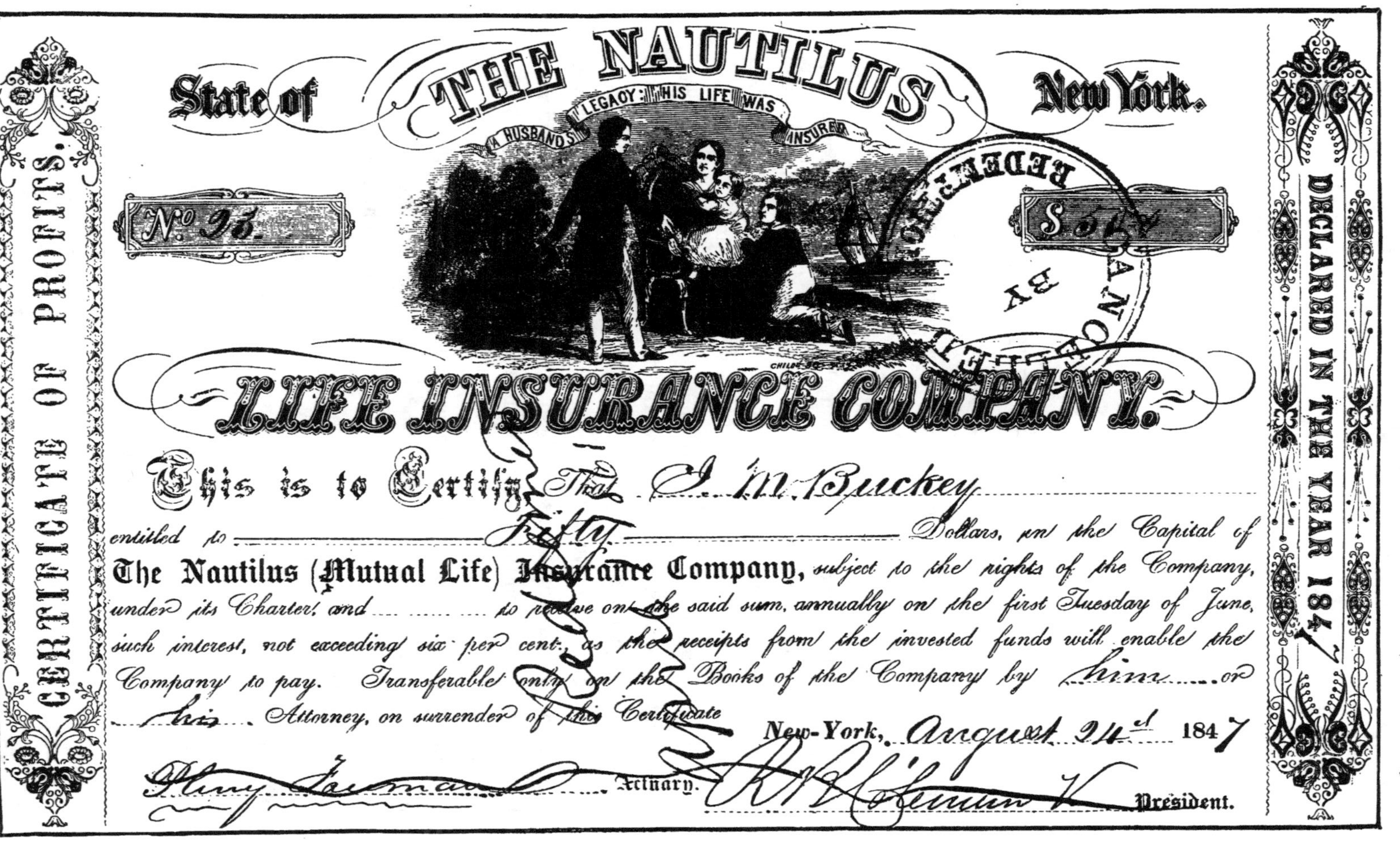

CERTIFICATE OF PROFITS.

DECLARED IN THE YEAR 1847

State of THE NAUTILUS New York.

No. 93.

$ 50

LIFE INSURANCE COMPANY.

This is to Certify That J. M. Buckey
entitled to Fifty Dollars, in the Capital of The Nautilus (Mutual Life) Insurance Company, subject to the rights of the Company, under its Charter, and to receive on the said sum, annually on the first Tuesday of June, such interest, not exceeding six per cent, as the receipts from the invested funds will enable the Company to pay. Transferable only on the Books of the Company by him or his Attorney, on surrender of this Certificate.

New-York, August 24th 1847

Actuary. President.

VII.

PERIOD OF THE CIVIL WAR.

1861–1865.

THE difficulties which surrounded the managers of Northern life companies in 1861 were little less perplexing than those which confronted the Government at Washington. Their contracts were of a peculiar kind; they required periodical payments, and the hazard under them was increased by a state of war. This increased hazard did not apply solely to those who might enter the military or naval service, but the hazards of civil life, especially in the Border States, were sometimes but little less than those of the camp and the battle-field. In Maryland, Kentucky, Tennessee and Missouri men were arming themselves against their neighbors, and there was constant fear of invasion and of mobs and incendiaries. Trade and commerce were almost at a stand-still; exchange between New York and distant points was held at ruinous rates; communication between the North and South was frequently interrupted, and finally cut off altogether.

Looking back upon these troublous times, it is easy now to see what course would have been consistent and easy; but then the future was a sealed book, and every new leaf, as it was turned, brought new surprises and new perplexities. Men found themselves driven along by the tide of events which they could not control, and compelled to re-adjust their plans from day to day to the new conditions which changing circumstances forced upon them. In the history of the NEW-YORK LIFE during this period there is nothing more touching, and nothing more creditable, both to the Company and to its Southern policy-holders, than the persistence with which they clung to the hope of peace. It is a pleasure also to record the fidelity and high sense of honor with which Southern agents discharged their trust as custodians of the Company's funds, notwithstanding contrary edicts and wide-spread repudiation. Agreeing to differ upon questions of a political character, officers and agents alike continued to discharge the duties growing out of their relations to policy-holders in such a manner that, when the war ended, both were prepared to resume those relations without recrimination, and with mutual confidence and respect.

1861. THE correspondence made necessary by the political events of 1861 was conducted by Hon. Morris Franklin, President of the Company. Mr. Franklin was in early life a lawyer, and had taken an active and honorable part in the political affairs of his native State and city. His letters manifest a high sense of personal honor, a fervent patriotism, a spirit of Christian charity, and the sincere hope of an honorable peace. The policy outlined therein received the cordial approval of the Board of Trustees, and in accordance therewith the Company continued to receive premiums and to pay losses in the seceded States until August twenty-sixth, when communication was forbidden by the proclamation of President Lincoln. A letter written by the Company's agent at Richmond, August twentieth, and received September 10, 1861, announced the death of John J. Faris, insured under Policy No. 14,315; the restrictions upon commerce between the North and the South were removed on June 24, 1865, and the claim under this policy was paid on the twenty-eighth of September following.

LETTER-HEAD OF 1861.

In order that the perplexities of this period and the spirit in which they were met by the Company may be fully understood, it will be necessary to examine the correspondence somewhat in detail. As has already been noted, the question of assuming a war risk under Southern policies had been asked in December, 1860, and answered in the negative. The beginning of the new year brought repetitions of the inquiry, and members of Northern militia organizations began to ask what their status would be in case they were called into active service. The answer was the same in substance to all, namely, that, although the policy forbade actual service, the Company would take the liberal view that the mere fact of service would not invalidate the policy, unless death ensued, or the insured's health was impaired thereby. Sometimes a policy-holder was concerned for the safety of his home and family. Rev. Peter Ainslie wrote from Dunneville, Va., January twenty-fourth: "I am a preacher. I have a wife, children and servants. Suppose an armed force approached my house, or forced themselves upon my premises, and in defending my family and my rights, I get killed—will my policy become null and void? Or suppose they steal my servants, and in my efforts to recover them I am killed—does my policy become null and void?" Mr. Franklin wrote in reply, January twenty-ninth: "The fact of war existing between the Federal and State Governments does not vitiate our policy. Should you be killed while acting in your own defence, or that of your family or property, the Company will pay the sum insured. Only in event of joining the contending forces will the policy become a forfeiture, should death ensue. In the sincere hope that all will yet be well, I am," etc.

Two days later a policy-holder in the far South presented his case in a manner that proved prophetic. Dr. Wm. H. Holcombe, dating his letter "Waterproof, Republic of Louisiana, January 31, 1861," wrote:

Please inform me what course is proper as to the renewal and payment of my life insurance policy. We are on the eve of a long and dreadful war between our respective nationalities. Communication will be interrupted for months, perhaps years. I might not be able to remit. If death occurred, could you or would you pay? Is it lawful for a citizen of one country to insure his life in a foreign and hostile country? Can the payments be made through neutral mediums, say Liverpool? If no arrangement is practicable or proper, will you refund, etc.? I make these inquiries because I know—what the North has not yet recognized—that the South will ***never*** submit to Lincoln's Administration.

To this the Company replied under date of February thirteenth, that he might pay in any way convenient to himself, and that "all the obligations of the Company to its policy-holders will be faithfully and honorably met under any and all circumstances."*

Meanwhile events in Charleston harbor were proceeding to that culmination which did so much to make Dr. Holcombe's prophecy come true. As Major Anderson's little band looked out from Fort Sumter upon the formidable preparations making for their overthrow, there was one of their number who remembered his policy in the NEW-YORK LIFE, and on February fourth he addressed a letter to the Company's Baltimore agents, through whom he had insured, as follows:

MAJOR-GENERAL JOHN G. FOSTER.
[This cut by courtesy of the "National Tribune," Washington, D. C.]

FORT SUMTER, S. C., Feb. 4, 1861.

Messrs. RICHARDSON & SONS, Baltimore, Md.

Dear Sir: Being insured in your Company, I am desirous to be informed whether, in case we are attacked by the forces of South Carolina, and I lose my life in the defence, the Company will pay the amount of my policy to my family.

Very respectfully yours,

J. G. FOSTER, Capt. Engrs., U. S. A.†

---

*Dr. Holcombe paid his next premium in February, and, in 1864, having removed to New Orleans, took out a new policy, the value of the old one at time of lapse being allowed in payment of the first premium.

†Captain Foster was the engineer officer in charge of the work of completing Fort Sumter when Major Anderson transferred his command thither on the night of December 26, 1860. He was promoted Brigadier-General October 3, 1861, and Major-General July 18, 1862; commanded a brigade under Burnside in the expedition against Roanoke Island, etc., in February, 1862; commanded United States forces in North Carolina July 6, 1862, to July, 1863; at Fort Monroe July 18, 1863, to November 11, 1863; Department of the Ohio December 12, 1863, to February 9, 1864; Department of the South May 26, 1864, to February 9, 1865; mustered out of service September 1, 1866.

Messrs Richardson & Sons
Agents of N-York Mutual
Life Insurance Co. Balt^o. Md.

Fort Sumter S.C.
Feby 4. 61

Dear Sir

Being insured in your company I am desirous to be informed, whether, in case we are attacked by the forces of South Carolina, and I lose my life in the defence the company will pay the amount of my policy to my family.

Very Respectfully Yours
J. G. Foster
Capt. Eng^rs U.S.A.

The letter was forwarded to the Company and was replied to through the Messrs. Richardson, on February eighth:

> We have your favor of yesterday, together with that of Capt. Foster to your address. Upon reference to our form of policy you will see that the risk referred to is not legally covered. Should it unfortunately happen that any of these brave men now doing duty at Fort Sumter should be attacked, and fall in defence of the trust committed to their care, we doubt not but that there is patriotism enough in our Trustees to waive the legal question which might arise under the policy and pay the amount insured; as in the case supposed, it would be an act in self-defence, and as such come within the spirit and intent of the contract. In the hope that this may be satisfactory to yourself and the Captain, I remain, etc.

Fort Sumter was fired upon April twelfth, and after a bombardment of over thirty-four hours, was surrendered on the afternoon of the fourteenth. On the fifteenth President Lincoln issued his proclamation calling for 75,000 men, and immediately the question of war risks under life policies became of new and pressing importance. A meeting of delegates from sixteen companies was held in New York April nineteenth, when it was recommended that the companies give their consent to the insured entering the military or naval service; that the insured have the option to pay a war extra of five per cent. per annum on the amount insured, with an additional five per cent. as a climate risk for service south of 34 degrees north latitude; that the option be given to the insured either to pay the war extra or to have their policies renewed upon discharge from the service, upon satisfactory evidence of good health; and that in case of death, the war extra not being paid, the companies should pay the surrender value of the policies. The NEW-YORK LIFE issued a circular April twenty-fourth, announcing that it would accept war risks on these terms, the extra to be paid by the insured after leaving the service, if the policy were continued, until he should be pronounced in sound health by one of the Company's Medical Examiners. New policies upon which a war risk was desired were to be issued for the term of life only.*

* The first war permit was issued April nineteenth, to Mr. Alex. George Wood, of New York; 14 were issued during the month of April, and 129 during the year 1861. Among the requests for war permits was one from Mr. Wm. P. Darst, of Lancaster, O., dated April twenty-first. It was written in a tremulous hand, and said: "Although I am somewhat advanced in years, I do not wish to stand idle while the flag of our country is dishonored and our laws defied. * * * Please obtain the consent

Although action was taken thus promptly, about fifty letters were received, during the ten days following the President's proclamation, inquiring if the Company would take war risks. Only two of these were from the South, the question having been previously discussed with Southern agents and policy-holders, as will be shown in correspondence soon to be introduced. Mr. G. H. Buckingham wrote from New Orleans under date of April fifteenth, asking what the war risk would be on his policy, and adding facetiously: "We are in a bad fix. Lincoln only gives us twenty days—to repent!" There was unconscious humor also in a letter received from Mr. Joseph S. Cook, of Boston, asking to have a war permit endorsed upon his policy, "so that there shall be no pull-back, *as I may get shot if I go.*" During the ten days spoken of, a score of letters were received in the ordinary course of business from the principal cities of the South, but only two made any reference to the new phase which military affairs had suddenly assumed.

The second of the two letters above referred to was from Dr. J. S. Copes, the Company's agent at New Orleans. On April ninth he had written:

> The necessity for giving answers to persons insured in your Company concerning the rate to be charged for military service becomes more and more pressing. They may be called upon by authorities they cannot disobey, to enter it, and as it concerns their wives and children, they want it settled. Also give me the construction your Board will put upon the words "or in the known violation of any law of the United States," as they relate to military or naval service in this Southern Confederacy. You fully understand these points. Please give me a frank and full explanation of your proposed course regarding them. I much need it. Other companies are charging one per cent. extra for military service.*

To this Mr. Franklin replied April sixteenth:

> We have fixed upon no rate to cover the war risk, for, as at present advised, we shall not under present circumstances assume it. We consider the present movement of some of the Southern States as embraced in the clause noted, *viz.*, "in the known

---

of your Company to my entering any military organization for the defence of our own State or of Washington City." A memorandum on the letter shows that Mr. Darst was 60 years of age, and a reference to the register shows that he actually took out a war permit and paid four quarterly war extras. His policy was paid as a death-claim February 24, 1876. A few permits were issued to chaplains without charge, and to sutlers at two and one-half per cent., although the latter usually paid the full rate.

* Only one—the American Life, of Philadelphia—was mentioned by name in the correspondence.

violation of any law of the United States," consequently should either of our insured fall in what he may consider to be the discharge of his duty, our Company will not hold itself responsible under the conditions of our policy. Regretting, as we most sincerely do, the necessity which compels us to this course, justice to our policy-holders at large requires us to assume this position, and we know of no company in this city or elsewhere disposed to take a different view of the present most unfortunate condition of our national troubles. In the ardent hope that the time is not distant when the notes of fraternal war shall cease to be heard in our once happy land, I remain, etc.

To this position Dr. Copes strenuously objected, in a letter dated April twenty-second, and the correspondence that ensued was voluminous and spirited on both sides, and resulted in the following statement, May thirtieth, of the course the Company would pursue with regard to Southern policies:

Under a strict legal construction of the policy, the entering into a military organization would vitiate it, but our Company have adopted the more liberal rule of only holding it in abeyance during such departure from the conditions. * * * * Your understanding is correct as regards re-instating policies. All we shall require at the termination of the war, which we pray God may speedily arrive, is that the back premium shall be paid and proof given of good health, the same as we now ask in all cases of lapsed policies, for non-payment at maturity. In speaking of the value of a policy forfeited in consequence of death by exposure from enlistment, we mean such an amount as we would have paid the party had he offered to surrender and sell his policy previous to its forfeiture. The renewals for May and June have gone forward, and if we misunderstood you in reference to premiums being confiscated, we very much regret it, but we think your language will bear that construction according to our recollection of it.* We shall continue to maintain, we fondly hope, the most friendly relations with our New Orleans agent, and although differing very materially upon national affairs, we have now, as we have always had, great confidence in his honor and integrity.

The excitement incident to the great uprising of the now awakened North caused a serious interruption of the business of the Company. Under date of April nineteenth Mr. S. R. Beckwith wrote from Cleveland, O.: "Jerry Ensworth, your agent, is Captain of the Cleveland Grays, and

* Dr. Copes' words were: "Up to this moment the NEW-YORK LIFE INSURANCE COMPANY stands unimpeached and unimpeachable; the next moment after your letter becomes known, its prestige has forever departed; its funds in my hands will be seized, and I shall be required to purge myself of all complicity in what will be regarded its dishonorable conduct." This he afterwards explained to mean that he feared "the assured would seize the funds." It was entirely creditable to Dr. Copes' high sense of honor that he felt more keenly on these questions as the guardian of policy-holders' interests than the policy-holders did themselves. On May tenth he wrote: "The members of the Local Board request me to say that in their opinion no interference will be attempted with my regular remittances to you, even in the heat of armed conflict."

received orders to march to Washington last night. * * * Mr. G. E. Smith has kindly offered to attend to his agency for the NEW-YORK LIFE, and I give him an office with me. * * * Mr. Richards' policy has been received, but he has gone with Mr. Ensworth's company, as Lieutenant. His firm wishes to pay his premium, and a percentage [war extra], if you allow policies on those who have enlisted." Mr. W. L. Evans, agent at Cincinnati, O., wrote the same day: "I have just returned from a business tour into the country. During my absence my clerk was called, with the company of which he is a member, to Washington. I am now without assistance in the office, but hope in a short time to get off my report for the present and last month's business." Mr. George C. Davis, also of Cincinnati, wrote on the twenty-second: "On my return home, some ten days ago, I found your favors of twenty-ninth and thirty-first, with the package of blanks, etc. Since then everything has been topsy-turvy—drums beating, colors flying, troops marching, people shouting, newsboys screaming. In short, our town is turned into a military camp, and business pretty much suspended." Messrs. E. J. Richardson & Sons wrote from Baltimore, April twenty-fourth: "We hear that dreadful accounts prevail in New York relative to Fort McHenry being captured, our city bombarded and in flames—all which is entirely untrue. Our city is perfectly quiet, but under strict military guard. Business of every kind is almost entirely suspended." And on the twenty-ninth: "Our office is constantly filled with insured parties inquiring about the war-clause. We can hardly find time to write a word."*

Another question, beset with difficulties, presented itself for solution early in 1861, and became urgent with the surrender of Fort Sumter, namely, the question of risk to policy-holders who entered the "Home

---

* The minutes of the Trustees for April twenty-third contain resolutions adopted respecting "J. Oscar Voute, a valuable and efficient clerk in this Company," then "making arrangements to join the Reserve Corps of the Seventh Regiment." It was voted "that his salary be continued during his absence, and his position reserved until he shall return, if such may be his fate." This particular organization was not called into service, but Mr. Voute afterward served in Baltimore, and at Suffolk, Va., from May till November, 1862, as a member of Co. G. ("Brooklyn City Guard"), 13th Regiment, N. Y. State Militia. He not only returned, but has been for many years the efficient Assistant Cashier of the Company.

Guard." Under date of February fifteenth, Dr. Copes wrote: "To-day Mr. James J. Bard, insured in your Company, inquires whether, as a member of the 'Civic Fossil Guard,' whose agreement* I inclose, he will be required to pay an extra premium. This corps is designed for protection and to preserve domestic tranquility. It became an organization during the late election struggle, and was composed of the friends of Bell and Everett. They now assume this semi-military organization for the purpose above-named." To this Mr. Franklin replied, under date of February twenty-third: "The mere fact of entering into such an association does not necessarily violate the policy, provided he is not killed, or his health impaired in consequence of such enlistment."

After April fourteenth inquiries of a similar character came from various points in the Border States. April twenty-fifth Mr. Franklin wrote, in reply to an inquiry from Mr. W. S. Vernon, the Company's agent at Louisville: "We think that, under the conditions of our policies, the assured are justified in 'forming themselves into a company for the defence of their homes, wives and children.'" It was necessary, however, to distinguish sharply between the protection of homes from mobs, and resistance to invasion of the State by a military force. Then, there were in some places two kinds of "Home Guards." Mr. Edward Morrison, the Company's agent at St. Louis, wrote on May eighth: "Though we are not quarreling, we are living in great uncertainty, almost on a volcano. There are about ten thousand men drilling nightly as 'Home Guards,' about half Union and half Secession. I am daily asked what would the NEW-YORK LIFE do in case they were called out to do active service, and any one insured lose his life. It is a question that has not been answered by

* CIVIC FOSSIL GUARD.—We, the undersigned, residents of the City of New Orleans, forty years of age, and over, do hereby pledge ourselves to form a Volunteer Corps, for the defence of the City of New Orleans, and the protection of the lives and property of its inhabitants; to obey the orders of such officers as may be elected to command us; and, also, to be subject to the civil authorities in case of insurrection or invasion. It is understood that, unless in cases of imminent peril—to be judged of by our superior officers—we shall not be required to do duty beyond the limits of our respective Districts, and then only in obedience to the orders of our superior officers; and in no case shall we be required to go beyond the City limits, except as a Volunteer Corps, and only, in such case, with the consent of the commanding officer. [Note by Dr. Copes: "These companies are not in the State service, nor furnished with arms by it."]

any other company." To this Mr. Franklin replied, May fourteenth: "Inquiry is made as to what effect the joining of a military organization for home protection will have on the policy; we answer that, should death occur in consequence of any riot or civil commotion within the limits of the city, among your own people, we should consider the Company liable; but we cannot assume or cover the risk of death if it occur in consequence of invasion from other States, as that would be an act of war not contemplated in the issuing of the policy."*

So far as the duty of "Home Guards" pertained to home defence against the disorderly elements of society, the Company made no distinction between North and South at this time. Mr. G. N. Robinson wrote from Memphis, May tenth: "We are all holding ourselves ready at a moment's warning to defend our families, if invaded. You see my position. How will it affect my policy? Please answer definitely, that I may make known your future policy to those of our friends who are insured in your Company, as we are all in the same condemnation." To this Mr. Franklin replied, May seventeenth: "We certainly recognize the right of every man to defend his home and property against riot or invasion, and should he fall in such defence the Company would, beyond all question, 'justly and honestly' pay the insurance; but we cannot countenance the entering into any military organization having in view a collision between

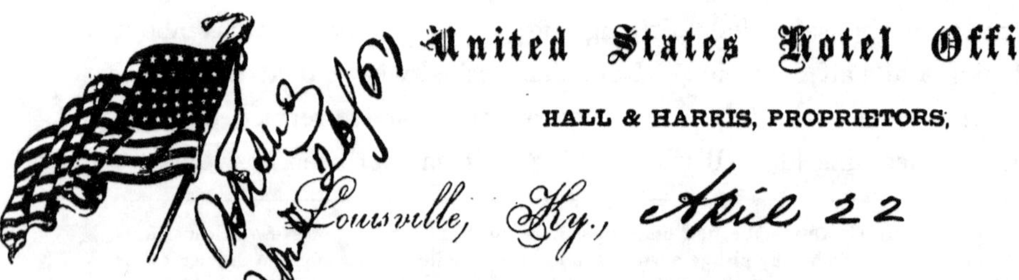
United States Hotel Office,
HALL & HARRIS, PROPRIETORS,
Louisville, Ky., April 22

HEADING OF LETTER OF MR. THEODORE HARRIS, ASKING FOR WAR PERMIT.

* One of the first policy-holders to apply for a "Home Guard" permit was Mr. Theodore Harris, of Louisville, Captain of the "Louisville Battalion." Later Mr. Harris took out a permit as sutler, but before he could use it his battalion was called into active service during Bragg's invasion of Kentucky, in 1862, and he took out a third permit, paying the "war extra."

the Federal Army and other portions of our people. Home protection we recognize, but if death occur in consequence of enlistment in opposition to the general Government, we could not, in justice to the great mass of our policy-holders, pay a loss under such circumstances; according to our construction of national law, it would render us liable as affording 'aid and comfort' in time of war to a legally acknowledged enemy."

Simultaneously with the question of war permits came the question of the effect of secession and a state of war, upon the Company's contracts. Upon this point Southern agents and policy-holders needed to be assured anew with every new phase of public events. On January 3, 1861, the Company's agent at Richmond, Mr. Charles E. Wortham, wrote: "I send you enclosed a short editorial from the Richmond 'Dispatch,' which is producing a very bad effect on the business of your Company, as well as that of other Northern life companies in this city and State." The article was a comment upon an editorial that had recently appeared in the New York "Commercial Advertiser," in which, referring to life insurance, it was said that, "the first blast of actual war between the South and the Federal Government would sweep away nearly $12,000,000 of Southern capital." Mr. Wortham declared himself satisfied of the Company's purpose to act liberally towards its Southern patrons, but wished a statement that would satisfy *them*. On January eighteenth Mr. Wortham wrote again, sending other newspaper articles, and asking for a statement of the Company's views, with permission to publish the same. On the twenty-first Mr. Franklin wrote:

From the tenor of several communications recently received, it appears that some of our Southern friends entertain the opinion that, in the event of a separation of the States, the policies issued by this and other companies in the Northern States will be repudiated. If, by any possibility, the legal contract could be annulled in such an unfortunate contingency, which we emphatically deny, this Company, and we believe all others, will fully recognize the moral obligation between their customers and themselves, faithfully and promptly to meet all honorable demands which can or may be made against them, without regard to locality or political views or sentiments. In our business relations we know of no distinction between the North and South, and certainly shall not inquire, when a demand is made upon us, whether the deceased was a citizen of the United States, as now organized, or of a Southern Confederacy—the only question being, as stated in the policy, whether he died while actually engaged in war or in consequence of having enlisted therein.

In the earnest hope that our Union may be preserved entire, and especially that Virginia will remain firm in her allegiance, I am, with great respect, etc.

Virginia passed the ordinance of secession April seventeenth, and the question of the validity of policies in Northern companies was again raised. On May sixth Mr. Wortham wrote: "I have heard to-day for the first time, through the agent of the Mutual Life, who has just returned from New York, that all the New York companies have decided not to pay in future losses in the Southern States, with probably a very few exceptions. Please inform me what your views are in regard to losses in the seceded States. I do not mean any death that might happen in war, for we all well know that you do not insure against such risks." In order, if possible, to stem the tide of distrust now growing stronger every day, Mr. Franklin on May sixteenth wrote to Mr. Wortham as follows, and gave authority for the publication of his letter in the cities of Virginia where the Company had agencies:

We apprehend that an impression exists in the minds of many of the Southern members of our Company that the present unhappy condition of our political relations has the effect to invalidate and make void the policies held by them, the consequence naturally being that many of them are surrendered and forfeited by the non-payment of premiums as they become due. We regret that any should labor under so great a mistake, for could it be established that a state of war between any States of the Union would work a legal discharge of the Company's obligations, which we emphatically deny, we should be recreant to our duty to recognize such a principle, and we therefore desire to be expressly understood when we declare in good faith that, notwithstanding the present most unfortunate position of the Union, we will never repudiate our contracts or fail promptly and cheerfully to respond to any claim which can or may be made against us either in equity or law; all we ask or expect is, that our policy-holders will faithfully discharge ***their part of the condition upon which the contract is based,*** and they may rest assured that the NEW-YORK LIFE INSURANCE COMPANY will never give just cause for complaint on the part of those who now are, or who may hereafter become our policy-holders.

Letters of similar import were addressed to other Southern agents, in response to similar inquiries, and the letter of January twenty-first was published, addressed to policy-holders of the Company. The position assumed by the Company gave general satisfaction. Mr. James H. Taylor, agent at Charleston, S. C., wrote under date of May eighteenth: "Your esteemed favor of the eleventh inst. came on sixteenth inst. I have furnished copies to all those who hold policies of you, and, so far as I have heard, your position is perfectly satisfactory. Our friends here are not unreasonable. If they are killed in war they know they have no claim under your policies, nor do they ask it. But they do most positively object to the position the ———————— of New York has taken, and look upon it as a mere bold, bald swindle."

Meantime the legal phase of the relations between the Company, its agents and policy-holders, was assuming importance. About May first, Governor Brown, of Georgia, issued a proclamation forbidding the payment of debts due to persons in the Northern States, and the Company inquired of its agent at Augusta, Mr. J. Milligan, what effect it would have upon collections. Mr. Milligan replied under date of May seventeenth: "The proclamation of Governor Brown has fallen, I think, still-born before him. That some persons may not pay what is due the North is likely enough, as the times are specially hard, and it is a season at which no great deal of money is to be had; but I do not believe that one man in a hundred regards the proclamation in any other light than as a recommendation to do a very unwise and dishonest thing, regarding it as mere clap-trap nonsense. I shall not give it the slightest regard; any moneys paid into my hands for you shall be held sacred, subject to such order and direction as you alone may give."

On the other hand, Dr. Copes wrote under date of May twenty-fifth:

A very intelligent gentleman informed me this morning that one of your courts had already decided that a life insurance company was absolved from all obligations to a Southern holder of its policy. Is this true? * * * A very general impression prevails among our assured that you may, ***nolens volens***, be prevented from meeting your policy engagements, under the present deplorable condition of political affairs. * * * It seems to me that one of three things will have to be done: (1) Allow all premiums to remain here for the present, invested and secured as you may direct; (2) assign for a proper consideration all your agency business here to a local company; or (3) make an arrangement for a general purchase of nearly all your policies. I am besieged daily for pledges of increased security for the payment of policies, and am obliged to spend so much time and meet so many prejudices that I weary of the duty. Please write me fully and freely.

To this Mr. Franklin replied, May thirty-first:

We know nothing of the decision to which you refer, but let that be as it may, we distinctly and unequivocally say to you, and through you to each of our assured, that, let the present unhappy controversy terminate as it may, whether in a separate or united Confederacy, in the Union as it has been, now is, or may hereafter be, the NEW-YORK LIFE INSURANCE COMPANY will fulfill and recognize in good faith all its obligations, let legal questions be decided as they may; for, independent of technicalities of law, justice and equity will continue to control all our operations. You have recently had evidence of our action in the anticipated payment of the policy of the late Mr. Davis. We cannot consent to adopt either of the propositions suggested, as that might imply a doubt as to the policy which we now pursue or may hereafter pursue in the transaction of our business. Until we have failed or hesitated in the performance of our contracts, our friends should rely upon our honor, and rather give us credit for what we have done, than cast suspicion upon our intentions.

With the end of May came new difficulties in the way of the transaction of business with the Southern States—by order of the Postmaster-General, the carriage of the mail in the States then in insurrection was discontinued. On May twenty-eighth the Company issued the following notice to its Southern agents and policy-holders:

Office of the NEW-YORK LIFE INSURANCE COMPANY,
112 & 114 Broadway,

NEW-YORK, May 28, 1861.

Sir: In consequence of the contemplated postal service being discontinued in the Southern States, and present derangement of the currency, the Company finds it impossible to forward, as heretofore, the usual renewal receipts to its agents, but, wishing to avoid unnecessary embarrassments in the renewal of policies, have to request those who may be able to do so, to forward their premiums to the Home Office, deducting 2½ per cent. for exchange, upon receipt of which the renewal will be sent, or disposed of as directed by the parties. In cases where the premiums cannot be so placed, upon the restoration of mail facilities and usual average rate of exchange, the Company will renew such policy as may have lapsed, in consequence of the above causes, provided the party should be in good health, and so certified by one of its Medical Examiners, upon payment of the premium during the suspension of such policy, or upon such terms as may be deemed equitable between the parties. On all premiums paid by the parties, commission will be credited to the different agents entitled to the same.*

---

* The first Southern agent to foresee the difficulties and inconsistencies involved in an attempt to continue business, was Major Rice W. Payne, of Warrenton, Va. On May twelfth he wrote: "In response to so much of your letter as requests my advice in respect to the transmission of premiums, etc., duty to my Government requires me to say—that as war now exists between the Confederate States and your Government, my agency for your Company necessarily terminates. Whenever hostilities shall have ceased, and our respective Governments resumed the attitude of friendly relations, it will then be my pleasure, if yours, to accept the agency I have heretofore held at the hands of your Company, and to renew my own insurance therein." On August 14, 1865, Major Payne wrote: "I am about to resume the practice of my profession, and in calling to mind old friends and clients who in past years sought my professional services, I cannot but recall your Company, and to say that the restoration of our business relations would be alike desirable and agreeable to me." He was re-appointed August sixteenth.

The item of exchange had already become a serious one to both the insured and the Company. On May tenth Messrs. Allen and Teasdale, agents of the Company at Springfield, Ill., wrote: "Exchange on New York is now fifteen per cent. for our currency, and as we can receive nothing else, I write to inquire if you will pay it or allow the funds to remain on deposit until exchange is less." On May eighteenth Mr. James H. Taylor wrote from Charleston: "I have some funds in hand for you, but how am I to get funds to you? I have tried to-day and every day for some weeks to get exchange, but it has been, when sold, in such shape as to be out of my reach. Gold is worth ten per cent. premium. Please advise me, and say how I am to manage in the future. I presume, at the end of the month post-office facilities will cease. Postmaster Reagan takes charge of the offices in the Confederate States." On May twentieth Mr. W. H. Bridgman, agent at Chicago, wrote: "The crisis in our currency has at last been reached and the worst is over, although the matter is not fully settled, but henceforth we take this wild cat stuff for its specie value only. What action the bankers will take in regard to deposits now on hand, is not yet made known. They have only taken deposits 'payable in like funds,' but as no two banks are of the same value, it remains to be seen whether they can pay their depositors off in the poorest. I cannot use your funds now and shall advise that you allow them to remain just as they are, in my name as agent, at the banking house of B. F. Carver & Co. I think they will pay in good funds in a short time. Business will be very dull now until we get money to do it with." On the twenty-first Mr. Bridgman wrote: "Excitement is great and currency is selling at fifty cents on the dollar to brokers. Gold very scarce." On May twenty-second Mr. William E. Burr, of Boonville, Mo., sent New York draft in payment of premium, saying "This draft cost me the round sum of fifteen per cent. premium." He asked to be allowed the agent's commission, and was allowed five per cent.

In order to overcome the difficulty with respect to the discount on Southern currency, the following letter was written, May first, to the agents most affected:

Dear Sir: With reference to the checks sent, or which may be sent to you for dividends—we would suggest that they be retained by you, getting the parties' endorsement, and in lieu thereof pay the amount due by your own checks out of the Company's funds in your hands. This will save us the exchange, and the checks can be returned us properly endorsed as a remittance to your credit.

With the stoppage of the mails between the North and the seceded States, the American Express Company organized the "American Letter

FROM CHARLESTON *via* LOUISVILLE, PER "AMERICAN LETTER EXPRESS."

Express," which undertook to deliver mail matter between Louisville (which was within the Federal lines) and Nashville (which was within the Confederate lines). In some cases they passed through the lines under flag of truce. On May twenty-eighth Mayor Lamb, of Norfolk, wrote to ask if his policy would be paid if he died a natural death, and said:

"Enclose your reply to me unsealed in an envelope directed to Commodore Prendergrast, Frigate Cumberland, Old Point." On May twenty-eighth Mr. James M. Muldon, agent at Mobile, sent a draft to balance his account by mail, and sent bulky documents by private hands. On June twenty-eighth Mr. Charles E. Wortham wrote from Richmond: "I am just in receipt of yours of the twelfth and fifteenth instants, one through W. S. Vernon & Co. (of Louisville), and the other through Commodore Prendergrast."

But this state of things could not long continue. On July thirteenth Congress passed an Act declaring certain States in insurrection, and on August sixteenth the President, by proclamation, prohibited all commercial intercourse with such States after August twenty-sixth. On August twenty-seventh the Company received a letter from Dr. Copes, dated August nineteenth; the letter was endorsed, "Not answered, as all mail and express were stopped yesterday, twenty-sixth." The Company had done its best to serve its Southern policy-holders in these trying times, but was compelled at last to yield to the inevitable.*

With respect to the general business of the Company, the one com-

---

*The legal aspect of commerce between the two sections had also had attention in the South. Early in June the Attorney-General of Louisiana gave to the President of the Mechanics and Traders' Bank, of New Orleans, an opinion to the effect that a power of attorney given on May twenty-second, by a citizen of New York to a citizen of Louisiana, to transfer bank stock, was not valid, as it was given after the beginning of the war and its recognition by the Confederate States. He continued: "No principle of international law is more firmly established than that the declaration of war arrests all intercourse between the belligerents. War puts every individual of the respective Governments, as well as the Governments themselves, in a state of hostility to each other. There is no such thing as a war for arms and a peace for commerce. The existence of civil contracts and relations is contradictory to a state of war, and hence it has been held that commercial partnerships existing between the citizens of one country and those of another are dissolved by the breaking out of a war between the two countries. * * * The remittance of money for any purpose, the making of contracts, the acceptance of trusts, the creation of any civil obligation, or commercial relation whatever, is unlawful and forbidden, simply because it is inconsistent with the hostile attitude of the parties. The belligerent Governments have placed their respective citizens in an attitude of hostility towards each other, and no relation inconsistent with hostility can be lawfully created by the acts of individuals without the express permission of the Government."

The Attorney-General of Mississippi decided that the licenses of foreign insurance companies could not be renewed in that State, as the law required evidence that such companies possessed certain amounts in stocks held "by citizens of the United States, and the United States no longer exists." "There are no longer 'citizens of the United States,' or other persons capable of holding the stocks contemplated by said law. * * * The ordinance of secession has put it out of the power of such companies to comply with conditions precedent to the issuance of such licenses."

plaint that runs through the correspondence of 1861 is that of hard times. On March sixth Messrs. E. J. Richardson & Sons wrote from Baltimore: "We have retained more receipts than usual, principally by request of parties, some of whom have been insured a long time, and have been prevented from paying at maturity by the dreadful state of the times." Again, on April fourth, they wrote: "With us at Baltimore prospects grow apparently worse every day. People failing by scores, and the mechanical classes entirely idle. New business is out of the question to any extent. We have done all we could to assist our policy-holders, and we have their promises to pay in various forms for about $800, not one dime of which we could realize to-day." On May seventh Mr. Edward Morrison wrote from St. Louis: "I am very sorry to send you back so many renewal receipts, but it is utterly impossible for people to get money." On the same date Mr. W. S. Vernon wrote from Louisville: "We have lost many of our policies, not so much in relation to secession—these are few—as the want of money to renew them. Great is the distress of our whole community. You may have some idea of it in the city of New York, but not to the extent it is here. This place is viewed by thousands as the battle-ground; we are between the upper and nether mill-stones, apparently doomed to be ground into dust. * * * Our business is nearly all gone, and what to do to maintain our families we know not."* A third letter of the same date, from Mr. E. T. Morrison, of Toledo, O., said: "The war feeling has prevailed here to such an extent that it has been a difficult matter to collect premiums falling due. In making my collections for April I had to take 'cats and dogs,' as we say in the West,—in other words, due-bills—orders on groceries, dry goods stores, and churches,—and I hope I may get my money back." On August thirteenth Mr. A. M. McLean wrote from Rochester, N. Y.: "If we are to make reports promptly on the first of each month, it will cause a mighty crushing of bones in our business. We think it not too large an estimate to say that our remittances would be reduced one-half."

*The distress in Kentucky was so great that the Legislature passed a "Stay Law," providing that property seized for debt should not be sold by the Sheriff until January 1, 1862.

Even far-off California felt the stress of the hard times incident to the war. Exchange on New York was five per cent. premium, and there was talk of secession there also, and of a "Pacific Republic." "Home Guard" permits were wanted by policy-holders. Mr. Samuel H. Lloyd, the Company's agent at San Francisco, wrote under date of May first: "We are a Union people. Of course there are many Southern people here, and secession is advocated here and there; but if you hear anything about a 'Pacific Republic,' or anything about California joining the separatists, please say there is not so much as a probability of any serious attempt at either." On September sixth he wrote announcing the election of Governor Stanford, the unconditional Union candidate, "by an overwhelming majority," but saying "Home Guard" permits would still be wanted.*

The Company met the difficulty in a liberal spirit, paying generous surrender values to such as gave up their policies, taking notes for forty per cent. of premiums due, and changing annual premiums to semi-annual and quarterly. Premium notes were also accepted on policies with quarterly and semi-annual premiums, the interest on the notes being paid in advance. This policy was reflected in the annual report for 1861, which showed $74,659.73 paid for surrendered policies, as compared with $31,373.90 paid in 1860, and $48,334.42 in quarterly and semi-annual premiums due subsequent to January first, as compared with $22,414.74 the year previous. The redemption of dividends proved timely and helpful, and the plan of redeeming one-fifth of all declared after 1850, in addition to all declared prior to that date, made every policy-holder of twelve months' standing a sharer in the benefit. The total amount paid for dividends was $124,330.84, or nearly twenty-five per cent. of the premiums received, including premiums on new policies.

On July ninth Dr. Henry W. Bellows, President of the United States Sanitary Commission, issued an address describing a recent tour among the soldiers in camp and field; and on the thirteenth the Executive Fi-

* On June twenty-seventh Mr. Lloyd had written: "After to-day we have a daily overland mail." The letter quoted above bears this memorandum: "Copy—original sent by Pony Express."

nance Committee in New York published an appeal for funds, in which they estimated that "every dollar, honestly and judiciously expended in sanitary measures, will save at least one soldier's life." On the seventeenth the Trustees of the NEW-YORK LIFE voted that "an amount not less than $1,000, and not exceeding $5,000, be appropriated to the use of the Commission." Under the authority thus conferred upon the officers two donations were made, the first of $1,000 and the second of $4,000. The Company's action was justified on the ground that many of its policy-holders were in the army, and that the contribution brought the Company into favorable notice before the public.*

On August thirty-first a resolution was adopted by the Trustees, to the effect that it was desirable that an investment be made in United States Treasury Notes, bearing interest at the rate of 7.30 per cent. per annum, to the amount of $100,000, and the subject was referred to the Finance Committee. At the meeting of October ninth the Committee reported that the officers, with the approbation of the Committee, had

HEAD QUARTERS

DOUGLAS BRIGADE, U. S. A.

DAVID STUART, Colonel, Commanding.

11599 = 1000 = 500.

Chicago Sept 5th 1861

HEADING OF LETTER FROM E. D. SWARTOUT, QUARTERMASTER AND COMMISSARY OF SUBSISTANCE, ASKING FOR WAR PERMIT UNDER POLICY NO. 11,599.

* It so happened that in the Commission's published list of subscriptions, the NEW-YORK LIFE'S was credited to the Mutual Life. Upon receiving the Commission's next appeal, Mr. Franklin called attention to the Company's previous subscription and to the error in the Commission's report. Dr. Bellows wrote in reply, under date of March 6, 1862: "We have greatly regretted the mistake to which you refer in our 40th publication. It was inexcusable, and no apologies can mend it. We propose, however, to correct the unintentional error of our Publication Committee by a special note in our republication of the report, and also by a line in each of the New York papers. If I had known of it I should not have had the effrontery to make any new application, and I hereby respectfully withdraw the petition you have received so forbearingly."

made a temporary loan of $80,900 at six per cent. interest, taking Treasury Notes as collateral, under an agreement that the loan should always be kept at least five per cent. below the market value of the Notes. The Committee urged in justification of their action that, while as individuals they should uphold the Government in every way possible, as Trustees of a sacred fund they should consider first of all the question of safety and of profit; that a temporary loan upon such securities enabled the owners to purchase more of them, and so the Government was helped as effectually as if they were purchased by the Company; and that in the event of a long continuance of the war such securities would probably depreciate, and could be purchased at a profit when the Government would require aid more emphatically than at that time.* There is no record of the discussion had upon the report, but it is followed by a resolution "that the temporary loan of $80,900 be called in and invested in United States Treasury Notes." At the meeting in November the Committee reported it done.

In September the question arose as to the effect of an Act of Congress upon the Company's treatment of its policy-holders in the seceded States. On September tenth Messrs. E. J. Richardson & Sons wrote:

> We note your remarks relative to policy-holders residing in Virginia and other Southern localities, and feel satisfied you will pursue a just and liberal course towards them. Another question of very great interest is now agitating our insurers, which is this: The late United States Congress passed an Act confiscating all property in disloyal States. Should Maryland secede from the Union (which God forbid), will the insured residing in this State be paid in the event of death?

To this Mr. Franklin replied, under date of September twelfth:

> As we understand the action of the late Congress in relation to confiscation, the mere passage of the Act does not, of itself, prevent our Company from paying to policy-holders any moneys belonging to them—some legal proceeding on the part of the Government must be had; should such be the case we, in common with all others, should be compelled to submit and unable to part with any funds in our possession belonging to parties residing in disloyal States. Should Maryland secede (which God forbid), the risk of a legal confiscation must be assumed by the persons immediately in interest, but

*There is no question but that, on general principles, the Committee's reasoning was eminently sound, and had it not been for the Legal Tender Act of February 25, 1862, investments in United States securities would have been temporarily, at least, unprofitable to life insurance companies.

without such action, we do not believe that our Company will take advantage of any technicality to avoid the payment of these policies.

The annual report for the year showed that, notwithstanding financial and national embarrassments, the business of the Company had increased. It was also said:

The result of our war risks has thus far justified the decision of the Board in fixing the rate of extra premium. After the unfortunate defeat of our army at Bull Run, and the apparent want of sufficient sanitary regulations, the officers, for several months, in the exercise of a discretion vested in them by the Board, discontinued the issuing of any new policies with war permits. Subsequent improvements, however, through the industry and zeal of the Sanitary Commission, induced them again to resume* the risks to an amount not exceeding $1,000 on any one life, where the insurance is effected for the benefit of the wife, children, or near relative of the soldier; but in all cases they have continued to issue permits upon existing policies.

The system of redemption of dividends inaugurated at the last annual meeting of the Board has met with very decided and general favor, and has removed a prominent objection which has heretofore been urged against the Company with great effect by agents of similar institutions, to wit: that our dividends were of no available value beyond the mere payment of interest, not being redeemed during the life-time of the assured, nor paid to his representatives at death. Besides, the rapid accumulation of premium notes, without any relief from dividends [beyond the payment of interest] was felt to be a great burthen, and was seriously complained of by many of our policy-holders; but under the present system they are gradually being liquidated, and will eventually be so reduced, should our business continue to prosper, that no more than five will probably be outstanding at the falling in of the policy. It is true that, in the first workings of the system, some few complaints were heard in relation to the non-payment of interest for the preceding year; but most, if not all, have become satisfied that the plan could not prudently be carried out except upon the principle adopted, and it is now almost universally conceded to be a safe and popular policy.

In the year 1860 we lost 56 lives, and during 1861 the same number; which, taking into consideration the increased number of lives and advanced ages of the assured, shows a very favorable result as to the risks assumed. The amount of losses reported during the year is $189,000, which, in comparison with the preceding, shows a decrease of $28,000. It must be kept in mind, however, that since the twenty-fifth day of August, the usual postal and express communications with most of the Southern States have been entirely discontinued; consequently we are not advised if any—and if any, how many—of our assured have died since that time. Owing to the interruption of mail facilities, it is to be presumed that many of our Southern policies have lapsed, as it has been impossible to forward the usual renewal receipts signed by one of the officers, without which agents are not authorized to renew, as is expressly stated in the margin of the policies. Besides which, it is reasonable to assume that most of the parties have, either

* The first of such policies was issued October tenth as "an exception," and on October eleventh the new course was announced.

directly or indirectly, violated their conditions by entering into military or naval service without the consent of the Company, or by being engaged in the known violation of some law of the State where they may reside, or of the United States. In the absence of any direct information on the subject, we have assumed, in making the valuations, that they either have been or will be renewed—deeming it prudent to set aside a fund in reference thereto, rather than consider them as having lapsed, and be obliged hereafter to make provision for the same.

A review of the mortality experience of the Company showed that there had been, since organization, 455 deaths, in lieu of 499 deaths expected by the Carlisle Table. This gain had been somewhat unevenly distributed among the different ages. The report said on this point:

The result of our business shows that, from 25 years and under, the actual losses have exceeded those called for by the table; from 26 to 46 there has been a gain; from 51 to 55 a loss; from 56 to 60 a gain; and from 61 and upwards a loss. The experience of this Company proves that the older ages are not profitable to insure; and consequently, for a number of years past, we have refused, as a general rule, applications for ages beyond 55—making occasional exceptions thereto, depending upon the longevity of the family of the party, and other circumstances calculated to extend the probable ordinary duration of life.

A scrip dividend of thirty per cent. on the premiums of all participating policies one year in force was declared, and a second twenty per cent. of all dividends declared from 1850 to 1860 was ordered paid in cash.

1862. EARLY in March, 1862, a bill was introduced in Congress proposing a stamp tax on life insurance policies and a three per cent. tax on dividends. The Convention of American Life Underwriters was called together on March thirteenth, by President Winston, to consider the subject of taxation and war risks. The Convention adopted resolutions to the effect that "a stamp duty on policies, proportionate to the amount of each, and of sufficient magnitude to realize the quota of taxation apportioned to life insurance companies, is the only safe and equitable form of taxation," and that this method be recommended to Congress in preference to any other. It was also recommended that the companies continue to take war risks in accordance with the rules adopted by the Convention in April, 1861.* The President of the Convention was ap-

* Four companies reported 429 war permits granted under policies insuring $618,300; three companies reported 304 permits, without giving amount of insurance; two companies reported $1,200,000 insured under war policies, without giving the number of permits. The figures given indicate about

pointed to present its views to Congress. The law as passed, laid a tax of one per cent. on premiums, three per cent. on dividends and a stamp tax of twenty-five cents on policies and renewals. It was amended in accordance with the recommendation of the Convention, the stamp tax being made twenty-five cents for $1,000 or under, fifty cents for more than $1,000 and not exceeding $5,000, and one dollar for policies of more than $5,000, and all other taxes were repealed.

With the capture of New Orleans, Norfolk and Memphis by the Federal forces in the spring of 1862, new questions arose for adjudication. The position of Southern agents had been a very trying one. Unable to receive instructions from the Home Office, anxious to do justice both to the Company and to policy-holders, they were liable to be regarded with suspicion by both. After these places came under Federal control communication was irregular, especially with New Orleans, and letters were sometimes lost in transit. Very little business was doing and everything was under military surveillance and control.

In August, 1861, there were two death-claims pending at the Norfolk agency. Mr. William P. Griffith, of that place, died July 10, 1861, at Warrenton, N. C., whither he had gone in the hope of improving his health. Proofs of death were not completed prior to August twenty-sixth. On September twelfth the Company wrote Messrs. E. J. Richardson & Sons, at Baltimore: "We are very anxious to communicate with our agent in Norfolk, if there is any way, either by private opportunity or otherwise, to accomplish it. We suppose there are persons constantly traveling between the two cities, and hope you may be able to assist us in this matter." The Messrs. Richardson replied, under date of September fourteenth, that a policy-holder wished to go South on business and wanted a territorial permit. This presented a new difficulty, and the Company wrote on September seventeenth :

Independent of the extra risk which he would incur in consequence of the present military aspects of affairs, we deem that, under the proclamation of the President, all

1,560 permits and about $2,250,000 at risk by the following companies: American (Philadelphia), American (Hartford), Berkshire, Charter Oak, Connecticut Mutual, Manhattan, Mutual Life, NEW-YORK LIFE, Penn Mutual. Six war losses were reported, aggregating $9,000.

commercial intercourse between the parties in rebellion against the Government, and citizens residing in the loyal States, is actually prohibited, and that our granting a permit for that purpose would be virtually, if not actually, a violation of the proclamation. We are unwilling to do anything either directly or indirectly, which can be construed, or even tortured, into the least semblance of opposition to the view of the general Government upon the political questions of the day.

Norfolk was occupied by the Federal forces May 10, 1862, and on July third following, Mrs. Griffith was given a safe conduct to New York by General E. L. Viele, Military Governor, and the claim was paid to her in person, July tenth.

The other policy was upon the life of Richard A. Worrell, and became due September tenth. The Company made strenuous efforts to pay this claim before it was due. Letters were written to the agents at Norfolk, Petersburg and other points in Virginia to collect all moneys due the Company and apply them, together with any funds in their hands, to the payment of this claim. Some of the Company's policy-holders were also requested to pay their premiums to the claimants under this policy, taking receipts therefor which would be duly recognized. On February 8, 1862, a letter was sent to Mr. Ferguson, of Norfolk, under flag of truce, asking if anything had been paid on the policy, and requesting an answer by the same channel. On the day following the payment of Mrs. Griffith the Company again wrote Mr. Ferguson. No reply was received to either of these communications, but word was received in August through Mr. H. C. Hardy, of New York, whose brother lived in Norfolk, that nothing had been paid on the policy.* The Company replied August fifteenth, reciting the circumstances, and saying payment would be gladly made as soon as it could be done understandingly. Miss Ellen Elizabeth Worrell, one of the daughters of the insured, was appointed guardian of her younger sisters September third, and soon afterward came to New York and was paid in full October second. She brought a letter of introduction from

* It is due the Company's agents to say that the reason of its non-payment by them was that most of the moneys in their hands had been paid subject to the decision of the Company as to the status of their policies, etc., which the agents were unable to obtain. Some of the Company's letters never reached their destination. As Mr. Ferguson had been in the military service of the Confederacy, some of his early letters were not allowed to be forwarded.

Hon. Wm. W. Lamb, Mayor of Norfolk, in which he said: "Your prompt payment to Mrs. Griffith, of this city, of the insurance on her husband's life, has sustained the high reputation of your Company in this community, which I hope it will long continue to enjoy."

New Orleans was occupied by the Federal forces May 1, 1862. Dr. Copes' first letter bore date May thirty-first, and was received about the middle of June. He had been sorely beset. When communication was interrupted, in 1861, there were two death-claims pending at his agency under policies on the lives of Jacob Boyd and Charles H. Sheafe, the first of which had been ordered paid. Another was incurred between August, 1861, and May, 1862, under policy on the life of E. M. Rice. The Boyd policy had been partly paid when the District Attorney of the Confederate States forbade the agent to pay out any more money, and it was with great difficulty that the Receivers appointed under the Sequestration Act of the Confederate Congress were dissuaded from taking charge of the agency. This was done by a skillfully drawn document in which Mr. Franklin's letters on the subject of Southern policies were freely quoted, and the relations between the Company and its policy-holders were shown to be such that the former was always under heavy liabilities to the latter; and it was argued that, if the Confederate Government confiscated the Company's resources it would become liable for its debts to policy-holders. Dr. Copes had been the most strenuous of all the Company's Southern agents in demanding liberal terms for Southern policy-holders, and he was equally faithful to his obligations to the Company. The letter reproduced on another page, written after the war was over and the Company was again doing business in the South, shows how he regarded his own action and the Company's course, in later years.

Mrs. Sheafe brought suit, with garnishment, against the agent for the amount of her claim, to prevent the funds in his hands from being seized by the Confederate Government. Soon after the city was captured Dr. Copes sent a messenger into the interior, whither these claimants had fled, to pay them with the Confederate currency left in his hands, the use of which was prohibited in New Orleans after May twenty-seventh, by order

ASSETS, $37,000,000, | Local Board of Directors in N. O.

BRANCH OFFICE

New York Life Insurance Company.

GENERAL AGENT FOR LOUISIANA:

J. S. COPES, 46 Carondelet Street.

Life, Term, Non-Forfeiture, Tentine and Endowment Policies.

RECEIVED APR 3 1879 HOME OFFICE.

New Orleans, March, 27th 1879

Hon. Morris Franklin, Pres.
N. York.

RECEIVED APR 3 1879 HOME OFFICE

Dear Sir

Having occasion to reexamine some press copies of former years, vivid memories of difficulties & perils are awakened by a reperusal of the letter a copy of which I enclose to you. I have thought that if you could in any considerable degree put yourself in my place at the time & under all the conditions then environing me, you would the more fully appreciate the relief & elation of feeling with which I quoted your language from the several letters cited. It has always been regarded by the wise & good as noble & just: worthy of the best days & the highest exemplars of Roman virtue & luminous with the spirit of christianity.

For myself, I regard ~~it~~ this appeal, all things considered, as one of the best efforts of my life in defending the right; & succesful only, as Ezra & Nehemiah declared in their straits, "by the good hand of my God upon me." You confided in me & I confidently, yea proudly believed & trusted in you, & the blessed Master who knew us altogether, guided us by his counsel. He will do it to the end. With great esteem, your friend.

J. S. Copes.

of General Butler issued May nineteenth. Communication with the interior was soon forbidden, and for many months nothing was heard from the messenger. In September Dr. Copes was obliged to take the oath of allegiance to the United States, in order to continue the Company's business or his own. Mrs. Sheafe returned to the city in November and claimed that she had not been paid. In January, 1863, she offered to withdraw the suit if payment were promised. The matter was left in Dr. Copes' hands and a final settlement was made in October. A creditor's policy on the same life was paid to a St. Louis firm on September 27, 1861. The Rice policy was paid in October, 1862, as soon as the necessary proofs were submitted. After the interchange of several letters, Mr. Franklin had written to Dr. Copes on July thirtieth:

> We are very much gratified at the course you have pursued in protecting the interests of our Company during the terrible ordeal through which we are now passing. We heartily approve of the disposition and contemplated disposition of the funds, and you will add another obligation by furnishing us at your earliest convenience a detailed account current between you and the Company.*

On May twenty-ninth the Company received *via* Havana, a letter dated April third, from Mr. James M. Muldon, agent at Mobile, saying he had previously sent statements of business to January, 1862, by same *route*. The letter continued:

> The New England Life Insurance Company, of Boston, have authorized their agent in this city (during the war) to receive notes at twelve months, bearing interest, for the full amount of premiums. As all our life policies are worth at least one year's premium there can be no loss to the Company on premiums, and [it] will enable many to continue their insurances who otherwise might be compelled to sacrifice their policies and all that has been paid on them. I have adopted the same course, and am receiving notes for premiums, bearing seven per cent. interest. I give a conditional receipt; in case it is not approved by the Company, the note is to be returned and premiums paid as formerly, otherwise the policy to be null and void. Do write me, if only to say my action in the matter is approved or not.

To this Mr. Franklin replied on the same day, sending his letter by the same *route*, in care of Mr. Walter Douglass, Havana:

---

*Dr. Copes had on hand about $4,800 in Confederate money when the city was captured. Of this amount he authorized the Company to charge him with $3,200, at fourteen cents on the dollar, in September, 1863, and the balance was charged to Profit and Loss in the Company's report for the year.

We are in receipt this morning of your valued favor of April third. It is indeed refreshing to look again upon the familiar handwriting of our esteemed correspondent at Mobile, from whom, for so long a time, owing to the melancholy situation of our national affairs, we have been debarred the privilege of hearing. The letter of January twenty-second, to which you refer, was received after its long journey and should have been answered, and I was not aware until this morning that it had not been. In reference to renewals of our policies in Mobile and other Southern cities, we are not at liberty, under present circumstances, to make any arrangements, and must leave the subject for future consideration and adjustment when a more healthy state of affairs shall disembarrass it of all the perplexing questions with which it is now encumbered; for the present, we are compelled to consider all of our Southern policies as cancelled, but we doubt not that our Board, in the exercise of a sound discretion, will do equal and exact justice between the parties. Your letter of August first, enclosing draft on London for £311-2-5, has not been received. Please therefore enclose the duplicate and forward at your earliest opportunity to South Cuba Western Express Co., Havana, Cuba. All of our Southern losses reported and to be reported, must be held in suspense until acted upon by the Board.

At the meeting of the Trustees on July 9, 1862, the officers presented a report to the effect that, as the Southern ports were gradually being opened, and postal communication restored, applications were received for the renewal of policies which had lapsed and for the payment of losses occurring in the seceded States. The report cited portions of the correspondence which has already been presented herein, and asked instructions from the Board with respect to the payment of losses and the renewal of lapsed policies within the districts named, also as to the acceptance of the notes taken at the Mobile agency, and of Tennessee currency received at Memphis in renewal of policies while that city was within the Confederate lines. The report was referred to a Committee, which reported adversely on each proposition on August thirteenth, basing their action as to the first two upon the law of July 13, 1861, and the President's proclamation of August 16, 1861, declaring all commercial intercourse between citizens of the United States and those of the seceded States unlawful so long as hostilities should continue. The report was referred to the officers, with instructions to take legal counsel on the subject. On September tenth the officers presented an opinion by Hon. William Fullerton, to the effect that the restriction upon commercial intercourse referred to in the law and the proclamation did not apply to those parts of the seceded States which maintained a loyal adhesion to the Union and Constitution, or which might from time to time be occupied and controlled by forces of the United States. A resolution was thereupon adopted that the officers be authorized to pay losses in the localities last mentioned, and to renew such policies as had lapsed upon such terms and conditions as might be deemed equitable between the insured and the Company.

This meeting of the Trustees affords a good illustration of how the Company was compelled to deal at the same time with questions arising out of two entirely different phases of the war then raging. Between September fourth and seventh the Confederate army, under General Lee, crossed the Potomac and advançed to Frederick, menacing both Baltimore and Washington, and on the ninth the Company's Baltimore agents wrote asking permission for policy-holders to join organizations for the protection of the city. Mr. Franklin replied on the same day:

> The proposition was submitted to the Board at a regular monthly meeting held this day, and it was unanimously decided, that permission be granted to the citizens of Baltimore to organize for the protection of their city from the violence of the rebels, without forfeiture of their policies. We recognize the principle that a home guard, such as you appear to contemplate, should not work a forfeiture, but in the event of your people going beyond a strictly home defence, and following the enemy outside of the limits of your city, it must be considered as a military organization not covered by the policy, although in the event of being obliged to pursue them so as to render the city perfectly secure, we shall hold that the risk is covered, provided the parties do not take the field as a general organization in defence of the Government.

At the same meeting the officers reported the death of Colonel Dudley Donnelly, from wounds received at the Battle of Cedar Mountain, August ninth;* and a peculiar case from the San Francisco agency: Mr. Edward Roepke applied for $3,000 insurance at this agency in July; he passed a satisfactory medical examination and received a temporary policy good for ninety days, or until the Home Office could act upon the application. Mr. Roepke embarked for Panama on the steamer "Golden Gate," July twenty-first, and his application was sent by the same vessel. On the twenty-seventh the steamer was found to be on fire, and of the

---

*The funeral of Colonel Donnelly, of the 28th New York Volunteers, occurred at Lockport, N. Y., August 19, 1862, and the 129th New York Volunteers (afterward the 8th Heavy Artillery), then in camp on the Fair Grounds, attended as a guard of honor. The writer was a member of this regiment, and this was his first military duty.

OFFICE OF THE

New-York Life Insurance Co.

112 & 114 BROADWAY,

New-York, June 25th 1861

Policy No. 10827 Life of Dudley Donnelly Amt. 3.000

In Consideration of the extra premium of Five per cent. to be paid in addition to the premium mentioned in the annexed Policy No. 10827 Dudley Donnelly the party insured, has PERMISSION during the next twelve months TO ENTER THE MILITARY OR NAVAL SERVICE OF THESE UNITED STATES, and to travel and reside North of the 34th degree of north latitude.

And on payment of the additional extra premium of five per cent. will have permission to travel and reside SOUTH of said 34th degree of north latitude while engaged in such service.

It being understood that the extra premium is to continue to be paid after the present war, or the return of the party insured therefrom, until, on re-examination, he can furnish the certificate of one of the Company's Examining Physicians that he is in good health.

Wm Franklin

Received $37.50 on account of the above FIRST mentioned extra of five per cent, the balance of same to be paid in the following instalments

September 25th 1861 = $37.50

December 25th 1861 = $37.50

March 25th 1862 = $37.50

Wm Franklin

347 persons on board 219 were lost, among them Mr. Roepke. Thus, within about ten days, and while the papers were in transit, the temporary policy became a claim. It was ordered paid in full.

In October the Company's traveling agent visited Norfolk and examined the affairs of that agency; as a result, Mr. Franklin wrote to Captain Ferguson under date of November seventh:

> Enclosed herewith we hand you receipt and statement of the unsettled part of the account as it stands on our books, and would express our extreme gratification at the honorable settlement you made with Mr. Bloss, and trust that nothing hereafter will occur to disturb our harmonious personal intercourse or business relations. We understand from Mr. Bloss that some of the old members in Norfolk would like to renew their policies. With the view of facilitating renewals, we would enquire if any of your savings banks will receive your currency on deposit and allow a specified interest, and if so, whether your policy-holders will agree that drafts on said deposits shall be received in payment of their policies when they become claims. We hope some arrangement satisfactory to all parties may be made, for be assured that instead of availing of the legal cancelment of the large number of policies now lapsed, as some have supposed, the officers will do everything in their power to aid in their revival in an equitable manner—which would appear to be by payment of back premiums and six per cent. interest, on satisfactory medical examination. The policies being revived, the dividends and benefits connected therewith would also revive.

No reply being received to this letter, another of the same purport was written to Dr. R. B. Tunstall, the Company's Medical Examiner at Norfolk, on December fourth. Answers were received from both during the month to the effect that the banks were paying no interest, and the plan was reluctantly abandoned.

At the October meeting of the Trustees, the following case was submitted for consideration: Mr. Hugh C. Irish, a resident of Paterson, N. J., insured for $2,000 in December, 1861. Premiums were paid to December, 1862. During the summer of 1862 Mr. Irish raised a company and joined the 13th New Jersey Volunteers, and was killed at the battle of Antietam. No war permit had been asked for and no war extra paid. Captain Irish had instructed his brother to pay the premium on his "war policy," and had assured his wife that if he was killed she would receive the money; from which it was inferred that he intended the war extra to be paid and supposed it was paid. His brother had paid the regular premium only. The case was referred to the officers with power, and the claim was paid.

The annual report for 1862 was presented at the meeting of the Trustees on January 28, 1863. The year had been the most successful of any since the organization of the Company. Of the 6,528 new policies issued by the eleven life companies in New York City, the NEW-YORK LIFE had issued 3,302, or more than one-half.* This phenomenal success was attributed by other companies, the report said, to the fact that the NEW-YORK LIFE had continued to take war risks on new policies when other companies refused; † but the Trustees, while admitting that such action had undoubtedly had a helpful influence, declared the main cause to be a change in agency methods. On this point, it was said:

> The officers are satisfied that no man can succeed in procuring applications for life insurance so long as his mind is occupied with other branches of insurance or with any general business; his time, talent and thoughts must be devoted to life insurance only. Experience has fully demonstrated that local agents absorbed in other pursuits are occupying unprofitably territory which might otherwise be cultivated to advantage, and the attention of the officers has been mainly directed during the past year to perfecting a new system. As a general rule, no man is appointed an agent except with the express understanding that all other occupations are to be discontinued, and his time devoted exclusively to the service of the Company. It is to this plan the officers attribute the success which has thus far more than surpassed their most sanguine expectations. In the selection and instruction of agents they have procured the services of men of character, industry and zeal who have labored to spread the blessings of Life Insurance in districts where it was comparatively unknown. The States of Indiana, Illinois, Wisconsin and Iowa have responded to the new method in a manner which promises large

---

* Superintendent Barnes said, in his fourth annual report: "The two most remarkable events of the year, in the American Life Insurance world are, the unprecedented dividends of the Mutual Life, for its quinquennium, amounting to $3,000,000; and the issue by the NEW-YORK LIFE, of three thousand three hundred and two new policies during the year."

† The Philadelphia offices decline all new business, or risks to go to the war. We believe this class of risks is also generally declined at New York, Hartford and Boston—though in the case of the NEW-YORK LIFE the office takes not to exceed $1,000 on a volunteer's life, where the policy is for the benefit of the wife and children. There may be other exceptions, but we have not heard of them.—*Circular of American Life Insurance Co., of Philadelphia, 1862.*

The annual reports of the New England Mutual for 1861 and 1862 indicate that this company also issued war permits with new policies.

There appeared in the "United States Insurance Gazette" for September, 1862, an unsigned letter "from one of our city life insurance officials to an agent seeking information concerning war permits." It is a violent attack on companies issuing such permits, and said, among other things: "Some of the large companies may combine and take war risks, but their object is to lead the younger companies on to do the same, in order that they may be used up, and thus lessen competition!"

results in the future. Competent men have been assigned certain territory, within which they select and instruct other agents who, after actual experiment, are appointed and assigned appropriate districts.

The 10-payment non-forfeiting policy, it was said, had been received with such general favor that several other companies had adopted the premium table without credit to the NEW-YORK LIFE as the originator.

The report noted the death within the previous four weeks of four of the Company's agents, Messrs. Henry Wingate, of Frankfort, Ky., Daniel Anthony, of Rochester, N. Y., L. Chapman, of Springfield, Ill., and E. Willard Trotter, of Albany, N. Y. All except Mr. Chapman had been long in the service of the Company. Of Mr. Trotter, whose service had been most conspicuous, it was said:

He was peculiarly adapted to his position, and there are probably few if any who were more successful in canvassing for life insurance. It was by his industry and zeal that a business in Norfolk and other places in Virginia, yielding a gross income of nearly one hundred thousand dollars per annum, was built up. He was always a welcome guest of all our local agents, for he was highly educated and had enriched his mind by extensive reading and by foreign travel. He possessed unusual conversational powers, was good-hearted and a very genial companion.

The results under "war policies" showed extra losses in excess of extra premiums to the amount of $815. The losses had been twenty-four: one at Fort Donaldson, five at Shiloh, one at Williamsburgh, two at Perryville, one at Cedar Mountain, two at Antietam, one by the explosion of the "Mound City," and eleven from disease. The losses had been almost evenly divided between risks in force at the beginning of the war and those afterward assumed. The action of the Company in assuming these risks was thus referred to:

When it was decided to assume these risks the Board had in view only the establishment of such a rate as would indemnify the Company against loss, and with no expectation that it would yield a profit. It felt that persons voluntarily exposing themselves to the deprivations and dangers of the camp and the battle-field were entitled to every facility to enable them to make provision for their families in the event of death.

Attention was called to the fact that there were included in the assets of the Company as reported "a large amount [$208,132.23] due for premiums from persons residing in the Southern States, a part of which was known to be in the hands of agents;" also that all the Southern policies had been considered in force and about $500,000 charged as a liability thereon.* It was unanimously voted that both items should remain in the report entire until the Company received more reliable information on the subject.

A scrip dividend of thirty-five per cent. on the premiums of whole life policies twelve months in force was declared, and it was voted to redeem and pay in cash a third twenty per cent. of all dividends declared from 1850 to 1860.

On June 14, 1862, the Company complied with the Massachusetts law, and was admitted to do business in that State. The report of the Company to the Commissioners, as of November 1, 1862, included in liabilities scrip dividends of a present value of $653,320.42, assuming that they would be paid in accordance with the plan already adopted, but which were still liable for any losses by the Company, and which could not be paid so as to impair the fund reserved against losses, nor without further action of the Board of Trustees. With this item charged as a liability and the policy reserve valued by the Actuaries' Table of Mortality with four per cent. interest, there was no surplus, but a slight deficiency. The Massachusetts Commissioners, however, decided, after the report was out, that the scrip dividends were not a legal liability, and by a circular, dated April 8, 1863, gave the Company credit for a surplus of over half a million dollars. The valuation of the reserve fund in the New York Report being made on the Carlisle Table as of December thirty-first, showed a surplus of $39,028.93, the scrip dividends being included as a liability at their full face value.†

---

*In commenting on the NEW-YORK LIFE'S report to the Massachusetts Department, the Commissioners said: "The value of these policies can hardly be less than three times the amount due on them, so that if they had been stricken off, as has probably been done by most of the other companies which had business at the South, the ratio of net assets to premium reserve would have been increased, probably to 117 per cent., at least."—*Consolidated Mass. Reports, page 200.*

†Competition was sharp in those days as well as now, and the statement of the Actuary accompanying the Massachusetts Commissioners' circular says: "In the synopsis of the standing of Life Insurance Companies doing business in Massachusetts, which appears in the last Report of the Insurance Commissioner of that State, the NEW-YORK LIFE INSURANCE COMPANY is represented as having only 99.41 per cent. of assets to liabilities (though a modification of this is found in a subsequent page of the report), and we learn that interested parties are making use of this statement to the prejudice of

1863. At a meeting of the Trustees held on February 4, 1863, a Special Committee previously appointed to consider a claim under a policy for $6,000, upon the life of Joseph G. Chandler, of Mobile, Ala., reported that Mr. Chandler died July 3, 1862; that the premium due July 9, 1861, was paid to the Company's agent at Mobile, who gave the Company's regular renewal receipt therefor. Mobile was still within the territory with which commercial intercourse was forbidden by law, but it was represented that Mrs. Chandler was then (February, 1863) in New York, and that the money was to be invested here for her children and not to be taken into a State then in insurrection against the authority of the United States. Under these circumstances the Committee recommended the payment of the policy, and it was paid February fifth. The New England Mutual paid $4,000 on the same life.*

The invasion of Maryland and Pennsylvania by the Confederate forces in June, 1863, again brought the war to the doors of Northern cities. In response to a question from Messrs. Lancaster & Gaskill, agents at Philadelphia, the Actuary telegraphed, June seventeenth, "We give thirty days' war permit at one-half of one per cent., to be continued if desired." On the nineteenth the Company's agents at Baltimore reported that the authorities had been "for the past three days barricading the streets and alleys in the north-western portion of the city, evidently expecting the storm to burst in that quarter." Reference was made to the action of the Company in the preceding September, and the request

---

this Company, by imputing to it a much smaller surplus than is possessed by other companies." Then follows an explanation of the item above referred to.

The New York Insurance Superintendent, on the other hand, required the item of dividends declared and not paid to be entered in full in liabilities, and the NEW-YORK LIFE again had reason to complain of comparisons made of the surplus shown by the New York Report, by companies that did not include such dividends as a liability. This led to a considerable correspondence between Superintendent Barnes and the companies in question, and the publication of corrected figures of surplus. The NEW-YORK LIFE did not contend specifically for either view of the status of dividends declared and unpaid, it only insisted—then as now—that in the same report all companies should be required to conform to the same standard.

*Mrs. Chandler had come to New York *via* New Orleans, having reached the latter place after a journey of five days on a small vessel, which made its way through creeks and across Lake Pontchartraine. She was obliged to leave her two children—the youngest only fourteen months old—in the South. She proposed, as soon as she could receive and invest the proceeds of her policy, to return for her children, and after a short visit to Europe to live with her mother in this city.

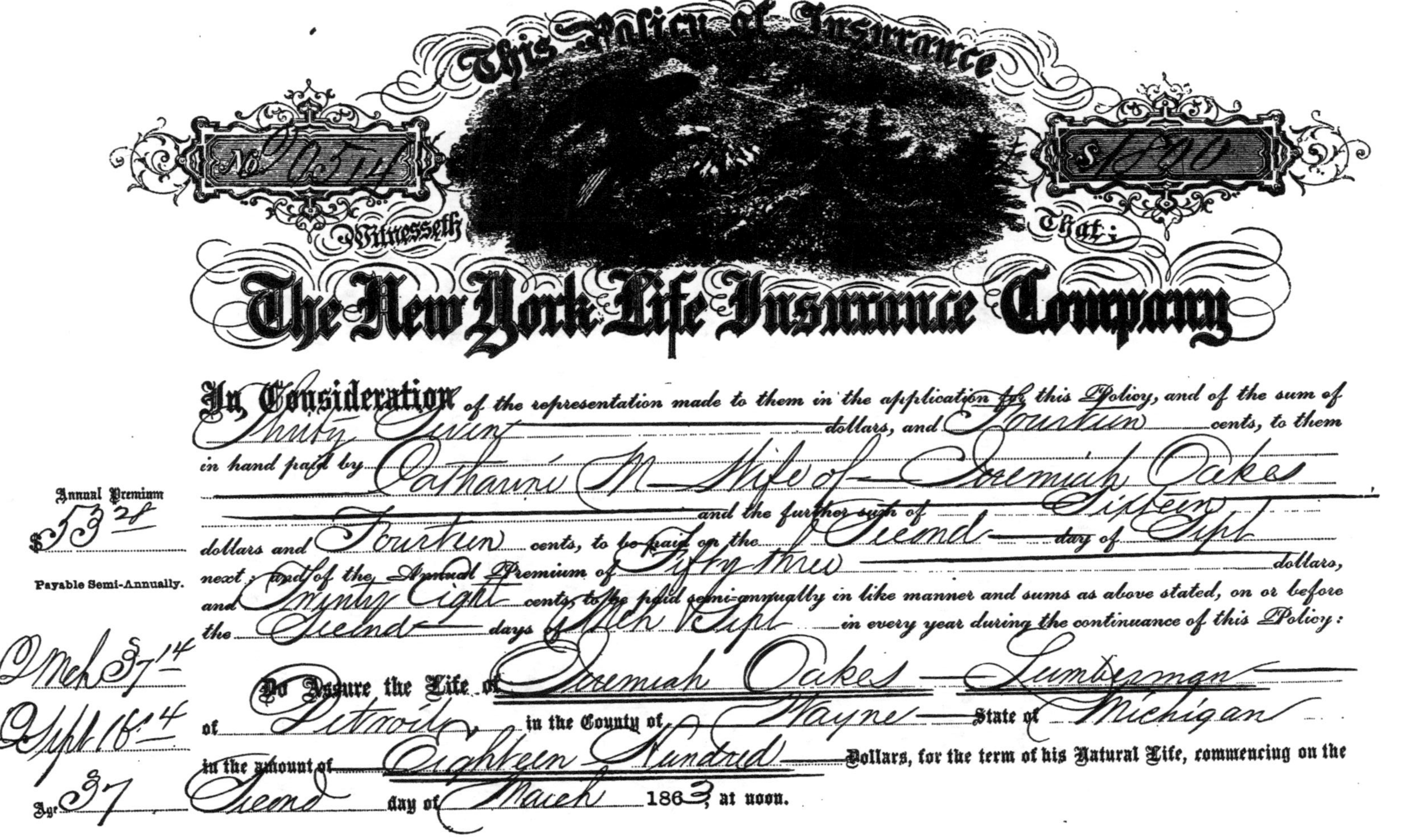

This Policy of Insurance

No. 03514 — $1800

Witnesseth That:

The New York Life Insurance Company

Annual Premium $53.28

Payable Semi-Annually.

Mch 2 $37.14

Sept 2 $16.14

Age 37

In Consideration of the representation made to them in the application for this Policy, and of the sum of Thirty Seven dollars, and Fourteen cents, to them in hand paid by Catharine M. Wife of Jeremiah Oakes and the further sum of Sixteen dollars and Fourteen cents, to be paid on the Second day of Sept next; and of the Annual Premium of Fifty three dollars, and Twenty Eight cents, to be paid semi-annually in like manner and sums as above stated, on or before the Second days of Mch & Sept in every year during the continuance of this Policy:

Do Assure the Life of Jeremiah Oakes — Lumberman of Detroit in the County of Wayne State of Michigan in the amount of Eighteen Hundred **Dollars, for the term of his Natural Life, commencing on the** Second **day of** March **1863, at noon.**

Policy Heading First Used in March, 1863.

[The reader will note a peculiar division of the premium; this was to give the insured the benefit of the premium note feature, as explained on page 87. On such a policy as the above the first payment would consist of a premium note for $21, and $16.14 in cash. To this was added one year's interest on the note.]

made that policy-holders be allowed to join in the defence of the city without prejudice to their contracts. The Company responded by telegraph the same day: "Policy-holders defending their firesides will be protected without extra charge." On the twenty-third the Company again telegraphed: "We advise that you remit all funds belonging to this Company by bank draft on this city, and remove valuables east to place of safety during this day." The funds were remitted as directed, but after consultation with "discreet friends," the Messrs. Richardson wrote that there were no signs of alarm, but if occasion arose papers would be sent to the Home Office. The battle of Gettysburgh was only a week away, and after that the war cloud drifted southward.*

On September twenty-eighth the Trustees voted that no more Southern policies that had lapsed for non-payment of premium be renewed or paid without the consent of the Board; and on October fourteenth it was resolved that all lapsed policies in the States then in insurrection be canceled.

At the May meeting of the Trustees a Committee was appointed to investigate and report "what salary, commission and perquisites have been paid during each year from January 1, 1858, to January 1, 1863, and with the probable amount on the same basis during 1863,—to the President, Vice-President, Actuary, and each of the General Agents, and employés of the Company, together with a statement of their respective duties; also what changes in the yearly expenses and management of the Company, if any, should be made." Ordinarily, the passage of such a resolution would be too much in the nature of office detail to be noticed in a formal history; but this resolution was destined to have a far-reaching effect upon the fortunes of the Company.

Under a resolution adopted February 13, 1855, the salaries of the

---

*The regiment to which the writer belonged was at this time in Fort McHenry. Unusual precautions were taken. The men were told off into gun squads every night, and slept near their pieces, and the approaches to the fort were picketed. One night there was an alarm; rockets were sent up and the garrison was aroused. Nothing came of it; but the next morning it was observed that the 10-inch columbiad in the north-western bastion was "in battery"—that is to say, run close to the parapet, in position for firing—and that it was elevated at the angle of longest range.

President and Actuary had been fixed at $1,500 per annum, together with commissions at the rate of two and one-half per cent. upon the "increased accumulated assets" of the Company. The amounts of these increased accumulations had been made up from year to year, and the Committee claimed that there should be deducted therefrom the uncollected premiums on Southern policies, bad debts charged off, losses on stocks sold, rent for the premises occupied by the Company, canceled notes, and returned premiums on policies surrendered,—forming an aggregate of $360,840.09. Attention was called, however, to the fact that by reason of policies surrendered, notes canceled, and premiums returned, the liabilities of the Company had been diminished by the sum of $154,569.20, and it was submitted whether strict justice would not be done by requiring these officers to refund commissions on the difference. The first report was made July fifteenth; on August twelfth the officers presented their side of the case; on September twenty-eighth both offered their resignations to take effect November first, which were ordered to lie on the table. At the meeting on October fourteenth the resignation of the Actuary was accepted, and that of the President was unanimously declined. It was then voted that William H. Beers be appointed Actuary *pro tem.*

The annual report for 1863 was presented to the Trustees on January 26, 1864; it showed a considerable larger business than that of the preceding year, the premium income having exceeded one million dollars. The lapsed policies in Southern States having been declared canceled in October, the Company in its report charged off the premiums, interest and premium notes due on such policies, and the balances due from Southern agents, and thus presented a schedule of assets free from doubtful items. The Finance Committee reported that, "after making reservation for the value of all policies at the highest rate of mortality adopted in the United States, together with an allowance of $131,756.30 for extra climate and war risks, and for liabilities which may have been incurred on Southern policies," the surplus of the Company was $158,137.63. A scrip dividend of thirty-five per cent. was declared upon the premiums of all participating life policies twelve months in force; and it was voted to pay in cash the fourth installment of twenty per cent. on dividends declared from 1850 to 1860. At this meeting Mr. Beers was elected Actuary, and the salaries of President and Actuary were fixed at $7,500 and $5,000 respectively.

1864. THE Massachusetts Commissioners, who had taken a deep interest in everything pertaining to non-forfeiture policies, called attention in their report for 1863 to the increasing number of policies issued on the 10-payment life plan, the whole number in force in all the companies being 3,751, of which number 1,707 were in the NEW-YORK LIFE. This was the result of the Company's precedence in the matter of non-forfeiture. The Commissioners had noted the fact that by the wording of the policy form a paid-up policy was promised on surrender of the original, and had addressed the Company as to the effect of a failure to surrender. In reply, Mr. Franklin wrote on March 4, 1864:

> We had supposed there could be no question in reference to the clause in our ten-payment policies. Whatever may be the legal construction, however, our practice has been, when such a policy ceases after two payments, to consider it a paid policy, even though the surrender should not have been made, and we consequently place it among our liabilities, and of course should pay it in case of death. Upon policies in which premium notes have been given, the Company now require that the surrender should be made within a year, as the interest on such notes is required to be paid annually; but for all cash policies no limit is fixed.

The subject of the renewal of policies lapsed by reason of non-payment of premium, while the insured were within the Confederate lines, which the Board of Trustees had forbidden (September 28, 1863,) without its approval in each separate case, was on March 9, 1864, referred to the Supervisory Committee, with power. In February Mr. Franklin had written to Dr. Copes and the Messrs. Richardson that the Board required in each case "evidence of loyalty and good health." In a letter dated April fourteenth, "loyalty" was defined to mean that the insured "had taken no part, either directly or indirectly, in the Rebellion."

At the annual election held on May eleventh, there was a change in the ticket that had been elected every year without opposition since 1851. Messrs. Franklin and Kendall were elected President and Vice-President, respectively, as before; Mr. Beers was elected Actuary. One result of the change was noted in the report of the officers for the month of July, in which it was said: "Notwithstanding the disadvantages under which they labored during the present year, in consequence of increased competition, the large excess of commissions paid in other companies, and the organization of another company* under the presidency of our late actuary, the business has steadily increased."

There was constant complaint through the year of agents and policy-holders being enticed away from the Company by larger commissions and by misrepresentations concerning the relative standing of companies, amount of dividends, non-forfeiture privileges, etc. All the companies, except those under the Massachusetts non-forfeiture law, seem to have adopted non-forfeiting policies on the 10-year plan, but to have made variations in the conditions under which the benefit could be received. On the question of competition for agents, the officers reported at the meeting already referred to:

In illustration of the competition with which we have to contend, it may be stated that an agent heretofore in our employ, and who has not equalled many others in the amount of business procured, has recently received an appointment in a very prominent and successful company at an annual salary of $5,000 and a large commission on all the new business which comes to the office in this city. Other instances might be mentioned of very advantageous offers made to our agents—and which in some cases have been successful—to induce them to leave our employ and canvass for other companies.

The course of the NEW-YORK LIFE with respect to agents and to controversy is indicated by two letters written late in 1863. On December twenty-first a letter was received from an agent of another company, inquiring what rate of commissions the NEW-YORK LIFE would allow to a traveling agent. Mr. Franklin replied: "Our invariable rule is never to interfere with an agent of any other company so long as he is in their employ, and not to engage an agent who is in connection with any other company." The letter referring to controversy said:

Although we do not fear comparison, yet our experience is that newspaper controversies are unprofitable, and tend rather to weaken than to strengthen public confidence

* The Globe Mutual, organized June 7, 1864. The Vice-President of the Globe was formerly a General Agent of the NEW-YORK LIFE. The Globe enjoyed eleven years of apparent success; it reported $4,353,516.02 in assets, and $543,516.02 in surplus December 31, 1875; from this point its surplus declined until May, 1879, when it became insolvent and was placed in the hands of a Receiver.

in Life Insurance. You are unquestionably correct in the position you have assumed, but there is room enough for all to work without attempting to disparage one another. My advice is, let Mr. N—— keep up his fire, if it suits him; but if we do not supply him with fuel, it will very soon burn out.

The year 1864 witnessed the most daring and heroic efforts of the Confederate forces to retrieve their waning fortunes. In addition to the stubborn resistance made by their main armies, both Maryland and Missouri were invaded and their chief cities threatened. A battle was fought at the Monocacy River, near Frederick, Md., on July ninth, after which General Wallace fell back toward Baltimore, while General Early marched to the very gates of Washington. A brigade of cavalry was sent to cut the railroads north of Baltimore, and for a few days communication with the North was interrupted. On the twelfth the Company's agents at Baltimore wrote:

> Understanding that a mail for New York will leave at one o'clock to-day, we avail of the facility to write you. Business here is virtually suspended. Gloom and apprehension have brooded over our city ever since Sunday morning [July tenth] when, at six o'clock, we were summoned to the trenches, where all good citizens repaired, where a gun could be obtained. My boys left home without waiting to get a mouthful to eat and are still on duty. The youngest, just seventeen, I found yesterday on picket duty out on one of the turnpikes. To us every hour is an advantage, as our defences are being strengthened. This morning we are somewhat relieved from immediate apprehension, hearing the main force of the enemy have turned back toward Washington. God forbid they should ever capture it. I would rather Baltimore should fall. We have nothing here now very valuable except our books, our accounts for June having all gone and remittances made. This morning we are packing up our books and such papers as are of moment to send away for safety. Our banks are doing the same, having sent all their valuables away on Saturday night, placing them on gun-boats anchored off the city. We do not know when business will be resumed, of course, but will write you again shortly.

On the thirteenth request was made that policy-holders be allowed to act in defence of the city without prejudice to their policies. To this the Company answered:

> We have upon former occasions recognized the privilege of our policy-holders to enlist for home defence, without prejudice to their assured rights, and we shall do so with reference to those in your jurisdiction; but the privilege must be confined strictly to the defence of their homes and not extend beyond them.

In September a raid equal in daring to that of General Early, was led by General Price across Arkansas and into Missouri. A battle was fought at Pilot Knob on the twenty-seventh, and from there Price advanced the next day and attacked the southern defences of St. Louis.* On the thirtieth Mr. Morrison wrote:

In consequence of the sudden invasion of our State and city, it became necessary for our officials hastily to organize a force for the defence of the city. In doing so, as a matter of course, many of our insured were enrolled. I have taken the responsibility to tell them to go, and if killed we would deduct one year's war premium from their policies. If the danger is over—which it will be, I think, in a few days—they will be disbanded. We are not obliged to go into camp or expose ourselves in any way except in case of attack. Will you please take as favorable a view of the case as you can and write me instructions for the future. I hope you will approve of what has been done. I believe others are doing the same.

To this the Company replied, October sixth:

We appreciate the situation in which you are placed and consider it our duty to protect the assured as far as possible; we have in similar instances held policies to be good so long as the party is only engaged strictly in defence of his home, and if killed in such defence we should deduct the regular war premium for one year and pay the balance. Should they, however, be obliged to go beyond the limits of the city, we would recommend that they pay the war extra, if circumstances permit, to put the matter beyond all question in case of death.

Among the claims paid in 1864 which call for special mention are those of Lieutenant A. J. Howard, of Brighton, Vt., Captain J. Sewell Reed, of Dorchester, Mass., and private Horatio Jones, of Fond-du-Lac, Wis. In each case there was evident the purpose on the part of the insured or the beneficiary to keep the policy in force by the payment of premium and extras, and in each there was a failure at some point. Lieutenant Howard died at Algiers, La., of disease; Captain Reed was killed at Dranesville, Va., by guerillas; and private Jones died at Port Hudson, La., of typhoid fever. Proof of death of the latter was furnished by a comrade while upon his death-bed. The acknowledgment from Mrs. Reed is addressed to Mr. Franklin, and says:

The action of your Board removes from me a heavy burden, for I have an invalid child dependent upon me and cannot leave him to go out into the world to labor for a support, and therefore very much needed the assistance you have rendered me. If any

---

*After leaving the vicinity of St. Louis, General Price marched westward, traversing the entire State, and destroying much property. No less than five pitched battles were fought in October, and his forces were finally driven into Arkansas.

of those dear to you are ever in need of a friend, may they find one as considerate and kind as you have been to me. Will you express my thanks to every member of your Committee, for indeed I am very grateful to them all.

In the absence of strict proof much always depends on the character of the claimants, and Mrs. Reed had the endorsement of Rev. James H.

Capt. Reed was a gallant & meritorious officer & the statement of Mrs. [illegible] should command full credit, & the condition of the bereaved widow of Capt Reed the sympathy & regard of us all.

J. H. Means

I strongly recommend the case of Mrs Reed to the favorable consideration of the Insurance Company, at which Capt. Reed's life was insured.

Edward Everett

Means, pastor of the Second Congregational Church, of Dorchester, of which she was a member, and of other prominent citizens of that place, as well as that of Governor Andrew and Hon. Edward Everett. It was not always easy to secure legal evidence of the death of a soldier, for the reason that the Government refused to furnish any evidence upon which a claim against it might be based. In the case of Lieutenant Howard, the Company accepted as proof of death the fact, duly authenticated, that the Government had granted his widow a pension on account of her husband's death in the service; and in the case of private Jones, proof of death was furnished by a comrade, then at home sick, and who died two days afterward.

During the year $2,250 was voted in gratuities for various purposes. One thousand dollars was contributed to the Mississippi Valley Sanitary Fair, held in St. Louis, to raise funds to be expended in the work of the Sanitary Commission along the Mississippi River; one thousand dollars was given to the Sanitary Association of the City of New York;* and two hundred and fifty dollars was given to a fund raised for Captain John Smith, of the propeller "D. S. Miller," who was instrumental in saving the lives of passengers on board the steamer "Isaac Newton," which was destroyed by fire.

In view of the increased cost of living and the general advance in wages, caused by depreciation of the currency, as compared with gold, a "bonus" of twenty-five per cent. upon their salaries for the year was voted to officers and employés of the Company.†

The annual report for 1864 was presented by the officers at the meeting of the Trustees on January 30, 1865. Special attention was called to the large increase in cash premiums ($439,195.95) and in net assets ($1,005,217.63). The general tendency to increased expenditure for business, and the loss of a number of the Company's most efficient agents were noted. It was said that greater care than ever had been used in the appointment of Medical Examiners and in the acceptance of risks, as a

*The Citizens' Association of New York held a meeting February 29, 1864, and appointed a Committee upon the sanitary condition of the city. From statistics gathered by this Committee it appeared that the death-rate per 1,000 of population of the several cities named was as follows: New York 28 (it was 21.05 in 1894), Boston 24.3, Philadelphia 22.9, Newark 23, Providence 21.8, Hartford 18.2.

†This increase was far from being sufficient to offset the increase in cost of living—which was probably nearer one hundred per cent. The Government allowance for clothing to enlisted men was $3.50 per month in 1862, and $7 per month in 1865.

result of which 299 applications for $892,000 insurance had been declined. Many of these had been accepted elsewhere, and losses among them to the amount of $35,000 had already come to the knowledge of the officers. The surplus of the Company, after making reservation for the value of all policies at the highest rate of mortality adopted in the United States (Actuaries' 4%), together with a liberal allowance ($45,000) for extra risks and other contingencies, was $426,317.06. The Finance Committee recommended a scrip dividend of fifty per cent. on the premiums of participating policies one year in force, the payment in cash of the last instalment of twenty per cent. on dividends declared from 1850 to 1860, and the payment in cash and in full of the dividends declared in 1861 and 1862. It was so voted. The schedule of policies showed 12,460 Whole Life Policies, 114 Term Policies, 378 Endowments, one Joint Life Policy, one Survivorship, and seven Annuities in force.*

1865. THE year 1865 opened with the end of the war near at hand. On January fifth Mr. Wyllie Woodbridge, the Company's agent at Savannah, wrote, expressing his gratification at restored communications, saying all his papers had been destroyed, and asking for a memorandum of his business, that his accounts might be adjusted at an early day. "I shall be happy," he continued, "to resume the agency if you so desire. This bloody war has existed long enough; let us hope that peace may soon be restored to our whole country, and civilization once more exist under our glorious Constitution. We are now passing through the worst agonies of the revolution in our social relations, and there must be much misery and want where once there was prosperity. But we will trust in God, who can bring light out of darkness." Mr. Franklin replied under date of the sixteenth, expressing his pleasure at hearing once more from "the Company's valued correspondent at Savannah," and saying that as soon as a definite rule of action had been decided upon in reference to Southern business he would be communicated with. "We are now," he

*The ordinary form of Endowment at this time was a policy due at a specified age, as at 40, 45, 50, etc., to 65, or at prior death. Non-forfeiting policies—both Life and Endowment—were paid up in ten years.

said, "heartily engaged in collecting funds for the relief of the sufferers among you. One vessel has already sailed with a good supply of provisions, and another is loading at our wharf and will very soon be on her heavenly errand."*

Five days after the fall of Richmond Mr. Wortham wrote from that place. Unfortunately, both this letter and one written April twenty-second are not on file; but in answer to the latter, Mr. Franklin replied April twenty-seventh:

> Be assured, my dear sir, that your attempts to alleviate the sufferings of your fellow men, without regard to national proclivities, as a member of the association to which you allude, have our hearty sympathy, and with you we most fondly hope that you and your associates "have ministered to the comfort and relief of thousands from both armies."

On May twenty-fourth Mr. Wortham wrote expressing his thanks "for the many kind acts and favors extended by the Company," including the balancing of his account, many of his papers having been lost or destroyed in consequence of the fire on April third. Among these papers was a scrip dividend.† Upon his affidavit that it had been lost, the Company paid it in cash, together with other similar obligations in his hands, which had been ordered redeemed subsequent to 1861. Eighty per cent. of the dividends declared from 1850 to 1860, and the dividends of 1861 and 1862, had thus become redeemable since 1861, and these were now paid upon demand, without reference to the status of the policies upon which they had been declared. The delay in their redemption thus proved a great boon to Southern policy-holders, giving them money when needed as never before.

---

* The two vessels referred to were the "Rebecca Clyde," which sailed January fourteenth, and the "Daniel Webster," which sailed January sixteenth. The first was in charge of Archibald Baxter, and was furnished with provisions by committees of the Chamber of Commerce and the Produce Exchange. The "Daniel Webster" was in charge of Colonel Julian Allen, representing the people of Savannah, by authority of General Sherman. To this vessel's cargo Boston contributed largely, besides sending the steamer "Greyhound" on the fourteenth. The last public address of Edward Everett was made at a meeting held in Faneuil Hall, January ninth, in aid of the Savannah fund. Mr. Everett died January fifteenth following. Philadelphia subscriptions to the Savannah fund were announced on the fifteenth as amounting to $21,000.— *See New York Herald for January 13, 14, 15 and 16, 1865.*

† This piece of scrip was afterward sent to the Company by Mr. Wortham, it having been found and restored to him by a negro.

Among the documents from the Richmond office that came to the surface in 1865, was a receipt for Policy No. 9,890, on the life of James H. Morrison, which was surrendered to Mr. Wortham March 27, 1862, for its "equitable value, as advertised and published by the said Company." This paper recited that the agent had no power to purchase policies, but the Company acknowledged the claim and paid the surrender value through the Baltimore agency in July, 1865.

Mr. Muldon wrote from Mobile on April nineteenth, saying he was "still in the land of the living," asking for Company news since 1862, and offering his services if business was to be resumed at Mobile. In a second letter, dated May fourteenth, he sent "third" of bill of exchange for £311–2–5, referred to in his letter of January 22, 1862, "first" and "second" of which had been sent through the blockade *via* Havana, August 1, 1862, and never received. This bill had a checkered history. When presented at the Union Bank of London, in June, 1865, it was refused acceptance; but the drawer (Southern Bank of Alabama) immediately wrote to its London correspondent, saying it was all right; and so, nearly three years after its date, it was paid, and thus both commercial honor and banking methods were vindicated. Mr. Muldon had on hand redeemable scrip in sufficient amount to pay back premiums and interest on two policies on his own life, which were thus re-instated, and a considerable amount of scrip in the hands of other persons was redeemed through his office.

Letters were also received during the next few months from Messrs. Martin and Taylor, of Charleston, Garland, of Petersburg, and Van Gilder, of Knoxville, all former agents of the Company. Two claims that had matured upon policies in force after communication was interrupted were paid through Mr. Garland. Mr. Van Gilder had been compelled to turn over to the Confederate Receivers at Knoxville and Jonesboro the cash and one note in his hands belonging to the Company, in lieu of which he forwarded copies of the decree of the court and receipts of the Receivers. Mr. Garland had escaped a like dilemma by refusing premiums on the ground that he would be obliged to report and pay them to the Confederate Receiver.

At the June meeting of the Trustees the subject of paying losses in Southern States was discussed, and it was voted to obtain the opinion of counsel as to the authority and liability of the Company with respect to the payment of such claims. On July twelfth the opinion of counsel was submitted, and it was voted to pay losses occurring during the war where the premiums had been received by the Company and the deceased had not taken up arms against the Government. At the same meeting the subject of renewing Southern policies lapsed during the war was discussed and referred to the Supervisory Committee. The Committee reported August ninth, and a resolution was adopted authorizing the officers to renew such policies on the payment of back premiums and interest, upon receiving a satisfactory certificate of good health and that the insured had taken no active part in the war. The end of the period within which such re-instatements might be made was at first fixed at October first, but on November ninth this limitation was removed, and on January 31, 1867, the limitation respecting those who had served in the Confederate Army or Navy was also removed. The war had continued so long that it was found to be more advantageous for most policy-holders, and to require much less ready money in all cases, to take out new policies. The Southern business had been largely on the part note plan, under which nearly the whole reserve on policies was in the form of notes given by the insured. These having been canceled with the policies, the holders had received nearly their full surrender value at the time of lapse. In the Report of the Officers to the Trustees, in January, 1862, the reserve on Southern policies was estimated at $500,000; and when these policies were canceled, in 1863, there was charged to Profit and Loss about $400,000 on account of premiums and interest due on the same, balances due from Southern agents and premium notes canceled.* The re-instatements made after the war must have reduced the amount of forfeitures to a very inconsiderable sum.† Owing to the unsettled state of affairs in the

* The total amount charged off was $469,067.86. This included an unknown amount of premium notes canceled in 1863 on Northern policies, of which there were in the preceding year $42,963.17.

† There was published in the "Morning News" (balance of name missing), in 1869, a list of Southern policies re-instated, amounting to $731,345.

South, the liability of agents to legal complications, and the unfavorable mortality previously experienced, no efforts were made in 1865 to extend the business in the Southern States.

In May, 1864, when the Governors of several Western States called out the militia to do garrison duty for one hundred days, the Company, in reply to inquiries on the subject, issued a circular stating that no extra would be required where the insured performed only garrison duty within their respective States, but when ordered beyond those limits, or engaged in actual hostilities, the regular war extra would be charged. One death-claim was paid in 1865 as a result of this circular. John Sandiland, of Mishawaka, Indiana, insured for $1,000 under Policy No. 22,335, dated July 3, 1863, went out under the call as a member of the 138th Indiana Volunteers, and died of typhoid fever at Tullahoma, Tenn., October 3, 1864. As he was doing duty beyond the limits of his State without a permit, he was not strictly covered by the terms of the circular, but the Company waived the technicality and paid the claim less one year's war extra, in February, 1865.

During the same month the Company was notified of the death of William W. Kaye, of Philadelphia, insured for $1,000 under Policy No. 13,822, taken out in 1860. Mr. Kaye enlisted in the 183d Regiment Pennsylvania Volunteers, in January, 1864, and paid the war extra. Two of his comrades certified that he was wounded at the battle of Cold Harbor, Va., June 3, 1864, and had been missing since that time, and that the dead were not buried until they were unrecognizable.* Upon being furnished with these facts, the Trustees directed the payment to his widow of one year's interest on the amount of the policy, the principal to remain in abeyance until further action of the Board. In 1866 Mrs. Kaye was granted a pension by the Government, on the ground of her husband's death, and upon this evidence the Company paid the claim in full.

---

*The Federal dead lay unburied where they fell, from the third until the eighth of June, when they "were in a horrible state of putrefaction" (Walker's History of the Second Army Corps, page 518). The regiment to which the writer belonged — the Eighth New York Heavy Artillery — took part in this bloody but fruitless assault, and the body of Colonel Peter A. Porter, who "was killed within a few yards of the enemy's works" (Gen. A. A. Humphreys) was brought off during the night of the fourth, under such difficulties and dangers that the men who rescued it were awarded medals by the Century Club, of New York, of which Colonel Porter was a member.

In May of this year the limit of insurance upon one life was increased from $10,000 to $20,000.

In December the cholera made its appearance in New York, and the Trustees approved a subscription of five hundred dollars made by the officers to the funds of the Sanitary Association. Precautions were evidently taken none too soon, as the Company paid one loss by cholera in 1865 and eighteen in 1866.

The annual report for the year was presented to the Trustees January 31, 1866, and showed a rapidly increasing business, the premiums being for the first year in the Company's history in excess of two millions of dollars. A dividend of fifty per cent. on participating life policies one year in force was declared, and the outstanding dividends declared in 1863 and 1864 were ordered paid in cash.

A review of the Company's experience under war risks showed that 731 permits had been granted, on policies amounting to $1,151,950; and that there had been 73 losses, amounting to $107,100. The total mortality above the probable was $91,897, and the total amount received as "war extra" was $72,754.86. The war risks under policies issued prior to December 31, 1860, amounted to $868,200, and the losses above the probable under these policies were $52,801.82; the new war risks were $283,750 in amount, under which the losses above the probable were $39,095.18. The insurance in force December 31, 1860, was $16,388,109, and the war continued four years; an extra charge of eighty-one cents per $1,000 annually upon the whole amount would, therefore, have made up for the extra losses incurred under old policies.

Although, as we have seen, Life Insurance felt severely the hard times incident to the beginning of the Civil War, yet it had prospered during its continuance beyond anything in its previous history, and almost beyond any other business. Life Insurance, like the Union, had stood the strain of war, and had emerged stronger than ever before. It had done something to mitigate war's sufferings, and to show to the adherents of each side how much they had in common, and how much they still loved and respected each other. It was yet to be influential in binding all sections of the country in closer bonds of brotherhood.*

FROM A LETTER-HEAD OF THE PERIOD.

---

* "One heart and one hand,
One flag and one land—
One nation evermore."

Quoted by Major Livingston Mims, of Atlanta, in an address before the NEW-YORK LIFE'S "Columbian Convention," Chicago, July 12, 1893.

TABLE SHOWING THE CONDITION OF THE LIFE COMPANIES DOING BUSINESS IN NEW YORK DECEMBER 31, 1865, THEIR BUSINESS FOR THE YEAR, THE SAME ITEMS FOR THE NEW-YORK LIFE, AND THE NEW-YORK LIFE'S SHARE OF ALL:

ITEMS.	THIRTY COMPANIES.	NEW-YORK LIFE.	N.-Y. L's SHARE.
Assets	$64,232,123	$5,018,449	7.8
Premium Notes and Loans in Assets	14,118,881	1,186,988	8.4
Surplus	17,890,624	685,967	3.8
Liabilities	46,341,499	4,332,482	9.4
Surplus to Liabilities, Per cent	38.6	15.8	....
Insurance in Force	395,703,058	45,485,726	11.5
New Insurance Written	245,427,057	16,324,888	6.7
Total Income	24,887,020	2,181,494	8.8
Premium Notes and Loans in Income	6,322,464	349,445	5.5
Death-Claims Paid	4,125,442	490,522	11.9
Death-Claims per $1,000 Insured	$10.23	$10.80	....
Total Paid Policy-holders	6,292,036	785,811	12.5
Expenses and Taxes	4,025,619	333,681	8.2
Per cent. to Income	16.1	15.3	....

VIII.

FROM PEACE TO THE PANIC.

1866–1873.

THE period following the Civil War was necessarily one of adjustment in industrial and commercial conditions, as well as in civil and political relations. The war had called from peaceful pursuits, for longer or shorter periods, upwards of three millions of men, and had caused the expenditure by the Government of over three thousand million dollars within the space of five years. The year 1865 saw more than a million men lay aside the implements of destruction and take up again those by which material and moral values are produced; it saw expenditures of the Federal Government reach the enormous total of twelve hundred and ninety-seven million dollars, from which they declined in a single year to five hundred and twenty millions, and in six years to less than three hundred millions.

The increased production of the years immediately following the war was chiefly in manufacturing, in mining and in railroad construction. The grain raised in 1870 was but little more than in 1860; the cotton and tobacco produced were less; but manufactures more than doubled; the output of mines and oil wells increased from fifty, to one thousand, per cent.; railroad construction, which was only 1,846 miles in 1860, was 6,070 miles in 1870. The hardy veterans turned to the tasks of peace with the same courage and energy they had shown in war; they occupied all the old fields and sought out new ones in the undeveloped West. Between 1860 and 1870 the increase in the total population of the United States was twenty-two per cent., and between 1870 and 1880 the increase was thirty per cent.; the States and Territories lying west of the Mississippi River—excluding the five States admitted to the Union prior to 1850—more than doubled their population in each decade.

This period saw a wide extension of the general agency system of the NEW-YORK LIFE, and a large increase in its agency force. It brought into the service of the Company many of the best field men it ever had, some of whom continue with it to this day. It saw the Company's business re-established in the South, while new fields were occupied in the West; the Company again entered Canada; and, crossing the Atlantic, this new-comer of the nineteenth century established itself in the foreign field in competition with companies that were old before it was born. It was a period of fierce rivalry at home and abroad; competition was never before so severe, and never since so openly unscrupulous. The new business of all the companies was largest in 1869, when it reached six hundred and fourteen million dollars, and this proved high-water mark for the next nineteen years.

1866. THERE was but little demand for life insurance in the South immediately after the war, and in 1865 the NEW-YORK LIFE transacted the business growing out of its former contracts either through its former agents, as correspondents, or directly with the insured. In 1866, however, a beginning was made in the re-occupation of the Southern field. Messrs. V. & F. A. Anderson, of Galveston, were appointed General Agents for Texas in January; in August Mr. Henry Harney was appointed General Agent for Georgia and Florida, with head-quarters at Savannah; in September the Trustees authorized the purchase of Virginia bonds to the amount of $50,000, for deposit with the Treasurer of the State, as required by the law of February 3, 1866. The purchase and deposit were made by Mr. J. C. Deming, who had succeeded Captain Ferguson in the agency at Norfolk. The same month (August) saw the re-appointment of Dr. Copes as General Agent for Louisiana, and the appointment of Mr. Thomas Frost as General Agent for South Carolina.

The Messrs. Anderson were to accept applications from acclimated persons on the 10-payment life plan only, and to charge one per cent. extra. In Georgia and Florida no extra charge was made on the 10-year table for acclimated persons; those unacclimated were charged one per cent. extra for residence in Savannah and vicinity, but none for residence in the interior of the State. The tax on premiums in Georgia was one per cent., and the city license in Savannah was $100. In Louisiana the extra rates for acclimated persons were one-half of one per cent. on Ordinary Life Policies, and one per cent. for ten years on 10-Payment Life Policies; unacclimated persons were insured only on the 10-year table at two per cent. extra for the ten years. The State license in Louisiana was $1,000, and the city license in New Orleans was $500. In South Carolina applications were received only on the 10-Payment Life table; one-half of one per cent. extra was charged acclimated persons in Charleston, but for those residing in other parts of the State there was no extra charge. In Virginia no extra was charged; the State tax was one per cent. on premiums and a license fee of $25 for each agency. Mr. Muldon continued to act for the Company at Mobile, where an extra of three per cent. was charged acclimated persons insured on the Ordinary Life tables. Mr. Muldon was succeeded in the following year by Mr. Thomas Carson.

As an illustration of the commissions paid at this time, the following alternative rates offered to Dr. Copes are cited: (1) Fifteen per cent. on new premiums and seven and a-half per cent. on renewals; or (2) twenty

From a Letter-head of the Period. The Office of the North American Fire Company was in the New-York Life Building, 112 & 114 Broadway.

per cent. on new premiums and five per cent. on renewals; or (3) twenty-five per cent. on new premiums and two and a-half per cent. on renewals. The rates given under the second option were selected.

During the early part of 1866 Mr. Nelson Sayler, of Cincinnati, Ohio, worked in New Orleans in connection with Dr. Copes; he was unable, however, to endure the climate, and returned to Ohio in June. From a long report made by Mr. Sayler, on business conditions and prospects in New Orleans, the following extract is made, as bearing on the subject of compensation and extra rates:

> The Southern people, and especially the peculiar element represented in New Orleans, do not look upon life insurance as we Northern people do. * * * Their climate, so balmy and genial, produces almost the whole year round what they use. There is little or no storing in summer for a long, cold winter. They live on the day's bringing forth, and from this they learn to think of to-day and almost ignore to-morrow. * * * This one feature will always render life insurance in New Orleans a business requiring much harder work, with less remuneration, than in any Northern city. Another point: there are companies insuring in the South at the same table rates as in the North. Whether it is safe to do so or not, is another question. The Mutual Benefit withdrew its agency—as I understand—for this reason. The Mutual Life of New York will not insure there, and the Connecticut Mutual has never done business in the Southwest. Though the experience of insurance companies may prove that longevity is not so great in the South as in the North, yet the almost universal belief *there* is that it is. Doubtless this is a mistaken notion, but it is firmly fixed and truly believed. Their daily papers laud their climate and affirm its healthfulness; their leading citizens do the same, and the *ignoble vulgus* takes up the cry and sounds it on the street corners. * * * They admit that a Northern man must become acclimated, but scout the idea that a native-born Southerner, or one who has had the yellow fever, or one who has passed through several epidemics of it, is any greater risk than a New Yorker in New York; and to tell an Alabama or Mississippi planter that he is shorter-lived than an Ohio farmer, would be considered the height of absurdity.

The letters of Southern agents of this period contain many references to other companies that were insuring Southern risks at Northern rates, and the records of the Insurance Departments and of the courts are now all that remain of most of these companies. They paid higher commissions and promised larger dividends than the old and well-established companies, and for a time enticed away from them both agents and customers; but many of these returned in the course of time, after a dearly-bought experience.

Extension of the Company's business westward was made during this year by Mr. Reuben Partridge, who had his head-quarters at Leavenworth, Kas. Mr. Partridge went as far west as Denver in search of business, and among the appointments made by him was that of Dr. W. B. Bancroft as Medical Examiner, a position which Dr. Bancroft held and honored for over twenty-five years. He is well-known throughout the western country as a giant in physical proportions, the Nestor of the medical profession, a skillful surgeon, and a man of unblemished character.

In 1866 there were five agencies which received over $100,000 each in premiums—those of D. W. Russell, of Boston, $306,244.84; E. J. Richardson & Sons, of Baltimore, $137,769.63; S. A. Mattison, Detroit, $127,423.00; Curtis L. North, of New York, $116,513.10; and Lancaster & Gaskell, of Philadelphia, $105,120.77.* Mr. Russell took charge of the Boston agency in July, 1864, and at once placed it in the front rank. For several years the premium receipts of the NEW-YORK LIFE in Massachusetts were larger than those of any other company; in 1869 they were over six hundred and thirty thousand dollars. Mr. E. J. Richardson had been the Company's representative in Baltimore since 1848, and his steady devotion to the interests of his clients bore fruit in a large and increasing business. He remained in the Company's service until his death in 1868. Mr. Mattison was General Agent of the Western Branch of the Company, and Superintendent of Agencies for the United States. Mr. Lancaster had been in the Company's service since the Company's entrance into Pennsylvania in 1849. If these achievements seem small to the most successful agents of to-day, they will probably be the first to acknowledge the changed conditions, and to say, "other men labored, and we have entered into their labors." According to an article

* The following memorandum of commissions paid in 1866, attached to the report for that year, further indicates the distribution of the Company's business at that time:

Massachusetts Agency	$55,390.04	Missouri Agency	$7,529.21
New York City Agency	46,769.00	Illinois Agency	4,554.16
Ohio Agency	12,555.04	California Agency	3,871.05
Maryland Agency	11,890.43	Wisconsin Agency	3,016.61
Michigan Agency	11,794.22	All other agencies	90,250.95
Pennsylvania Agency	10,379.32		

written by Mr. W. F. Morrill, General Eastern Agent of the Company, and published in the "Kennebec Journal" of April 13, 1866, "the largest life insurance in the United States" was then carried "by a gentleman in Philadelphia," who was insured for $150,000. "A gentleman in Philadelphia"* still holds the record for the largest insurance on his life, but the amount is ten times as much as that mentioned by Mr. Morrill, and this is a fair illustration of the increased popularity of Life Insurance.†

Early in this year the Company began the custom of attaching to each policy a copy of the application upon which it was issued. It seems strange that so natural and proper a thing should not have been done before, and stranger still that it should not have become the universal custom. All companies make the application a part of the contract; from which it follows that, if a copy is not attached to the policy, the insured is not in possession of the whole contract and cannot know what his rights and privileges are under it. It is made obligatory to furnish such copy in some States, and it does not speak well for the State of New York that bills to this effect have been introduced in several Legislatures and have failed to pass. The best preventive of litigation, after a policy becomes a claim, is a perfect understanding of its provisions during the time it is in force.

At the meeting of the Trustees, held January 31, 1867, it was voted to pay the dividend of 1865 in cash, and to declare a new dividend of fifty per cent. on the premiums of Ordinary Life Policies one year in force.

1867. It was now nine years since the Company took possession of its offices at 112 and 114 Broadway. Its business had increased beyond all expectations. Its assets were more than four times as much, its annual income was over five times as much, and its new business was more than ten times as much, as they were nine years before. Its present quarters had become too strait for it. At the meeting of the Trustees, held on March 13, 1867, the Finance Committee reported that the prem-

* Hon. John Wanamaker.

† Since this was written it is reported that Mr. Wanamaker has increased his insurance to $2,000,000.

ises did not afford sufficient accommodation for the Company's employés, nor adequate security for its books, papers and assets. The Committee called attention to the plot of ground on the south-east corner of Broadway and Leonard Street—occupied formerly by the Society Library, and latterly by the publishing house of Messrs. D. Appleton & Co. and the dry goods house of Messrs. S. B. Chittenden & Co.—as offering unusual advantages for an office building. The building recently occupying the site had just been burned;* the plot had a frontage of sixty feet on Broadway and was about one hundred and seventy feet deep on Leonard Street and Catherine Lane, thus giving light and air on three sides. After a full discussion, the Committee was authorized to make the purchase at a price not exceeding five hundred thousand dollars. On April tenth the Committee presented the purchase contract, which was approved, and a Committee on Plans was appointed. The Company subsequently acquired the lot adjoining, in the rear, making a plot 196 feet deep. Plans were invited from five prominent architects, each to receive one thousand dollars, and the return of his plan if unsuccessful. The successful competitor was Mr. Griffith Thomas, who designed the Park Bank building, Pike's Opera House, and other noted structures of the day. The Building Committee, as finally appointed, consisted of the President and Actuary, and Messrs. William Barton, William H. Appleton, George Osgood and David Dows, Trustees of the Company. On December eleventh it was voted to build, in accordance with the plan adopted, a white marble structure, at a cost not to exceed one million dollars. The contract was awarded to Mr. Thomas Gardner, Jr., and the building was finished and ready for occupancy on May 1, 1870.

When the Company declared its first dividend in 1846, there was no established usage on the subject in this country. The only dividend declared to life policy-holders prior to that time was one by the Girard Life and Trust, in 1844, which was added to the policies in the form of

---

*On the morning of the fire, and while it was still burning, Mr. Beers called on Mr. Appleton and made a proposition for the site, subject to the approval of the Trustees. This proposition became the basis of the Committee's report.

reversionary insurance. The NEW-YORK LIFE adopted the percentage plan, which, with various modifications to adapt it to the new forms of policies, had been continued during twenty-one years. While preserving a fair degree of equity between policy-holders insuring in the same year and on the same premium table, this plan failed to take account of the surplus factors which vary according to the kind of policy taken and the number of years it has been in force. As a result, policies recently issued were paid too much and policies of long standing too little. In order to remedy this inequality, the officers of the Company submitted to the Finance Committee in October, 1867. a proposition to adopt the Contribution Plan,* devised by Messrs. Sheppard Homans and David Parks Fackler, at that time Actuary and Assistant Actuary, respectively, of the Mutual Life Insurance Company. The proposition was reported to the Trustees with the approval of the Committee, October ninth, with examples of its practical working. It was proposed to allow policy-holders thereafter the option to have the value of their dividends added to their policies in the form of reversionary insurance, payable with the policies, or to receive them in cash on the policy anniversaries. The report and recommendation were unanimously adopted.

The State of Louisiana, in which the Company had just re-established its business, was sorely afflicted during this year. In April the Mississippi

* With the report of January 1, 1868, was printed the following explanation of the "Contribution Plan": "Each policy is credited with the premium paid and its reserve from the preceding year, if any, and the interest earned thereon; it is charged with the net cost of insurance for the year, and the reserve (or amount requisite to be retained in the re-insurance fund). The difference between these constitutes the dividend, or sum which the assured has contributed during the year in excess of the amount actually required. The dividend (the conditions remaining unaltered) naturally increases each year, for the reason that the 'reserve' grows rapidly with the age of the policy, and is estimated to yield an interest of only four per cent. per annum, while it actually realizes a much higher rate, and the difference goes to increase the returnable sum on each particular policy. * * * Some of the older policies of the Company will the present year realize a cash dividend on the policy proper (without reference to profits on dividend additions) of over sixty-eight per cent. of the annual premiums."

The Contribution Plan—which is now in almost universal use—was adopted by the older companies in the following order: Mutual Life 1863, NEW-YORK LIFE and New England Mutual 1867, State Mutual 1868, Connecticut Mutual 1869, Mutual Benefit 1870, Penn Mutual 1871. (See article by D. P. Fackler, in Proceedings of Actuarial Society of America, October 3, 1889.) The percentage plan being more favorable to new insurants and more easily understood, companies which were paying large percentage dividends were loth to abandon it because it helped to secure new business. To the new companies the Contribution Plan offered an easy method of concealing their small dividends, and a fertile field for estimates of increasing returns to policy-holders.

and its tributaries overflowed their banks to such an extent that vast areas were swept of nearly everything movable by water. A committee of forty was formed in New Orleans to solicit subscriptions for the sufferers, of which Dr. Copes was a member. Upon his application the Company made a donation of one hundred dollars to the relief fund. Pestilence followed the flood; in July the yellow fever appeared; on September eighth it was declared epidemic; between July seventh and October twenty-fourth, out of 5,767 deaths occurring, 2,876 were from yellow fever. The Company paid five yellow fever losses, and contributed $250 to a relief fund raised for the sufferers.

As regards competition in the South at this time, the following extract from a letter written by Dr. Copes under date of April thirtieth gives an inside view:

> I think, in view of the number of new life agencies coming in here, it would be well, as you have paid the license fee, to expend a little more in advertising. You have many objections to contend with, and it requires all the resources I can command to meet them. Your tables are objected to as being higher than others; your restrictions in the matter of acclimation far more rigid, and your credit on premiums less; and you have an agent who is a poor hand at the work of deceiving his neighbors, or at telling a competitor he is a cheat and a swindler. * * * I have several times brought to the notice of the tax collector here the Knickerbocker, the Globe, the Columbia (of Cincinnati), and other companies not licensed; but he tells me he cannot find their offices, and if he does find them, they tell him they are doing no business. The St. Louis Mutual is doing business here without discrimination between Northern and Southern risks and on a very low table of premiums.

A death-claim paid in 1867, under a Southern policy which lapsed during the war, deserves brief mention. Mr. Joseph George, Jr., of Savannah, Ga., insured in May, 1850, for $2,000 under Policy No. 5,837. Mr. George paid his premiums regularly until May, 1861, when the Company's agent at Savannah refused to receive the premium then due—which was tendered in gold—not having the Company's renewal receipt. No further payment was made, and Mr. George died in January, 1865. The Trustees ordered the policy to be paid in full.

During these years of large dividends the most extravagant calculations and predictions were made concerning future returns from life insurance policies. In order to meet these claims with a guarantee that should have a solid mathematical basis, the NEW-YORK LIFE devised and introduced, in 1867, a Return-Premium Endowment Policy. This contract agreed to pay the face of the policy, together with all premiums received thereon, at age sixty-five or at prior death. This was a straightforward offer to give the insured the face of his policy for the use of his premiums while the policy was in force—the premiums themselves to be returned at the maturity of the contract. It was something new—even the standard works on the theory of Life Insurance contained no formulas for the return of the gross premiums paid in case either of death or survival. But there was a young man in the Mathematical Department of the Company who thought such a formula could be made, and he made it. He is still in the Company's service, being none other than the present Actuary, Mr. Rufus W. Weeks. The large premium required for such a policy prevented it from becoming popular, but the results under maturing policies were very satisfactory.* The form of Premium-Return now in use by the Company, which guarantees, in addition to the face of the policy, a return of the whole or half of the annual premiums paid (as may be desired) in case of death within a stipulated period, is more in accord with

* Policy No. E-2,788, issued in 1868, on a life aged 31, for $5,000, annual premium $319.80, matured by death in 1886, with the following result:

Nineteen premiums, $319.80 each,	$6,076.20	
Less eighteen cash dividends,	1,810.00	
Cash cost of policy 18½ years,		$4,266.20
Face of policy,	$5,000.00	
Return-Premium additions,	6,076.20	
Paid at maturity,		$11,076.20
Profits over cost after 18 years' insurance,		$6,810.00

Policy No. E-3,162, issued in 1868, on a life aged 43, for $5,000, annual premium $898, matured as an endowment in 1890, and was paid to the insured. The costs and results were as follows:

Twenty-two premiums, $898 each,	$19,756.00	
Less twenty-one dividends,	5,368.72	
Cash cost of policy 22 years,		$14,387.28
Face of policy,	$5,000.00	
Return-Premium additions,	19,756.00	
Dividend at maturity,	240.50	
Total paid at maturity,		$24,996.50
Profits over cost after 22 years' insurance,		$10,609.22

the genius and purpose of Life Insurance, and involves but slight additional outlay.

The annual report for the year 1867 was presented to the Trustees January 31, 1868. It gave, in addition to the usual items of receipts, disbursements, assets and liabilities, the following schedule of policies in force: 12,888 Ordinary Life Policies, insuring $39,330,099; 7,364 10-Payment Life Policies, insuring $24,645,963; one 20-Payment Life Policy for $5,000; 1,483 Endowment Policies, insuring $4,469,032; 1,165 Paid-up Policies, insuring $964,884; 91 Term Policies, insuring $213,900; and two Joint Life Policies, insuring $8,600. A dividend of $955,463.98 was declared, to be credited on the policies, or paid in cash, at their next anniversaries, in accordance with the new plan; and the scrip dividend of 1866 was ordered to be paid in cash. It was also voted that, in making the apportionment of dividends to each policy-holder under the new plan, the officers be authorized, at their discretion, to deduct therefrom the *pro rata* of taxes that were then, or might thereafter be, imposed by the States in which the respective premiums were collected. This measure was made necessary by reason of the varying rates of tax laid upon premiums by different States. By this means the policy-holders of each State were made to bear the taxes imposed by their own State, and one State was not permitted to tax the citizens of another. This was the course and the reasoning generally adopted by life companies at this time; but the taxing States have since insisted that the tax is in the nature of a license to do business, and the companies have acceded to this view. No deductions are now made from dividends on account of taxes paid by the Company.

1868. THE increase in the Company's new business during the last six years had been over seven-fold—the Company was not only outgrowing its office accommodations, but the capacity of its official staff to supervise it. A committee of three Trustees was therefore appointed January 31, 1868, to take into consideration the need of additional assistance to the officers of the Company. The committee reported on April eighth, recommending that the Vice-President be made an active officer, and that William H. Beers be elected to that office. The report was accepted, and at the annual election on May thirteenth following, Mr. Beers was elected Vice-President and Actuary. Meanwhile Mr. Henry A. Dyer, who had been in the employ of the Company for several years as a Special Field Agent, was transferred to the Home Office and made Superintendent of Agencies. In August of the same year Mr. P. S. Lincoln, an accomplished mathematician, was placed in charge of the mathematical work of the Actuary's Department, thus enabling Mr. Beers to devote his whole time and energies to executive duties. Mr. Franklin was at this time nearly sixty-seven years of age, and gave his special attention to the adjustment of policy claims, a duty for which his amiable disposition and legal training peculiarly fitted him.

In March, 1868, was issued Volume I., Number 1, of the "New-York News-Letter," which is described in a sub-title as "a Journal of Instructive and Entertaining Literature." The first number was in the eight-page form, in which it continued to be published until September, 1878, when it took its present form. It was not illustrated, but contained the Annual Report for 1867; a full-page article entitled "Two Hours at the Home of Dickens"; a story, showing how Mrs. Buffon surprised her husband with a sewing-machine purchased by saving a few cents a day, and how Mr. Buffon surprised his wife with a life insurance policy purchased by saving the money he usually spent for cigars—which his wife detested; shorter articles on Life Insurance and other topics; and three pages of advertisements. One of the shorter articles noticed a policy taken in the NEW-YORK LIFE in April, 1863, by Horace Greeley, at the age of fifty-two. This policy was kept in force until maturity, and was paid at Mr. Greeley's death in 1872. No one was named as Editor; the publishers were Messrs. Francis Hart & Co., who (and their successors, Messrs. Theo. L. De Vinne & Co.) continued as such until August, 1886, from which time it has been printed on the Company's own presses.

During this year the Company made arrangements for the extension of its work in the South in an energetic and systematic manner. In April Messrs. B. G. Humphreys & Co. were made General Agents for the State

N. York Oct. 27/68

M. Franklin Esqr
Pres. of "N. Y. Life Insurance Co"

Dear Sir

I desire, in this way, to express my acknowledgement of the promptness and courtesy with which you settled my claim against your Company for the amount due on my policy, after a suspension of payments on my part for more than seven years. I have no doubt ~~the~~ but that the settlement was a perfectly fair one, and I acknowledge with pleasure the courteous and friendly manner in which it was made

Very respectfully
Yr's

W. M. Green
Bp. of Mississippi

of Mississippi, with head-quarters at Jackson; and in December Messrs. J. E. Johnston & Co. were made General Agents for Georgia and Florida, with central offices at Savannah. The two firms were in reality one, and the partners were ex-Governor Humphreys, of Mississippi, General Joseph E. Johnston, and Major Livingston Mims. Although the "cause" of the Confederacy was "lost," the Southern people cherished their old leaders with a love all the more fervent, because they represented all that survived of the cause for which they had sacrificed so much. These three gentlemen were able, therefore, to command the best talent in the South in the work of soliciting life insurance, and under their hands the "Southern Department," into which the two firms were finally consolidated, became one of the Company's most prosperous agencies. In May the Trustees authorized the purchase of Tennessee bonds to the amount of twenty thousand dollars, for deposit with the Treasurer of that State, and Mr. Daniel O'Dell, who had been a General Field Agent since August, 1866, was made General Agent at Memphis, from which point the business of the Company was extended into Arkansas and Texas.

At the August meeting of the Trustees the Finance Committee reported that, at the suggestion of the Officers they had considered the policy of doing business in the Dominion of Canada, which would necessitate the deposit with the Canadian authorities of seventy-five thousand dollars in United States stocks. The Committee approved the proposition, and the Trustees authorized the deposit. At this time American currency was worth in gold about sixty-one cents on the dollar, while the Canadian currency was on a gold basis. The Trustees authorized the Officers of the Company to use their discretion with respect to the money in which Canadian policies should be payable. In order to meet all preferences, two kinds of policies were issued, one on a gold, and the other on a currency, basis. The gold-policy holder paid his premiums in gold or its equivalent, and was guaranteed payment in the same; the currency-policy holder paid his premiums in American currency, and was guaranteed payment in the same. The latter class got the better bargain; they bought American currency for premiums at a discount during the next ten years, and received payment in currency that constantly appreciated until it reached par with gold on the resumption of specie payments, January 1, 1879. The deposit was made with the Dominion Government August twenty-eighth, and Mr. Walter Burke was made General Agent and Attorney for the Company. Mr. Burke managed the agency with marked ability and success until his death, in January, 1878. On account of a law passed by the Dominion Government in 1877, the Company withdrew from Canada March 1, 1878; no successor was, therefore, appointed to Mr. Burke until 1883.

Mr. Edward Jones Richardson, for twenty years the representative of the Company in Baltimore, died in that city August 29, 1868. Mr. Richardson succeeded Mr. J. Smith Homans, under whom he had been a successful solicitor, and by whom he was highly commended. During the period of his agency Mr. Richardson took two of his sons, Edward A. and George I., into partnership with him. The style of the firm, E. J. Richardson & Sons, was continued by the sons after the father's death, until 1872, when Mr. George I. Richardson became the Company's representative in Baltimore, a position which he still holds after a longer period of service than that of his father before him. At the meeting of the Trustees in September, 1868, resolutions were adopted expressive of the loss sustained "in the death of one who had been a most faithful and efficient agent, who for more than twenty years had discharged all the duties devolving upon him to the entire satisfaction of the officers, and to the promotion of the best interests of the Company."

The Company's scrap-books for this period contain many competitive circulars of other companies, but very few of its own. The subject that gave rise to more "claims" and "refutations" than any other was the subject of dividends, involving as it did, both the plan of the company—whether organized on the purely mutual, stock, or mixed, basis—and the method of distributing surplus to policy-holders. Under the charters and by-laws of many of the younger companies on the mixed plan, stockholders were not only given entire control of the company, but also a large share of the surplus earned. A company paying—or claiming that it would pay—large dividends, might not begin paying any dividends whatever until the fifth or sixth year; while others which declared dividends annually, beginning with the second year, might be a long time in redeeming them. The only NEW-YORK LIFE circular of the year found on file contains such a plain statement of facts from official sources, that it is printed herewith. The original is dated, "Branch Office New-York Life Insurance Company, Norwich, Conn., July 1, 1868," and signed "J. E. Linnell, M. D."

LIFE INSURANCE.

Life Insurance Companies are multiplying so rapidly of late, and State Legislatures are granting charters *without stint*, and frequently to men who have not the practical knowledge of the fundamental principles of Life Insurance adequate to conduct the business for the interests of the insured, it has become a matter of serious import to the community that they have at command a list of companies doing business in a given locality, from which they can determine whether the interests of the *policy-holders* or those of *stockholders* are best cared for.

To this end the following exhibit of the several companies doing business in New York is presented from *official returns* made to the Insurance Commissioner of that State for the year ending December 31, 1867:

NAME OF COMPANY.	When dividends are paid to policy-holders	STOCKHOLDERS' SHARE OF PROFITS UNDER CHARTERS AND BY-LAWS.
Ætna	3d year,	1½ per cent. on participating premiums; $78,654 paid to stockholders in 1867, being 134 44-100 per cent. on cash capital.
American Popular	None,	All profits to be paid to stockholders.
Atlantic Mutual	3d year,	20 per cent. of the profits credited to the stockholders, besides interest on capital.
Berkshire Life	3d year,	All profits now paid to policy-holders.
Brooklyn Life	3d year,	20 per cent. of profits paid to stockholders and interest on capital.
Charter Oak	2d year,	Stockholders are limited to 8 per cent. per annum of profits. $50,000 of stock notes paid up last year. Charter gives power to loan one-fourth of the capital, and other funds, upon endorsed promissory notes not having more than twelve months to run.
Connecticut Mutual	5th year,	All profits paid to policy-holders.
Connecticut General	None,	All profits paid to stockholders.
Continental	4th year,	12½ per cent. of profits over legal interest. [$28,000 paid stockholders, 1868, being 28 per cent. on paid-up capital.]
Economical	2d year,	20 per cent. of residue over an annual reserve toward a reserve fund of $200,000 to be applied to payment of stockholder's notes; 7 per cent. of profits to be paid yearly as dividend on capital stock, and when notes fully paid 20 per cent. to be paid stockholders as a surplus dividend over the 7 per cent.
Excelsior	3d year,	10 per cent. of net profits paid to stockholders.
Equitable	2d year,	All profits paid to policy-holders annually on contribution plan, except 7 per cent. interest on capital of $100,000, paid in gold.
Germania	4th year,	Stockholders, after 1869, are limited to 5 per cent. on capital, over legal interest.
Globe	3d year,	Cash paid-up capital of $100,000 may be increased out of the profits to $600,000, and the interest thereon paid to stockholders.

NAME OF COMPANY.	When dividends are paid to policy-holders	STOCKHOLDERS' SHARE OF PROFITS UNDER CHARTERS AND BY-LAWS.
Great Western........	5th year,	20 per cent. of profits paid to stockholders, besides interest on capital.
Guardian	4th year,	All profits paid to policy-holders, except interest on capital.
Home.............. .	3d year,	Stockholders now receive 5 per cent. on capital, over legal interest. A reserve fund of $200,000, to be made up out of the profits, at discretion of Directors.
Hahnemann..........	3d year,	10 per cent. set apart for retirement of capital.
John Hancock........	4th year,	All profits paid to policy-holders, except interest on capital; dividends on cash premiums on 2d year; on cash and note 4th year.
Knickerbocker	6th year,	Stockholders are entitled to 13 per cent. annually on capital, over legal interest. Dividends declared to policy-holders the 6th year, and annually thereafter.
Manhattan	5th year,	12½ per cent. of profits paid to stockholders. Up to January, 1867, $140,786.82 had been paid, which included $31,285.81 apportioned January 1, 1867, being over 31 per cent. per annum, besides interest on capital stock.
Massachusetts Mutual,	2d year,	All profits paid to policy-holders, except interest on capital.
Mutual Life..........	2d year,	All profits paid to policy-holders, annually, on contribution plan.
Mutual Benefit.......	5th year,	All profits paid to policy-holders.
National, N. Y........	4th year,	10 per cent. of profits paid to stockholders, and interest on capital.
National Travelers ...	4th year,	10 per cent. of profits paid to stockholders, and interest on capital.
National Life, Vt.....	6th year,	All profits paid to policy-holders. Dividends declared once in five years only.
N. Y. Life and Trust..	None,	All profits paid to stockholders.
NEW-YORK LIFE	2d YEAR,	ALL PROFITS PAID TO POLICY-HOLDERS, ANNUALLY, ON CONTRIBUTION PLAN. DIVISIBLE SURPLUS JANUARY 1, 1868, $1,642,425.59.
N. J. Mutual.........	3d year,	10 per cent. of profits paid to stockholders, besides interest on capital.
N. Y. State Life......	None,	All profits paid to stockholders.
N. E. Mutual..... ...	2d year,	All profits paid to policy-holders, annually, on contribution plan.
North American	4th year,	12½ per cent. of profits paid to stockholders. $30,000 paid stockholders in 1867, over legal interest, being 30 per cent. per annum on the capital.
Phœnix Mutual	5th year,	Stockholders received 31½ per cent. on paid-up cash capital of $16,000, over legal interest thereon.
Standard.............	4th year,	All profits paid to policy-holders, except interest on capital.
Security..............	4th year,	20 per cent. of profits paid to stockholders, and interest on capital.
Travelers	None,	All profits paid to stockholders. This company is preparing a table for mutual rates.
Universal.............	None,	All profits to be first applied to create a permanent reserve capital fund of $1,800,000, and then the interest and profits to go to stockholders.
U. S. Life............	4th year,	20 per cent. of profits paid to stockholders, besides annual interest on capital. At last triennial dividend of profits the stockholders received $39,932 over legal interest, being 39 93-100 per cent. on capital.
Union Mutual........	6th year,	All profits paid to policy-holders, except 3 per cent. on note capital of $50,000.
World Mutual........	3d year,	12½ per cent. of profits paid to stockholders, besides interest on capital.
Widows and Orphans	3d year,	All profits paid to policy-holders, except interest on capital.
Washington..........	2d year,	All profits paid to policy-holders, annually, on contribution plan, except interest on capital.

From this table it will be observed how few of the different companies are doing business on the mutual plan. It will, moreover, be apparent to any one using ordinary business sagacity, that, other things being equal, those four companies which have been in existence about a *quarter of a century*, have in their favor, besides ***mutuality of interests, the sure test of prosperous experience*** and the accumulation of a *large surplus capital, never divisible to speculators in the misfortunes of widows and orphans*, in opposition to the interests of stockholders, always having the precedence over those of the insured; the uncertainty of continued solvency even for a score of years, and the necessary greater cost of conducting a new business.

In November of this year the NEW-YORK LIFE re-insured the risks of the General Life and Accident Company of Newark, N. J. The business thus acquired consisted of 41 policies, insuring $77,500, with annual premiums amounting to $3,614.68.

The annual report for 1868 was submitted to the Trustees, January 29, 1869. The Policy Schedule showed a decided tendency toward Endowments, the increase being 1,958 policies, as compared with an increase of 1,579 Ordinary Life, and of 1,134 10-Payment Life, Policies. The year had been one of great prosperity, the new business larger than ever before, and the securities showed a market value of nearly four hundred thousand dollars over cost, in view of which a vote of thanks was tendered the Finance Committee.* The annual dividend declared on the "Contribution Plan" was $1,109,009.11, and it was voted to pay in cash the scrip dividend of 1867. This completed the redemption of all outstanding

*Of this excess $177,599.38 was on United States bonds. People are so accustomed in these days to consider Government bonds as the best of securities, that they have forgotten that they were ever questioned. Yet in June, 1867, Dr. Copes wrote the Company that its large investments in these bonds stood in the way of business among wealthy foreigners who wished large insurances. He called attention to the talk of repudiation, even in Northern newspapers, and said the whole negro vote would be used, if occasion offered, for repudiation. Repudiation in various forms became so much of an issue that Secretary McCulloch referred to it at length in his report of December, 1867. Mr. Blaine says: "The Secretary argued bravely and wisely in his report, in favor of paying the principal and interest of the Government bonds in coin. His argument was designed to meet heresies which had found favor in unexpected quarters. The plea was urged by the new and short-lived school of finance that the notes of the national banks should be withdrawn and greenbacks substituted for them, that all payments by the Government on the principal of the bonds should be in its own paper. It was admitted by these novel theorists that the bonds on their face promised coin for interest; but they maintained that the bonds had been issued in large part when gold was at a heavy premium for paper, and could be rightfully liquidated for paper at its advanced value. Propositions were frequently presented to stop the issue of bonds and to pay out notes for any obligations of the Government offered at the Treasury or becoming due in any form."—("Twenty Years in Congress," Vol. ii., page 330.) The National Democratic Platform of 1868 urged "that all the obligations of the Government, not payable by their express terms in coin, ought to be paid in lawful money." President Johnson, in his annual message for 1868, said: "The holders of our securities have already received upon their bonds a larger amount than their original investments, measured by the gold standard. Upon this statement of facts it would seem but just and equitable that the six per cent. interest now paid by the Government should be applied to the reduction of the principal, in semi-annual instalments, which in sixteen years and eight months would liquidate the entire national debt."

dividends.* In each of the years 1868 and 1869 old policy-holders received two dividends, that for the current year and the scrip dividend of two years before, the total value of which exceeded in many cases the annual premium due.

1869. THE large amount of money put in circulation by the expenditures of the Civil War gave an impetus to business which, in the nature of things, could only be of transient duration. The prosperity which marked the years immediately following was based upon a depreciated currency, and was fictitious in many lines where the supply created was greater than the demand, and where important enterprises were intrusted to unskillful hands. About 1869 the tide began to ebb; the time was at hand that would try every man's work. In 1865 there were thirty life companies doing business in New York State; the number increased year by year until 1870, when there were seventy-one; from this point the number fell off gradually until, in 1880, there was the same number as in 1865. The first failures were in 1869, when two British companies re-insured their American risks in American companies which subsequently failed. Yet, so slow were men to discern the signs of the times that, on April 1, 1870, there were on file in the Insurance

* The following table shows the dividends declared under the percentage system, and when they were redeemed:

YEAR.	DIVIDEND RATE.	WHEN REDEEMED.
1846	50 per cent.	In 1861.
1847	50 "	
1848	50 "	
1849	40 "	
1850 (8 months)	40 "	
1851	50 "	Twenty per cent. in 1861, 20 per cent. in 1862, 20 per cent. in 1863, 20 per cent. in 1864, and 20 per cent. in 1865.
1852	40 "	
1853	00 "	
1854	30 "	
1855	30 "	
1856	30 "	
1857	30 "	
1858	30 "	
1859	30 "	
1860	30 "	
1861	30 "	In 1865.
1862	30 "	
1863	35 "	In 1866.
1864	35 "	
1865	50 "	In 1867.
1866	50 "	In 1868.
1867	50 "	In 1869.

Department at Albany, the charters of twelve projected companies, two of which were afterward organized and had a brief existence. Of sixteen New York companies that re-insured their risks, fourteen re-insured in companies that subsequently failed; and of six other-State companies that re-insured, three did so in companies that subsequently failed.

In the light of the foregoing record, the Trustees of the Southern Life Assurance and Trust Company of Mobile, Ala., must be accounted wise, and their policy-holders fortunate. This company was organized in 1866, and on February 11, 1869, published the following "Notice to Policy-holders":

> Notice is hereby given to the policy-holders of this Company that, in accordance with the Resolution of the Board of Trustees, passed on the twenty-second day of January last, to discontinue the issue of new policies, and to re-insure those already issued, the Trustees have effected the re-insurance with the old-established and dividend-paying NEW-YORK LIFE INSURANCE COMPANY, of which Gen. Joseph E. Johnston is the General Agent for Alabama and Mississippi. The Cash Assets of this Company on the first of January, 1869, were $11,000,822.60. During the year 1868 it issued 9,105 new policies. Dividends not used in settlement of premiums will be added to the policy. A Circular, containing full information, will be sent to every policy-holder at an early day.
>
> ROBERT S. BUNKER, President.

The number of policies taken over was 279, insuring $1,376,700, upon which the annual premiums were $62,869.63. These policy-holders were placed on the same footing as others, except that their dividends were subject to the actual mortality experienced—a wise provision, as it proved, for the mortality experienced was considerably above the expected.

In March of this year the Trustees authorized the purchase of bonds of the States of Alabama, Georgia and Louisiana to the amount of two hundred and fifty thousand dollars, for deposit in these States in accordance with their laws.

The extension of the Company's business westward, begun by Mr. Partridge in 1866, had been continued. Early in 1867 Colonel Alexander Hawes became a sub-agent of Mr. Partridge; before the year closed, the partnership of Partridge & Hawes was formed; and in 1868 the work was pushed along the line of the Union Pacific Railroad, the terminus of which was then at Julesburg. On May 10, 1869, the "golden spike" was driven,* to commemorate the completion of the roadway which united the Alantic with the Pacific, and during this year agencies were established in Utah, Montana and Nevada. Colonel Hawes personally wrote the first life applications taken in Salt Lake City, and found the field so ready for the harvest that he received fifteen thousand dollars in advance premiums before the first policy was ready for delivery. Mr. William B. Crane, who worked under Messrs. Partridge & Hawes, took fifty thousand dollars in premiums during this year in a single mining town in Nevada.

The Company took advantage of the general prosperity and the increasing popularity of Life Insurance in 1869, to place its business more exclusively on a cash basis. It always maintained that loans upon policies, if kept within proper limits, were absolutely safe for a life insurance company, and of advantage to the policy-holder who was compelled to do business on credit. Of the advantage to the insured of all-cash payments, *if he had the money*, there was never any more question than there is that it is better to own the whole of a valuable property than it is to own a part. The arguments of the all-cash companies were based upon the tacit assumption that every man could pay his whole premium in cash if he would. The Company had, since the war, urged the all-cash plan more and more, and in May, 1869, it limited future credits to twenty-five per cent. of the premiums on Ordinary Life Policies, and to twenty per cent. on 10-Payment Life Policies. No premium loans were to be allowed unless the premium exceeded fifty dollars per annum, and none where the premiums were payable quarterly.

September 27, 1869, is known in the annals of the New York Stock Exchange as "Black Friday." Customs duties and interest on Government securities were payable in gold, while for other purposes greenbacks were a legal tender. Gold was an article of commerce and of speculation—being necessary chiefly to the importer and the Treasury. A clique of speculators stealthily bought up most of the private stock east of the Rocky

*There were really two golden spikes, and two of silver used on this occasion. They were presented by the four States—Montana, Idaho, California and Nevada. The junction was made at Promontory, just north of Great Salt Lake. Telegraph wires throughout the country were connected with this point so that every stroke of the hammer was noted wherever there was a telegraph office.

Mountains and thus obtained control of the market. Importers with duties to pay in gold and speculators who had sold gold for future delivery, were at the mercy of the clique. The highest price in August had been 136⅝; on September twenty-fourth, after several days of excitement, it rose to 164. Upon the announcement that the Treasury would sell gold,

From a Circular Used in 1869.

the price dropped to 135. The NEW-YORK LIFE owned at this time gold bearing bonds to the amount of over two million dollars, and as some of its policies were payable in gold, a gold account was necessarily kept. Its profits on gold sold during the year were over forty thousand dollars, the highest sale being made in September, at 155.

During this year two cases occurred where the insured became sick and delirious just before a premium fell due, and died leaving it unpaid. In both cases the Trustees ordered payment of the policy in full. The necessity of some such provision as has since been incorporated in the Company's policies—namely, a month's grace in the payment of premiums, and automatic non-forfeiture conditions which assume that the insured intends to keep his policy in force—was probably then seen, but the time to supply it had not fully come.

Another case of hardship came to light during this year against which it would be difficult for any Company to provide. In August, 1862, the Company issued a policy for $1,000 upon the life of Mr. Alden Josselyn, of Lawrence, Mass., the beneficiary being the mother of the insured. In April, 1863, Mr. Josselyn died of consumption, and when the attending physician filled out proofs of death he certified that he had treated the deceased before he insured, for hemorrhage of the lungs. As it was expressly stated in the application that the insured had never had any disease of the lungs, and as the Company would not have accepted the risk had the hemorrhage been acknowledged, payment of the claim was refused. It was placed in the hands of a lawyer, who wrote the President that he had a good case against the Company. The President replied that if he would make out a good case for the Trustees, they would be just as willing to pay the claim as a jury would be to compel payment. Thereupon affidavits were submitted from both parents, two sisters and an intimate friend of the deceased, to the effect that they had never known him to have any hemorrhage or disease of the lungs. Being convinced that a jury would accept this evidence rather than that of the attending physician, the Trustees ordered the payment of the claim. In 1869 the lawyer was arrested for not having turned the money over to his client.

For many years the Company has printed with its "Instructions" for preparing proofs of death the statement that, "the intervention of any third person is not necessary for the collection of any approved claim, and the payment of a commission to any person for services in regard to such claim is unnecessary."

The annual report for 1869 was submitted to the Trustees January 31, 1870, and showed a larger amount of new business than ever before; it proved to be the largest business of any year prior to 1882. The insurance in force, for the first time in the Company's history, exceeded one hundred million dollars.

POLICY HEADING USED FROM OCTOBER, 1869, TO JANUARY, 1895.

1870. THE year 1870 saw the agencies of the NEW-YORK LIFE extended westward to the Pacific Coast. Colonel Hawes was made Superintendent of Agencies west of the Mississippi River. Mr. W. B. Crane, who had been for a short time General Agent for Nevada, Idaho, Oregon, Washington and British Columbia, became associated with Col. Hawes under the style of Crane & Hawes, Managers for the Pacific Coast, with head-quarters at San Francisco. On March twenty-sixth, of the same year, Mr. Harry S. Homans was appointed "General Agent for the Kingdom of Great Britain and the continent of Europe." The Company thus entered upon a course that has since made its agencies as widely extended as the British military posts, whose morning drum-beat, Webster said, "following the sun and keeping company with the hours, circled the earth every day with the unbroken strains of the martial music of England." Mr. Homans established his head-quarters at Numbers 76 and 77 Cheapside, London, and soon afterward associated with himself Mr. Cornelius Walford, who was probably the best known writer on insurance

HOME OFFICE IN 1870.

topics in the United Kingdom. During the same year Mr. Homans established a General Agency in Paris, the offices being at No. 1 Rue Scribe, with Mr. Albert Lee Ward in charge, as General Agent.

On May eleventh the Trustees held their first meeting in the new building, at 346 and 348 Broadway. It was an occasion for general congratulation, and to Mr. William Barton, Chairman of the Building Committee, a vote of thanks was tendered for his untiring industry and zeal in bringing to completion the plans of the Board. The structure was at that time one of the handsomest in the city. It was modeled after the Erectheum at Athens; the exterior was of pure, white marble; and it was finished and furnished in a style at once massive and elegant. The insignia of the Company—an eagle feeding her young—was sculptured in the marble architrave crowning the front entrance, and the arms of the State of New York appropriately crowned the center of the balustrade surrounding the roof. The building seemed complete and large enough for the needs of the Company for all time, but the march of Invention and of Progress have since compelled many changes. The Company had scarcely occupied it three months when it was found necessary, in order to rent the upper floors, to put in an elevator—a means of conveyance which had come into fashion since the building was begun. Other changes and enlargements, made necessary by the increasing business of the Company and the increasing value of land in lower New York, will be noted in their order.

With the growth of the Company's business in the Southern States came various demands under old policies, and all sorts of attempts to discredit the Company in the eyes of the Southern people. The latter was chiefly the work of companies which had little or no business in the South before the war. Such as had here and there a policy made a great show of liberality;* while others traded upon the grievances of a few dissatisfied policy-holders in the NEW-YORK LIFE, and upon their own disregard of sound principles of underwriting. The names and character of the Company's agents in the South proved, however, a tower of strength; and they challenged all comers to gainsay the record, that "the NEW-YORK LIFE received more Confederate money for premiums during the

---

* The Knickerbocker Life Insurance Company, which had only 760 policies in force in the whole country on December 31, 1860, published a letter, dated Mobile, Oct. 5, 1869, and signed Ellen B. Nicholson, saying her husband was insured before the war; allowed his policy to lapse; was offered the option of reviving it or accepting its surrender value; accepted the latter and died about a month afterward; whereupon the Company very generously paid her one thousand dollars additional! This statement was said to show that "no insurance company, North or South *can*, or *will*, deal more liberally with all its assured than that good and reliable old company, the Knickerbocker Mutual!" For further particulars, see records of Receiver of the company, appointed June 25, 1888.

war, and paid more money for lapsed policies after the war, than all other companies combined." The dissatisfaction of a few policy-holders at the amount received as a surrender value for lapsed policies, it was said, grew out of "the wrong impression that they ought to have received back very nearly the entire amount of premiums paid, and for which they have received insurance"—an impression, it should be noted, which has always prevailed to a considerable extent.* A typical case of this kind was widely published in 1870, to which Mr. Franklin replied in a letter to Dr. Copes, dated March 26th, as follows:

My attention has been called to a letter in the "New Orleans Times" of the thirteenth inst., the evident intention of which is to give notoriety to certain alleged facts which could not be attained by a correspondence in regular course.

I do not propose by a lengthy newspaper controversy to aid General Gaines by giving advertising value to the letter for competing companies, who are envious of the NEW-YORK LIFE, and whose interests he may or may not be desirous to advance.

In justice to ourselves, and for the information of the numerous policy-holders of the NEW-YORK LIFE, we feel compelled to deny the statements made by General Gaines, through the same channel in which they were made. The documents and vouchers for our statement will be deposited with you, our esteemed agent, and may be investigated by any parties interested. The facts are as follows:

1. The Company did not forfeit this policy in 1862. Gen. Gaines had ample opportunity to pay his premium in New Orleans, for, by an express, special arrangement, made by you as our agent, with the Confederate States authorities, such moneys were to be held in trust by you, and were not to be confiscated. Other parties paid their premiums, and Gen. Gaines could have done the same on the 11th March, 1862, when it was due, or at any time thereafter till May of that year, in the currency which you were then receiving. By his failure so to do, he voluntarily abandoned the policy and forfeited all claims under it.

2. The Company have, since the war, offered to re-instate this policy upon the payment of the back premiums, and to deduct from such amount all the dividends which the policy would have earned had it been in full force all the time, the effect of which would be that Gen. Gaines, had he accepted the proposition, would have been in exactly the same condition as if no lapse had occurred.

3. It being understood that some of the parties wishing to revive their policies could not conveniently pay the amount required for back premiums in cash, the Company offered to charge the whole amount of them against the policy as a loan, to be

* It is not an unheard of thing, even to this day, for a policy-holder to present his policy and say, seeing he has not died he has cost the Company nothing, and if his premiums are returned he will give the Company the interest on them and call it quits. The guarantee of the amount of one's policy in case of death appears very intangible to those who live, but it must be made substantial with the money of the living to those who die.

paid by future dividends or otherwise, at the convenience of the policy-holder, and required only the future premiums to be paid in cash. This offer was made to Gen. Gaines, and he was at liberty to accept either mode of settlement.

4. The Company offered to make this adjustment, and to revive his policy without any oath or affidavit, the Medical Board having accepted the risk.

5. The surrender value of this policy at the time of its lapse was $1,068. We proposed to settle this (notwithstanding it had lapsed early in March, 1862,) by the cancellation of a debt which Gen. Gaines owed the Company, and for which we hold his note for $927.12, and by the payment to him of cash for the balance, $140.88. In addition to this, we authorized a further payment of $300 cash, if, in your estimation, under all the circumstances, it would be equitable and proper to do so. This, we are aware, you promptly offered him.

6. In reply to all these earnest endeavors of the Company to do what was fair, and even liberal, to the utmost verge of equity in regard to other policy-holders, we received a demand for the payment of $2,500 in cash, under penalty of being "published in the newspapers." As we are willing to go before any tribunal, North or South, on the record alone, without any argument, and could not, in justice to other policy-holders, concede this demand, the infliction of the threat was consequently risked.

7. The total cash paid to the Company by Gen. Gaines is $1,738.50, for which sum, divided into annual installments, it carried the amount of $5,000 insurance on his life for fifteen years, during all of which time it [the Company] was liable to pay his family, at any moment, had he died, this $5,000. He now demands that, for the privilege of carrying this risk for fifteen years, we should return to him all the cash part of the premiums paid by him, and $761.50 additional, to say nothing of his indebtedness for loans as above mentioned, or he will "publish a full history of the case in the newspapers."

We think further comment than this brief exhibit of the facts unnecessary, and are content to submit it to the public to decide whether faithfulness to the trust committed to us by the whole body of our policy-holders would permit any greater degree of liberality in the case of Gen. Gaines.

One of the charges of General Gaines was that the Company refused any redress in the case of Colonel T. D. Merrick, of Little Rock, Ark. Colonel Merrick's policy lapsed during the war, for non-payment of premiums, and no attempt was made to revive it. After his death, in 1866, its payment as a death-claim was of course refused, but upon a representation of all the circumstances by General James F. Fagan, the Company's agent for Arkansas, a liberal allowance was paid as a surrender value of the policy. Upon having his attention called to this fact, General Gaines promptly retracted so much of his letter as referred to this case, saying, "General Fagan's well-known gallantry is a sufficient guaranty that Mrs. Merrick has been justly settled with."

Among the death-claims paid in 1870 was one for $15,530.99, upon the life of General George H. Thomas. General Thomas was insured under Policy No. 49,112, dated June 18, 1868—a fifteen-year endowment.* He was at that time fifty-one years of age, and was the embodiment of physical strength, courage and will power, which, a few years before, had made him the "Rock of Chickamauga." He died in San Francisco, March twenty-eighth, after an illness of a few hours. The certificate of death said: "Died of apoplexy; probably rupture of blood-vessel in the brain from atheromatous degeneration of the vessel. No symptoms previous to day of his death to indicate this condition." Probably General Thomas could have passed a medical examination for insurance the day before his death. So near men may be to death from internal causes, and yet not know it!

The annual report for the year 1870 was presented to the Trustees January 31, 1871. It showed a slight falling off in new business. The influences which culminated in the financial crisis of 1873 were already making themselves felt. The Company's standard of valuation of its policy liabilities was the Carlisle Table of Mortality, with interest at four per cent. for participating policies, and at five per cent. for non-participating policies. By this standard its surplus January 1, 1871, was $1,152,408.04. The New York State standard by the law of 1868 was the American Table of Mortality, with interest at four and one-half per cent., and by this standard the surplus was $1,946,612.76. The Massachusetts standard was the Actuaries' Table of Mortality, with interest at four per cent., and by this standard the surplus was $587,795.89. An attempt, made in 1868, to secure the adoption of a common standard in these two States having failed, the NEW-YORK LIFE Trustees now took the initial step toward

---

George H Thomas
Maj Genl U.S.A.

*FROM GENERAL THOMAS' APPLICATION.

increasing its reserve fund to correspond with the more rigid standard, by voting to open a special reserve fund account, to be credited annually with $50,000 and its accumulations during the next ten years.

1871. WHEN the NEW-YORK LIFE began business in England, it encountered the opposition that usually besets the foreign competitor. But when its first policy matured by death, in January, 1871, it received considerable kindly notice by reason of the promptness with which the claim was paid. It arose under Policy No. 73,754, issued August 17, 1870, upon the life of Mr. George W. Watts, of Brompton, the amount being £300. Mr. Watts died December sixth following, under circumstances that might have delayed payment of the claim had the Company's policies contained the usual clause making them void in case of death by the insured's own hand. Mr. Watts died in Salisbury, at the house of a friend, whither he had gone to make arrangements for a business partnership. A coroner's inquest was held and the following verdict rendered: "That George Watkins Watts, suffering from extensive disease of the brain, and being in the habit of taking a medicine containing prussic acid, did, on the date first mentioned, and at the time and place named, accidentally, by misadventure and misfortune, take an overdose of the medicine, by means of which he, the aforesaid George Watkins Watts, then and there instantly died." Proofs of death were made to the Company's office in London, late in December—the certified copy of the coroner's verdict bearing date December twenty-third—and the claim was paid in London, January 19, 1871. Such expedition was something new in life insurance in England, and the newspapers published full accounts of it under the head of "Yankee Enterprise."

In January of this year the Company began the issue of Ten-Year Dividend Policies, upon what afterward became known as the Tontine plan, which will be more fully described in connection with the introduction of the Company's "Tontine Investment Policy" in 1872. The Ten-Year Dividend Policy had nearly the same features as the Tontine Investment Policy with 10-year Tontine period, except that only one option was offered at the end of the period, namely, to continue the policy and apply the surplus to purchase an annuity to be used in reduction of future annual premiums, the excess, if any, to be paid in cash.* When these policies matured, however, they were allowed the regular Tontine options. The NEW-YORK LIFE, as a purely mutual Company, holds to the principle that no privileges should be extended to any policy-holder not accorded to every other policy-holder holding a policy in the same class or of a similar character. In pursuance of this principle, it considered its old policies non-forfeiting when it adopted non-forfeiting policies on the same premium tables; and the new privileges of the Accumulation Policy—first issued in 1892—were at once extended to all other policies paying the same premium for the same risk.

In May, 1871, a Convention of Commissioners and Superintendents of Insurance, of the various States having Insurance Departments, was held in New York City, and the life insurance companies were invited to lay before the Convention such matters as they might regard important to be considered. Representatives of the companies met at the office of the Mutual Life Insurance Company, on May twentieth, by invitation of President Winston. Mr. Winston was made Chairman of the meeting, and Mr. John E. De Witt, of the United States Life Insurance Company, was made Secretary. After discussion, it was voted that "the following are regarded by this meeting as of primary importance:

"1. Uniformity in the forms of annual reports and other requirements made by the different State Departments of Insurance.

"2. The adoption of the same basis, principles and system in the valuation of policies and computation of reserves by the different State Departments, where such valuations and computations are to be made.

"3. The acceptance by each State Department of the valuations made by any other State Department (in which the companies were incorporated) when properly performed on sound and recognized principles, and a uniform basis.

"4. The lists of policies and securities in detail required in the annual statements to be made to one State Department only, and the certificate of the total amount of such policies, and amount and value of such assets from said Department where made, to be deemed sufficient in all other State Departments.

---

* Instead of one month's grace in the payment of premiums and the privilege of re-instatement during a second month, the grace under these policies was for as many months, not exceeding six, as there had been full years' premiums paid at the time of lapse.

"5. The deposit of securities by the companies to be made in the State only in which the company was incorporated, if there required, and the certificate of such deposit from the Insurance Department of the State where made, to be accepted by all other State Departments.

"6. The appointment of one agent or attorney only in each State to be required by it to accept legal service in behalf of a company, thereby avoiding great possible dangers.

"7. Taxation. If not practicable to have it entirely removed from Life Insurance, to be made uniform and reasonable in the different States, and not complicated and oppressive, as at present in many portions of the country."

The following-named officers were appointed a Committee to present these views to the Convention: Messrs. F. S. Winston, of the Mutual, William H. Beers, of the NEW-YORK LIFE, Henry Stokes, of the Manhattan, Henry M. Alexander, of the Equitable, Hugo Wesendonck, of the Germania, and Jacob L. Green, of the Connecticut Mutual.

This statement of what, in the opinion of the companies, should be, indicates by the rule of contraries what was not, and what obstacles beset the path of all life companies—the NEW-YORK LIFE included—at this time. The State insurance officials have held annual meetings since 1871, and in 1874–5 adopted a uniform blank for the statements of the companies, and the conditions set forth as desirable under the first, second, third and sixth heads above have been practically realized. The taxation of Life Insurance, however, continues very unequal in the different States.

Mr. Henry A. Dyer, who had been for nearly three years Superintendent of Agencies for the Company, and who brought to the discharge of his duties marked executive ability and great fidelity and earnestness of purpose, died July 2, 1871. He was succeeded by Mr. Daniel O'Dell, who had been in the service of the Company since 1865, and who at this time was General Agent at Memphis.

In October of this year occurred the great Chicago fire, which destroyed property to the amount of $190,000,000. The insurance thereon was about $100,000,000, of which nearly $50,000,000 was paid. The losses were distributed among over two hundred companies, of which sixty-four were made bankrupt. The necessity which the fire companies would be under to realize upon their securities, and the consequent disturbance of the money market, were foreseen and, indeed, exaggerated at other money centers; the nominal shrinkage of values at the New York Stock Exchange during the week following the fire was greater than the insurance held by all the companies. A greater Chicago has since risen, as if by magic, upon the site of the blackened ruins of October, 1871, but had it not been for the fifty million dollars received from the insurance companies, Chicago's upbuilding must have been much more slowly accomplished and with much greater losses to her commerce and wealth. Although no such sweeping losses could occur in Life Insurance—except as the result of a calamity greater than has ever befallen the human race since the Flood—the Chicago fire, in its illustration of the value of the insurance principle, could not fail to be helpful in the long run to the progress of Life Insurance.

In addition to the money paid by the fire companies, the whole country resolved itself into a vast insurance society whose contributions in money, provisions and clothing were estimated at over seven millions of dollars.* Toward this relief fund the Trustees of the NEW-YORK LIFE, on October eleventh, voted a donation of five thousand dollars. At the same meeting five hundred dollars were voted to the Committee of Seventy who were endeavoring to put a stop to the misappropriation of the funds of the city by the Tweed ring.

The annual report for the year 1871 was presented to the Trustees on February 3, 1872. It showed an increase in everything except new business, dividends and expenses. The increase in policies in force—over seventeen hundred—was nearly half in endowments. Over one-

---

* For down from the West came the bidding, "O Queen, lift in courage thy head!
Thy friends and thy neighbors awaken, and hasten with raiment and bread!"
And up from the South came the bidding, "Cheer up, fairest Queen of the Lakes!
For comfort and aid shall be coming from out our savannas and brakes!"
And down from the North came the bidding, "O City, be hopeful of cheer!
We've somewhat to spare for thy sufferers, for all of our suffering here!"
And up from the East came the bidding, "O City, be dauntless and bold!
Look hither for food and for raiment—look hither for credit and gold!"
And all through the world went the bidding, "Bring hither your choicest and best,
For weary and hungry Chicago, sad Queen of the North and the West."
—*Will Carlton.*

Roxbury: Oct. 3 1871.

My dear Mr. Russell:—

I can tell you in a moment, what were my reasons for applying to you for a ten years' Endowment. ~~I am now in good health and~~ I have six boys for whose future education I must look forward. I should be sorry to die, leaving their mother without means to take care of them in the best way. I am so fortunate that I have a good income— and, with a little extra effort with my pen, I can enlarge that income now, as I know I shall not be able to when I am sixty years old. I determined therefore, to purchase an Endowment in some Life Company now which would enable me ten years hence, to send my boys to college if I wished to,— or which would permit my wife to do so if I were not living.

Having made this determination I took the best advice I could as to the standing of different Companies,— their reserves,— and the certainty that my investment would be safe. Yours was named to me as one of two which I could rely upon and I came to you.

Respectfully Yours.

Edw. E. Hale

(It may be proper to explain that the above letter was addressed to D. W RUSSELL, Agent of the New York Life Ins. Co., 13 Merchants' Exchange, Boston, and was entirely unsolicited, as was the insurance referred to therein, hence we regard it as more complimentary to the Company than it would otherwise have been.)

CIRCULAR USED IN 1871, AND LATER.

fifth of the Company's business was under endowment policies—a proportion which continues to this day. It was voted to set aside $50,000 as a real estate sinking fund; and a recommendation of the Officers to establish Local Boards in the larger cities of the State, and to loan money upon desirable property therein, was approved.

1872. THE marked favor with which the NEW-YORK LIFE'S "Ten-Year Dividend Policy" was received induced its Officers to develop more fully the principles embodied therein, and to add other attractive features. The new form was called the "Tontine Investment Policy." It provided for dividend periods of either ten, fifteen or twenty years, selection to be made upon applying for the policy. In case of death, the beneficiaries received the amount insured only, all claims to surplus being waived in favor of survivors. In case of lapse, no paid-up or cash value was given, all claims to such values being waived in favor of those who survived and kept their policies in force. To guard against loss by forfeiture, so far as possible, a month's grace was allowed in payment of premiums, and a re-instatement was allowed during the month following lapse, provided the health of the insured continued good, as shown by satisfactory medical examination. In case the grace was availed of, or re-instatement was had, a fine at the rate of ten per cent. per annum was collected for the time the premium remained due and unpaid.

At the termination of the dividend, or Tontine, periods the following options in settlement were allowed:

1. To continue the policy, and with the surplus apportioned to purchase an annuity to be applied to the payment of future premiums on the policy, or to be received in cash.

2. To continue the policy by the payment of premiums, if not already paid-up, and to receive the surplus apportioned in cash.

3. To withdraw the entire cash value of the policy, consisting of the reserve thereon and the surplus apportioned.

4. To convert the entire cash value into a paid-up policy, provided that in case such paid-up policy exceeded the amount of the original policy, a satisfactory medical examination be passed.

5. To convert the entire cash value into an annuity for life.

The new and most valuable feature which these options introduced into Life Insurance was the cash surrender value of the entire reserve upon the policy before its natural termination. It is a fundamental principle in Life Insurance that a certain amount—fixed by the rates of mortality and interest assumed, the age of the insured and the year of the policy—must be in the company's hands. The State had already declared what rates of mortality and interest should be assumed, and remorselessly wound up every company that failed to comply with this condition. If a policy was in force, its reserve, or re-insurance fund, was the company's contingent liability therefor; if the policy ceased to be in force by sale and cancellation, the company's liabilities were correspondingly reduced. Yet it was not customary for companies to pay this amount in full, upon the surrender of a policy, nor to guarantee any surrender value in cash.* Some companies refused to pay any cash value whatever, contending that the money had been paid for insurance, and that nothing but insurance should be given for it. Others made a surrender charge, upon the ground that, as a class, discontinuing policy-holders were the best risks, and, seeing the company could be held to its contract, the party wishing to retire should leave behind him enough to secure another member in his place. This surrender charge was fixed by law in Massachusetts, but companies of other States were each a law unto themselves, and the insured who wished to surrender his policy for cash could demand nothing, and must accept whatever was offered. This privilege of receiving a cash surrender value of the entire reserve fund before the natural termination of the policy, was all the more valuable because it was not obligatory. A man might wish to continue his policy; if so, the way was open under several options. In short, the

---

*The single exception to this rule, in 1872, was the Brooklyn Life Insurance Company, which, in 1869, inserted in its policies a table of cash values showing how much would be paid in cash on the anniversary of the policy, or within thirty days thereafter, for its surrender to the company provided three annual premiums had been paid. According to a circular issued by Mr. D. P. Fackler, in 1879, the Brooklyn was still the only company which guaranteed a cash surrender value *at any time* after a certain period. This value was not, however, the full reserve on the policy.

policy-holder was allowed to re-adjust his insurance to his changed circumstances—if change there should be. Instead of a policy that gave insurance only, or cash only, at the end of a selected period, the "Tontine Investment Policy" gave either insurance or cash.

The prospectus of the new policy announced that it divided the profits of insurance between those who died soon after insuring and those who lived long, that policies maturing by death during the Tontine periods would give large returns without sharing in the surplus; and that the surplus being accumulated at compound interest and divided among a diminished number, would give a large share to each survivor, and so an incentive would be created which would tend to keep policies in force. Nevertheless, these advantages were purchased at some risk, and the policy was recommended only to those who had a reasonable prospect of being able to keep it in force. The clause making the policies null and void in case of non-payment of premium appeared less harsh at that time than it does now, after an experience of thirty-five years of non-forfeiture. It was then less than twelve years since the NEW-YORK LIFE had originated and introduced its Ten-Payment Life Non-forfeiting Policy, and considerably less since policies on the Ordinary Life tables had been made non-forfeiting. Moreover, the Tontine Policy was forfeitable during a limited period only; the policy-holder had unusual privileges in the month's grace and the privilege of re-instatement, and unusual advantages at the end of the period. Tontine Policies proved popular, notwithstanding their forfeitability—as the records of the Tontine companies conclusively show—; but it was found in actual practice that this feature added very little to their profitableness and entailed sacrifice where it was hardest to bear; the Company, therefore, began in 1884 the issue of a Non-forfeiting Tontine Policy. Meanwhile it continued to issue annual dividend policies with non-forfeiture provisions to all who preferred that form of contract.*

---

* The word "Tontine" is derived from the name of a Neapolitan, Lorenzo Tonti, who in the seventeenth century introduced into France a system of Tontine Annuities. Under this system a number of persons joined in forming a fund, the income of which was divided among the living at stated periods. At the death of a member, his share of the principal passed to the survivors. The principal

The prospectus explaining the Company's Tontine plan was accompanied by estimates of results at the termination of the several periods. Much criticism has since been indulged in, by opponents of the Company and the system, because these estimates were not fully realized; but the same thing is true of all estimates of life insurance dividends made at that time, and all companies made estimates. Every company then paying dividends assumed that it would continue to do so at the same, or at higher rates, and such dividends were always taken account of in estimating the future cost and benefits of a policy. The Tontine estimates of 1872 were based upon the dividends of the time and previous experience as to lapses, and were certified by competent and disinterested actuaries to be conservative.* The NEW-YORK LIFE took pains to print

---

was divided when the membership reached a point agreed upon at the formation of the fund. The system has been used quite extensively in France, Germany and South America, and occasionally in Great Britain and the United States. A Tontine Association was formed in New York City in 1791, consisting of 203 persons who paid in $200 each, the contributors having the privilege of nominating the persons to enjoy the benefits. It was agreed that the original fund should be divided when the shareholders should be reduced by death to seven. The fund was invested in a building at the corner of Wall and Water Streets, which was known as the "Tontine Coffee House." The appointees were all children, and the number was reduced to seven in 1871 by the death of Mr. John P. de Wint, of Fishkill, N. Y. The property, which had meantime become very valuable, then passed to the seven survivors.

It will be seen from the foregoing that the word "Tontine" as applied to Life Insurance is, to a certain extent, a misnomer. The holder of a Tontine Policy who dies does not forfeit his premium payments, but receives a large return for his money. The only real forfeit was of the reserve—under the early Tontines—of policies which lapsed after two or three premiums had been paid. The long-term dividend system can hardly be called a system of forfeitures. The premiums of all participating policies are made somewhat higher than it is *expected* will be necessary to meet all claims; but as the whole system rests upon assumptions as to mortality and interest running through the life-time of the longest livers, it is an open question how soon surplus should be divided. The Tontine principle was first applied to life insurance in this country by the Equitable Life Assurance Society, in 1868. These Tontines were forfeitable for non-payment of premium, and the dividend period was fixed by the length of time required for the premiums, with compound interest at ten per cent. per annum, to equal the face of the policy. Policies maturing by death under this plan could, therefore, never return less than this rate. The dividend, when apportioned, was payable in cash or in reduction of future premiums. There was no cash surrender option. In 1870 the Mutual Life began the issue of Tontine Policies with 10-, 15- and 20-year dividend periods, and in 1872 the Equitable introduced its "Tontine Savings Fund Policies," with substantially the same features as the NEW-YORK LIFE'S Tontine Investment Policies. The Mutual Life discontinued the issue of Tontine Policies in 1872.

WILLIAM H. BEERS, Esq., *NEW YORK, January 19, 1872.
Vice-President NEW-YORK LIFE INS. CO.

Dear Sir: As requested by you, I have made a careful examination of your circular and estimates in relation to the "Tontine Investment Policy" issued by your Company.

The assumed rates of interest, mortality and expense, upon which the estimates of probable results are based, are, in my opinion, less favorable than the experience of yours and other compain all its pamphlets on the subject, this caution—which is certainly more than was done by other companies with respect to estimates of annual dividends:

While much larger results than these have been approved and endorsed by some of the most competent and experienced life insurance experts, and by men of great financial and business experience, it is expressly stated that the foregoing examples are presented as estimates only, and are not to be considered as promises or guarantees. The elements involved—viz., mortality, interest and miscellaneous profits—being variable in their nature, exact results cannot be foretold.

In December of this year the officers of the Company were called upon to face a peculiar question. There appeared in the "Herald" of November thirtieth a communication from President Winston, of the Mutual Life Insurance Company, proposing to reduce premium rates by making the loading on all net premiums ten per cent. This reduction was recommended by the Actuary of the Mutual Life, Professor Bartlett, and the experience of the company was said to justify it. The expenses of the Mutual Life during the preceding year had been 7.87 per cent. of its gross premium receipts, and during the three years preceding they had

---

nies would have justified, and therefore the estimates may be considered such as are likely to be realized.

The *benefits* you propose to extend to those selecting this class of policy *are more varied in their character and advantages than are afforded by any plan of insurance now in use by any company* within my knowledge, and are such as cannot fail to render the Tontine Investment Policy a popular, safe, and highly remunerative form of insurance. Very truly yours,

SHEPPARD HOMANS, Consulting Actuary.

WILLIAM H. BEERS, Esq., NEW YORK, January 19, 1872.
Vice-President NEW-YORK LIFE INS. CO.

Dear Sir: In accordance with your request, I have carefully examined the scheme of the Tontine Investment Policy, issued by your Company.

The estimates of the benefits likely to accrue to the holders of this class of policies (after the expiration of the term during which distributions of surplus are forborne) are based upon what I regard as very moderate assumptions of profit from the elements of mortality, interest, margins and gains from policies discontinued. I have no hesitation in saying that I think it *more probable that the actual results will exceed, than fall short of your estimates.*

The *various advantages of this form of policy* are well presented in the circular explaining it, and I notice among them several methods of applying the surplus which *do not appear to have ever been offered by any other company.*

I see no reason why the Tontine Investment Policy should not at once become as popular as any other plan of insurance now known. Yours truly,

EDWIN W. BRYANT, Consulting Actuary.

Substantially the same opinions as to the estimated results under these policies were expressed by Hon. Elizur Wright and Mr. David Parks Fackler.

averaged 9.22 per cent. In seven of the preceding ten years the rate had exceeded ten per cent. The expenses of other companies doing business in Massachusetts had averaged 30.51 per cent. during the three years preceding. It was evident, therefore, that the Mutual was proposing to do business on a perilously narrow margin, and that many of the weaker companies must inevitably go to the wall in the competition that would follow. The three companies having the next higher expense ratios in 1871 were the NEW-YORK LIFE (10.90), the Mutual Benefit of N. J. (10.06), and the Equitable (15.52). The NEW-YORK LIFE and the Mutual Benefit could evidently have met this reduction, if necessary; but it would have been a crushing blow to the business as a whole, and they resolved to make common cause with the weaker companies. In doing this they did not prevent policy-holders from securing their insurance at the lowest possible rates, since the higher premium need only be paid the first year; after that, whatever reduction was possible, by economy of management, was made by dividends.

Mr. Beers headed a Committee of eighteen life insurance officers who, on December fourth, addressed a letter to Messrs. Elizur Wright, Sheppard Homans and David Parks Fackler, asking their views on the subject. Mr. Wright had won great and deserved fame as Insurance Commissioner of Massachusetts, and Messrs. Homans and Fackler were familiar with the business of the Mutual Life by reason of their previous official connection therewith. These gentlemen, under date of December sixth, gave it as their opinion that the proposed reduction was "a virtual abandonment of those cardinal principles of security and equity upon which the claims of the Mutual Life Insurance Company to the confidence of its policy-holders and of the community have rested"; and that "it cannot be carried into effect without injustice to existing policy-holders and a decrease in their security." On December twelfth an Executive Committee representing eighteen companies, and composed of Messrs. Henry B. Hyde, of the Equitable, William H. Beers, of the NEW-YORK LIFE, N. D. Morgan, of the North American Life, and John E. De Witt, of the United States Life, addressed a letter to President Winston, disclaiming any wish to advise him as to the management of the Mutual Life, but expressing their belief that great injury to Life Insurance generally would result if the proposed change were carried into effect. Upon this ground they requested the Mutual Life to reconsider its action. To this Mr. Winston responded, on the same day, that he would lay their communication before the Board of Trustees and recommend their favorable action thereon. This was done, and the Board directed "that the proposed reduction of rates be not carried into effect until the further action of the Board." Subsequent events have confirmed, beyond all question, the wisdom of the associated companies. In 1879* the Mutual Life made a reduction in rates much less radical than that proposed in 1872, and after an experience of six years under the reduced scale it abandoned the project and adopted premium tables higher than those in use in 1872. In only six, of the twenty-three, years that have elapsed since 1871, have the Mutual's expenses been as low as ten per cent. of its entire income.

In November of this year the Company paid the Colvocoresses claim,† the details of which form one of the most remarkable cases in

---

* In September, 1877, the Mutual Life announced that it had accumulated a vitality fund from the reserves of policies surrendered (the difference between reserve and surrender value paid in 1876 was stated at $569,390 before the Assembly Committee in 1877), which it proposed to use in securing new members by allowing them a rebate of thirty per cent. on the first two annual premiums. Early in 1879, however, this plan was abandoned for a uniform reduction of fifteen per cent. on Ordinary Life Policies.

† At a late hour on the night of June third, Captain George M. Colvocoresses, a retired naval officer, was found in the streets of Bridgeport, Conn., in a dying condition, and he soon after expired without recovering consciousness. He was a resident of Litchfield, and had left home during the afternoon intending to take the eleven o'clock boat from Bridgeport to New York, where he had an engagement the next day with an agent who had recently placed a large amount of insurance on his life. He carried with him a leather valise, a small morocco traveling-bag, a sword-cane and an umbrella. He purchased a ticket for the boat, put his valise in the state-room, and went to a restaurant for his supper. During supper he kept his traveling bag in his lap. He was last seen by a druggist, from whom he purchased two sheets of writing paper and two envelopes, and who at half-past ten o'clock pointed out the nearest *route* to the boat, which left at eleven. Just as the boat was putting off a pistol-shot was heard, and a police officer ran to the spot whence the sound proceeded and found the Captain in a dying condition.

His clothing was unbuttoned, and his shirt where the bullet entered his body was on fire; his sword-cane covering was broken and the sword was bent, but bore no stain; the cane and umbrella were found near him; the traveling bag was gone, but was subsequently found on the Naugatuck wharf, having been cut open with a dull knife, and rifled of its contents, except a blank check-book.

Life Insurance history. At the June meeting of the Trustees, it was voted to contribute $250 to the fund raised for the Committee of the New York Bar for the prosecution of corrupt judges.

1873. THE year 1873 was comparatively uneventful in the history of the Company, but was big with events in the world at large. It was a year of disaster and distress upon sea and land. Of all the lives lost on transatlantic vessels between 1841 and 1873, nearly one-third were lost in the year 1873 alone. No less than twenty-one vessels hailing from New York or sailing thence were wrecked, burned or never heard from more. Among the most noted of these were the "Atlantic," the "Britannia," the "City of Washington," the "Erie," the "Ismailia," and the "Ville du Havre." The propeller "George S. Wright" was stranded in February, 1873, while *en route* from Sitka to Portland, Oregon. All on board were

---

Diagonally across the street from the body was found a large, old-fashioned, percussion-lock horse-pistol. The stock had been broken and glued together, and further secured by tarred twine; it was broken again at the old fracture. The bullet had entered his body about six inches below the left breast, taken a somewhat downward course, passed out of his back, struck the fence and lodged in the earth, where it was found. On the following day there was found, about sixty feet distant from where the body lay, a pill-box containing percussion caps, and a bullet about the size of the one which had passed through the body. Near this box was also found an old powder-horn, containing powder. Both the pill-box and the powder-horn were tied up in pieces of soiled cotton cloth.

Query: Was he murdered or did he commit suicide? The first supposition seemed the more probable at the coroner's inquest, and a verdict was rendered that he came to his death from a pistol or gunshot wound at the hands of some person or persons unknown. Subsequent developments seemed to favor the theory that he committed suicide. The facts in support of the latter supposition are as follows:

The deceased was, so far as known, and according to his oath before the assessors in the preceding October, a man of small means, yet he had insured his life during the preceding year for nearly two hundred thousand dollars. He had endeavored to give the impression that he had made considerable sums on Erie Railroad stock, through a certain broker in New York, and that he had a large claim for prize money pending at Washington—neither of which could be verified. Just before his death he told his executor that he was going to deposit some bonds in a safe deposit company in New York when he next visited that city, and that he would leave a memorandum of them in his tin box in the Litchfield bank. This memorandum included twelve bonds of the Connecticut River Valley R. R. Company, and it was claimed that all the bonds of this company had been traced to other owners and possessors. (This, however, was ascertained by the representative of the NEW-YORK LIFE to be not true.) It was also claimed that a few grains of powder were found in the Captain's empty bag, and that it showed an indentation into which the hammer of the pistol fitted when placed in the bag.

The weak points in the suicide theory were—if the expression may be allowed—very strong ones. First, there was the physical impossibility—as claimed by physicians—of a man shooting himself in such a manner and then throwing the pistol across the street with force enough to break the stock. Second, no sufficient motive for the deed could be shown: the Captain's pay as a retired naval officer enabled him to live in comfort; he was suffering from no painful disease; and his domestic relations were unusually happy.

lost. One of her passengers, Major John S. Walker, Paymaster in the United States Army, who had been to Alaska to pay off the troops stationed there, was insured in the Company for $10,000 under Policy No. 58,582, taken in Washington February 13, 1869. The loss was paid August 13, 1873, as soon as the fate of the vessel was established and the claim made.

Both yellow fever and cholera were epidemic at various points in the South and along the Mississippi River, cholera cases being reported as far north as Chicago. The yellow fever caused over three thousand deaths, and the Company paid nineteen losses from this cause, thirteen of which occurred in October. At the meeting of the Trustees held October eighth, it was voted to contribute five hundred dollars to the fund in aid of sufferers from yellow fever at Shreveport and Memphis, where it

---

The deceased held four policies in the NEW-YORK LIFE, amounting in all to ten thousand dollars. The first was taken in 1847, and contained the usual clause making it void in case of suicide; the other three were taken after the clause had been expunged, the last one being for $3,500, and dated March 8, 1872. The Company paid these policies in full on November 25, 1872. Policies were held in nineteen other companies, to the amount of $185,500. These companies made the agent who had negotiated the insurance chairman of a committee to investigate the case, and submitted the facts, as ascertained, to Judge Charles J. McCurdy, who gave his opinion that it was a case of suicide with intent to defraud the companies, and advised resistance of the claims. Upon this recommendation the companies refused to pay, and suit was brought by the executor, Mr. George M. Woodruff, in the Superior Court of Litchfield County, to recover. The case never came to trial, but, after repeated adjournments, the companies compromised the claims against them by paying fifty per cent. of the face of the policies.

The writer hereof had a pleasant interview with Mr. Woodruff during the preparation of this narrative. He said no new light had been thrown on the case since the payment of the policies. The story published in a New York paper, in 1885, to the effect that a dying sailor had confessed to the murder, was acknowledged by the reporter to be a pure fabrication. Mr. Woodruff confessed to being a good deal puzzled in his own mind by the strong array of facts tending to confirm the suicide theory, coupled with the contrary evidence—especially the absence of any sufficient motive. The latter phase was evidently the determining factor in the decision of counsel for the companies to compromise. Governor Hubbard, who was retained by the companies, said to Mr. Woodruff—"How a man with the blue sky above him and the green earth beneath his feet, could ever voluntarily plunge into such a hole, is more than I can see. Only the Almighty himself," he continued, "knows whether that man committed suicide or was murdered." Mr. Woodruff said the money received from the NEW-YORK LIFE was his main-stay in prosecuting the claims against other companies; and he related this incident in confirmation of the danger to the insured of the suicide clause in his policy: A physician went into the office of a life company, said he contemplated taking a policy, and asked if the company paid suicide claims. He was told it did not, and was asked if he expected to die in that way. He said no, but that he had been a physician in an insane asylum long enough to know that men sometimes became suddenly insane without having previously exhibited any signs of insanity. The representative of the NEW-YORK LIFE, however, was convinced that it was a case of murder, and in this opinion he was upheld by Mr. Robert Pinkerton, the famous detective.

was most virulent.* There were over seven thousand cases of cholera and about thirty-eight hundred deaths, and the Company paid eight cholera losses.

The last policy written in 1872 was numbered 94,700, and it was evident that Policy No. 100,000 would be issued during 1873. The privilege of placing this policy was given to Mr. Winfield M. Clarke, Manager for Indiana, who in return offered the privilege to the agent who should receive and pay over the largest amount in new premiums one week prior to the issuing of the One Hundred Thousandth policy. The prize was won by Mr. D. B. Sheidler, of Muncie, who began work for the Company on February first. The policy was issued August first, on the life of Mr. Marcus Claypool, of Muncie, and was a "Tontine Investment Policy" for ten thousand dollars.

From the organization of the Company until 1866 the Company's Medical Department had been under the exclusive control of Drs. Wilkes and Bogert. With the beginning of 1866 the Department received a new accession in the person of Dr. Charles Wright. Dr. Wright had been employed by the Company, during the previous three years, to make examinations in New York and Brooklyn, and had developed a remarkable aptitude for the work. Upon being made a member of the Medical Board, he at once put into practice a system by which lives were classified according to their assumed insurable value, and all examinations were made to conform to the new system. The mortality experience of the Company, as afterward tabulated, showed a considerably lower death-rate in the years following this change.

In December, 1873, the Company, after reviewing the mortality among its policy-holders in certain parts of the South, adopted, in conjunction with several other prominent companies, new premium rates for persons residing south and east of a line beginning at the point of intersection of the northerly boundary of North Carolina with the Atlantic

---

* The number of deaths from yellow fever at various points were as follows: Pensacola 61, Mobile 27, Montgomery 102, New Orleans 225, Shreveport 759, Memphis 2,000, Calvert (Tex.) 125, Marshall (Tex.) 36.

coast, thence running westerly along the said northerly boundary to a point one hundred miles from the coast, thence in a south-westerly direction, continuing one hundred miles from said coast to the thirty-fourth parallel of latitude, thence westerly along said parallel to the westerly border of Alabama (excepting the city of Atlanta and an area within a radius of fifty miles around it), thence northerly along the westerly border of Alabama and along the Tennessee River to the northerly boundary of Tennessee, thence westerly along the northerly boundary of Tennessee and Arkansas extended to the ninety-seventh degree of west longitude, thence southerly to the thirty-second parallel of north latitude, thence westerly along the said parallel to the Pacific Ocean. The climate extra included in these rates was $10 per $1,000 on Ordinary Life Policies, Twenty-Payment Life Policies and Twenty-Year Endowment Policies; $12.50 per $1,000 on Fifteen-Payment Life Policies; and $15 per $1,000 on Ten-Payment Life Policies.

This year saw an important change in the law governing the purchase of life policies. The law of April 1, 1840, authorized a married woman to insure the life of her husband for her sole use, free from the claims of the representatives of her husband, or any of his creditors, except that such exemption should not apply where the amount of premiums annually paid should exceed three hundred dollars. In case of the prior death of the wife, the insurance might be made payable to *her* children. This Act was so amended by subsequent Acts that the insurance in the latter case might be payable to *his*, *her*, or *their* children, and the amount of premiums which might be paid for insurance for the sole use of the wife and children was made five hundred dollars. Such policies, the courts ruled, were not assignable, and could not even be purchased by the issuing company. This sometimes involved hardship to an aged couple, to whom the cash value of the policy was more valuable than the insurance. On June 23, 1873, it was enacted that such policies might be surrendered to, and purchased by, the company issuing the same. On May 5, 1879, the law was further amended so that such policies may now, with the written consent of the husband, be assigned to any person whomsoever. These amendments, however, are regarded as applying only to policies issued since the date of the amendments.

In September occurred the great financial crisis, from which the country did not recover for many years. The immense destruction of wealth by the Chicago fire in 1871, and by the Boston fire in 1872, and the large indebtedness contracted by individuals, by municipalities, and by the unprecedented extension of railroads which followed the war, had laid upon the country greater burdens in the way of interest than could be borne. The gradual tendency of prices to a gold basis wiped out the margin upon which many traders were doing business, and left them no alternative but bankruptcy. The suspension of Jay Cooke & Co. on September eighteenth precipitated the crisis, and the credit of thousands was soon involved in a common ruin. With 1873 the era of prosperity which followed the war came to an end. The stimulus to business which had been imparted by unnatural conditions had spent its force, and there was now to follow a long period of reaction and convalescence.

TABLE SHOWING THE CONDITION OF THE LIFE COMPANIES DOING BUSINESS IN NEW YORK DECEMBER 31, 1873, THEIR BUSINESS FOR THE YEAR, THE SAME ITEMS FOR THE NEW-YORK LIFE, AND THE NEW-YORK LIFE'S SHARE OF ALL:

ITEMS.	FIFTY-SIX COMPANIES.	NEW-YORK LIFE.	N. Y. L's SHARE OF ALL.
Assets	$360,140,684	$24,342,452	6.7
Premium Notes and Loans in Assets	57,628,863	962,113	1.7
Surplus	48,589,757	1,623,288	3.3
Liabilities	311,550,928	22,719,164	7.3
Surplus to Liabilities, Per cent	15.6	7.1	....
Insurance in Force	2,086,027,178	123,672,386	5.9
New Insurance Written	465,614,001	26,621,460	5.7
Total Income	118,396,502	7,456,424	6.3
Premium Notes and Loans in Income	10,764,581	236,327	2.2
Death-Claims Paid	27,124,575	1,446,123	5.3
Death-Claims per $1,000 Insured	$12.83	$11.70	....
Total Paid Policy-holders	66,840,264	3,828,384	5.7
Expenses and Taxes	17,661,182	820,522	4.6
Per cent. to Income	14.5	11.0	....

THE FOLLOWING TABLE SHOWS THE PREMIUM RECEIPTS IN 1870 AND 1873 OF ALL AGENCIES OF THE NEW-YORK LIFE RETURNING OVER $100,000:

		1870.	1873.
Boston	D. W. Russell	$506,299.13	....
"	Stocking & Austin...............	....	$332,994.02
Chicago	S. McElroy......................	170,175.51	248,547.28
"	O. P. Curran	109,414.25	....
"	Curran & Perkins	....	165,616.80
Louisville	Howe & Burdge.................	184,579.17	....
"	R. C. Howe	....	149,628.37
Baltimore........	E. J. Richardson & Sons	183,990.57	153,980.90
Savannah........	J. E. Johnston & Co.............	195,716.19*	148,807.66
New Orleans	J. S. Copes.....................	140,300.32	....
"	Copes and Ogden	....	175,907.96
Memphis	O'Dell & Spicer.................	†	....
"	L. A. Spicer....................	....	128,396.87
Philadelphia	T. J. Lancaster	121,713.27	†
"	R. C. Hill & Co.	†	126,541.21
Leavenworth	Partridge & Hawes	144,552.81	....
San Francisco	Crane & Hawes ‡................		134,004.86
St. Louis	W. G. Bentley..................	207,436.02	....
"	W. L. Hill	....	126,461.87
New York	J. A. Rhodes	179,039.99	....
"	McConnell & Moore.............	....	201,893.09
Montreal	Walter Burke...................	†	223,573.82
Cleveland........	O. C. Kendrick	....	180,910.75
London, Eng.	H. S. Homans	†	159,708.51
Lawrence, Mass...	C. E. Kimball	158,163.62	†

* About 30 per cent. of this amount was returned by B. G. Humphreys & Co.

† Returned less than $100,000.

‡ This firm was formed in 1870.

IX.

EFFECT OF THE PANIC ON LIFE INSURANCE.

1874–1879.

THIS is the dismal period of American Life Insurance. It was a period of great industrial depression and of wide-spread commercial disaster. During the five years immediately preceding, railroad obligations—many of them bonds at high rates of interest—had been incurred to the amount of nearly seventeen hundred million dollars. The increase in State, county and municipal indebtedness between 1870 and 1880 was over two hundred and fifty million dollars. Manufacturing and mining corporations had floated large amounts of securities while the currency was depreciated and prices were high. The day of reckoning had now fully come. During these six years one hundred and seventy-three railroads, with obligations outstanding to the amount of over nine hundred and seventy-seven million dollars, were sold under foreclosure or went into the hands of receivers. The commercial failures aggregated over one thousand million dollars. Nearly fifty national banks went into liquidation, with liabilities of over sixteen millions. Even savings banks were drawn into the financial maelstrom created by the general depreciation in prices. Of the one hundred and sixty-six such banks in New York, twelve went into voluntary liquidation, and twenty-six, having liabilities of nearly thirteen million dollars, failed. In Massachusetts there were eighteen failures—one-tenth of the whole number—with liabilities of nearly ten million dollars and an ultimate loss of nearly two millions. Over nine million dollars worth of real estate was acquired under foreclosure proceedings. The average earnings of all savings banks in the commonwealth declined from over six, to less than four, per cent. The Superintendent of the

Banking Department of the State of New York, in commenting on the savings bank failures between 1871 and 1877, by which he estimated that depositors would lose $4,500,000, said, if the funds of all savings banks had been invested in United States bonds in 1871, the shrinkage would have been $7,000,000; if in the best bank stocks, it would have been $35,-000,000; if in the best railroad securities, over $30,000,000; and if in real estate, from $40,000,000 to $50,000,000.

In such a general financial upheaval, Life Insurance did not escape heavy losses. Nine New York companies went into the hands of receivers, and two others re-insured their risks in companies that became insolvent during the period. Eleven other-State companies retired from the State; two of them re-insured in a company that has continued solvent; six finally went into receivers' hands; and the remaining three voluntarily wound up their affairs.* The liabilities of the New York companies, when they were found insolvent, were nearly twenty-seven million dollars, and the deficiency was nearly seven millions. Other-State companies, by their last reports to the New York Insurance Department, had liabilities of nearly twenty-five million dollars and a surplus of nearly three millions. Somewhat over three millions in assets were held by the companies that re-insured or went into voluntary liquidation, and the premium notes and loans of both classes of companies—which were never paid, and therefore were not lost—aggregated over twelve millions more. During this period there were also nineteen other small companies in the South and West that went out of existence with more or less loss and scandal. The total assets of the solvent companies doing business in New York in 1879 was somewhat over four hundred million dollars. Although careful estimates made at the time showed that the deficiency of failed companies was not much in excess of one per cent. of the total receipts of all companies since organization, and was a mere bagatelle as

*The situation, in 1876, as regards the re-insured and the re-insuring companies, is graphically set forth in the "Life Insurance Tree," reproduced on another page from the "Herald" (a Chicago insurance journal, predecessor of the present "Argus," of Chicago.) Of the eighteen companies which there appear as independent branches, ten have since failed, and one (the National Life U. S. A.) has ceased to be an active company.

compared with the losses in other lines of investment, yet the fact remained that companies holding about nine per cent. of the entire life insurance accumulations of the country either failed or ceased to do new business during this brief period of six years.

The shock to public confidence by these cumulative failures in different fields of investment, was something almost unparalleled in financial history.* The actual losses sustained were aggravated by disclosures of flagrant mismanagement—of false returns to cover up deficiencies; of the enrichment of managers and their favorites; and of hard and unscrupulous dealings with patrons. A single life company had forty law-suits pending when it went into the hands of a receiver. The people were angry and vindictive. A crusade against corporations began, which has continued with varying degrees of intensity and rancor until the present time. Life Insurance was specially singled out as the object of attack.† In nearly every large city there were prominent journals which sought by one-sided and exaggerated statements to cast discredit upon the system—upon all companies, both bad and good. Politicians, who are ever ready to use public opinion for selfish purposes, found in hostile legislation a means of public preferment and a source of private gain. The number of bills introduced in the various legislatures for the regulation of Life Insurance was unprecedented. Many of these were the work of "strikers" and of men who wished to pose as the champions of the people against corporations; many failed of passage, and some were vetoed after pas-

---

*One of the worst features of the financial situation in America is the all but universal distrust of corporate management, whether as applied to railroads or to financial institutions.—*N. Y. Cor. London Telegraph, March 8, 1877.*

† For more than two years the press of the whole country has rung with the story of life insurance failures. A war more relentless and cruel in its effects has seldom been waged against any commercial interest; nor seemingly with greater cause. Public confidence in the business has everywhere been shaken to its depths. Courts, officials and legislatures have been driven by the prevailing sentiment into an organized legal crusade against it, and this ill-starred movement has entailed a greater loss than all the previous company failures, resulting from ordinary business causes, that have ever taken place in the entire history of Life Insurance in this country. The persecution is still actively maintained, and gives little sign of abatement. * * * The greatest danger to life insurance just now is not depreciated securities, nor excessive expenditures, nor fraudulent management; it is in blind legislation, official interference, and the loss of public confidence. The policy-holders' worst enemies are his professed friends, who lend their aid in denouncing without knowledge or discrimination the assumed maladministration of the business.—*Insurance Monitor, February, 1878.*

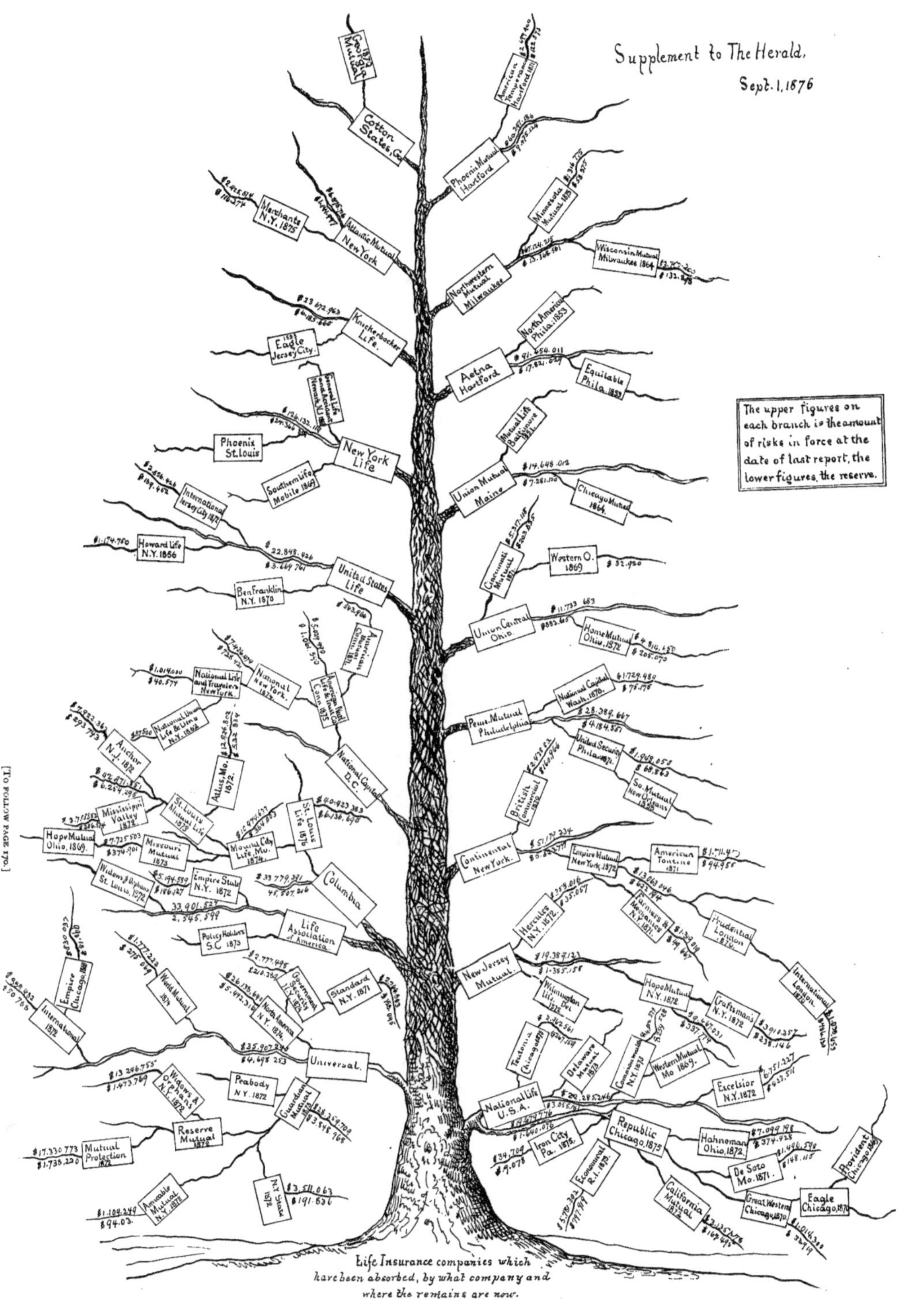

[To follow page 170.]

sage, yet no less than forty-two laws relating to life companies were placed upon the statute books of the various States during this period. The temper of legislators is indicated by the Iowa law of March 8, 1876, which was entitled "An Act relating to Life Insurance, *and to prevent injustice to the assured.*" A compilation of the receipts and expenditures of the principal life companies of the country, from organization to the close of 1878, showed that nearly eleven per cent. of their total expenses had been for taxes, licenses and fees to government officials.*

As a measure of self-defense, the life companies formed the "Chamber of Life Insurance," through which they proposed to act together in securing the favorable attention of the community and in securing just legislation in the interests of Life Insurance.† The reference to legislation aroused the antagonism of some portions of the press, and threw suspicion upon the motives of the Chamber. The NEW-YORK LIFE, although a member of the organization, does not appear to have been very zealous in its support; it did not furnish its vital statistics for the compilation made by the Chamber, nor did it adopt the application and policy forms devised with a view to prevent fraud. These forms included a stringent suicide clause; warranted all statements full, complete and true, and made all statements warranties, whether material or not; and voided the insurance absolutely in case of impairment of health by stimulants or narcotics, residence or travel beyond certain limits, or in case of engaging in forbidden employments. The light in which the proposed new contract was represented to the public may be judged by the cartoon‡, reproduced

* By A. F. Harvey, Actuary of Missouri Ins. Dept., in "Insurance Times," August, 1879.

† The objects of the organization were thus stated by itself: "1. To attract the favorable attention of the community to Life Insurance and its advantages. 2. To promote by all proper means, in any of the United States, such just and equitable legislation as may be in the interest of policy-holders, and by like means to oppose such proposed legislation as may be prejudicial to such interests. 3. To obtain by all proper means the repeal of obnoxious legislation now in force in any of the United States respecting Life Insurance, and particularly all statutes for unfair taxation of Life Insurance. 4. To diminish the expense of Life Insurance in such manner as may be accomplished by means of co-operation, as compared with independent action. 5. Generally to promote and protect the interests of the holders of life policies, and the interests of the associated companies respectively."

‡ For a full understanding of the cartoon, it is necessary to know that the initials "F. S. W." refer to President Winston, of the Mutual Life; "C. T. L." to Prof. Charleton T. Lewis, Secretary of the Chamber; "H. B. H." to President Hyde, of the Equitable; "W. H. B." to Vice-President Beers, of the NEW-YORK LIFE; and "J. G. B." to President Batterson, of the Travelers.

THE SITUATION.

Driver (F. S. W.).—Keep that door shut, Mr. Secretary Lewis. Let no one out!
Secretary (C. T. L.).—Ay, ay, sir! I'll do my best, but they are getting very nervous.
Passenger (H. B. H.).—Look here, Mr. Driver, do you call this friendly or equitable?
Passenger (W. H. B.).—We have never objected to suicide heretofore, but this is too deliberate.
Traveller (J. G. B).—Gentlemen, I always told you that an accident policy was the best.

(Hon. R. J.)—"It seems to me; therefore, that it will be almost impossible for the representatives of the deceased who has been insured, to recov such a policy, if the underwriter thinks proper to avail himself of the defences which the form of policy will afford him. And I rather suppose, there Companies will find it difficult to carry on their business, when the public shall see that the value of the policy rests upon so frail and uncertain a foun upon another page from the Baltimore "Enquirer," in which also appeared an adverse opinion by Hon. Reverdy Johnson. The forms criticised were somewhat modified before final adoption.

Between January 1, 1875, and January 1, 1880, the New York Insurance Department examined all the life companies chartered by the State, twenty-one in number. While the results of these examinations were re-assuring in the case of the eleven sound companies, the fact that nearly half of all were found insolvent, and the scandalous disclosures made with respect to several, kept public opinion in constant excitement and suspense. The Department itself did not escape criticism and charges of malfeasance. Under the law of 1873, bills for services rendered by persons employed by the Department in making examinations were to be audited by the Superintendent and the Comptroller of the State, and paid out of the State Treasury, which, in turn, was to be re-imbursed by the company examined. This law had been passed for the express purpose of preventing extortion by the Insurance Department, and a bill repealing it was vetoed by the Governor during the legislative session of 1877. The Superintendent, Hon. John F. Smyth, disobeyed this law in several cases in 1877, and the Governor recommended his removal therefor in February, 1878. The case was tried before the Senate, and resulted in a failure to remove by a vote of nineteen to twelve. The Superintendent's excuse was that there was no money available in the State Treasury for the payments required, and that there was no way of continuing the examinations except to require payment direct from the companies. In his annual message in 1879 the Governor recommended the abolition of the Insurance Department, and the return of its few necessary powers to the Comptroller's office, whence they had been taken. Nothing came of this recommendation; but the fact that it was made shows the spirit of unrest and suspicion which characterized the time.

The imperfection of the laws relating to the winding up of insolvent life companies contributed much to the loss and demoralization resulting from Life Insurance failures. Those who invoked the law against dishonest managers found they had only exchanged one oppressor for another.* The Continental Life went into a receiver's hands October 25, 1876; its first dividend was declared October 1, 1879; meanwhile three receivers and one referee had been appointed by the courts, after tedious and expensive litigation. The fourth and last receiver was discharged August 11, 1886, to which time $1,396,328.40 had been paid policy-holders, $455,814.29 for receivership expenses, and the balance of assets, which the first receiver reported at $3,949,727.20, in addition to premium notes and deferred and uncollected premiums, had disappeared as depreciation, or been paid out for care of property. The waste and scandal of receiverships became so great that, in January, 1878, Governor Robinson called the attention of the Legislature to the subject, and the annual Conventions of State insurance officials, of 1877 and 1878, passed resolutions deploring the evils which had grown out of receiverships, and pledged themselves to make every effort to preserve the existence of corporations before consigning them to receivers' hands. There are now in the hands of receivers the remains of eighteen life companies which failed during, or prior to, this period.†

Although all of the failing companies but three had come into existence after 1860, and the practices of many of them had been vigorously protested against by the older companies, the public did not make nice discriminations. So long as the new companies issued policies at lower rates, or promised larger dividends than others, people were content to patronize them, and to treat the protests of the better-managed companies as the empty clamor of business competitors; when the crash finally came, the uprightness of the sound companies availed but little to stem the tide of popular indignation and distrust. The aggregate new business of all the companies reporting to the New York Department fell off nearly fifty per cent. between 1874 and 1879; the insurance in force decreased nearly thirty per cent.; and the premium income declined about forty per cent.

---

* Some receivers insist that premiums in all cases shall be paid to them, or the policy must lapse, and very many have so lapsed, because the holders had no confidence that they would receive their money back again. Other receivers refused to accept premiums, believing it to be their duty to wind up, not to run, the company.—*New York Insurance Report, 1876.*

† "Insurance Year Book," 1894, p. 122.

The NEW-YORK LIFE succeeded somewhat better in the amount of new business, and very much better in retaining its old business and income, as the following tables show:

AMOUNT OF NEW INSURANCE ISSUED ANNUALLY, AND OF INSURANCE IN FORCE DECEMBER 31, OF THE NEW-YORK LIFE AND OTHER LIFE COMPANIES DOING BUSINESS IN NEW YORK, 1874–1879:

BUSINESS YEAR.	NUMBER OF COMPANIES REPORTING.	NEW INSURANCE ISSUED.		INSURANCE IN FORCE.	
		NEW-YORK LIFE.	ALL OTHER COMPANIES.	NEW-YORK LIFE.	ALL OTHER COMPANIES.
1874	50	$21,809,389	$329,994,281	$122,835,123	$1,874,401,107
1875	45	21,964,190	277,312,147	126,132,119	1,795,911,027
1876	38	20,062,111	212,603,378	127,748,473	1,608,246,717
1877	34	20,156,639	158,126,978	127,901,887	1,428,203,436
1878	34	15,949,986	140,551,143	125,232,145	1,355,689,078
1879	31	17,098,173	150,767,217	127,417,762	1,312,543,403

ANNUAL INCOME RECEIVED AND AMOUNTS PAID POLICY-HOLDERS BY THE NEW-YORK LIFE AND BY OTHER LIFE COMPANIES DOING BUSINESS IN NEW YORK, 1874–1879:

BUSINESS YEAR.	NUMBER OF COMPANIES.	ANNUAL INCOME.		TOTAL PAID POLICY-HOLDERS.	
		NEW-YORK LIFE.	ALL OTHER COMPANIES.	NEW-YORK LIFE.	ALL OTHER COMPANIES.
1874	50	$8,182,564	$107,550,150	$4,559,421	$60,250,618
1875	45	7,944,363	100,700,721	4,131,137	61,352,803
1876	38	7,729,559	88,629,024	4,242,868	59,082,532
1877	34	7,574,385	78,587,759	4,367,770	56,285,200
1878	34	7,647,887	72,815,112	4,807,593	56,084,654
1879	31	7,887,126	69,813,277	4,821,490	46,825,475

The table showing amounts of insurance written and remaining in force indicates how great must have been the volume of insurance terminated. Times were hard and taxes were high, and there was the ever present spectre of life insurance failures. Although the columns of new insurance include all policies issued, about two hundred millions of which were not taken, yet the lapses in all the companies were nearly seven hundred millions and the policies surrendered were nearly five hundred millions. Upon not taken policies nothing was paid to the companies; upon policies lapsed nothing was paid by the companies; for surrendered policies either paid-up insurance or a cash value was given. The following table shows the Paid-up Policies in the NEW-YORK LIFE, at December thirty-first of each year, the total amounts allowed for surrendered policies, and the amounts actually paid in cash or in cancelation of notes and interest each year upon policies surrendered:*

YEAR.	PAID-UP LIFE POLICIES.		PAID-UP ENDOWMENTS.		TOTAL ALLOWANCE FOR SURRENDERED POLICIES.	PAID IN CASH, NOTES AND INT.
	NUMBER.	AMOUNT.	NUMBER	AMOUNT.		
1874	7,917	$13,410,746	2,930	$2,414,157	$1,539,974.96	$240,172.30
1875	9,205	16,399,395	3,274	2,826,475	1,111,742.01	181,927.81
1876	10,172	18,711,584	3,568	3,324,488	1,107,372.12	219,573.15
1877	10,989	20,200,179	3,846	3,701,462	980,911.61	317,187.40
1878	11,793	21,995,348	3,834	3,805,099	732,999.60	197,382.80
1879	12,319	23,062,489	3,652	3,672,976	516,280.61	167,168.60

The severest test of a life company during this period was the financial test—the manner in which its securities retained their value. The following table shows the NEW-YORK LIFE'S assets and surplus, as admitted by the Insurance Department, at December thirty-first of each year; also the amounts marked off for depreciation, and the market values in excess of book values after such deductions:

YEAR.	ASSETS.	SURPLUS.	MARKED OFF FOR DEPRECIATION.	EXCESS OF MARKET VALUES.
1874	$27,179,395	$4,520,402	....	$331,316.50
1875	30,505,122	5,690,507	....	479,052.95
1876	33,163,715	6,180,973	$205,539.51	580,515.76
1877	34,787,610	6,274,841	473,142.72	504,345.64
1878	36,643,924	6,799,569	97,203.98	623,837.62
1879	38,858,831	7,688,547	135,966.93	811,520.98

The total amount marked off for depreciation was $911,853.14; there was an increase in the excess of market values over book values of

*The present custom of the Company is to report in disbursements only the amounts paid in cash or in liquidation of notes and interest. The reasons for the change will be found in full in Chapter XI.

$480,204.48, and the profit realized on bonds, stocks and gold sold in 1875 was $84,645.60, making a total offset of $564,850.08; the net loss on assets, averaging over thirty-two million dollars, was, therefore, only $347,003.06—or a trifle over one per cent. This included all the reductions recommended by the Insurance Department, as a result of its examination of the Company in 1877.

1874. HAVING made this general review, it now remains to sketch briefly, in their order, the events particularly affecting the NEW-YORK LIFE.

In March, 1874, the Legislature of California passed a law requiring every other-State insurance company doing business there to appoint an agent in California who should, in effect, have all the powers of the executive officers of the company—"any act, statement, representation or agreement" made by him was to have the same force and effect as if done by the company. All policies upon the lives of citizens of that State were to be issued in the State, and be subject to the laws thereof and no other; the companies being required to agree that the State courts were to have exclusive jurisdiction in all cases of litigation. Every company must pay, upon surrender of a policy, three-fourths of the reserve value thereof in cash, within sixty days. The law went into effect July first, and upon that date twenty-nine companies, including the NEW-YORK LIFE, withdrew from the State.

During this year the Company brought to light certain fraudulent practices which had been carried on in Ireland—against English and Scotch companies for several years, and against itself for a short time. Two local agents and two medical examiners had united in a scheme to secure policies upon the lives of invalids, pay the premiums themselves, and appropriate the proceeds of the policies at death. The persons were real, but the papers, including declaration of interest in the life insured, were all false. The matter was brought to light by certain documents which the NEW-YORK LIFE sent direct to the insured, who immediately wrote that they held no policies in the Company. Investigation and legal proceedings followed, which resulted in the conviction of all the

12

conspirators, who were sentenced to from twelve to eighteen months' imprisonment.

1875. IN 1875 the Department of Cuba and the Antilles was established, with head-quarters at Havana. Colonel A. G. Dickinson was placed in charge, and the Department was gradually enlarged to include Mexico, Central America and South America. As the Spanish language is spoken in most of these countries, the name was changed to Spanish-American Department, and it continues as such until the present time. Col. Dickinson retired in 1886 and was succeeded by Messrs. J. Sanchez and J. Merzbacker, both of whom had been long in the employ of the Department. The latter became a defaulter to his firm in 1890, since which time Mr. Sanchez has been in sole charge.

1876. AMONG the thousands who every year witness "Buffalo Bill's" mimic representation of "General Custer's Last Battle," probably few recall the excitement and sorrow caused by the report, in July, 1876, that five companies of the Seventh United States Cavalry, with their gallant commander, had been utterly destroyed by the Sioux Indians. In all the annals of savage warfare in the West, there is no parallel to the battle which took place June 25, 1876, on the banks of the Little Big Horn River,* in Southern Montana. It was a case in which the danger of converging columns and of divided forces, in the presence of an enemy, found a terrible illustration. General Terry arrived at the point of junction at the time appointed, only to find that Custer had fought the enemy two days before, with a divided command, one part of which had been exterminated and the other besieged until the approach of General Terry's force saved them from the fate of their companions. Two hundred and sixty-five killed, including fifteen officers, and fifty-two wounded, were the dread sacrifices of this bloody field.

This engagement cost the NEW-YORK LIFE more than any battle of the Civil War. It had policies upon the lives of General Custer and four of his brother officers, amounting in all to forty thousand dollars.

---

* Now called Custer River.

The names and amounts were as follows: George A. Custer*, $5,000; Captain George W. Yates, $5,000; Captain Myles W. Keogh, $10,000; Lieutenant James Calhoun, $5,000; Lieutenant John J. Crittenden, $10,000; Lieutenant James E. Porter, $5,000. These officers paid the regular premium and had permission to travel and reside in any part of

THE CUSTER MONUMENT ON THE BATTLE-FIELD, SHOWING CUSTER'S CROW SCOUT "CURLEY."

[This cut is used by the permission and courtesy of Chas. S. Fee, General Passenger Agent of the Northern Pacific Railroad, St. Paul.]

the United States, when acting in the discharge of their duties, in time of peace, with the proviso that if they died from any disease contracted outside the ordinary traveling limits named in the policy, the Company might deduct in paying the loss such extra premium as would have been charged had the extra traveling privileges been applied for in the usual

---

* G. A. Custer.

FROM GENERAL CUSTER'S APPLICATION.

course. They all appear to have supposed that the same course would be taken in case of engaging in hostilities, as none of them applied for a war permit. One year's war premium was therefore deducted from each policy in payment. The proofs of death, signed by comrades of the dead, who buried them upon the field where they fell, are affecting mementoes of this tragic episode in the history of the great West. The claims were all paid in November, and were published in the list for that month, in the "News-Letter" for January, 1877. The following comment in the same issue is so pertinent to the loss of valuable lives at any time, that it may well find a place here:

> The recent payment of $40,000 by the NEW-YORK LIFE to the families of General Custer and his brave companions, brings up anew the subject of their woeful fate. The country was aglow with indignation for a few weeks thereafter, and thousands clamored for an opportunity to avenge their deaths. And now we have so far forgotten them that it may seem out of place to refer to their cases as illustrations of the value of Life Insurance. But the more we reflect on it the more it will be seen that nothing could be more appropriate. All the enthusiasm and indignation awakened by their heroic conduct and their tragic fate brought them not back from the dead, and these emotions have long since given place to others awakened by more recent events. But now, when come the silence and the calm, when the world returns to its own and forgets to be sympathetic or helpful, and men are intent each upon providing for his own household, then the life company comes and in the name of the dead provides that substantial aid and comfort which would have been a part of their duty and joy had they lived.

Two of the worst life insurance failures of this period, and several amalgamations no less scandalous, occurred during this year. While the excitement incident thereto was at its height, the following advertisement appeared in a New York paper: "Policy-holders in the NEW-YORK LIFE INSURANCE COMPANY can learn some interesting and confidential information, important to them, concerning that Company, by sending their names, address and number of policies and amounts of insurance to 'Investigator,' P. O. Box ——, New York."

The Company immediately issued the circular, a *fac-simile* of which will be found on the following page. The "Spectator" of December, answering a correspondent who had asked what it meant, said: "This matter was alluded to in the November number of the 'Spectator' and explained as the probable work of strikers, and we have no additional

Office of the New York Life Ins. Co
346 & 348 Broadway
New York Oct. 27. 1876.

To the Agents:

Gentlemen, — Your attention may have been called to an Anonymous advertisement over the signature of "Investigator" which is going the rounds of the newspapers in reference to this Company. We have to say, relative thereto, that in our opinion the object of the Author is black-mail in some way, or to disturb the policy-holders and induce them to surrender their policies, or, for some ulterior purpose to impair the confidence and enviable esteem which this Company enjoys throughout the Country.

We assure you, and through you, all our policy-holders, that if anything had occurred to mar the prosperity of our Company the officers would be the first to know it, — Such is not the case and certain it is that there is nothing in its past and present history that will not bear the most critical examination.

Please send us a copy of every paper in which you see the Advertisement above referred to, — And much oblige

Yours, Very truly,

Wm. H. Beers

Vice Prest.

information or different opinion now. The person who advertises gives no sort of information in response to repeated inquiries both by mail and personally." No reputation was so high in those days but that sharks and wolves in human form sought to snap at it, and wreckers and strikers were continually on the hunt for prey. Policy-holders in failed companies were beset by circulars from persons who wished to represent them and collect their claims; and these communications were sometimes so worded as to give the impression that they were sent by order of the court. How the senders became possessed of the names and addresses of policy-holders, was a question often asked but never satisfactorily answered. It would seem that, either papers in the custody of receivers were not carefully guarded, or else receivers were greatly maligned.

During this year the yellow fever was epidemic at Savannah, although New Orleans, Mobile, Charleston and Pensacola escaped. The NEW-YORK LIFE paid one loss caused by yellow fever, and gave $250 to the fund raised for yellow fever sufferers in Savannah.

1877. EARLY in January, 1877, the Cashier of the NEW-YORK LIFE, while comparing checks paid by the Union Trust Company with the stubs in the check-book, discovered a check for $64,225 for which there was no corresponding stub. The check number corresponded to the number used on the same day, but there was another check bearing the same number and corresponding to the stub. Upon careful examination the check for $64,225 was declared to be a forgery. It was, however, such a skillful imitation, both as to the body of the check and the signatures, that a discovery of the guilty parties seemed quite as important to the NEW-YORK LIFE as to the Trust Company which had paid the check. Much time was spent in unraveling the mystery, when the facts were found to be as follows: A clerk in the employ of the Company had taken from a file of vouchers to which he had access a genuine check that had been paid. From this a noted forger named Becker had produced by lithography a *fac-simile* of the blank check, and the signatures had then been skillfully traced. To get it paid, a letter purporting to be written by an officer of the Company to a Wall Street broker, asking him to purchase sixty thousand dollars worth of gold certificates, was also forged. The letter was sent by a man named Elliott, who represented himself to be from the Company. The broker bought the gold, and in due time received from Elliott the forged check in payment, and delivered the gold certificates to him. The first clue to the guilty parties was discovered in this way: A Mrs. Chapman was murdered in London, and among her papers was found a letter from the Company's clerk referring to other rascalities in which her husband had been engaged, and who, at the time the letter was written, was in Smyrna prison with Becker and Elliott, charged with forging Turkish bonds. Becker and Elliott escaped from prison and returned to this country, and were arrested and indicted with the Company's clerk. Becker turned State's evidence, and produced in court the lithographic stone from which the body of the forged check was printed, and developed the drawing in the presence of the jury; Elliott was sent to Sing Sing for four years; the Company's clerk was already in the last stages of consumption, and the jury, evidently by reason of sympathy for his unfortunate condition and family, disagreed, and he died before a new trial could be had. The Trust Company lost the money paid on the check—less about ten thousand dollars recovered from the conspirators; the NEW-YORK LIFE probably spent more than the total amount of the check in bringing the guilty parties to justice, and in demonstrating its own blamelessness in the matter.

During the session of the Legislature of 1877 life insurance matters were hotly discussed, and so many remedies were proposed that nearly all legislation on the subject failed. There was for a time something like a panic among policy-holders, lest all companies should be found as badly managed as those which had failed. Legislators were beset on the one hand by insured persons who wished an honest inquiry, and on the other by wreckers and strikers who were endeavoring to use the occasion to extort money from the companies. The Legislature called for a statement of various items of loans and expenses, and summoned to Albany the officers of several of the larger companies which had failed to answer certain questions asked by the Superintendent of Insurance, with respect to their own salaries, etc. The information elicited did not bear out the secret charges and open denunciations which had been so freely made, and the general result was to re-assure the public mind as to the general management of the business.*

In pursuance of the plan of the Insurance Department to examine all life companies chartered by the State, an examination of the NEW-YORK LIFE was begun in May, 1877. It was continued during the summer, and the report of the same was made public October twenty-fourth. On September sixth an article appeared in the New York "Herald" to the effect that a shortage had been discovered in the "Builders' Loan Account" of the Company. (As a matter of fact, the Company had no such

---

* Under the pressure of charges that the failure of some three or four life insurance companies was brought about by the payment of enormous salaries to their officials, and other extravagant expenditures, the Insurance Committee of the House was directed to summon before it the officials alluded to (and others), and make them declare under oath what salaries, commissions and other compensation they received. The officials were summoned; they came promptly, took the stand, and were subjected each one to hours', some of them to five hours', examination. Of course, it did not take them all this time to tell what salaries they received. They were subjected to every imaginable question, and it seemed to make no difference whether it was pertinent or impertinent. But the officials answered fully and frankly. There was testimony enough taken to fill several volumes, and these, of course, must be printed, and counsel and stenographers paid. We are glad that such worthy people as the printer, Counselor Moak, and Stenographer Edwards have had the opportunity to earn the money these bills will amount to, and we are very sorry the over-burdened tax-payers of the State are made to suffer. The worst part of the business is that the people, frightened as much at this movement on the part of the Legislature of the State as at the failure of a few weak and poorly-managed companies, have ceased investing their surplus funds in the policies of life insurance companies to a considerable extent. Thus we see an honorable and worthy business interfered with by a Legislature directly, simply because one or two of its members, protected from suits-at-law through their membership, rise in their places and make serious charges against them. There should be discrimination used in judging of charges made on the floor of a Legislature. Members, being human, are as apt to be imposed upon by evil-disposed persons as any one else; and it has been shown in this investigation that the source of the charges which instigated this investigation was one of disappointment and revenge. If what is now known could have been made public at the time the investigation was moved, there never would have been any investigation.—*Albany Press.*

If the Assembly Committee on Life Insurance imagined that they would unearth some startling facts in their examination of the Officers of the NEW-YORK LIFE INSURANCE COMPANY, they have been greatly disappointed. That Company is one of perhaps half-a-dozen that stand in the forefront of Life Insurance in this country, and conducts its business excellently and on business principles. The questions asked by the Committee frequently imply, however, a different opinion. To read the questions by themselves would lead one to imagine that the Committee regarded life insurance companies as in some measure the foes of their policy-holders. It cannot be too carefully considered, during this investigation, that, in a well-managed mutual company, whatever benefits the company, benefits its policy-holders. Wild attacks upon the management of such a company may, of course, do it harm; whatever harm is done will be done to policy-holders, and nobody will benefit thereby.—*New York Tribune.*

account.) The information was said to come from the Deputy Superintendent, John A. McCall (now the President of the Company), and the possibility of a receiver was hinted at. During the day Mr. McCall, who was in Albany, and had not yet examined a single book of the Company, sent for an Associated Press reporter and authorized him to deny the article *in toto;* he also sent the following telegram to President Franklin:

"Herald" article absolutely untrue regarding your Company and myself. Never exchanged a word with reporter or any one else except Superintendent, since investigation commenced, about your affairs.

Truth got her boots on so quickly in this case that the lie was soon overtaken; but the incident illustrates the malignant spirit that was abroad, and the readiness with which reputable newspapers opened their columns to the most damaging reports, without investigation and regardless of the injury that might be inflicted upon the innocent. Mr. McCall had made for himself a reputation as an expert and incorruptible examiner—one who neither received favor nor showed it to any one in connection with his duties—and there were not wanting those who would have been glad to discredit his word and to smirch his fair fame.

The text of the Superintendent's Report was as follows:

INSURANCE DEPARTMENT, ALBANY, October 24, 1877.

The Superintendent having personally, and through the services of the Deputy Superintendent, aided by the force of the Department, commenced and completed a searching examination into the affairs of the NEW-YORK LIFE INSURANCE COMPANY of the City of New York, it affords him unqualified pleasure at being able to announce and make public the gratifying fact that the result of this examination is most satisfactory, and that, from the data in possession of the Department, the solvency of this, or other companies undergoing a similar test, can be readily ascertained, at little expense, for many years to come.

This Company was organized in 1845, and no investigation having been made, either by the Department or other properly constituted public authority, prior to the date when the Department was formed, much time has necessarily been expended to bring the matter to a conclusion.

The services of forty-one gentlemen of character, standing and experience, have been procured, who have valued and appraised the property situated in forty counties in this State and in the State of New Jersey, covered by 2,629 mortgages amounting to the sum of $17,354,847.84, and forty-nine pieces of property owned by the Company amounting in value to the sum of $2,541,576.46; which services have been intelligently and efficiently performed. The abstracts of title to each and every piece of these large amounts of property have been closely examined and reported on to the satisfaction of the Superintendent. All other investments, amounting to $10,311,045.67, have been carefully looked into, and evidence of payment by the Company, either by check or otherwise, for such investments, demanded and given, although many of these payments were made twenty years ago. The cash securities of the Company, the cost of which on the books amounts to $9,730,529.91, are of the most unexceptionable character, and are worth $580,515.76 more than cost.

The Superintendent personally examined these securities, taking the letter, number, and denomination of each security, and preserving the record of the same in the Department. In every instance where securities had depreciated in value, such depreciation had been promptly charged to profit and loss account, and all items of doubtful character had been stricken off by the Company from its assets, and omitted from its reports. Complete ***seriatim*** lists of policies, premium loans, and uncollected and deferred premiums have been made, and are on file in the Department.

Every item of liability, real and actual, or contingent, as sworn to by the officers in the last annual report made to the Department, a copy of which is herein embraced, has been closely scrutinized, and the statements in said report found to be true to the letter, and no other liabilities were found to exist.

The different Departments — Medical, Actuarial and Agency — have been reviewed, with the most satisfactory results — gentlemen entirely competent and assiduous having been found in charge of each branch, to whose conduct and performance of their duties much is due.

Agents collecting funds of the Company at different points are held to a rigid accountability, remittances being required at the larger points tri-weekly, while at the smallest points settlements are not allowed to be delayed longer than one week. Bonds are required where the sums handled are sufficient to justify the same.

The system of book-keeping adopted by the Company, after many years of experience, seems to be perfect, — the checks by one division on another being so complete, that no wrong can be done to policy-holders by false entries of any kind short of wide-spread collusion among many employés, all of whom were found to be exceedingly courteous, and, acting under instructions from the principal officers of the Company, were prompt in furnishing full information as to every detail.

Judged by the hardest test that could be applied under the law, and with every doubtful item eliminated from their resources, the net surplus, as shown by the detailed statement of this Company, which follows, amounts to $5,962,878.79.

This exhibit clearly establishes the fact that where a life insurance company is honestly, ably and prudently managed, there is no occasion to force a showing of solvency by including in its assets prospective value of real estate, and excesses of premium payments to be received.

For the reasons above given, the Superintendent has no hesitation in stating that this great corporation is entitled to public confidence, and its officers to his warmest commendation.

During this year — in June — the Company's limit on a single life was increased from $20,000 to $30,000.

At a meeting of the Trustees held October 10, 1877, it was voted, in view of the valuable services to the State and city, of the Seventh Regiment National Guard, State of New York, to contribute one thousand dollars toward the erection of a new armory for its use.

In November of this year Dr. C. R. Bogert, Medical Examiner of the Company from June, 1845, died at the age of seventy-nine. He was succeeded by Dr. Henry Tuck, who had been for ten years Medical Examiner and Referee for the Mutual Life, the NEW-YORK LIFE, and the United States Life, at Boston, where he had gained a high reputation in his profession.

1878. THE life insurance failures in the United States naturally caused distrust of American companies in Canada, and in 1877 a law was enacted there requiring all foreign companies to deposit with the Canadian Government an amount equal to the reserve upon Canadian policies. This Act took effect March 1, 1878, at which time the NEW-YORK LIFE and several other American companies withdrew from the Dominion. This requirement was subsequently modified so as to allow the funds to be deposited in the hands of Trustees in Canada under a trust-deed approved by the Finance Minister. The Company resumed business in Canada in 1883. Mr. David Burke, a brother of the former representative of the Company, was appointed Superintendent, with headquarters at Montreal. Mr. Burke was subsequently given the title of General Manager for Canada, and still later was made one of the Trustees under the Insurance Act mentioned.

The Legislature of California during its session of 1878 so modified the conditions of its insurance law of 1874, as to give to agents only their proper powers; the surrender value clause was so amended as to conform to the law of Massachusetts, except that the American Table of Mortality with four and one-half per cent. interest was to be used in computing the same. The NEW-YORK LIFE, therefore, re-established its agency there in August. Colonel Hawes again became the Company's representative, and has remained such until the present time.*

*Colonel Hawes was appointed General Manager for Great Britain and Ireland in June, 1895.

1879. DURING the last days of the session of 1878 the New York Legislature passed a bill forbidding the removal of suits brought against insurance companies from State to Federal Courts, but it failed to receive the Governor's approval. This was a favorite enactment with the average legislator of the period, as the companies were by this means brought under whatever laws a State chose to enact. The Supreme Court of the United States, however, decided that an agreement by a company to abstain in all cases from such removal was void, being against public policy, but that a State law revoking the license of a company that made such removals contrary to State law was constitutional. So many requirements were made by the different States that in December, 1879, the Trustees authorized the Officers to change the Company's policies at their discretion to conform to the laws of any State in which agencies were established.

During this year the Company paid several claims that were notable either by reason of the prominence of the insured or of peculiar circumstances connected with their death. Robert Dunlap, a reputable citizen of Lockport, N. Y., who was insured in the Company for $10,000, mysteriously disappeared in November, 1876. The premium due in April, 1877, was paid by his heirs. In August of the same year, evidence having been submitted to the Surrogate of the county showing that Mr. Dunlap had probably been drowned in Niagara River, letters of administration were granted on his estate. Under these, application was made for the payment of his insurance. A bond being given to indemnify the Company in case of his re-appearance, the policy was paid and the last premium refunded. William M. Tweed died during this year, holding the Company's policy for $10,581. When Mr. Tweed made his last journey abroad* he neglected to inform the Company or to obtain a permit—which action, by the terms of the policy, rendered it void. As the permit would have been granted without charge had Mr. Tweed been free to ask for it, the NEW-YORK LIFE paid the claim to his daughters, without question. The Knickerbocker Life resisted payment under a policy on

* He escaped from jail and went to Spain, but was returned by that country as an act of good will.

Mr. Tweed's life, on the ground of a violation of the conditions of the policy in making this journey, and was upheld by the courts.

The Policy of John Kreig, paid in December of this year, did not present any unusual features, so far as the NEW-YORK LIFE was concerned; but the circumstances attending its payment, which are related in the following reproduced extract from the Chicago "Tribune," set forth in a striking manner the Company's uniform action:

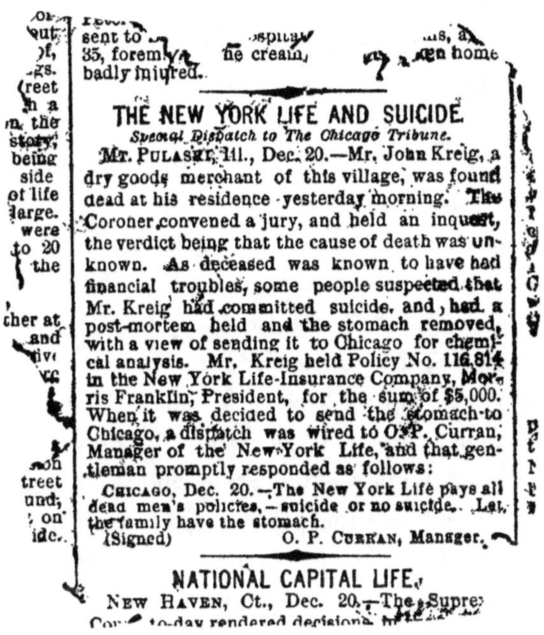

THE NEW YORK LIFE AND SUICIDE.

Special Dispatch to The Chicago Tribune.

MT. PULASKI, Ill., Dec. 20.—Mr. John Kreig, a dry goods merchant of this village, was found dead at his residence yesterday morning. The Coroner convened a jury, and held an inquest, the verdict being that the cause of death was unknown. As deceased was known to have had financial troubles, some people suspected that Mr. Kreig had committed suicide, and had a post-mortem held and the stomach removed, with a view of sending it to Chicago for chemical analysis. Mr. Kreig held Policy No. 116,814 in the New York Life-Insurance Company, Morris Franklin, President, for the sum of $5,000. When it was decided to send the stomach to Chicago, a dispatch was wired to O. P. Curran, Manager of the New-York Life, and that gentleman promptly responded as follows:

CHICAGO, Dec. 20.—The New York Life pays all dead men's policies,—suicide or no suicide. Let the family have the stomach.

(Signed) O. P. CURRAN, Manager.

NATIONAL CAPITAL LIFE.

NEW HAVEN, Ct., Dec. 20.—The Supre[illegible]

It was a general complaint of the period that the life companies were inclined to a rigorous enforcement of the conditions of the policy. There was some ground for the complaint—and some reason for the practice. During the last years of the companies that became insolvent they naturally resisted every claim that afforded opportunity for legal defense. It was, moreover, an era of attempted fraud, and several men were hanged for murders committed in connection with attempts to defraud the companies. Suspicion was in the air, and a wise discrimination was needed to distinguish between cases that could be resisted and cases that should be resisted.

This year witnessed the last but one, and the most extended, outbreak of yellow fever in the history of the country. Deaths occurred in one hundred and thirty-two towns of eight different States. The total number of cases exceeded seventy-four thousand, and the deaths were 15,934. Memphis led the list with 5,000 fatal cases; New Orleans reported 4,900; and 1,172 occurred in Vicksburg and vicinity. The NEW-YORK LIFE paid twenty-six losses caused by yellow fever—the largest number of any year in its history.

In October, 1879, the Finance Committee submitted to the Trustees plans and estimates for the addition of two stories to the Home Office building. Desirable tenants were ready to occupy the additional stories as soon as they were completed, at a rental that would make a fair return on the cost. The plans were approved November nineteenth, and a committee appointed to supervise the work. The new floors were ready for occupancy about a year later, and returned over ten per cent. upon their cost until they were required for the Company's use.

The year 1879 closed the period of disaster in Life Insurance—three more New York companies being added to the list of failures—and it is rather suggestive of the old saw, that "the door is locked after the horse is stolen," to find that, in the State where life insurance interests were largest, laws regulating the proceedings to be taken in the event of an impairment of the funds of life companies, and preventing the forfeiture of policies after three years' premiums have been paid, were enacted during this year. During this whole period the sound and well-managed companies had been kept in a state of constant suspense by the hostile legislation that was threatened, and the volume of talk finally ended with a non-forfeiture law less favorable to the insured than the custom of the companies under a large class of contracts, and in a statute for winding up insolvent companies that does nothing but expedite their dissolution. Under its provisions, one or two companies that might have been saved by careful handling have been "judicially but not judiciously strangled."*

---

*Hon. John A. McCall, in the "Chronicle," December 24, 1891.

The Act of 1877 preventing the re-insurance of risks without the policy-holders' consent, but authorizing receivers to re-insure the whole or any part of the policies of an insolvent company, has never been availed

THE HOME OFFICE AS REMODELED IN 1879.

of by receivers. It is not attributing overmuch wisdom to the actuarial profession to say that, there is not a reputable actuary in the country who, if left to himself, could not wind up an insolvent company with greater advantage and less loss to policy-holders than it has ever been done, or is likely to be done, under the law.

TABLE SHOWING THE CONDITION OF THE LIFE COMPANIES DOING BUSINESS IN NEW YORK, DECEMBER 31, 1879, THEIR BUSINESS FOR THE YEAR, THE SAME ITEMS FOR THE NEW-YORK LIFE, AND THE NEW-YORK LIFE'S SHARE OF ALL:

ITEMS.	THIRTY-ONE COMPANIES.	NEW-YORK LIFE.	N.-Y. L'S SHARE.
Assets	$401,515,793	$38,858,831	9.7
Premium Notes and Loans in Assets	24,632,710	621,403	25.2
Surplus	65,277,722	7,688,547	11.8
Liabilities	336,238,071	31,170,283	9.3
Surplus to Liabilities, Per cent	19.4	24.7	....
Insurance in Force	1,439,961,165	127,417,762	8.8
New Insurance Written	167,865,390	17,098,173	10.2
Total Income	76,174,954	7,887,126	10.3
Premium Notes and Loans in Income	2,265,825	66,589	3.0
Death-Claims Paid	16,892,573	1,569,854	9.3
Death-Claims per $1,000 Insured	$11.60	$12.40.	....
Total Paid Policy-holders	56,007,146	4,821,490	8.6
Expenses and Taxes	10,893,197	1,158,365	10.6
Per cent. to Income	14.3	13.0	....

X.

TEN YEARS OF RAPID GROWTH.

1880–1889.

THE decade ending December 31, 1889—which closed the first century of the Government under the Constitution,—was one of the most peaceable and prosperous in the history of the Republic. The political and financial questions entailed by the Civil War had at last been settled, and the *débris* of the conflict had been cleared away. The Act of Congress providing for the resumption of specie payments, which was passed January 14, 1874, had gone into effect January 1, 1879, without causing any monetary disturbance; and this demonstration of the nation's wealth and sincerity straightway made its credit the best in the world, and gave to business transactions a definiteness and stability which they had lacked for seventeen years. In the South, slavery was dead and had no mourners; the unfortunate *régime* which followed had also passed away. Freed from these impediments, the Southern States were producing larger crops of cotton and tobacco than ever before; new and diversified industries were springing up on every hand; and, under the leadership of such men as Lamar and Gordon and Grady, the New South became in sympathy, as well as in fact, an integral part of the Republic, and a potent and salutary factor in the councils of the nation. There was a New West, also—as there has been in every decade for the last half century—; the population of the newly settled States and Territories west of the Mississippi River increased over one hundred per cent.; their accumulated wealth increased nearly two hundred per cent.; and their annual output of gold and silver was greater than when placer mining was at its best in California, or when the Bonanza mines of Nevada were dazzling the world by their richness.

In the whole country the Census reports show an increase in 1889 over 1879 of eleven per cent. in the value of farm products, of sixty-nine per cent. in the value of manufactures, of forty-four per cent. in railroad earnings, and of forty-nine per cent. in accumulated wealth. The average wealth per capita in 1879 was $870, in 1889 it was $1,039. Deposits in savings banks nearly doubled during the period, and in 1889 exceeded fifteen hundred million dollars. Our foreign commerce showed an increase of almost exactly two hundred million dollars per year, or nearly thirty-five per cent. over the figures of the previous decade, and our exports of merchandise exceeded our imports by nearly fifty millions per annum. There was, during the same period, a decrease in the national debt, from $40.86 per capita to $15.92 per capita; a decrease in the annual interest charge, from $1.71 per capita to $0.53 per capita; a decrease in the total expenses of the national Government, from $5.33 per capita to $4.78 per capita; and a decrease in State, city, county and school debts, from $22.40 per capita to $18.13 per capita. With an increase in the total population of twenty-five per cent., the enrollment of children in the public schools increased thirty-four per cent., the expenditures for public schools seventy-nine per cent., and the endowments for institutions of higher education fifty-two per cent. The average yearly immigration from 1869 to 1879 was 247,212; from 1879 to 1889 it was 524,857.

Yet this general increase in so many of the elements and indications of prosperity was attended with trying conditions in commercial circles at times, and it was only the solid basis of the currency and the general hopefulness of the people that prevented another panic in 1884. The mercantile failures during the ten years, 1870–1879, had averaged about one hundred and sixty million dollars in liabilities per year, reaching two hundred and seventy-eight millions in 1873, and two hundred and thirty-four millions in 1878; during the ten years, 1880–1889, they averaged—on larger transactions—over one hundred and thirty-two millions per year, and in 1884 reached two hundred and twenty-six millions. There was enough danger to induce prudence, and to suggest the wisdom of being prepared for adversity.

Life Insurance shared in the improved conditions and general prosperity. The failures of the previous period had cleared the field of much rubbish and pretence, and the thorough examinations of the Insurance Department had shown that the companies doing about nine-tenths of all the business were well-managed and sound to the core.* There came a time when the people ceased to be frightened by rumors of weakness, or deceived by allegations of fraud. The scandal of receiverships gave the Legislature something new to wrangle over, and attacks upon, and investigations of, the Tontine system of insurance only strengthened that system in popular favor. The old animus against life companies was still strong enough in 1880 to secure the passage of a law taxing certain items of income, but the general belief that the law was unconstitutional made it a dead letter until 1887, when it was repealed. In 1884 was enacted the law requiring the life companies to base their reserve fund upon the Actuaries' Table of Mortality with interest at four per cent., instead of upon the American Table with interest at four and one-half per cent. The law went into effect December 31, 1887,† and although the new method of valuation required the addition of about thirty million dollars to the reserve funds of companies doing business in the State, not a single company withdrew, or was embarrassed by the change. Meanwhile the business grew as never before, save in the five years immediately following the Civil War. The new insurance issued in 1879 had been less than one hundred and seventy million dollars; in 1885 it was over three hundred and seventy-five millions, and in 1889 it was over seven hundred and eighty-five millions. This time the increase came to well-established and tried companies, it was based upon healthy financial condi-

* Of the companies operating in New York, all of them have submitted to rigid investigations, and with possibly a single exception, no one of them can be said to be an experiment. All are believed to be honorably conducted and free from the speculative and litigious management that has done so much in the past to bring Life Insurance into disrepute. To the writer, who has been, by reason of his connection with the Department during the past fourteen years, a participant in the investigations of all the companies incorporated under the laws of this State, and who has had frequent occasion to criticise them, it is a positive pleasure to state that at no time has there been so little necessity for criticism as now.—*New York Insurance Department Report, 1884, John A. McCall, Superintendent.*

† The law was drawn by Hon. John A. McCall, then Superintendent of Insurance, and now President of the NEW-YORK LIFE INSURANCE COMPANY.

tions, and it came to stay. As the NEW-YORK LIFE had felt the stress of the hard times following the panic less than other companies, so it now responded more fully to the improved conditions of business. The general tendencies of the period with respect to insurance written and remaining in force, income, disbursements and accumulations, are shown in the following tables:

YEAR.	NEW INSURANCE.		INSURANCE IN FORCE.		TOTAL INCOME.	
	N.-Y. LIFE.	All other Co's.	N.-Y. LIFE.	All other Co's.	N.-Y. LIFE.	All other Co's.
1880	$22,229,979	$165,274,277	$135,726,916	$1,340,268,256	$8,824,172	$68,579,273
1881	32,374,281	190,208,202	151,760,824	1,388,087,757	10,332,945	69,487,568
1882	41,325,520	216,191,696	171,415,097	1,466,233,775	11,494,144	73,575,990
1883	52,735,564	255,329,329	198,746,043	1,664,983,972	13,207,532	79,355,231
1884	61,484,550	259,825,620	229,382,586	1,641,362,935	13,832,752	83,141,624
1885	68,521,452	309,693,071	259,674,500	1,763,842,988	15,905,141	89,622,723
1886	85,178,294	363,335,948	304,373,540	1,918,039,510	18,831,758	98,029,557
1887	106,749,295	424,421,488	358,935,536	2,115,571,584	21,590,845	109,066,681
1888	125,019,731	506,711,976	419,886,505	2,341,690,623	24,871,174	122,153,257
1889	151,119,088	634,977,653	495,601,970	2,649,075,341	28,830,123	139,354,576

YEAR.	PAID POLICY-HOLDERS.		ASSETS.		SURPLUS.	
	N.-Y. LIFE.	All other Co's.	N.-Y. LIFE.	All other Co's.	N.-Y. LIFE.*	All other Co's.†
1880	$4,499,891	$48,053,184	$43,031,142	$374,919,867	$6,703,968	$62,309,102
1881	5,091,820	47,391,048	47,044,269	382,233,190	7,218,561	62,628,245
1882	6,210,310	46,426,746	50,550,982	399,051,365	7,072,012	66,739,923
1883	6,699,390	49,468,237	55,202,314	416,603,606	7,156,322	70,005,122
1884	6,734,955	51,412,651	58,941,739	432,545,980	6,618,157	71,914,618
1885	7,681,874	53,256,503	66,515,406	457,149,272	9,799,176	79,534,440
1886	7,627,230	53,300,824	74,921,927	485,203,432	11,764,377	85,713,107
1887	9,535,211	58,558,346	82,506,354	513,173,123	11,846,793	60,580,873
1888	10,973,070	63,156,290	92,685,062	549,062,808	13,549,099	65,807,929
1889	12,121,122	67,152,545	104,415,322	592,528,405	15,654,263	71,090,763

*Actuaries' Table with four per cent. interest all years.

†American Table with four and a half per cent. interest to and including 1886, Actuaries' Table with four per cent. thereafter.

1880. THE year 1880 was an uneventful one for the NEW-YORK LIFE in one sense—there is nothing of striking interest to be recorded—but it was a year of diligent work, and of increased business and resources.

The new insurance, insurance in force, income, assets and surplus showed gains of from six to thirty per cent. The total increase of new business by all companies was a little less than twenty million dollars, of which the NEW-YORK LIFE'S share was over five millions; the total increase in surplus was a little less than three million dollars, of which the NEW-YORK LIFE'S share was over one and a-half millions. The Company was now in its thirty-sixth year, and some results of old and new policies were thus noted in the "Record" for that year:

> Two men may appear to have equally good prospects of long life, and yet one die within a month, and the other live many years. For example: Policy No. 7, issued May 19, 1845, is still in force,* while Policy No. 142,835, issued June 24, 1880, matured by the death of the insured just five days afterward. Policy No. 15, issued May 24, 1845, upon a life aged twenty-nine, is still in force,† while Policy No. 17, issued three days afterward, upon a life five years younger, matured by the death of the insured January 13, 1880. The latter policy was for $1,000, and its total cash cost, less dividends, was $406.24, an average of $11.61 per year. If this $11.61 per year had been put at compound interest at 4½ per cent. per annum, it would have brought at the end of thirty-five years only $988.75.

Among the bills affecting life companies that were introduced in the Legislature in 1880, and failed of passage, there were two of special interest in connection with the history of the NEW-YORK LIFE. One of these bills authorized life companies organized under the laws of the State to lend money on bonds secured by pledge of their own policies, such loans not to exceed the reserve value of the policies pledged; and if such loans were refused by the issuing company, any other life company was authorized to make them to the amount of one-half of the reserve value of the policies pledged. Another bill required life companies to attach to each policy issued by them within this State a copy of the application upon which the policy was based. The first of these bills was only permissory—it compelled nothing—and it would have been of great value to the companies and to the insured; the second required what the NEW-YORK LIFE had been doing of its own accord for fourteen years, and had

---

* Surrendered for cash value May 27, 1891.

† This policy was in force on the fiftieth anniversary of the organization of the Company, and was then the oldest policy on the Company's books. Since the above reference to it was made in 1880, the Company has paid over sixty-six million dollars in death-claims.

Worcester. Massachusetts. Jan. 14th 1880

Morris Franklin Esq

President of New York Life Insurance Co. New York

My dear Sir.

It has been my purpose, ever since I received your check, (on Jan. 1st inst.) for $5089.24 cts in payment of my Endowment Policy. No. 919. to acknowledge to the Company the great gratification I have felt, after fourteen years of Insurance in the New York Life Ins. Co. and payment of premiums; in thus receiving the full amount for which I was insured, with the addition of a dividend at its close. This comes at a time when it affords me great help in throwing off the financial burdens which necessarily accumulated during these years that I have been carrying this Policy.

In looking the matter over, I find that adding to the amount now paid to me, the Dividends received from year to year, the investment has yielded me rather more than 4 per cent compound interest, besides giving me the protection of $5000. insurance for the whole period, free of charge.

I also wish to state the complete satisfaction I have always felt, at the manner in which my business with the Co. has been done, through the various agents with whom I have been connected. Reliability, and uniform courtesy and promptness have always characterized them, in their dealings with me. So that now as this Insurance is completed, and I reflect upon the past fourteen years, it is a source of pride to me, that I have been connected with the N.Y. Life Ins. Co. so long, and that I still hold a Life Policy in the Company.

Wishing you, Sir, and the N.Y. Life Ins. Co. still greater success in the future. I remain. Most sincerely yours

George E. Gladwin.

not found burdensome, but helpful in bringing to light errors during the life-time of the insured, and so preventing disputes after his death. Not until the enactment of the Insurance Law of 1892 was a life company of this State authorized to make loans on the security of its own policies; and there is not to this day any statute in New York State which requires a life company to place in the hands of the insured a complete copy of the contract for which he pays his money and upon which the future welfare of his family depends.* As the NEW-YORK LIFE was a pioneer in the matter of furnishing a copy of the application, so it was the first Company to place the benefits of the law of 1892 with respect to loans at the service of the insured by incorporating a loan feature in its policies.

1881. THE year 1881 repeated the triumphs of 1880, and with respect to new business it surpassed the previous year's work, the increase being over forty-five per cent. The time had now come in the history of the Company to make much of what it had accomplished, and during this year was published a complete list of the matured endowments paid by the Company to December 31, 1880. The total number paid was twelve hundred and ninety-four, and the total amount was over two million six hundred thousand dollars ($2,622,824.83). The Ten-Year Dividend Policies, issued in 1871, also matured this year, and with such excellent results that their publication proved the best advertisement of the value of the Company's Tontine Investment Policies, with which they were practically identical. The Tontine options allowed under these policies emphasized the value of a contract that allowed a re-adjustment of one's insurance to the new and changed circumstances in which he may find himself after a considerable period of time. Those who no longer needed insurance were able to withdraw from the Company, receiving as a surrender value the entire legal reserve, and, in addition, their share of the surplus accumulated. Those who still needed insurance could continue their

* A bill embodying this requirement was introduced for several years in succession; in 1881 separate bills were passed, one by the Assembly and one by the Senate, but neither of them became a law. A similar bill introduced in the Assembly in 1882 failed to pass both houses. It looked as if legislators were not so much interested in real measures of reform as they were in those which harassed the companies.

policies and take their dividends either in cash or in reduction of future premiums. The annuity option called attention to this form of investment as nothing else could, and where a policy had been on the Ten-Payment Life plan the insured found himself with a paid-up policy participating in the future earnings of the Company, and a dividend which, by conversion into annuity, yielded him an annual income during the remainder of life. A Wall Street broker, whose name is withheld at his request, wrote to the Company as follows, respecting such a policy for ten thousand dollars upon his own life:

> Ten years ago I took a Ten-Payment Life Policy on the Tontine principle. I paid to your Company a little over seven hundred dollars a year premium for ten years. I now have a paid-up policy for $10,000 and an annuity of $280 per annum, payable as long as I live. I had the choice of commuting this annuity for $2,660, but prefer the annuity and such additional profits as the policy may secure. The advantage to me has been the risk of my life borne by the Company, to the extent of $10,000, for ten years. The policy has been, and will be in future, relied upon as one of my choice assets for my family in the event of my death. I had other insurance on my life ten years ago, and was unwilling to assume the payment of additional premium for life. Now the payments are ended, and I have a reasonable prospect of receiving enough from this policy to pay the premiums on my other policies and keep them accumulating while I live. The results so far are such as I carefully arranged for, and desired to realize, and I am well pleased with them.

In proof of the value of such policies as investments, a policy-holder, who accepted the cash value of his policy, wrote: "Since the date of the issue of this policy I, with others, have learned the sad lesson that the most promising investments may turn out badly. In the case of this policy, however, it is a pleasure to state that the returns are equal to my expectations." Another wrote, under date of November 9, 1881: "From the options now offered me I have selected paid-up insurance and the return of the surplus in cash, and I must say, in justice to your Company, that the results far surpass anything I have ever seen in Life Insurance, and I have for years carried insurance in the largest companies of this country."

During this year ten policies matured which were issued prior to 1852; upon the oldest of them thirty-five premiums had been paid, upon the youngest, thirty. The total amount of premiums less dividends paid on these policies was $20,656.05, and the total amount paid by the Company at their maturity was $36,895.62. For each $100 paid by policyholders the Company returned—after over thirty years' insurance—$178.61. Such results on policies long in force, coupled with the results on Ten-Year Dividend Policies during shorter periods, demonstrated the value of the Company's contracts for any period through which they should be carried to maturity as contemplated.

Among the claims paid during 1881 were quite a number upon the lives of well-known persons. Among these were Rev. Stuart Robinson, D.D., of Louisville, Ky., who was insured in the Company over thirty-two years; Professor Quackenbos, the author of many school-books; William G. Fargo, founder of Fargo's Express Company; ex-Governor A. B. Gardner, of Vermont; Professor O. A. S. Hursh, of Heidelberg College, Tiffin, O.; Benjamin F. Hedges, Principal of the Pope School, St. Louis, Mo.; Isaac Lohman, an argonaut of '49, of San Francisco, Cal.; Philetus W. Vail, of Newark, N. J.; David Carroll, of Mount Vernon, Md.; and, most notable of all—whose death awakened the keenest sorrow wherever manhood is prized and statesmanship honored,—James A. Garfield. Principal Hedges held four policies amounting in all to $7,879. The first was taken to secure a friend from whom he had borrowed money; shortly after he took a policy in favor of his family, and later two more, of which they did not know the existence until after his death. When he was examined the last time, the examining physician pronounced him the best risk he had ever examined, and said he ought to live one hundred years. He died within four months, of *cerebro-spinal meningitis.* Mr. Vail held a life policy for $10,000, and a return-premium endowment for the same amount which would have matured by its terms in 1886. Upon the latter he had paid the Company $40,661.60; dividends in reversion had added $4,421.98 to the policy; and the Company paid the beneficiaries under this policy $55,083.58.

The pathetic circumstances of President Garfield's death do not need to be repeated here. That there was such a man as James A. Garfield, that he was President of the United States in 1881, that on July second

Cleveland. Nov 14th 1881

H C Hopkins Esq

Dear Sir

I have this day received
check from The New York Life Insurance
in full payment of proceeds of Policy
149056 for Twenty Five Thousand
llars on the life of the late James A
rfield. This sum, together with the
ount of Ten Thousand Dollars received
m The Equitable Life Association of New
rk being the full amount of the
surance on his life.

Please accept my thanks
the prompt payment of this sum
thout discount & before the expiration
the allotted time Yours very truly

Lucretia R. Garfield

Mentor O. Nov 4th 18

Morris Franklin, Prest.
New York.

Sir.

I enclose herewith my certificate of appointment as Administrator of the estate of James A. Garfield. We are much obliged for the accomodation proposed in the letter of the 27th ult to Mrs Garfield. Please forward check at your convenience

Very Respy Yours
Joseph Rudolph
Administrator

of that year he was shot by an assassin in the city of Washington, and that after seventy-nine days of suffering patiently and heroically borne, he died on the nineteenth day of September,—these things are all written so large in his country's history that the NEW-YORK LIFE waived the usual proofs of death, and paid twenty-five thousand dollars upon President Garfield's life as soon as letters of administration were granted on his estate. The President's policy was taken in May preceding his death, and was on the Ten-Payment Life table, with Tontine period of fifteen years, and only one premium of $1,887.25 was paid thereon. As it was in favor of his estate, it could not be paid until an administrator was appointed, but on October twenty-seventh* President Franklin wrote Mrs. Garfield that it would be paid immediately after such proceedings had been taken. Payment was eventually made on November 4, 1881.†

Mrs. JAMES A. GARFIELD. * October 27, 1881.

Dear Madam: Your late husband was the holder of a life policy in this Company for $25,000, payable to his legal representatives. We are not at present advised as to the appointment of an administrator, but when so informed, together with certificate of such appointment, we will, without delay, forward a check for the amount due, without awaiting the expiration of the 60 days when the same becomes due and payable according to the terms of the policy. With great respect, I am,

Very truly yours, MORRIS FRANKLIN.

Mrs. JAMES A. GARFIELD. † November 4, 1881.

Dear Madam: We notice in the "Times" of this morning that you have qualified as administratrix of the estate of your late husband. We, therefore, without delay, waiving discount and the usual formality of proofs, enclose herewith a cheque to your order, as administratrix, for $25,000, proceeds of Policy 149,056, upon the life of our late President. Please sign and return to us the enclosed receipts, together with policy and certificate of appointment. I remain, with great respect,

Yours very truly, MORRIS FRANKLIN.

In the "Tribune Life of Garfield," written by Whitelaw Reid in 1867, and published in "Ohio in the War," it is told how Garfield, when a young man, availed himself of the advantages of a life policy to secure a loan made by a friend to enable him to finish his course in college. Mr. Reid says: "He was now (1854) nearly twenty-three years old. The struggling, hard-working boy had developed into a self-reliant man. He was the neighborhood wonder for scholarship, and a general favorite for the hearty, genial ways that have never deserted him. He had saved from his school-teaching and carpenter-work about half enough money to carry him through the two years in which he

J A Garfield

FROM PRESIDENT GARFIELD'S APPLICATION.

During the year 1881 (June eighth) the limit of risk upon a single life was increased from thirty, to fifty, thousand dollars.

On September fourteenth, the Trustees voted to contribute five hundred dollars to the relief fund raised for the benefit of the sufferers from the forest fires which ravaged several counties in Michigan.

1882. In 1882 the Company's first regular Tontine policies upon the ten-year dividend period began to mature. The benefits under these policies have already been explained, both in connection with the adoption of the Tontine plan (see page 155), and in commenting on the results of Ten-Year Dividend Policies, which were allowed the same options in settlement. It will be of interest, however, to examine at this time the results as respects the proportion of lapses under the ordinary, and the Tontine, plans. The tables printed in the margin were furnished by the Company to the Committee appointed in 1885 by the Ohio Senate, to investigate Tontine insurance.

---

thought he could finish the ordinary college course. He was growing old, and he determined that he must go that fall. How to procure the rest of the needed money was a mystery; but, at last, his good character, and the good will this brought him, solved the question. He was in vigorous, lusty health, and a life insurance policy was easily obtained. This he assigned to a gentleman, who thereupon loaned him what money was needed, knowing that if he lived he would pay it, and if he died the policy would secure it."

Ten Years' Tontine Experience upon the Issues of 1872 and 1873.

Tontines.

Policy Year.	Total of Insurances for which Premiums were paid.	Deaths.	Total Remaining in Force at end of Policy Year.	Lapsed—next Premium unpaid.	Percentage of Lapses.
1st	$17,889,000	$114,000	$17,775,000	$3,933,000	22.1
2d	13,842,000	70,000	13,772,000	1,031,000	7.4
3d	12,741,000	76,000	12,665,000	702,000	5.5
4th	11,963,000	69,000	11,894,000	696,000	5.8
5th	11,198,000	68,000	11,130,000	467,000	4.1
6th	10,663,000	70,000	10,593,000	200,000	1.9
7th	10,393,000	122,000	10,271,000	84,000	.8
8th	10,187,000	170,000	10,017,000	31,000	.3
9th	9,986,000	121,000	9,865,000	......	....
10th	9,865,000	66,000	9,799,000	......	....
	$118,727,000	$946,000	$117,781,000	$7,144,000	6.1 Av.

The amount remaining in force at the end of ten years, $9,865,000, is fifty-five per cent. of the amount originally in force.

It will be noted that the first table shows the actual course, year by year, of the Ten-Year Tontine policies issued in 1872 and 1873; the second table shows the actual course, year by year, of non-Tontine policies issued in 1872 and 1873; while the third table shows the course, as to

TEN YEARS' NON-TONTINE EXPERIENCE UPON THE ISSUES OF 1872 AND 1873.

NON-TONTINES.					
Policy Year.	Total of Insurances for which Premiums were paid.	Deaths.	Total Remaining in Force at end of Policy Year.	Lapsed—next Premium unpaid.	Percentage of Lapses.
1st	$19,748,000	$229,000	$19,519,000	$4,734,000	24.2
2d	14,785,000	111,000	14,674,000	2,232,000	15.2
3d	12,442,000	141,000	12,301,000	2,208,000	17.9
4th.........	10,093,000	174,000	9,919,000	1,152,000	11.6
5th........	8,767,000	93,000	8,674,000	983,000	11.3
6th.........	7,691,000	77,000	7,614,000	585,000	7.6
7th.........	7,029,000	82,000	6,947,000	385,000	5.5
8th.........	6,562,000	89,000	6,473,000	210,000	3.2
9th.........	6,263,000	75,000	6,188,000	124,000	2.0
10th.........	6,064,000	106,000	5,958,000	......	....
	$99,444,000	$1,177,000	$98,267,000	$12,613,000	12.8 Av.

The amount remaining in force at the end of ten years, $6,064,000, is thirty-one per cent. of the amount originally in force.

HYPOTHETICAL EXPERIENCE UPON TONTINES ASSUMING NON-TONTINE RATE OF LAPSE.

Policy Year.	Total of Insurances for which Premiums were paid.	Deaths.	Total Remaining in Force at end of Policy Year.	Lapsed—next Premium unpaid.	Percentage of Lapses.
1st	$17,889,000	$114,000	$17,775,000	$4,302,000	24.2
2d	13,473,000	68,000	13,405,000	2,038,000	15.2
3d	11,367,000	68,000	11,299,000	2,022,000	17.9
4th.........	9,277,000	53,000	9,224,000	1,070,000	11.6
5th.........	8,154,000	49,000	8,105,000	916,000	11.3
6th.........	7,189,000	47,000	7,142,000	543,000	7.6
7th.........	6,599,000	77,000	6,522,000	359,000	5.5
8th.........	6,163,000	103,000	6,060,000	184,000	3.2
9th.........	5,876,000	71,000	5,805,000	116,000	2.0
10th.........	5,689,000	38,000	5,651,000	......	....
	$91,676,000	$688,000	$90,988,000	$11,550,000	12.8 Av.

Actual totals for first, second and fourth columns (see above), $118,727,000; $946,000; $7,144,000. Excess of insurance carried in consequence of the Tontine feature, $27,051,000. Excess of losses paid in consequence of the Tontine feature, $258,000. Amount of lapses prevented by the Tontine feature, $4,406,000.

lapses and deaths, which the Tontines would presumably have taken had they been upon the non-Tontine plan. The first notable difference is seen in the much lower rate of lapse among Tontine policies, or in other words, the greater persistency of the assured on this plan. It is to be noted, also, that the Tontine lapses are chiefly in the first years of the insurance, when no surrender value is allowed under any form of policy; hence the losses from forfeiture were not so much as is generally assumed by opponents of the Tontine plan.* The third table, taken in connection with the first, shows the larger benefits to the community of a certain amount of insurance on the Tontine plan, as compared with the same amount on the non-Tontine plan. At the end of a ten-year period the Tontine plan showed an excess of 29.5 per cent. of insurance carried one year, and an excess of 37.4 per cent. in the amount of death-claims paid. As the chief reason for the existence of Life Insurance is the payment of death-claims, and as the same amount of insurance on the Tontine plan results in the payment of a larger amount of death-claims, the plan, by this token, vindicates its right to be considered a valuable adjunct in providing for the

* If the insurance were all taken at age 35 on the Ordinary Life table the forfeiture of reserves would be $182,062.89 on the Tontine plan, and $191,944.68 on the non-Tontine plan. On other forms of policy the forfeitures would be less on the non-Tontine plan in most companies.

Policy Year.	Tontines.		Non-Tontines.		
	Insurance Lapsed.	Reserve Value.	Insurance Lapsed.	Reserve Value.	Reserve Values † Forfeited under N. Y. Law of 1879.
1st........	$3,933,000	$45,150.84	$4,302,000	$49,386.96	$49,386.96
2d........	1,031,000	24,063.54	2,038,000	47,546.92	47,546.92
3d........	702,000	24,984.18	2,022,000	71,962.98	23,987.66
4th.......	696,000	33,582.00	1,070,000	51,627.50	17,209.17
5th.......	467,000	28,645.78	916,000	56,187.44	18,729.15
6th.......	200,000	14,972.00	543,000	40,648.98	13,549.66
7th.......	84,000	7,462.56	359,000	31,893.56	10,631.19
8th.......	31,000	3,201.99	184,000	19,005.36	6,335.12
9th.......	....	....	116,000	13,706.56	4,568.85
10th.......	....	....	....	....	....
Totals..	$7,144,000	$182,062.89	$11,550,000	$381,966.26	$191,944.68

† The law allows a forfeiture of the reserve value of the discontinued policy, during the first two years, and of one-third of such value after three years' premiums have been paid, as a surrender charge.

future of families bereft by death of their ordinary means of support. Nor do the benefits of the Tontine plan end here, as it will be seen from the tables that the actual amount of insurance in force at the end of the tenth year on the 10-year Tontine issues of 1872 and 1873 was $9,799,-000, while had the same rate of lapse prevailed as in the non-Tontine class the amount in force would have been only $5,651,000. This shows a difference of over seventy-three per cent. in favor of the Tontine plan, in the amount of insurance then held by these policy-holders; and as this insurance had now a cash surrender value of the entire legal reserve, the Tontine plan is seen to have accomplished much more in saving the money of surviving and persistent policy-holders.*

At the meeting of the Trustees held on May 10, 1882, the Officers of the Company were authorized thereafter to pay death-claims immediately upon the receipt of satisfactory proofs of death.

At the December meeting of the Board, the Finance Committee presented a special report recommending the purchase of an office building in the city of Paris. The advantages of such a purchase in giving confidence to intending insurers were forcibly set forth and illustrated by references to the experience of other companies, and the estimated cost and income of the present property of the Company, at 16 Boulevard des Italiens, were stated. The Committee having had the matter under consideration during a period of about eighteen months, and the property having been personally examined by one of the members, and the opinions of experts taken, it was voted after full discussion, that the matter be referred back to the Committee with full power to act. In due course of time the purchase was made, and the Company entered into possession in March, 1884. This property now stands upon the Company's books at $750,000. Other property has since been acquired in Europe for office purposes, as follows: Ground was purchased in Amsterdam in August and September, 1890, and a building erected thereon in 1891–2; the

*The non-Tontine insurance lapsing after the second or third years would have had a small surrender value, but on the other hand that in force at the end of the tenth year could not in 1882 and 1883 have been surrendered for its full reserve value.

property stands upon the Company's books at a valuation of $200,000. Lots were purchased in Berlin in April, 1884, and the erection of a building thereon was begun during the following year; this property stands on the Company's books at $425,000. In April, 1885, land was purchased in Vienna, and the building erected thereon was completed in July, 1887; the property stands on the Company's books at $375,000. The purchase of land for a building in Budapest was authorized January 7, 1891, and the building was completed October 25, 1894; the property stands on the Company's books at $565,000.

The Committee submitted, as a part of its report, the following statement of premiums and annuity considerations received through the European Branch Office during the years 1876 to 1882, both inclusive. This statement does not include the business done in Great Britain and Ireland, that having been made a separate department under charge of Mr. J. Fisher Smith, reporting directly to the Home Office:

Statement of Business of European Branch Office, H. S. Homans, Director for Europe.

Year.	Premiums.	Annuity Considerations.	Total.
1876	$162,390.04	$211,909.74	$374,299.78
1877	201,864.04	163,347.89	365,211.93
1878	263,778.51	350,146.23	613,924.74
1879	350,313.35	516,803.84	867,117.19
1880	424,670.05	882,605.97	1,307,276.02
1881	498,360.98	1,216,187.65	1,714,548.63
1882	533,553.74	850,636.93	1,384,190.67
Total...	$2,434,930.71	$4,191,638.25	$6,626,568.96

Early in 1882 the Superintendent of Insurance called upon the stockholders of the Western New York Life Insurance Company, of Batavia, N. Y., to make good an impairment of the capital stock of the company, which had been doing no new business since August 21, 1879. As policy-holders were fully protected the stockholders declined to put any more money into the company, which was notified in November that application would be made for the appointment of a receiver. In noting this action, the Associated Press reporter shortened the name of the company at both ends, making it the "New York Life Insurance Company."

THE NEW-YORK LIFE BUILDING, PARIS, FRANCE.

This report coming to the notice of Hon. Charles G. Fairman, Superintendent of Insurance, he at once addressed the following letter to the Vice-President of the Company:

ALBANY, Nov. 16, 1882.

The assets of the NEW-YORK LIFE INSURANCE COMPANY, as shown by its last report to this Department, are $47,044,269.28, and its liabilities are $37,259,351.37, leaving a surplus of $9,784,917.91.

I do not hesitate to say that, in my judgment, it is one of the soundest and most reliable life companies in the world. The report prejudicial to its reputation arose entirely from a thoughtless and ignorant confounding of names on the part of some person sending a telegraph dispatch to the Associated Press. The dispatch referred to the Western New York Life, located at Batavia, N. Y. It seems just and fair under the circumstances, that this statement should be voluntarily and promptly made by this Department.

CHARLES G. FAIRMAN, *Superintendent.*

Attorney-General Russell added the following comment: "I concur entirely in the foregoing, and no proceedings against the NEW-YORK LIFE INSURANCE COMPANY have been commenced by me or even contemplated or suggested to me."

The Company's annual report for December 31, 1882, showed another remarkable increase in new business—the business for 1882 being nearly double that of 1880. It also showed $36,000 in contested claims, a ratio of one and eight-tenths per cent. of the total death-claims of the preceding year; the resisted claims of all companies doing business in the State were $577,854, a ratio of two and one-half per cent. of the total. As two of these claims against the NEW-YORK LIFE have become famous in insurance annals, a statement of the facts is here given as published in 1883, in reply to attacks upon the Company:

To the AGENTS OF THE NEW-YORK LIFE INSURANCE COMPANY.

Gentlemen: The report of the Company for the year ending 31st December, 1882, covers four claims, amounting to $36,000, which *technically*, under the form of returns made to the Insurance Department, are classed as "contested." As invidious comparisons have been made against the Company, and as these comparisons will doubtless be continued, the facts as to these four cases are given you herein, that you may be ready to meet any attacks on account of them.

1. Wisner Murray, of Goshen, Orange County, N. Y., was insured by this Company on 13th June, 1872, in the amount of $5,000, and on 23d June, 1874, in the amount of $1,000 additional—both policies being in favor of his wife. Both policies provided that in case of Murray's death in or in consequence of the violation of law, the insurance should not be binding on the Company, that being a risk against which the Company does not insure. On 13th July, 1876, Murray, then a man thirty-three years of age, went with his younger brother, Spencer Murray, to the Erie Railway Station at Goshen, armed with a revolver and with a rawhide tucked inside his coat, to await the arrival of the train from New York upon which Mr. R. H. Berdell, with whom he was

at variance, was in the habit of coming every afternoon. It was Mr. Berdell's custom, when arriving, to pass through the station house to his carriage at the rear platform. On the afternoon in question, Berdell, who was a gray-haired man of sixty to seventy years of age, alighted from the train, and started, as usual, to go through the station

THE NEW-YORK LIFE BUILDING, AMSTERDAM, HOLLAND.

house. About the middle of the room he found the two young Murrays standing in such position that he had to pass between them. As he attempted to do so, Spencer Murray, the younger brother, grasped both his arms from behind, put his knee in his back forcing him backward, and Wisner Murray, the insured, drawing his rawhide, rained a shower of blows on the upturned face of the old man, filling his eyes and covering his clothing with blood and dangerously wounding him. Berdell had a pistol in his pocket, and as his arms were pulled toward it he drew it, and pointing it in the direction of Wisner Murray, fired, killing him. As soon as the smoke cleared away, Berdell was apprehended and held to await the coroner's inquest, and his numerous enemies in Orange County, with a very capable and powerful backing of legal talent, endeavored to have it so conducted that Berdell should be declared responsible for the death. They failed, and Berdell was at once set at liberty; and in spite of the efforts of these enemies, no Grand Jury has ever ventured to find any indictment against him. Under these circumstances, when claim was made for the insurance, the Company declined to recognize it, but offered, as a courtesy, to return an amount exceeding the total premiums paid, with interest, upon surrender of the policies. This was refused, and upon the trial the evidence showed that the time that elapsed between the first blow struck and the shot was not thirty seconds, and that at the time Berdell fired he was still being held, could not stand erect, and could not take any aim. On this evidence the jury found that the killing was the natural and immediate consequence of the malicious, wanton, cowardly, unlawful and murderous attack by Murray, a young man in the prime of life, upon an old man, and that by his own act he had voided the policies.

2. Walton Dwight, of Binghampton, N. Y., was insured by the Company on 26th Aug., 1878, in the amount of $10,000, premiums payable quarterly. Fourteen days after the policy was issued, and before the first quarterly premium had been received by the Company, it was learned that Dwight had misrepresented his physical history in his application. As no risk would have been taken on his life if the facts had been stated in his application, the return of the policy for cancellation was accordingly demanded. Dwight refused to surrender it and the Company's counsel was instructed to institute proceedings in Equity for its recovery, but the Court was not in session, and before it met Dwight was reported dead. Suit has been brought under the policy, but has not yet come to trial. At the outset, the Company offered to submit the case to any competent judge mutually agreed upon, and abide by his decision, but the offer was not accepted. This case is somewhat widely known from the facts that Dwight, at the time the Company's policy was issued, took out insurance amounting to some $250,000 in some twenty-one companies; that the premiums were all payable quarterly; that he was without means to pay the second quarterly premiums; that he was reported dead on the 15th November, 1878, a few days before these second quarterly premiums became due; that the circumstances attending his reported death were such that it is charged that he either committed suicide or is still living, and that in either case the entire transaction was a deliberate conspiracy to defraud the insurance companies; that with few exceptions the companies interested refused to pay the insurance; that suits have been instituted against all of them, and that none have come to trial, although it is over four years since Dwight was reported dead. It is hardly necessary to say that the question of suicide does not concern the NEW-YORK LIFE, and that if there had been no other question the Company would have promptly paid the claim. The claim is resisted upon the ground that the policy was never properly in force, having been issued upon misrepresentations, ***and no premium having ever been received by the Company.***

3. John W. Hillmon, of Lawrence, Kansas, was insured by the NEW-YORK LIFE under two policies, on 30th November and 10th December, 1878, each in the amount of $5,000, premiums payable semi-annually. About the same time he took out $5,000

in the Connecticut Mutual Life, and $10,000 in the Mutual Life of New York. On 27th March, 1879, he was reported as having been accidentally shot dead, in Southern Kansas, by his partner, one J. H. Brown, while on their way to locate a cattle ranche. Simultaneously with the report of his death came a report that he was not dead, that

THE NEW-YORK LIFE BUILDING, BERLIN, GERMANY.

another body had been substituted for his, and that the affair was a conspiracy to defraud the insurance companies. An inquest had been held at Medicine Lodge, Kansas, near the place of reported death, a verdict given, upon the evidence of his partner, of accidental death by shooting, and the supposed remains buried, but they were disinterred and brought to Lawrence, Kansas, where a second inquest was held. From the evidence presented at this inquest, and from other information, including a confession made by the man Brown but subsequently retracted, the companies interested were satisfied that Hillmon and others conspired to defraud the three companies; that the man whose remains were claimed to be Hillmon's was one F. A. Walters, of Fort Madison, Iowa, who had been murdered for that purpose, and that Hillmon was still living. A trial of the case, with all the evidence that could be brought by the claimant, failed to establish any claim, the jury disagreeing, and the presiding judge so plainly evincing his belief, upon the evidence, that Hillmon was not dead, that the claimant declines another trial before him upon the ground that he has prejudged the case. It therefore remains upon the docket awaiting further action on the part of the plaintiff.

4. C. S. Alford, of St. Louis, Mo., was insured by the Company on 22d December, 1877, in the amount of $10,000. He died on 25th September, 1880. The proofs of death show that he died from diabetes, and that he had been treated for that disease before his application to the Company. That application stated he had never had kidney or any other serious disease; that he had never been sick, and had no family physician. Enquiry as to this disagreement elicited the facts that *on the same day* he applied to the NEW-YORK LIFE, he also made application to the Penn Mutual Life Insurance Company for insurance; that in his application to that company he acknowledged having had diabetes and having been treated for that disease. As this Company would not have insured Mr. Alford if his application had stated the facts, it offered to return the premiums paid, with interest, upon surrender of the policy for cancellation, and this offer not having been accepted, and suit having been brought, the Company declines to pay the claim until its liability has been judicially determined.

Attention is called to the fact that when a claim is once disallowed it appears as resisted in every report thereafter until settled, and, consequently, as the same claims appear over and over again, the Company is unjustly credited with these claims as newly-contested every year they appear. Thus the Murray claim has been in every report for six years, the Dwight claim for four years, the Hillmon claim for three years, leaving the Alford claim of $10,000 as the only new claim resisted in 1882, while the Company's report shows $36,000 in claims resisted. As a matter of fact, during the five years ending 31st December, 1882, it has disallowed claims amounting to $72,500, and so fair have been the reasons assigned therefor that not one of them has been decided against the Company, while during that time it has paid nearly nine millions of dollars ($8,957,746.52) in death-claims, without question.

The Dwight case was in the courts, under a test suit brought against the Germania Life Insurance Company, until 1887, when the New York Court of Appeals decided in favor of the company.* The Hillmon case has been tried four times. On the first two trials the jury disagreed. On the third, a death in the Walters' family prevented the introduction of testimony respecting F. A. Walters; a letter of his, offered in evidence by the Company, was ruled out, and the verdict was for the plaintiff. The

* Col. Walton Dwight has been seen in Chicago recently, according to the statement of Thomas Grannin, a commercial traveler. Grannin says that he knew Dwight well before his alleged death November 15, 1878, and cannot be mistaken.—*The Weekly Underwriter, August 10, 1895.*

Supreme Court of the State overruled this decision and ordered a fourth trial—in which the jury disagreed again. This case was examined by the Insurance Officials of seven States, in 1894, and six of them pronounced it a fraud; the seventh declined to approve it.

THE NEW-YORK LIFE BUILDING, VIENNA, AUSTRIA.

1883. THE marked success of the Tontine plan, as shown by the settlement of matured Tontines in 1882, made the plan and the Company objects of attack both in the Legislature and in the courts.

Resolutions calling for an investigation of the companies doing a Tontine business were introduced in both houses at Albany early in 1883, and the information asked for was significant. The companies were to report all the details of their Tontine business, including a list of all Tontine policies issued, *with the names of the insured,* etc. It was openly charged that the resolution was drawn by a New York lawyer, who was thus fishing for clients among holders of lapsed policies. The resolutions never got further than the committee stage, because the Insurance Committee of the Assembly demanded that some one should give a reason why they should be adopted. They invited the advocates of the resolution and representatives of the companies to appear before them, but none of the former responded. The Committee therefore reported that no grievance had been shown calling for action on the part of the Legislature.

The attacks in the courts were made to compel the return of premiums and for damages where policies had been allowed to lapse, on the ground that the Company had not carried out in good faith the plan as set forth in the prospectus. Two suits were brought under different policies by the same attorney—one in the Supreme Court of Brooklyn, and one in the Court of Common Pleas of New York. In the Brooklyn case* the court overruled the demurrer of the Company that the plaintiff, not having completed his part of the contract, had no cause of action, and this judgment was affirmed by the General Term in February, 1883, and the case sent to trial. Upon the trial, in January, 1885, the Company's books were produced, and Mr. Rufus W. Weeks, then mathematician of the Company, testified as to the method in which the Tontine accounts were kept. The judge thereupon dismissed the complaint with costs, stating that it was clear from the evidence and the books that the Company had complied with its contract in every particular. In the New York case† the demurrer of the Company was sustained, and the decision of the General Term affirmed the judgment of the lower court. The case was taken to the Court of Appeals, where the judgment was affirmed in

* Simons *vs.* NEW-YORK LIFE INS. CO.

† Bogardus *vs.* NEW-YORK LIFE INS. CO.

January, 1886. When the decision of the General Term of the Supreme Court was made, in February, 1883, sending the case to trial, the opponents of the Tontine plan seem to have carefully laid their plans in ad-

THE NEW-YORK LIFE BUILDING, BUDAPEST, HUNGARY.

vance to have the report of the case appear in the newspapers as if it had already been tried on its merits and the averments of the complaint proved true. These reports, with flaming head-lines and misleading comments, were reprinted in circular form and scattered far and wide. In order to give them the odor of respectability, some of them concluded by commending the policies of the Mutual Life Insurance Company, but that company promptly and indignantly disavowed their authorship. From the manner in which the attacks in court were coupled with the resolutions introduced in the Legislature, the public were justified in believing that they had a common origin.* A third case† was brought in the Court of Common Pleas of New York by a policy-holder who had completed his payment of premiums and was dissatisfied with the result of his policy; an accounting was demanded showing how the amount apportioned to his policy had been arrived at. Although the Company makes no secret of the method by which surplus is apportioned to Tontine policies, and has published a full account of it, yet to do this in detail, with every policy-holder who demanded it, would involve a vast amount of labor to no purpose. This case was first tried before a judge, without a jury, and decided in favor of the plaintiff. The General Term reversed this decision, and the Court of Appeals affirmed the decision of the General Term. It was held that, in the absence of any evidence of a want of equity, the plaintiff was not entitled to an accounting. It is difficult to see how great corporations could do business at all if any other theory prevailed. A railroad, or a bank, or a telegraph or telephone company, could not permit its records to be ransacked and its apportionments of surplus to be questioned by every dissatisfied stockholder, without annoyance that would speedily prove intolerable. The Trustees of a purely mutual life company have every inducement to be fair and to make as large dividends as possible, and at the same time provide for the undoubted solvency of the company.

At the meeting of the Trustees held on May 9, 1883, the Officers represented that by reason of the decline in interest rates capitalists were

---

* The inevitable trouble in regard to Tontine life insurance has arrived, and the victims are appealing to the Legislature to investigate the system, and the Supreme Court has been called upon to see that justice be done to the victims.—*Anonymous Circular.*

† Uhlman *vs.* NEW-YORK LIFE.

becoming interested in Life Insurance as an investment, and that a sufficient number of large risks could probably be obtained to give a satisfactory average; also that a careful review of the total re-insurance effected by the Company from organization showed that it would have been perfectly safe in carrying its own risks; it was thereupon voted to increase the limit of risk upon a single life from fifty, to seventy-five, thousand dollars.

In August, 1883, Dr. Charles Wright, the senior Medical Director of the Company, who had been in failing health for some months, was given a leave of absence for six months. He at once sailed for Europe, but the voyage only aggravated his condition, and he died of Bright's Disease on September second, a day or two after landing in London. Dr. Wright had been connected with the Company for over twenty years; since January 1, 1866, he had been a member of the Medical Board; and since the death of Dr. Bogert, in 1877, he had been the Chief Medical Director. He was also elected a Trustee during the same year. He was a man of good professional ability, of great energy and industry, and had a natural aptitude for the duties connected with his office. At the meeting of the Trustees held on September eleventh, resolutions were adopted expressive of the loss sustained by the Board and the Company.

The great age of President Franklin and the rapidly-increasing business of the Company made necessary during this year an increase in the executive staff, and the Finance Committee, to whom the subject was referred in November, reported on December twelfth, recommending that the office of Second Vice-President be created, and nominating Dr. Henry Tuck for the position. The recommendation was adopted, and Dr. Tuck was elected.

The death-claims paid in 1883, for the second year in the Company's history, exceeded two million dollars within twelve months. Among the six hundred and odd claims there were many that illustrated in a striking manner the value of Life Insurance to the family and to the estate of the insured; two cases will suffice as examples; the account of the first is taken from the "News-Letter" for August, 1883:

During the month of April an acquaintance entered the office of the Editor of the "News-Letter" bearing a letter from a lady whose husband's name appears in the list of death-claims paid in April. The letter said that she was greatly in need of the insurance on her husband's life, as, among other heavy expenses, she would be obliged to pay two hundred dollars for a lot to bury him in—for the want of which he was then lying in the cemetery vault. Would her correspondent kindly see if anything could be done to expedite the payment of the policy? Upon investigation, it was found that the delay was caused by the failure of the family physician to complete and return to the Company proofs of death. Fortunately, these proofs arrived on the following day, and on the day after the check went to the widow.

The other claim was that under the policies of Colonel Verling K. Hart, of Wyoming, the full significance of which did not transpire until several years later, when a member of the family wrote Mr. C. W. Moore, the Company's Manager at Detroit, through whom the insurance was originally effected, that the money paid on the NEW-YORK LIFE'S policies saved an estate which afterward proved to be worth over a million dollars.

1884. THE Company had now been settling matured Tontine policies for two years, with larger cash results than those attained by any other company on policies running through the same period of time, and with such other options in settlement as made its Tontines—to a large class of people—the most desirable policies issued. Although, as has been shown, the aggregate forfeitures under this plan were but little more than under the ordinary plan, owing to the greater persistency of holders of Tontine policies, yet there was opportunity for cases of individual hardship such as the general spirit and scope of Life Insurance seeks to mitigate or prevent. As the Tontine method of deferring dividends and compounding surplus and the options in settlement at the end of Tontine periods included the substance of the plan, it was now determined to issue a Limited-Tontine Policy with the same non-forfeiture conditions as policies on the non-Tontine plan. This policy was announced with the beginning of the year 1884.*

* What people *fear may happen*, rather than what actually will happen, often properly determines their action, and the number of persons who have been deterred from taking Tontine policies from *fear* of forfeiture has probably been far greater than the number who have forfeited their policies from inability to pay the premiums. This caution is so entirely praiseworthy that, to meet the wishes of the large class who desire Tontine Benefits without the risk of forfeiting their policies, the NEW-YORK LIFE announces that it will begin, with 1884, the issue of a Non-forfeiting Limited-Tontine Policy. This

The correspondent of the "Spectator," writing from Albany under date of January 14, 1884, said: "The Insurance Committees of both houses are more favorable to the important interest of insurance than usual. * * * They will be more likely to treat insurance, both life and fire, as one of the legitimate lines of business, rather than an interest to be preyed upon." Under date of February eleventh the same writer reported the introduction in the Senate of resolutions requiring the NEW-YORK LIFE to report to the Committee on Insurance the investments made by the Company since January 1, 1874, the amount of real estate owned, and the amount of judgments held for deficiencies, together with all details of persons, places, fees, etc., in connection therewith, and authorizing the Committee, if deemed proper, to examine the Company.* Under date of February twenty-fifth he wrote: "Senator Coggeshall on Thursday last introduced the annual resolution calling upon the Equitable and NEW-YORK LIFE companies for a particular detailed statement about Tontine policies, covering the entire period during which each company has issued such policies. As the resolution was being read, one of the senators turned to his colleague, and said: 'Do you hear the bell tinkle?'† The Senate, by a decisive vote, referred the resolution to the Insurance Committee as the best mode summarily to dispose of it." No action was taken on either of these subjects; reference is made to them here to show the hostility to which the Company and the Tontine plan were subjected.

The death of Mr. William Barton, a member of the Board of Trustees, on September 1, 1884, calls for something more than formal notice. Mr. Barton had been a Trustee since 1849, was chairman of the committee which superintended the erection of the Company's present building, and for over twenty-one years was chairman of the Finance Committee.

---

policy has the ordinary Tontine Options and Benefits, and is non-forfeiting according to the terms and conditions specified in the policy, which are the same as those of policies not Tontine.—*Extract from Circular, January 1, 1884.*

* It will be remembered the Company was examined by the Insurance Department in 1877.

† One of the fads of the day was a small bell in the shape of a chestnut worn on the watch chain, to be rung when a threadbare story was told.

To him was due much of the skill and success with which the Company's funds were handled during the Civil War and the trying times subsequent thereto. He was a gentleman of the old school, who felt the importance of his trusteeship, and labored unremittingly to discharge the duties growing out of so sacred a trust. On one occasion, a would-be borrower made to him a proposition which to Mr. Barton's mind seemed like an attempt to bribe him; although nearly eighty years of age, he was with difficulty restrained from committing a personal assault upon the offender.

In December of this year the Officers represented to the Trustees that the experience of the NEW-YORK LIFE and of other companies fully demonstrated that insurances upon individual lives to the amount of one hundred thousand dollars were not only desirable as average risks, but that as a class such policies were more likely to be continued to the end of their respective terms than policies for smaller amounts. It was therefore voted to increase the limit of risk upon a single life to one hundred thousand dollars.

Among the death-claims paid in 1884 were thirty-one policies that had been in force over thirty years, and sixty-seven policies that had been in force less than one year. The premiums, less dividends, on the older policies were $64,176, and the amount paid under them was $91,157. A case, illustrating several points, was thus described in the Company's publications of the time:

In 1866 a gentleman, then forty-nine years of age, insured in the Company for $20,000 on the Ten-payment Life plan—a plan, observe, upon which a man can soon pay up his policy. Two years later he took $15,000 additional with the Company, on the same plan. In 1871 he took paid-up policies for both, his paid-up insurance being about $15,000, upon which he has since received annual dividends. During the past year he died. One week after his death the Company received notice thereof, and with the notice came an order from the widow, duly executed, empowering and directing the Company to pay over to the Tax Collector of the city wherein she lived ***over six thousand dollars***, his receipt therefor to be a full discharge in that amount of the Company's obligations to her under her husband's policies. Tax bills were inclosed, showing that the amount was due upon four pieces of real estate, the assessed value of which was nearly four hundred thousand dollars, and that the property was to be sold for taxes within four days. The Company was asked to give to the Tax Collector such assurance of the validity of the claim as would secure the withdrawal of the property from sale. This the Company was able to do, and a few days later formal proofs of death were presented, the taxes were paid, and the balance paid to the widow.

1885. THE year 1885 was destined to see the controversy between the Tontine, and non-Tontine, plans revived in another form, and to draw into the discussion the managers of the leading companies and the Legislatures of two great States. The President of the Connecticut Mutual Life Insurance Company, in his annual report for 1884, published in the New York "Tribune" of March 22, 1885, assailed the plan with great bitterness, denouncing Tontine policies as "gambling" contracts. Life Insurance was declared to have but "a single function—the distribution among the heads of families of the loss incurred by each family in the death of its head." These strictures were replied to by the officers of the NEW-YORK LIFE, of the Equitable and of the Mutual, the latter company having begun in 1884 the issue of a five-year distribution policy, with essentially the same features as the non-forfeiting Tontines. As the Vicar of Wakefield said of his discussion with his neighbor: "It was managed with proper spirit on both sides. He asserted that I was heterodox; I retorted the charge; he replied; and I rejoined." In neither case could the personal element be eliminated. Tontine insurance in its various forms had been before the public for fifteen years; the companies practicing it were the growing companies; the results of maturing classes, while not showing as large results as had been predicted, were yet better than on any other plan; and—most important of all—people would take Tontine policies when they would not insure at all on the ordinary plan, and would keep Tontine policies in force when other policies would be dropped.* For the president of a company that had not only fallen hopelessly short of the results attained by its competitors, but also of its own

* It was charged that large amounts of Tontine insurance were written chiefly in order that it might lapse; but if this were true, the plan miscarried. The new insurance paid for in the NEW-YORK LIFE from 1872 to 1883, both inclusive, was $274,706,944 (not all of which was Tontine), and the lapses from 1873 to 1884, both inclusive, were $86,367,524, a ratio of 31.4 per cent. During the same period the paid-for issues of the Connecticut Mutual were $142,001,775, and the lapses were $54,877,295, a ratio of 38.6 per cent.

previous record,—to bring a railing accusation against Tontine policies at this late day, seemed too much like an afterthought to solace failure.

The specific charge that the old form of Tontine policy was a gambling contract, had been expressly dissented from by the Supreme Court, in the Simons case already noted;* while the larger proportion of lapses under the ordinary plan and the larger amount of death-claims paid under the Tontine plan, showed the greater public benefits under the latter. The "single function" theory of Life Insurance was only an assumption, made to preclude the legitimacy of the benefits which the Tontine plan provided for policy-holders who survived certain periods. This theory would exclude all endowment policies—which the Connecticut Mutual had issued for many years—and was inconsistent with any cash surrender values on life policies, although a guarantee of such values had been introduced into the Connecticut Mutual's policies for the first time in the year the NEW-YORK LIFE'S Tontines began to mature (1882). Although President Green has renewed the assault upon all forms of long dividend-period policies in several of his annual reports since 1885, the impression made upon the public mind and upon the progress of this plan of insurance seems to have been practically *nil.* Nearly all the life companies, except those organized under the laws of Massachusetts, now issue policies on this plan, and the companies adopting it do about eighty per cent. of the total business.

The philippic of the Connecticut Mutual's President in 1885 had, however, one result which he probably did not anticipate or desire, and for which he should not be held responsible. The New York Legislature being then in session, resolutions were introduced in the Assembly, March twenty-fifth, citing the statements made by President Green in the "Tribune," and providing for a Special Committee to ascertain the nature of the Tontine plan and to report what legislation, if any, was necessary in relation thereto. The Committee on Insurance was entirely ignored, and

*It was claimed by the counsel for the appellant, on the argument, that this insurance contract was a gambling contract. * * * We cannot assent to this view.—*Judge J. O. Dykman, re Simons vs. New-York Life.*

a proposition to refer the matter to Superintendent McCall, of the Insurance Department, was voted down. The resolutions were passed and the Committee was ordered to report within ten days. They came to New York, called a few witnesses, and at the expiration of ten days asked the Assembly for an extension of time. The appointment of the Committee had been characterized from the first, by correspondents of the leading newspapers of the State who were on the spot, as "a strike of the lobby," "a raid of the black horse cavalry," and "an alliance of the thieves and the noodles." It was found that one of its members and the "expert actuary" employed by it were agents of the Connecticut Mutual. The Tontine companies showed no fear of the investigation and no disposition to purchase immunity from it. The Assembly, which had been deaf to appeals to reason and propriety, was apparently susceptible to the keener shafts of ridicule, and the Committee's request for an extension of time was refused. Their report was published in full—evidently as paid matter—in the New York "Tribune" of May twenty-sixth. It was chiefly an effort to justify the Committee's appointment, and closed with a recommendation that the law of 1879, providing for a surrender value for life insurance policies, after the payment of three annual premiums, should be so amended as to prohibit all companies from issuing policies that did not provide for a surrender value. No action was taken on the recommendation. The non-forfeiting Tontines, already adopted by the companies, made such legislation unnecessary, and this form soon after came to be issued exclusively.

An Investigating Committee was appointed by the Ohio Senate, on April 15, 1885, instigated, according to the preamble to the resolutions adopted, by complaints in Ohio against "the unjust plans and methods of the Tontine insurance business as conducted by such companies foreign to Ohio," and by the "startling exposures recently made by the leading journals of this and other States of such plans and methods." The Insurance Commissioner of the State was made a member of the Committee, and Mr. Sheppard Homans, of New York, was appointed special assistant. This Committee made a thorough investigation of the plans and methods of all life companies doing business in Ohio on the Tontine plan, and were given every facility by the companies for forming an intelligent opinion as to its actual working and results. Their report —embracing the testimony taken and the Committee's conclusions—was made in August, 1885. "Every person in favor of, or opposed to, the Tontine plan, of whom knowledge was furnished the Committee, was examined, and whatever information was obtained in this direction will be found in the record." Comments upon the evidence by the three senators, and a *resumé* of the same by Superintendent Reinmund and Actuary Homans, follow the testimony. The senators refused to condemn Tontine or semi-Tontine insurance, saying that insurance officials equally conscientious and competent differed on this point, and that it was a question for individuals, rather than the public, to determine. They expressed the opinion that the alleged misapplication of surplus Tontine funds had caused much of the controversy,* but declared that "no evidence was furnished the Committee of corrupt diversion of funds, or intentional covering up of anything of interest either to the policy-holder or the public."†

The following extracts from the conclusions of Messrs. Reinmund and Homans, cover the essential points in dispute:

(1) *As regards the charge that Tontine insurance is a gambling scheme.*—Gambling, as usually understood, is a scheme by which one gets something for nothing—where no valuable consideration is given by the winner to the loser—where the gain to one is precisely offset by the loss to the other—and where the gain or loss depends, not on the will or power of either party, but rather upon mere chance or skill. It is usually condemned as a vice, as subversive of public morals, as wicked and unlawful. Nothing in the evidence obtained by the Committee shows, or even tends to show, that such grave charges can justly be brought against Tontine life insurance. On the contrary, the evidence clearly proves that Tontine companies derive solid advantages from Tontine contracts, and can safely promise, and in fact do give, great and solid benefits to Tontine

* These allegations were made chiefly by anonymous circulars, and by sensational newspapers at the instigation of others than policy-holders. The NEW-YORK LIFE, in reply to a question on this point, made the following answer in writing: "We have, with great expenditure of labor, examined the papers in connection with the *last thousand* Tontine settlements, and find, in *fifteen* cases, expressions of disappointment with the results. In only *four* of those cases is any charge made of bad faith. In *none* of them have legal proceedings been brought against the Company."—Report, page 65.

† Report, page 202.

policy-holders. Statistics abundantly prove, for instance, that when applicants for insurance deliberately elect to pay larger premiums than are absolutely necessary, as Tontine policy-holders do when they elect to forbear the usual yearly dividends, they thereby give evidence, unconsciously perhaps, or by instinct, that they expect to live to enjoy the benefits promised in case of long life—in other words, they give evidence of superior vitality, which is more reliable in determining the value of the risk than the most skillful medical examination. It is clearly proven that the rates of mortality, and also the rates of lapses, or discontinuances, are far less among Tontine than among non-Tontine policy-holders. These constitute the solid advantages of Tontine contracts, and the companies can give, and in fact do give, in return ample and compensating advantages in the way of larger dividends, or surplus, and larger surrender values than can be safely promised or given under ordinary policies.

(2) *As regards the charge that Tontine contracts tend to deprive families of the protection which they would otherwise have obtained under ordinary policies.*—The whole testimony obtained by the committee disproves this charge. The rates of discontinuances, except in the first two or three years when the conditions of the two contracts are similar, are far less among Tontine than among non-Tontine policies, and this is easily accounted for. The penalty in case of lapse, and the reward in case of persistence, are both greater. The definite promise to pay a large sum in cash at the end of the Tontine period, as surplus and guaranteed surrender value, furnishes a substantial collateral, available, if necessary, to borrow money to pay premiums, and would thus enable a Tontine policy-holder to keep up his insurance when an ordinary policy-holder would be compelled to lapse, or to accept (as a semi-Tontine policy-holder might also do) a small paid-up insurance. Human nature is so weak that it often neglects duties which are for our own interest or benefit, unless there is a penalty for the non-performance, or a reward for the performance of the same.

(3) *As regards the charge that expenses are greater in Tontine companies.*—Here, again, the evidence and statistical information disproves the charge. The heaviest expenses are generally those incurred at the time the policy is issued, and the greater the volume of new business the greater the apparent expenses. The Tontine companies issued seventy-four per cent. of the new insurances in 1884, but their expenses are actually smaller than those of the non-Tontine companies when compared to new business, or to insurances in force when properly classified.

(4) *As regards the methods of keeping accounts, and the proper application of the funds.*—No evidence of wrong-doing has been offered to the Committee, or that the funds properly belonging to Tontine policy-holders are not managed with fidelity and integrity, and are not held intact for the benefit of the proper beneficiaries. In fact, no charge or complaints of this nature have been made, or are known to the Committee as having been made against any company. In conclusion, the evidence obtained by the Committee demonstrates that the Tontine system of life insurance is lawful; that while the penalties enacted in case of discontinuance are greater than upon ordinary policies, the advantages in case of continuance are also greater. These penalties differ in degree, not in kind, and hence the term "gambling" is no more applicable to Tontine than to non-Tontine insurance, and in fact is applicable to neither. The fulfillment of the Tontine contract is encouraged rather than discouraged by these penalties, and the greater benefits given on these contracts.

THE NEW-YORK LIFE INSURANCE COMPANY'S BUILDING.
Draped in Memory of Gen. U. S. Grant, Aug. 8, 1885.

In October, 1885, the Company began the issue of a Five-Year Dividend Policy. This was practically a non-forfeiting Tontine policy with successive Tontine periods of five years each. It contained, however, new privileges. After two years there were no restrictions as to residence and travel, and none with respect to occupation except military and naval service in time of war, the manufacture of explosives, dueling and violation of law. In case of death after two years while engaged in the occupations prohibited, the reserve value of the policies was to be paid. A mortuary-dividend, or premium-return of one-half of all premiums paid during the five-year period in which death should occur, was paid with the policy. At the end of each five years the regular Tontine options were allowed in settlement or continuance of the policy. The cash surrender value consisted of the full reserve and surplus, except at the end of the first period, when it was the surplus and eighty per cent. of the reserve. The guarantee of immediate payment of death-claims was first inserted in this policy, although that had been the custom of the Company under other policies for several years. The Premium-Return feature of the Five-Year Dividend Policy proved very attractive, and has since been added to the Company's policies issued for longer dividend periods, and the amount of the return made either one-half or all of the premiums paid, taken at the tabular annual rates. Under the larger guarantee the policy-holder dying within a dividend period of ten, fifteen, or twenty years, receives his insurance for the use of his money, the face amount of the policy, plus the annual premiums paid, being paid at his death.

There came a day in October, 1885, when the "good, gray head which all men knew," was seen no more at the office of the NEW-YORK LIFE INSURANCE COMPANY;—Morris Franklin, President of the Company for over thirty-seven years, was dead. The announcement was made to the Trustees by Mr. Beers, at a special meeting held October twenty-seventh, in substantially the following words:

With a feeling of sadness it becomes my duty as Vice-President and Actuary of the Company to make official announcement of what is already known to each member of the Board;—Morris Franklin, our venerable and honored President, died at his home in Flushing on the twenty-second instant. This event suggests a review of Mr. Franklin's connection with the Company, which has been so long, so pleasant to his associates, so full of honor to himself, and of growth and prosperity to the NEW-YORK LIFE.

In all his life previous to his acceptance of the Presidency of this Company, in 1848, Mr. Franklin belonged to a past generation. He was born not far from this spot, when the business portion of the city was below Wall Street. He grew up as a contemporary of the founders of the older business houses of the metropolis. His early teacher, Goold Brown, and his kinsman, Lindley Murray, were authors of school-books which have been authorities for two generations of youth. Admitted to the bar soon after attaining his majority, he was a member, and for two years President, of the Board of Aldermen of this city, when such positions were sought by leading citizens, and when only such were considered competent to fill them. He was a member of the old Volunteer Fire Department, was for many years foreman of a company, and as such served with distinction at the great fire of 1835. He was four terms a member of the State Legislature, serving in both houses, before the anti-slavery agitation began.

Having thus given his early life largely to the service of his native city and State, and having thereby gained valuable experience and the confidence of his fellow men, he became, in 1848, the President of this Company. It had already had two Presidents within less than four years, but only a limited business. It had issued in all less than four thousand policies, and had less than $165,000 in assets. Yet, considering the state of the business, this was a fairly creditable record. The theory of Life Insurance was new and crude; its methods were for the most part yet to be wrought out; prejudice was to be overcome and confidence inspired. It is not to be wondered at that progress was slow; it is honor enough that the Company survived this experimental period, and slowly grew in elements of strength and permanence. In spite of all hindrances, in 1855 it passed the one million dollar mark in accumulated assets—of which about $400,000 was in premium notes.

My own connection with the Company began in 1851, first as accountant and then as mathematician and cashier. While occupying these positions, I always found Mr. Franklin a most appreciative and considerate chief executive. I was made Actuary in 1864, and Vice-President and Actuary in 1868; and, with Mr. Franklin's hearty concurrence, the active management of the Company was from the latter date largely committed to my hands, while he, already past his three-score years, devoted himself more particularly to office and supervisory work. But with this partial retirement from the more active duties of the Presidency, Mr. Franklin did not abate anything of his interest in the work and prosperity of the Company, and for seventeen years we have been harmonious co-laborers in making the NEW-YORK LIFE INSURANCE COMPANY what it is to-day. This relation was maintained until the last; and, as many of you can bear witness, it was never disturbed or marred by the infirmities of disposition which age so often brings. To the last Mr. Franklin was the same genial, kindly man, interested in the success of the Company, appreciative of the work, and considerate of the feelings and happiness, of his associates. He lived beyond the time allotted to most men, and, with nothing wanting to his happiness, either in official or private life, he at last laid down life's burdens as cheerfully as he had borne them. After a life full of labors and full of honor, at the ripe age of eighty-four years, he has entered into rest.

Resolutions expressive of the high esteem in which Mr. Franklin was held by his associates were adopted.

PRESIDENT NEW-YORK LIFE INSURANCE COMPANY, OCTOBER 27, 1885—FEBRUARY 10, 1892.

There was no doubt as to who should succeed Mr. Franklin. Mr. Beers had long been recognized as the inspiring force in the Company's management, and his election to the Presidency was by the unanimous vote of the Trustees present. The subject of the election of a Vice-President and Actuary was referred to a special Committee consisting of Messrs. Welch, Appleton and Booth, who were to report at the next meeting. Dr. Tuck was made Actuary, *pro tem.* On November eleventh the Committee reported, recommending that the office of Vice-President and that of Actuary be made distinct, and nominating Dr. Henry Tuck as Vice-President, and he was so elected. Mr. Rufus W. Weeks, the mathematician of the Company, was recommended by the Committee for Actuary, and was duly elected. In the matter of Second Vice-President the Committee, through its Chairman, Mr. Welch, asked for more time, whereupon Mr. Booth said that without the knowledge or consent of the Chairman of the Committee, he presented the name of Mr. Welch. The ballot was taken, and Mr. Welch was declared elected.

1886. In January, 1886, the Company began the issue of a Nonforfeiting-Tontine Limited-Endowment Policy which presented several new features. It was payable as an endowment in either ten, fifteen or twenty years, the amount of the endowment for each thousand dollars' insurance being three hundred dollars on a ten-year endowment, four hundred dollars on a fifteen-year endowment, and five hundred dollars on a twenty-year endowment. It served the purposes of an endowment policy, in providing a definite sum to those who survived certain periods, at much lower premium rates than the full endowment policy. It also gave more insurance for the same premium paid than the regular endowment, and thus obviated the objection sometimes made to the latter—that during the last years of such a policy there is very little insurance under it, the funds for its payment having been nearly all contributed by the policy-holder. The dividend periods of this policy corresponded with its endowment periods. The Premium-Return feature, first introduced in connection with the Five-Year Dividend Policy, in 1885, was incorporated in the new contract in two forms, and provided for the return either of half or all the premiums paid, in case of death while the policy was in force. The non-forfeiture provisions were new, and provided that, in case of lapse after three years' premiums had been paid, the legal reserve on the policy would, on request within six months, be applied to extend the insurance for its full amount for as long a time (within the endowment period) as such value would carry it, according to the Company's single premium rates for temporary insurance; and if such value were more than sufficient to continue the insurance to the end of the endowment period, such excess would be applied to the purchase of a pure endowment, payable at the end of the period if the insured were then living. This was the first introduction of the feature of extended insurance into the Company's policies. A *fac-simile* of the first Non forfeiting-Tontine Limited-Endowment Policy is given following this page.

While the Tontine discussion was going on, in 1885, Superintendent McCall, of the New York Insurance Department, without making any ado about it, directed the Actuary of the Department, Mr. John S. Patterson, to make an examination of the Tontine accounts of the NEW-YORK LIFE and Equitable. This was done, and Mr. Patterson's report was made early in 1886. Regarding the methods of the companies in keeping their accounts, Mr. Patterson said:

> Practical accuracy is undoubtedly secured by these methods, and absolute accuracy is as nearly secured as is feasible in the calculation of large accounts of a complicated kind, and as is considered practicable in the apportionment of surplus on either ordinary or Tontine policies.

On other points raised in the discussion, Mr. Patterson said:

> I am at a loss to see how any extraordinary or improper expenditures could be charged against the Tontine funds, with any greater safety to the officer so wrongly charging them, than if charged to the general fund of the company.
>
> The introduction of the semi, or non-forfeiting, Tontine does away with that which, in the minds of some, is another (if not chief) ground of complaint; though the actual cases of hardship chargeable to the absolute forfeiture of the old style, full Tontine policies, are surprisingly small.
>
> As to the charge that these policy contracts are gambling ones, it is, I think, hardly worth serious consideration. See decision of the General Term New York Supreme Court, second department, lately handed down.*

---

* Quoted on page 226.

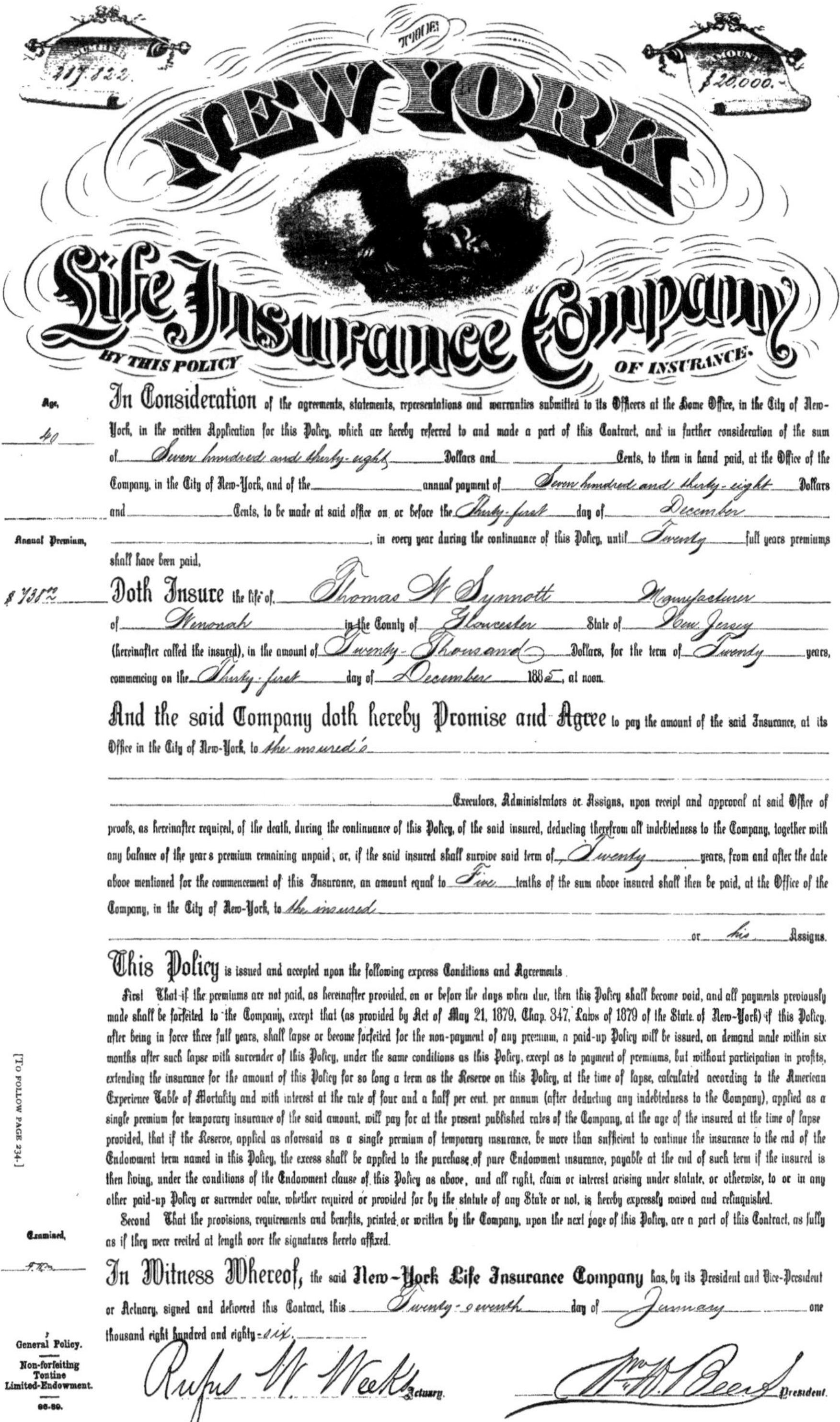

217.822.

Amount $20,000.

THE NEW YORK LIFE INSURANCE COMPANY

BY THIS POLICY OF INSURANCE.

Age. 40

In Consideration of the agreements, statements, representations and warranties submitted to its Officers at the Home Office, in the City of New-York, in the written Application for this Policy, which are hereby referred to and made a part of this Contract, and in further consideration of the sum of *Seven hundred and thirty-eight* Dollars and ______ Cents, to them in hand paid, at the Office of the Company, in the City of New-York, and of the ______ annual payment of *Seven hundred and thirty-eight* Dollars and ______ Cents, to be made at said office on or before the *Thirty-first* day of *December* ______, in every year during the continuance of this Policy, until *Twenty* full years premiums shall have been paid,

Annual Premium, $738.00

Doth Insure the life of *Thomas W. Synnott* *Manufacturer* of *Wenonah* in the County of *Gloucester* State of *New Jersey* (hereinafter called the insured), in the amount of *Twenty-Thousand* Dollars, for the term of *Twenty* years, commencing on the *Thirty-first* day of *December* 188*5*, at noon.

And the said Company doth hereby Promise and Agree to pay the amount of the said Insurance, at its Office in the City of New-York, to *the insured's* ______ Executors, Administrators or Assigns, upon receipt and approval at said Office of proofs, as hereinafter required, of the death, during the continuance of this Policy, of the said insured, deducting therefrom all indebtedness to the Company, together with any balance of the year's premium remaining unpaid; or, if the said insured shall survive said term of *Twenty* years, from and after the date above mentioned for the commencement of this Insurance, an amount equal to *Five* tenths of the sum above insured shall then be paid, at the Office of the Company, in the City of New-York, to *the insured* ______ or *his* Assigns.

This Policy is issued and accepted upon the following express Conditions and Agreements.

First That if the premiums are not paid, as hereinafter provided, on or before the days when due, then this Policy shall become void, and all payments previously made shall be forfeited to the Company, except that (as provided by Act of May 21, 1879, Chap. 347, Laws of 1879 of the State of New-York) if this Policy, after being in force three full years, shall lapse or become forfeited for the non-payment of any premium, a paid-up Policy will be issued, on demand made within six months after such lapse with surrender of this Policy, under the same conditions as this Policy, except as to payment of premiums, but without participation in profits, extending the insurance for the amount of this Policy for so long a term as the Reserve on this Policy, at the time of lapse, calculated according to the American Experience Table of Mortality and with interest at the rate of four and a half per cent. per annum (after deducting any indebtedness to the Company), applied as a single premium for temporary insurance of the said amount, will pay for at the present published rates of the Company, at the age of the insured at the time of lapse provided, that if the Reserve, applied as aforesaid as a single premium of temporary insurance, be more than sufficient to continue the insurance to the end of the Endowment term named in this Policy, the excess shall be applied to the purchase of pure Endowment insurance, payable at the end of such term if the insured is then living, under the conditions of the Endowment clause of this Policy as above, and all right, claim or interest arising under statute, or otherwise, to or in any other paid-up Policy or surrender value, whether required or provided for by the statute of any State or not, is hereby expressly waived and relinquished.

Second That the provisions, requirements and benefits, printed or written by the Company, upon the next page of this Policy, are a part of this Contract, as fully as if they were recited at length over the signatures hereto affixed.

[TO FOLLOW PAGE 234.]

Examined, F.K.

In Witness Whereof, the said **New-York Life Insurance Company** has, by its President and Vice-President or Actuary, signed and delivered this Contract, this *Twenty-seventh* day of *January* one thousand eight hundred and eighty-*six*.

General Policy.
Non-forfeiting Tontine Limited-Endowment.
86-89.

Rufus W. Weeks Actuary.

Wm. H. Beers President.

On April 16, 1886, President Beers reached his sixtieth birthday. In order to celebrate it in the manner that would please him best, the general agents passed the word around, about ten days before, that as many applications for insurance as possible should be procured for presentation at the Home Office on that day. The day came, and with it applications for insurance to the amount of over three million dollars. It was specially significant of the growth of the Company's business that a similar effort on the part of the agency staff three years before had produced applications to the amount of but little over one and one-half millions. But the time was coming when even the larger achievement would be similarly surpassed by the Company's agency force under the inspiration of new methods and a better policy contract.

With the increasing age and business of the Company, its list of policies maturing by death presented remarkable illustrations of the value of insurance either for a short time or a long time. In 1886, for example, policies were paid upon the lives of sixty-one persons who died within less than one year after insuring, and twenty-four policies were paid that had been in force over thirty years. The distribution through the year of the deaths under the first class, no less than the fact that so many died so soon after passing a careful medical examination, illustrates how deeply seated is the law of mortality. Eleven of the sixty-one lived less than three months, thirty-two less than six months, and forty-nine less than nine months, after their policies were issued. Compared with the number of new policies in force, the mortality rate was about five per thousand, showing no lack of care in selection. The largest insurance on a single life was fifty thousand dollars, and the insured, Mr. Robert F. Hurlburt, of Minneapolis, Minn., with two friends, was drowned in Lake Minnetonka, during a severe storm. The twenty-four policies in force over thirty years were upon the lives of twenty-two persons. The total premiums, less dividends, were $37,010.28, and the total return was $55,927.22. The total cash dividends used in reduction of premiums were $20,895.24.

Among other notable claims paid in 1886 were those upon the lives of ex-President Arthur, John B. Gough, Senator John F. Miller, of California, ex-Senator George W. Morrill, of Vermont, Dr. John P. Gray, Medical Superintendent of the Utica Insane Asylum, Hon. Edwin G. Halbert, the Company's General Manager for Minnesota and Dakota, and George W. Perkins, General Manager for Ohio. President Arthur's insurance was taken in April, 1863, on the Ten-Payment Life plan, and the policy then issued was exchanged for a paid-up policy in favor of his wife, in February, 1875.* His wife's death occurred prior to his own, and the policy was paid to his two children, one of whom was still a minor. Mr. Gough's policy was taken in December, 1865, in favor of his wife, and was on the Ten-Payment Life plan.† At that time Mr. Gough was lecturing five nights in a week from October to May, at from fifty, to two hundred and fifty, dollars per night—a valuable life, surely, and one that ought to have been insured. Mr. Gough's place of birth is given in his application as Sandgate, England, and his occupation as "lecturer"; then follow the statements that he was forty-nine years of age, married, and "temperate for the last twenty years." Every one who has heard Mr. Gough's affecting description of his early struggles with the appetite for drink will appreciate in some degree how much those six words meant to him, and will feel more fully the force of the closing words of his last lecture, delivered the night before his death:—"Young men, keep your record clean!"

In the deaths of Messrs. Halbert and Perkins the Company suffered not only an ordinary money loss, but the loss of two valuable general managers. Mr. Halbert was a member of the New York Legislature in 1881, from the Binghamton district, and entered the service of the NEW-YORK LIFE in 1885. On April 14, 1886, Benton County, Minnesota, was swept by a cyclone that completely destroyed the village of Sauk

---

* C. A. Arthur

FROM PRESIDENT ARTHUR'S APPLICATION.

† Mary E. Gough by John B. Gough

FROM MR. GOUGH'S APPLICATION.

Rapids, and did great damage at St. Cloud and Rice's Station. About sixty persons were killed, over one hundred wounded, and several hundred thousand dollars' worth of property was destroyed. Mr. Halbert had gone to Sauk Rapids on business with Mr. Edgar Hull, President of the German-American National Bank of St. Cloud, and they were walking along the street together when the cyclone reached the town. Both were killed. Mr. Hull had made application for a policy that day and was to have been examined on the day following. Mr. Perkins first entered the service of the Company in 1872, having previously been Superintendent of the first Reform School in Chicago. He was associated for several years with Mr. O. P. Curran, under the firm name Curran & Perkins, Managers of the Northwestern Branch of the Company, with head-quarters at Chicago. Mr. Perkins was afterward made Assistant-Superintendent of Agencies, and spent most of his time in the field; later still, he was made Manager of the Ohio Agency, with head-quarters at Cleveland, and he held this position at the time of his death. He was succeeded as Manager for Ohio by his son, George W. Perkins, now Third Vice-President of the Company. Upon the latter's election to his present position Hon. John A. Finch, formerly Chairman of Insurance Commission of the State of Indiana, sent a message of congratulation, saying he knew not which to congratulate most—the son of such a father or the father of such a son.

1887. EARLY in 1887 the Company made preparations to erect office buildings in Kansas City, Omaha, St. Paul, and Montreal. The ground for the first three was purchased in December, 1886, and for the latter in February, 1887. All the buildings were begun in 1887 and completed in 1889. The Kansas City Building is situated at the corner of Ninth and Wall Streets and covers a lot 120 x 160 feet; the property, together with four other lots and buildings adjoining, since acquired, stands on the Company's books at a valuation of $1,535,000. The Omaha Building is situated at the corner of Farnam and Seventeenth Streets and covers a lot 132 feet square; it stands on the Company's books at a valuation of $950,000. The St. Paul Building is situated at the corner of Sixth and

Minnesota Streets and is 100 feet square, with additional lots considerably larger; the whole property stands on the Company's books at a valuation of $725,000. The Montreal Building is situated at the corner of

THE NEW-YORK LIFE BUILDING, KANSAS CITY, MO.

Place d'Armes and St. James Street and covers a lot 72 x 116 feet; it stands on the Company's books at a valuation of $475,000. The latter is eight stories in height; all the others are ten stories; all are solidly built of the very best material, and are fire-proof. Lots were purchased in Minneapolis in July, 1888, and a similar building erected there in 1888–1890; this property comprises a ten-story office building 99 x 150 and an additional lot 99 x 180 feet, and stands on the Company's books

THE NEW-YORK LIFE BUILDING, OMAHA, NEB.

at a valuation of $925,000. These valuations were placed upon these properties by a committee of the Insurance Officers of seven States during the examination made of the Company's condition and securities, in 1894.

Reference has already been made to Chapter 534, Laws of 1880, imposing a tax of "one per cent. upon the gross amount of premiums, interest and other income received by life companies during the year

THE NEW-YORK LIFE BUILDING, ST. PAUL, MINN.

from persons residing in this State, or from investments represented by or based upon property situated in this State." In February, 1887, Comptroller Chapin sent a communication to the Legislature stating that reports were received under the law in 1880 from fifteen companies; that several of the reports were made under formal protest, accompanied by a refusal to pay the tax, on the ground of the unconstitutionality of the law. Less

THE NEW-YORK LIFE BUILDING, MONTREAL, CA.

than six thousand dollars had been received, and a part of this had been returned by previous Comptrollers who, being convinced that the law was not valid because it did not state the object to which the tax should be applied, had made no attempt to enforce it. The clause in the Constitution to which reference was had certainly seemed plain and positive; but a decision of the Court of Appeals, affirming the constitutionality of the collateral inheritance law, where the same question was raised and the

THE NEW-YORK LIFE BUILDING, MINNEAPOLIS, MINN.

same clause relied upon, left no doubt as to the construction that would be placed upon the insurance tax law. The clause in the Constitution and the decision of the Court, were as follows:

Every law which imposes, continues, or revives a tax shall distinctly state the tax and the object to which it is to be applied, and it shall not be sufficient to refer to any other law to fix such tax or object.—*Constitution, Act* 3, *Section 20.*

We do not think that the policy embodied in the section had any reference to special taxes, and which may be collected in a variety of ways under general laws, such as auction duties, excise duties, taxes on business or particular trades, avocations or special classes of property.—*Court of Appeals, State vs. Mary McPherson.*

The Comptroller recommended that a special Act be passed remitting the taxes for the years 1880 to 1883 upon the payment of those for the years 1884 to 1886; taxes thereafter to be paid annually as imposed by the law. Three bills were introduced—one to carry out the suggestions of the Comptroller, one to collect the taxes as recommended and to repeal the law, and one to remit the taxes and repeal the law. The latter was passed June 25, 1887. While the subject was in Committee, Hon. John A. McCall, ex-Superintendent of the Insurance Department, who had become Comptroller of the Equitable Life Assurance Society, addressed the Committee in favor of the law as passed. Referring to the authority exercised over the companies by the State with respect to investments, and to the requirements imposed as to the earning power of investments in order to secure solvency, Mr. McCall said:

Wisely or not, the State has curtailed the kind of securities that the companies of this State could invest in, in a way that has interfered with their operations when compared with the liberal actions of other States. Until lately, without regard to where the premium receipts came from, this State has required the money to be invested within its borders or in the States adjoining. When you consider that the policies issued to residents of New York are not one-fifth of the total policies in force, it will be conceded that in competition with companies of other States they have been placed at a disadvantage. The Chinese wall that was erected around them has been quoted time and time again by the agents of foreign companies as an example of the selfish use by Eastern people of Western money, and by authority and direction of New York's Legislature. It has resulted generally in the taxation of the receipts in each State, and then when we get them here and convert them into securities, as compelled by law, you tax them again.

Not only that, but to-day you tax the capital and interest and dividends of the corporations and institutions that issue the securities in which we find rest for our money, and by this Act you tax us for receiving said earnings, which the moment they were declared were taxed to the respective corporations by another enactment. So it is true of the premiums. You say, in order to pay your claims you must set aside a sum from your premiums and add to it every year from the same source, so that when the time arrives for the payment of the claim—and nothing is surer than death except New York taxes—you will have in hand the sum due. But in order to keep this amount safe and unimpaired in your hands, we will enact—paradoxical reasoning—to take away one per cent. of the sum each year until the claim matures, and then if you do not hold, which, of course, you cannot, the full one hundred per cent. at maturity, we will take away ***your*** life for the consequence of ***our*** act.

During this year the first of the Company's Fifteen-Year Tontines matured. The results were proportionally larger than under policies running through shorter periods, and gave a correspondingly greater impetus to the business of the Company. From the time the Company's Tontines began to mature, agents found in the results and options under them the most convincing arguments for level premium insurance, as opposed to insurance on the co-operative, or assessment, plan. The latter plan had done this, at least, for the average man—it had taught him that protection, the promise of money in case of death, was worth something and cost something to the man who lived. That point being conceded, it was easy to show that, deducting a fair price for this protection from the annual premium charged by the NEW-YORK LIFE, the cash value of its maturing Tontines was equal to the balance of the premiums paid, increased at a high rate of interest. The Tontine plan was seen, therefore, to do two things, and to do them well, namely, it kept men insured, and so protected the families of those who died; and it saved and returned, with large interest, the investment portion of the premiums.

The value of the Premium-Return feature, first introduced in 1885, was illustrated during this year in the payment of thirty-four policies which became death-claims. Eighteen of these were written with guarantee of a return of one-half, and sixteen with guarantee of all, premiums paid in addition to the face of the policy in case of death during a specified period. The total amount of premiums paid on these policies was $14,517.57, the total amount of the policies was $204,737, and the total premium-return was $11,472.33, making a total to beneficiaries thereunder of $216,209.33.

Among the policies paid as death-claims during 1887, were four upon the life of Mr. J. B. Cornell, of New York, aggregating $46,144.61; two on the life of Mr. Seymour L. Husted, of Brooklyn, aggregating $15,-435.37; and one, for $5,000, upon the life of Professor Spencer F. Baird,

Secretary of the Smithsonian Institution at Washington. Mr. Husted's policies were for $5,000 each and were taken, one at age fifty-seven and the other at age sixty. Additions to these policies by dividends in reversion were over fifty per cent. of the original insurance, and they returned $15,435.37 at a cash cost of $7,788.35. Another claim upon the life of a man unknown to fame was thus described in the "Burlington (Vt.) Free Press" of April 20, 1887:

The "Free Press" contains a card from the attorneys of Mrs. Jane Allen, of Burlington, widow of Noah Allen, acknowledging the prompt payment of a $10,000 policy, on the life of Mr. Allen, by the NEW-YORK LIFE. Mr. Allen was at one time a leading merchant of Burlington, and reputed to be worth $50,000 or $75,000. In the days of his prosperity, some twenty years or more ago, he effected an insurance upon his life, as already indicated. Misfortunes came upon him in a body, and his estate was swept away, all except this. His creditors pressed him hard, and squeezed him most unmercifully for the amount laid away in the policy, but it was not surrendered. The policy alone has survived the wreck, and it is the staff upon which the widow now leans.

The attorneys of Mrs. Allen, in acknowledging payment of the policy, said: "We are requested by Mrs. Allen, the beneficiary of the policy, to express to you her sincere appreciation of the prompt adjustment of her claim, and we are happy to add the assurance of our own admiration of the generous treatment which Mrs. Allen has received from your Company in its waiver of certain apparent errors in the application which would have materially reduced the amount coming to her if the Company had insisted upon its legal rights."

At the meeting of the Board of Trustees held on October 12, 1887, the President called attention to a letter, copies of which had been placed in their hands by the cashier of the Company, which contained serious charges against the management of the Company and against the President personally. He asked that an investigation be made. After a full discussion, on motion of Mr. Strong, a committee of five Trustees, of which Mr. Potts was Chairman, was appointed to nominate a special Investigating Committee. The Committee, as reported later, consisted of Messrs. Wm. L. Strong, Benj. H. Bristow,* John Claflin,

* Mr. Bristow was unable to serve on the Committee, owing to important engagements, but approved its findings, and upon his motion all papers connected therewith were placed in the personal custody of the President.

Richard Müser, John N. Stearns, and C. C. Baldwin. This Committee reported in February, 1888; and, while virtually admitting "slight shortcomings," they exonerated the Officers from any bad faith or fraudulent dealing, and commended their ability, zeal and disinterestedness.* The conclusions of the Committee were submitted to the cashier, who thereupon addressed a letter to the Chairman, saying that he should leave the

---

* Your Committee, after careful investigation of the affairs of this Company by every means in their power, have satisfied themselves that the Officers of the Company have honestly endeavored to administer the affairs of the Company with a single eye to the good of the Company. No instance has been brought to our attention where any pecuniary advantage of a personal kind has been brought home to the Officers in any act on their part.

Your Committee, therefore, without hesitation, report that there is no evidence whatever of bad faith or fraudulent dealing on the part of the Officers, but, on the contrary, there is evidence of the utmost good faith and zeal on their part for the welfare of the interests committed to their charge. The success or failure of a company must be judged not by isolated transactions, but by the whole course of the business of the company, and when we remember that under the present management the increase of the business is almost without parallel, while its assets have steadily increased and its surplus has been maintained and increased, and when we remember that the Company has passed through very severe financial crises without serious loss, we feel that it would be most ungracious in the Trustees of this Company to set over against these merits any slight shortcomings which, in the judgment of your Committee or of individual members of the Committee, may have from time to time been committed.

We consider ourselves exceedingly fortunate in the character, ability, zeal, and disinterestedness of the present Officers, and we think that no company can point to a better record than ours in its business management. It is the opinion of this Committee that this Company has been managed with marked ability and integrity, and throughout the close investigation which we have made, every detail, so far as we are able to judge from the examination of every record and paper which we saw fit to call for, and with which the Officers willingly furnished us, has tended in every instance firmly to establish our former belief and confidence in the Company as to its stability, character, and responsibility.

Having so thoroughly satisfied ourselves regarding the able management of the Company and the excellence and value of its assets, we regret that we cannot go further and ourselves estimate the amount of reserve for insurance obligations which ought to be counted as a liability. This, it is evident, can be done only by an expert in actuarial calculations.

We have not the slightest reason to doubt the accuracy of the calculations of the Actuary of this Company. On the contrary, we are fully convinced that his figures are correct, but it seems to us the present time is especially opportune for an examination of the insurance accounts by an expert not connected with the Company, to the end that the investigation of your Committee may be so supplemented and completed that a full exhibit of this Company's affairs will have been made by persons in no wise obligated to the Officers of this Company.

We suggested to Mr. Banta that we thought it desirable that the Insurance Department of this State should be asked to make a careful and exhaustive computation of the liabilities of this Company. Mr. Banta replied to the effect that the Insurance Department of this State might not make a fair examination, and that the Insurance Department of Massachusetts could alone be relied upon for accuracy.

It is evidently impracticable for this Company, a corporation of the State of New York, to call upon the State of Massachusetts for assistance in determining its liabilities, but (Mr. Banta not adducing any sufficient reason for his doubts as to the reliability of the Albany officials) we would suggest the issue in the hands of the Trustees, and should abide by their action in good faith.*

1888. IN January, 1888, the Company announced an "Insurance Bond with Guaranteed Interest," which contained desirable investment features. These bonds were paid up by either fifteen or twenty annual instalments, and after all payments were completed bore interest on their cash cost (taken at the tabular annual rate) at the rate of four per cent. per annum during the life-time of the bondholder, the face value being payable at his death. In case of death during the instalment-paying period, the face of the bond was paid immediately; and in case the instalments paid at death, together with compound interest at four per cent. per annum, exceeded the face of the bond, such excess was to be paid with the claim, as a mortuary-dividend. A non-forfeiture clause provided that in case of discontinuance after three annual instalments had been paid, a paid-up bond would be given for as many fifteenths or twentieths of the original bond as there had been annual instalments paid.

---

advisability of the Insurance Department of this State making a complete and exhaustive estimate on a four per cent. basis of all reserves which ought to be counted as liabilities by this Company.

Finally, your Committee express their gratification that these charges have brought about this investigation, the result of which has strengthened in the minds of your Committee the confidence which we have heretofore felt in the management and in the good faith and ability of the Officers.

W. L. STRONG, RICHARD MÜSER,
JOHN CLAFLIN, C. C. BALDWIN.
JOHN N. STEARNS,

The Committee's report was accepted and unanimously adopted by the Board of Trustees. The President stated that a valuation of all policy liabilities was being made by the Albany officials, and that he hoped to be able to present it to the Board when submitting the annual report. This was afterward duly submitted to the Board of Trustees.

*144 ST. JAMES PLACE, BROOKLYN, N. Y., Jan. 31, 1888.

WILLIAM L. STRONG, Esq.

Dear Sir: I have consulted with my counsel, the Hon. D. H. Chamberlain, in reference to my interview with you and Mr. Welch on Saturday last, and have received from him a letter, copy of which I enclose. You will see that he admits the force of the considerations you presented to me that a public scrutiny of these affairs, no matter in what conclusion it might terminate, would be fraught with peril to the Company, to individual policy-holders, and possibly to other interests which might be involved, and that he advises me that I am absolved from any duty to further prosecute this investigation.

I beg to say, therefore, that I shall leave the issue of this matter to the Board of Trustees, and shall abide in good faith by such action as they may deem their responsibility calls upon them to take.

Yours respectfully,

THEO. M. BANTA.

Surplus was accumulated during the instalment-paying period, and cash and annuity options were provided at the end of the period, in lieu of the interest-bearing bond, if preferred. During the instalment-paying period, the restrictions were the same as under the Free Tontine Policy noticed below; after the bond was paid for, there were no restrictions whatever.

In March, 1888, the Company began the issue of a "Non-forfeiting Free Tontine Policy" which was distinguished from the Non-forfeiting Limited Tontine by a slightly higher premium rate, and by greater freedom of action on the part of the insured with respect to occupation, residence and travel. After two years no restrictions were placed upon policy-holders except as to dueling, violations of law and service in war, in which cases, if death occurred, the reserve value of the policy was to be paid.

During the year the Company paid two claims for over one hundred thousand dollars each—one on the life of Royal M. Pulsifer, of Boston, for $102,794, and one on the life of David Hostetter, of Pittsburg, Pa., the well-known manufacturer of patent medicines. Mr. Pulsifer was for many years the publisher of the Boston "Herald," and at the time of his death was insured in fourteen companies, for an aggregate of over two hundred thousand dollars. He held four policies of twenty-five thousand dollars each in the NEW-YORK LIFE, to which additions had been made by dividends. In acknowledging receipt of payment the executors of Mr. Pulsifer wrote the Company's Boston Manager: "You were the first representative of the numerous companies in which he was interested to call on us as to the settlement of the claim, and everything that could have been done by the Company or yourself to facilitate matters, has been done." Dr. Hostetter's policies were among the first written by the Company with premium-return, and he had paid the Company $52,648 in premiums on two policies of $50,000 each. The policies and return-premiums amounted to $126,324. Dr. Hostetter, besides being one of the earliest and most successful manufacturers of patent medicines, was largely interested in railroads and in natural gas companies. He died from the effect of an operation for calculus.

Other claims paid to which unusual interest attaches were those of Hon. Daniel Manning, ex-Secretary of the Treasury, Mr. John Ogilvie, of Montreal, and Mr. Edward B. Paul, of Boston. Mr. Manning is on record as commending life insurance as an investment, and his practice was consistent therewith. He held three policies in the Company at the time of his death, the first having been taken in 1863, the second in 1868, and the third in 1877. Mr. Ogilvie was one of the best-known millers and grain dealers in Canada and was a brother of Senator Ogilvie. Mr. Ogilvie held four policies in the Company at the time of his death, amounting to $52,418.80, two of which, being taken when American currency was at a discount, both premiums and policies were made payable in gold. This was a case in which the Company profited by the extreme caution of the policy-holder. The policy of Mr. Paul was taken eighteen years before, in favor of a then infant daughter, and would have matured as a Tontine in two years more. Evidently it was intended as an investment for the child, to mature when she reached womanhood. Living or dying, it was sure to provide for her. It was paid to her guardian in December, 1888.

Among the matured Tontine policies settled in 1888 was one on the life of Hon. William F. Parrett, Circuit Judge of the First Judicial District of Indiana. Judge Parrett not only expressed his entire satisfaction with the results of his policy, but added the following commendation of the Company's Tontine plan and policy contracts generally: "From past experience as a Judge and a member of the legal profession, I prefer your Company's policy contract and its valuable Tontine policy to any other."

1889. THE annual report for 1888 was presented to the Trustees on February 14, 1889, and called forth many expressions of commendation for the ability with which the Company was managed. In replying to these expressions the President spoke of the fierce and increasing competition in the life insurance business, referring to the great advance in commissions, and to the excessive rebates given the insured by agents, and advising that he be authorized to make the Company's policies incontestable. The Trustees thereupon adopted a resolution authorizing the President to make all policies—issued and to be issued—incontestable, and to take such further measures as he should consider best from time to time to protect and advance the business of the Company. An incontestable clause was inserted in the principal policies of the Company in June, and was in the following form:

> If this policy shall become a claim by death after having been in force two full years, the Company will not contest its payment on account of any incorrect statement in the application or in the accompanying declarations to the Medical Examiner (except in case of fraud), provided, however, that if the age of the insured is understated the amount of insurance payable shall be such proportion of the amount of the policy as the premium paid bears to the required premium at the true age.

The practice of rebating a part of the first premium to the insured, already noticed by Mr. Beers in his annual report to the Trustees, had for some time been recognized by agents and managers alike as a great evil. Its effect was to increase the cost of business and to introduce inequality among the insured. The Life Underwriters Association of New York, at its annual meeting held in May, 1888, adopted a memorial to the companies, with a view to securing concerted action for the suppression of the practice. In pursuance thereof, a meeting was called of representatives of the various companies in July of that year, and a plan was formulated by which each company was to forbid the giving of rebates by its agents. Some of the companies, however, refused to sign the agreement, and the whole plan fell through. Meanwhile, efforts were made to secure the passage of a law forbidding the giving of rebates. Several bills were introduced, and one drafted by ex-Superintendent John A. McCall became a law on May 14, 1889. It provides that no life company doing business in the State shall make any discrimination between persons of the same class or expectation of life, either in the premium charged or in dividends or other advantages; and that no life company or agent thereof shall pay or allow, or offer to pay or allow, as an inducement to any person to insure, any rebate of premium, or other special favor or advantage, not specified in the policy. Every agent is required to procure from the Insurance Department a certificate of authority to do business; violation of the law is a misdemeanor; and it is made the duty of the Superintendent to revoke the certificate of any person convicted of its violation, and no certificate may be issued to the offender within the three years following his conviction.

The month of June, 1889, was marked by one of the most appalling disasters that ever happened in this country. A dam on the North Fork of the Connemaugh River in western Pennsylvania overflowed and was washed away, and the flood of waters thus let loose swept down the narrow valley carrying death and destruction in their path. Seven or eight villages were destroyed, involving a loss of millions of dollars' worth of property and of several thousand lives. The life insurance companies paid in all about three hundred thousand dollars, and subscribed liberally to the relief fund raised for the sufferers. The NEW-YORK LIFE had about seventy-five policy-holders in Johnstown and vicinity, fifteen of which, insuring $43,600.49, became claims by death.

The local agent of the Company, Mr. John McDermott, had a narrow escape, saving his immediate family but losing fifteen relatives. Owing to the peculiar circumstances—whole families lost, papers lost, etc.,—the Company sent a special agent* to the scene of the disaster, in order to facilitate the proving of claims under its policies. Six policies, amounting to $17,573, were paid on June twenty-sixth, and these were the first policies paid in Johnstown. Other payments followed as soon as the loss papers could be completed. A policy for $1,000, upon the life of Mr. Charles A. Kies, was found three miles below Mr. Kies' residence in a heap of *débris*, covered with sand and badly water-stained. Both Mr. Kies and his wife were drowned, and the Company gave notice of its readiness to pay the policy to his legal representatives upon proof of right to inherit. Mr. Kies had been married but a short time and left no family; the parents of both himself and wife were living, however, and the question arose whether he or his wife was drowned first—as the parents of the last to die would inherit under the policy. The Company paid the policy to the administrator, and it was understood that the

---

* Mr. Charles Langmuir, now Agency Director for Europe.

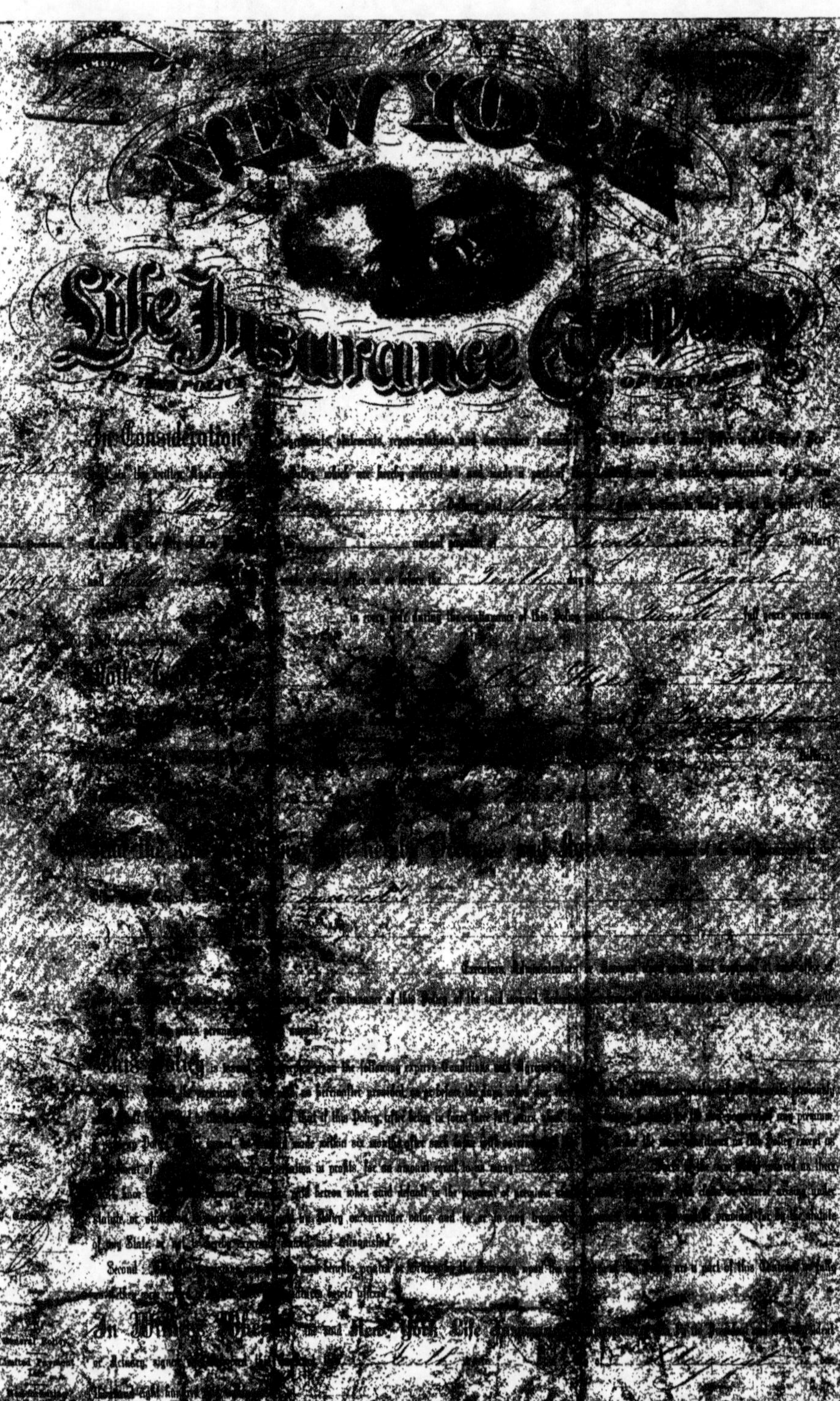

New York Life Insurance Company

parents of the couple agreed to share the proceeds. A representation of Mr. Kies' policy is given on page 252. Another of the Company's policy-holders, Mr. John Fenn, insured for $5,000, floated down stream on a house-top until another building struck him and knocked him into the water, from which he never rose. His wife, seven children and a servant girl, were imprisoned in their own house by the water and carried away. As the house rose and fell and swayed to and fro upon the current, one after another the inmates were all drowned, except Mrs. Fenn. Finally, the house was crushed and an opening made through which she escaped. Her husband's policy was all that remained of former prosperity.

In June, 1889, the Company began the issue of a "Distribution Policy." This policy provided for the accumulation of surplus during periods of fifteen or twenty years, as elected by the applicant, as under the Tontine plan, and provided the usual Tontine options in settlement for policy-holders who survived and kept their policies in force. It differed from other policies of the Company in the following respects: (1) The premiums for the first two years were paid in one sum, when the policy was issued, and were considerably less than two annual premiums on the ordinary policy; subsequent premiums were slightly higher than the annual premiums on the ordinary policy.* (2) Paid-up insurance was given after the payment of premiums for four years' insurance (three premiums) instead of after the payment of premiums for three years. (3) After the payment of premiums for a specified number of years,† the Company agreed to loan the policy-holder the amount of any subsequent premium during the distribution period, such loan to be used to keep the policy in force. (4) If death occurred during the period in which the premium-loan was available, a premium-return feature provided for the return of all premiums paid during that period; thus, if the loan were

---

* At age 40 the insured paid $49.70 per $1,000 in one sum for the first two years' insurance, and $35.60 per year thereafter. Under the Free Tontine Policy he paid $32.20 each year, or $64.40 for the first two years.

† Ten years on a 15-year policy, unless the insured was over age 60 at time of insuring; ten years on a 20-year policy, unless the insured was over age 45; at ages above 45 the number gradually increased to 15 at age 59.

availed of and death occurred, the return-premium would cancel the loan and leave the face amount of the policy intact for the insured's family or estate.

As this policy became the subject of fierce debate early in the following year, particular attention is called to its advantages. The great bane of Life Insurance then was the rebating practice of agents, which resulted in immense amounts of insurance being allowed to lapse after being in force one year. This policy allowed and required payment for two years' insurance when issued, at a rate somewhat more than the term rate for two years and considerably less than the full annual rate.* The man who paid a single premium got two years' insurance at least, and having paid more than the first premium on an ordinary policy, was more likely to continue. The premium-loan feature enabled the insured to keep his policy in force when it might otherwise be impossible, and the premium-return feature paid the loan in case of death. This loan feature was entirely different from the old premium-note plan, which created a debt against the policy from its inception and made no provision for payment of the debt except such as was afforded by annual dividends. The new feature was designed to be available in case of emergency after the insured had paid sufficient premiums to acquire a valuable equity in the policy. In such case, the policy-holder would not be at the trouble of assigning his policy to a creditor, nor be at the mercy of money-lenders. The loan was to be made by the Company at six per cent. interest, and to be a lien against the policy until paid.

Early in the year the Company prepared and forwarded to the Paris Exposition certain exhibits showing the Company's business for the preceding year, the total receipts and expenditures from organization, and the benefits under its Free Tontine Policy with Premium-Return. These were entered, together with pictures of the Company's buildings in the United States and Europe, in the Department of Social Economy, and

---

* The annual premium for $1,000 on a Twenty-Year Term Policy, at age 40, is $21.08; the first premium, covering two years' insurance, on a Twenty-Year Distribution Policy for $1,000, taken at same age, is $49.70. See also note on page 253.

San Francisco Sept 11th 1889

Col. A. G. Hawes Manager

Dear Sir

I have this day received from you a check for $27.483,64 in full payment of amount due me under my matured Endowment Policy in the New York Life Insurance Co.

My Policy was for $20.000 taken twenty years ago, on which I paid ten annual premiums of $1574.60 each or a total of $15.746.00

You now return me $11.737.64 more than I paid which gives me a compound Interest Investment of nearly four per cent for the whole period in addition to my Life Insurance

My Policy was an annual dividend one and therefore less profitable by far than the investment Policies now now issued by your Company. but the result speaks for itself and I Commend your Company to any one Seeking Life Insurance

Yours Very truly

A. H. Rutherford

attracted much attention. Upon these exhibits the Company was awarded, on September 29, 1889, a Diploma and a Silver Medal. The correspondent of the "Insurance Post," of London, said concerning the award:

A Silver Medal has been awarded the NEW-YORK LIFE, which it may be proud of, considering that no company has won a Gold Medal in connection with insurances and annuities for the public, and that the committee of the four French life companies, which had the management of the section, and the *Caza Nazionale di Associazione*, of Milan, which is a semi-State accident insurance association, alone secured each a grand prize. Gold Medals, however, were awarded to certain native insurance companies in respect of pension and annuity schemes for their clerks, and to four of the officers of French companies who acted as "collaborateurs," etc.

Reduced *fac-similes* of the principal exhibits and the Diploma, and full size representations of the Medal, are given on the following pages.

The Company paid in 1889 two losses for one hundred thousand dollars and upwards, one upon the life of Mr. E. P. Allis, of Milwaukee, and one upon the life of Mr. John H. Maginnis, of New Orleans. Mr. Allis was proprietor of the Reliance Iron Works, an establishment employing about twelve hundred men and having an annual output valued at about three million dollars. He was a representative of the best type of American manufacturers, a man who had made his way in the world by virtue of talent and industry, whose shops were models of their kind, and who found his chief happiness in his home and family and in efforts to improve the condition of his workmen. An entire floor in one of the buildings was set apart for their use, as a dining-room, reading-room, and hall for social and literary meetings. Mr. Allis failed in business at one time, and ever after had a wholesome skepticism concerning the certainty of business ventures. He left an estate estimated at about two million dollars, with an indebtedness of about two hundred thousand. He carried in all $361,000 in life insurance, making his claim the largest ever paid in this country. He came of a long-lived family, but died at the age of 65 from a gall-stone. Mr. Maginnis was President of the Maginnis Cotton Mill and of the Maginnis Oil and Soap Works, and was prominent in various social and commercial organizations. His first policy was taken in 1869 at the age of 24, and was for $10,000. He gradually added to this amount, until at his death he was insured for $127,464.10—all but

NEW-YORK LIFE INSURANCE COMPANY.

WILLIAM H. BEERS, President.

INCREASE IN ASSETS 1845-1888.

The part of the square printed in black represents the Surplus of the Company, by the present standard of the State of New York.

ASSETS

JANUARY 1, 1850,

$211,802.52

ASSETS

JANUARY 1, 1855,

$902,062.70

ASSETS

JANUARY 1, 1860,

$1,769,133.24

ASSETS

JANUARY 1, 1865,

$3,741,078.48

ASSETS

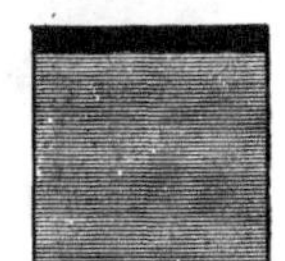

JANUARY 1, 1870,

$13,327,924.63

ASSETS

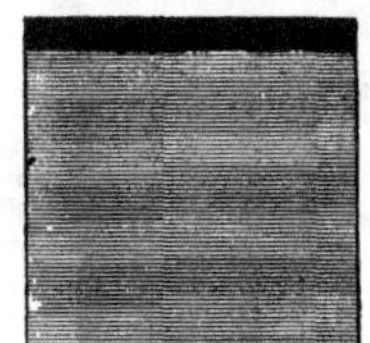

JANUARY 1, 1875.

$27,348,667.08

ASSETS

JANUARY 1, 1880.

$38,996,952.66

ASSETS

JANUARY 1, 1885,

$59,283,753.57

ASSETS

JANUARY 1, 1889,

$93,480,186.55

$20,000 of which was in the NEW-YORK LIFE. His death was due to a cause that no family record, good habits, or healthful surroundings could insure against;—during a violent storm, he was struck by lightning and instantly killed.

Several losses for smaller amounts invite comment. Professor C. H. McCay, of Baltimore, was a writer upon actuarial subjects before the NEW-YORK LIFE was organized. He was insured in the Company in 1853, at which time he was Professor of Mathematics and Astronomy in

the University of Georgia. He was at one time Actuary of the Southern Mutual Life Insurance Company. He was a contributor to insurance, and scientific, journals until the close of his life. His policy in the NEW-YORK LIFE was for $10,000, and was in force over thirty-five years. The cash dividends paid were equal to over one-third of the whole premiums, and $384 was added to the policy in reversion. John F. Hartranft, of Pennsylvania, who was insured in the Company for $10,000, had been Colonel, Brigadier-General, Major-General, Auditor and Governor, holding each of the last two offices during two terms. He distinguished himself on many battle fields during the Civil War, and received a medal

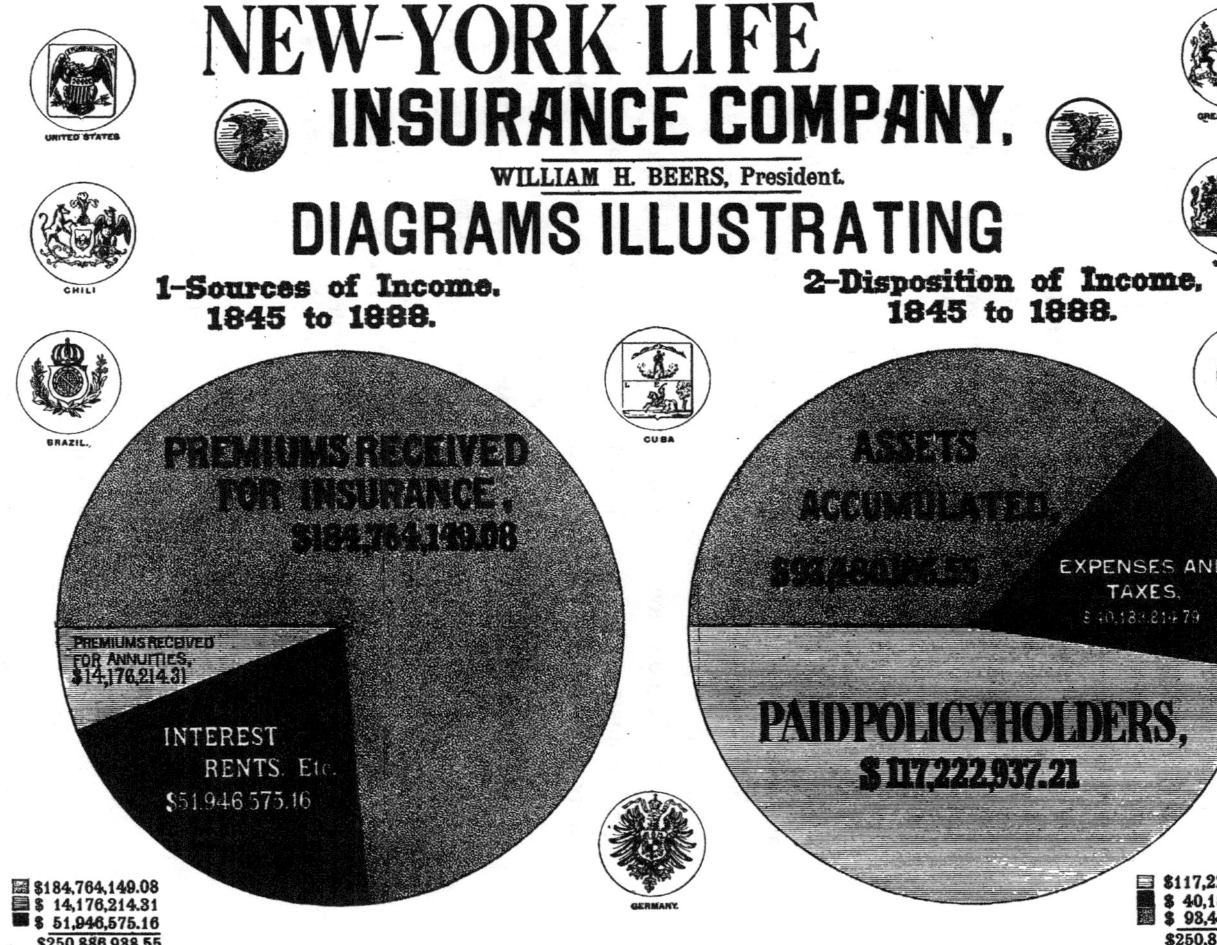
NEW-YORK LIFE
INSURANCE COMPANY.
WILLIAM H. BEERS, President.
DIAGRAMS ILLUSTRATING
1–Sources of Income.
1845 to 1888.
2–Disposition of Income,
1845 to 1888.
UNITED STATES
CHILI
BRAZIL.
CUBA
GERMANY.
GREAT BRITAIN.
SWEDEN
SPAIN
PREMIUMS RECEIVED
FOR INSURANCE,
$184,764,149.08
PREMIUMS RECEIVED
FOR ANNUITIES,
$14,176,214.31
INTEREST
RENTS. Etc.
$51,946,575.16
ASSETS
ACCUMULATED,
$93,480,186.55
EXPENSES AND
TAXES.
$40,183,814.79
PAID POLICYHOLDERS,
$117,222,937.21
$184,764,149.08
$ 14,176,214.31
$ 51,946,575.16
$250,886,938.55
$117,222,937.21
$ 40,183,814.79
$ 93,480,186.55
$250,886,938.55

from Congress for distinguished bravery; but, after passing through so many dangers unscathed, he died, at the age of 58, of Bright's Disease. Another man, unknown to fame, deserves mention here because of the peculiar circumstances under which his policy was paid. Under date of April 17, 1889, Mr. J. J. Pierce, Administrator of the estate of Mr. John T. Gardner, wrote from Wilmington, Del., to Mr. C. A. Wray, State Agent, as follows: "I desire to thank you and the Company for your kindness and unusual haste in the payment of this claim, the proofs of death being in the New York office of the Company but twenty-eight hours before I received the check. I stated to you that, if I did not receive the money within two days it would cause a loss to the estate, as there were payments to be made within that time. You and the Company have complied with my request, and, in addition to the benefits of the life insurance, the estate is saved this loss by your promptness, which certainly has my heartiest commendation."

Early in the year the Company suffered the loss by death of its European Manager, Mr. H. S. Homans, who died in Paris, January 12, 1889, of cerebral congestion, after an illness of only a few hours. Mr. Homans came of a distinguished family, his grandfather, Benjamin Homans, having acted as Assistant Secretary of the Navy under Presidents Madison,* Monroe, and Adams, and his father was a distinguished naval officer. The following extract from "Galigani's Messenger" of January 15, 1889, indicates the esteem in which Mr. Homans was held in Europe:

H. S. Homans was specially gifted with the faculty of organization, and when, in 1870, the NEW-YORK LIFE decided upon the extension of its business to Europe, he was intrusted with the execution of this project. No better choice could have been made. We cannot now recall the manifold difficulties which confronted the enterprise in its earlier stages; suffice it to say they were formidable enough to dismay any ordinary pioneer, and that, on more than one occasion, even the staunchest believers in Mr. Homans advised him to desist. His energy, however, was indomitable, and now, after a lapse of twenty years—a short space of time for so arduous an undertaking—the NEW-YORK LIFE is recognized by every government of Europe as the foremost representative of American assurance, and, what is still better, has by its competition and its

---

* Washington was captured and the public buildings burned by the British, August 24, 1814, and early in that day Mr. Homans sent two wagon loads of public documents up the Potomac on a canal boat and hid them in the woods. See Philadelphia "Ledger," August 5, 1895.

NEW-YORK LIFE INSURANCE COMPANY.

WILLIAM H. BEERS. President.

ESTABLISHED 1845. PURELY MUTUAL.

THIS COMPANY HAS BRANCH OFFICES IN ALL CIVILIZED COUNTRIES.

DIAGRAMS ILLUSTRATING

1–New Insurance Written in 1888.

2–Sources of Income in 1888.

3–Disposition of Income in 1888.

WITZERLAND

SOURCES

OF INCOME IN 1888.

$19,617,946.82
$ 1,509,643.93
$ 4,273,692.08
$25,401,282.83

NEW INSURANCE WRITTEN IN 1888:

$125,019,731.

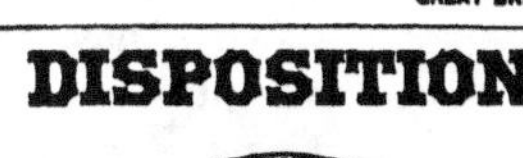

DISPOSITION

OF INCOME IN 1888.

$10,973,070.05
$ 4,516,193.76
$ 9,912,019.02
$25,401,282.83

HOME OFFICE:

346 & 348 BROADWAY, NEW YORK, U. S. A.

better methods contributed greatly to the general progress of life assurance on the continent. Mr. Homans was the main factor in this good work, and the high distinctions conferred upon him by four European governments, attest that his merits were not allowed to remain unrecognized.*

The annual report for 1889 was presented to the Board of Trustees on February 18, 1890. Mr. William H. Appleton, Chairman, presented the report of the Finance Committee, calling attention to the fact that the last year had been marked by greater advances than those of any previous year in the Company's history, and that the assets exceeded one hundred million dollars. The report was, in part, as follows:

It is with feelings of no ordinary satisfaction that the Finance Committee reports to the Board to-day at its Forty-fifth Annual Meeting, that the assets of the NEW-YORK LIFE INSURANCE COMPANY now exceed $104,000,000. In announcing this gratifying fact, we desire to lay particular emphasis upon the further fact that the Company has already paid to policy-holders over $129,000,000. We emphasize this second fact because it is easy to accumulate money if you do not pay it out. But in the history of the NEW-YORK LIFE INSURANCE COMPANY its benefits to policy-holders have gone hand-in-hand, nay, have kept in advance of its accumulations for their security and future benefit. It is interesting to look over the history of the accumulation of this vast fund. By reference to the figures of the Company it is found that there has been an increase in every year of its history, the smallest increase being in the first year, $17,496, while the largest increase was in the last year, $11,573,414. In the second year the total amount paid policy-holders was less than $7,000; during the last year over $12,000,000 were paid to policy-holders. It required eleven years to accumulate the first million dollars; during the last year the accumulations were over eleven million dollars, showing an increase one hundred and twenty-one times the average of the first eleven years.

We beg leave also to refer briefly to the investment record of the Company, because, when a company has one hundred million dollars in its keeping, it ought to be able to show that it is worthy of the trust. A reference to the books of the Company shows that the net amount of gains already realized in the profit and loss account is over $700,000; while the present market value of securities over cost value on the Company's books is $4,000,000. Certainly this is a remarkable record, running over a period during which the country has passed through several commercial crises—through two wars—and in which Life Insurance has grown from practically nothing to be one of the greatest financial institutions of the country.

The total receipts of the Company from interest, rents, and profits on investments have been over $52,000,000, exceeding death losses by over $2,000,000, and exceeding total expenses of all kinds, including taxes, by over $8,000,000.

---

*Mr. Homans was Officer of the Legion of Honor of France, Chevalier of the Crown of Italy, Commander of the Order of Isabella the Catholic, and Chevalier of the Order of Christ of Portugal,—which distinctions were conferred upon him for services in the cause of Life Insurance.

NEW-YORK LIFE INSURANCE COMPANY.

WILLIAM H. BEERS, President.

ESTABLISHED 1845. PURELY MUTUAL.

PREMIUMS RECEIVED IN 1888
$21,127,590.75

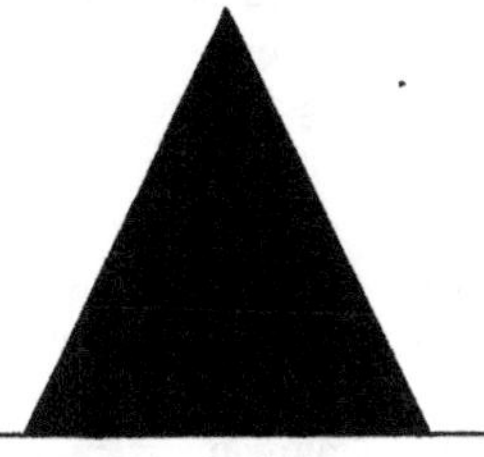

BENEFITS TO POLICY-HOLDERS IN 1888:
$10,973,070.05

ITALY

NORWAY.

MEXICO.

RUSSIA.

AUSTRIA.

DENMARK.

INSURANCE IN FORCE

JANUARY 1, 1889,

$419,886,505.00

HOLLAND.

BELGIUM.

The total dividends paid by the Company have been over $37,000,000; and the total surplus accumulated for dividends is now over $15,000,000, making a total of over $52,000,000 saved to policy-holders from the table rates. This is an average of about twenty-five per cent. on all premiums received for insurance; and twenty-five per cent. is about the present average of surplus gained each year in proportion to the insurance premiums received.

It seemed fitting that this report, which shows the assets of the Company to have passed the one hundred million dollar mark, should be introduced by this *résumé* of the Company's history. It is a history of which every one now connected with the Company and its management may well be proud, and it reflects the greatest credit upon all who have been instrumental in bringing about so grand a consummation.

Turning to the report which is presented to the Board to-day, and comparing it with that of last year, which we thought at the time was the greatest report ever presented, we find that the figures for 1889 show the following remarkable increases over 1888: Increase in interest, $303,653; increase in payments to policy-holders, $1,148,051; increase in surplus, $1,716,849; increase in premiums, $3,458,330; increase in total income, $3,761,983; increase in total assets, $11,573,414; increase in new insurance, $26,099,357; increase in insurance in force, $75,715,465.

The ratio of death-claims paid to average insurance in force shows a decrease during 1889 as compared with 1888, the ratios being 1.09 per cent. in 1889 against 1.13 per cent. in 1888.

It is gratifying to note that the interest receipts of the Company were 4.8 per cent. on the average net assets for the year, and 4.9 per cent. on the average invested assets. It is proper to make this distinction, because a part of the net assets consists of quarterly and semi-annual premiums due subsequent to January 1, 1890, and of accrued interest on investments, neither of which items the Company has yet had opportunity to invest, although it makes itself whole as regards the deferred premiums by a larger premium charged for the same amount of insurance.

To sum up the strong points of the report, we have only to note the immense revenue of the Company, now nearly thirty million dollars per year; the character of its securities, as shown by the market value over cost; the magnificent sum of its total assets; its strong financial position, as shown by its large surplus; and the immense volume of its current business, amounting during 1889 to over $151,000,000 of new insurance. The amount at risk is now nearly $500,000,000, and the growth of the Company during the last five years has been so rapid that I think we hazard nothing in saying that the day is not far distant when the Company will have one thousand millions of insurance on its books.

Mr. Loomis L. White, of the Finance Committee, following Mr. Appleton, said that this was an era in the history of the NEW-YORK LIFE INSURANCE COMPANY. "The Finance Committee," he said, "best appreciates, perhaps, the vast work which has been accomplished during the past year, and for the last ten days we have been wading ankle-deep in figures that are so immense and colossal in their proportions as to

NEW-YORK LIFE

INSURANCE COMPANY.

WILLIAM H. BEERS, President.

DIAGRAMS ILLUSTRATING THE NEW-YORK LIFE INSURANCE COMPANY'S NON-FORFEITING FREE TONTINE POLICY, WITH MORTUARY-DIVIDEND EQUAL TO ALL PREMIUMS PAID, IN CASE OF DEATH WITHIN TWENTY YEARS.

Age of Insured, 35 years. **Amount of Policy, $100,000.** **Annual Premium, $4,100.**

The portion of the circles printed in parallel lines represents the face of the Policy; the portion printed in black represents the Mortuary-Dividend equal to all Premiums paid. Both together represent the Amount Payable in case of death in any year of the Tontine period.

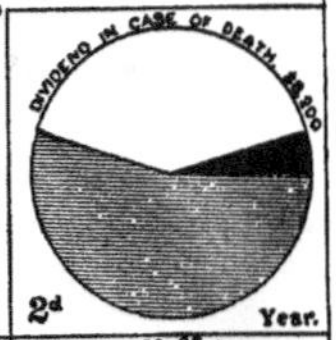

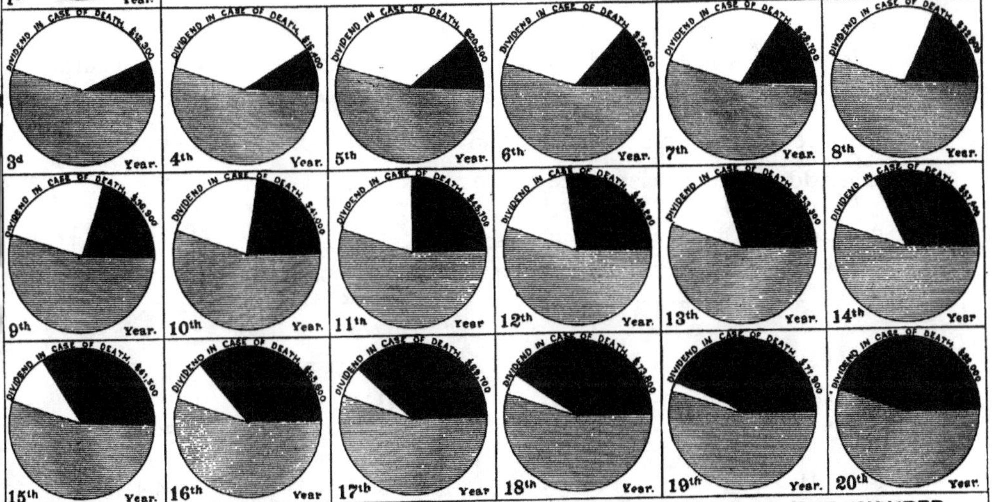

COST OF THE POLICY

ANNUAL PREMIUM.

$4,100

PAID IN 20 YEARS

$82,000.

METHODS OF SETTLEMENT AT THE OPTION OF THE INSURED, AFTER THE PAYMENT OF TWENTY ANNUAL PREMIUMS.

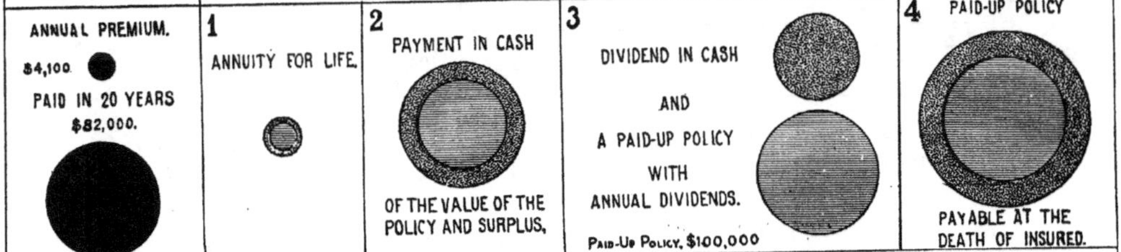

1 ANNUITY FOR LIFE.

2 PAYMENT IN CASH OF THE VALUE OF THE POLICY AND SURPLUS,

3 DIVIDEND IN CASH AND A PAID-UP POLICY WITH ANNUAL DIVIDENDS.

PAID-UP POLICY, $100,000

4 PAID-UP POLICY PAYABLE AT THE DEATH OF INSURED.

The amounts represented by those parts of the circles printed in parallel lines are guaranteed; those represented by the parts printed in dots are estimated additions from Surplus.

excite the admiration of all interested in great financial interests. These results have been attained only by the constant and untiring vigilance and energy of the Officers of the Company." Mr. John Claflin, of the Finance Committee, followed Mr. White, endorsing fully all that had been said by the Chairman of the Committee and by Mr. White, and adding that in commercial circles the wonderful ability that marked the management of this institution would be recognized in a more emphatic manner than it was by the Board of Trustees.

A review of the ten years fully justifies the encomiums of the Committee. Comparing the figures of 1889 with those of 1879, the new business is seen to be nearly nine times as much, the income and insurance in force are more than three times as much, the amount paid policy-holders is two and one-half times as much, and assets and surplus are each nearly three times as much. The substance of two companies, each greater in some respects than the NEW-YORK LIFE in 1879, had been added in the brief space of ten years.

BUSINESS OF 1879 AND OF 1889.

ITEMS.	1879.	1889.
New Insurance Written	$17,098,173	$151,119,088
Income	7,887,126	28,830,123
Paid Policy-holders	4,821,490	12,121,122
Assets, December 31	38,858,831	104,415,322
Surplus, December 31	5,374,403	15,654,263
Insurance in Force, December 31	127,417,762	495,601,970

TOTAL IN TEN YEARS, 1880–1889.

New Insurance Written	$746,737,754
Total Income	167,720,585
" Paid Policy-holders	77,174,873
" Increase in Assets	65,556,491
" " " Surplus	10,279,860
" " " Insurance in Force	368,184,208

SCIENCES
1789
INDUSTRIE
1889
ARTS
AGRICULTURE
PROGRES
RÉPUBLIQUE FRANÇAISE
DE L'INDUSTRIE ET DES COLONIES
EXPOSITION UNIVERSELLE DE 1889
LE JURY INTERNATIONAL DES RÉCOMPENSES
MÉDAILLE D'ARGENT
A La New-York, Compagnie d'Assurances sur la Vie
FRANCE
GROUPE DE L'ÉCONOMIE SOCIALE — SECTION VII
LE PRÉSIDENT DU CONSEIL
COMMISSAIRE GÉNÉRAL
PARIS, 29 SEPTEMBRE 1889
FRANCE
PARIS
OCÉANIE · AMÉRIQUE
ASIE · AFRIQUE
MDCCCLXXXIX
FORCE DOMPTÉE
EUROPE RENAISSANTE

TABLE SHOWING THE CONDITION OF THE LIFE COMPANIES DOING BUSINESS IN NEW YORK, DECEMBER 31, 1889, THEIR BUSINESS FOR THE YEAR, THE SAME ITEMS FOR THE NEW-YORK LIFE, AND THE NEW-YORK LIFE'S SHARE OF ALL:

ITEMS.	THIRTY COMPANIES.	NEW-YORK LIFE.	N.-Y. L'S SHARE.
Assets	$696,943,721	$104,415,322	15.0
Premium Notes and Loans in Assets	19,028,751	367,394	1.9
Surplus	86,745,026	15,654,263	18.0
Liabilities	610,198,695	88,761,059	14.5
Surplus to Liabilities, Per cent.	14.2	17.6	....
Insurance in Force	3,144,677,311	495,601,970	15.8
New Insurance Written	786,096,741	151,119,088	19.2
Total Income	168,184,699	28,830,123	17.1
Premium Notes and Loans in Income	978,977	68,869	7.0
Death-Claims Paid	42,668,529	5,032,466	11.8
Death-Claims per $1,000 Insured	$15.45	$10.15	....
Total Paid Policy-holders	79,273,667	12,121,122	15.3
Expenses and Taxes	34,898,168	5,754,828	16.5
Per cent. to Income	20.7	19.9	....

XI.

A PERIOD OF CHANGE.

1890–1895.

THIS period, though brief in time, was destined to be big with events. It was to be a time of trial and of triumph—a time in which all the forces of official criticism, of anonymous spite, and of the open hostility of former friends were to be directed against the Company, by which its history and its records were to be held up to "the fierce light that beats upon the throne." It was to see the Company come forth from the struggle with but few blemishes, strong in the devotion of its friends, strong in resources and strong in recuperative power. Under the inspiration of a new management it was destined, in a brief space, to regain all it had lost; and, by enlarging the scope of its contracts and making their benefits more definite and certain, it was to spring forward in a new career of popularity and usefulness to which the annals of Life Insurance furnish no parallel. By openness of method and truthfulness of statement it compelled the attention and approval of those to whom the people have committed the oversight of insurance matters, in such manner that the whole business of Life Insurance is now presented to the public in a truer light than ever before—a light which must eventually compel retrenchment and reform. Under the influence of these salutary changes the name of the Company has become a synonym for fair-dealing, for mutuality, and for helpfulness to the insured; and, under the conditions thus created, the security furnished by its policies has become the nearest perfection ever attained in a life insurance contract. No other five years of the Company's history have been so crowded with stirring events in its management, and in no other period has so much been done to make it "a Company of the policy-holders, by the policy-holders, and for the policy-holders."

1890. THE beginning of the year 1890 brought with it a controversy between the Company and the Massachusetts Insurance Commissioner, that disrupted for a time the cordial relations so long maintained with the people and the authorities of that Commonwealth. The controversy arose over the Company's "Ordinary Life Distribution Policy," which, the Commissioner claimed, violated the anti-rebate law of Massachusetts, and was a combination of assessmentism and regular life insurance. The Commissioner communicated to the Company, under date of December 28, 1889, his objections to the policy, and notified the President to discontinue its issue while the Company was authorized to transact business in Massachusetts. A note was added, saying: "As it is not impossible that other companies may have been impelled to consider similar questionable expedients in order to meet the competition of this policy, this letter is made open for their information and guidance." The letter appeared in the Boston papers on the day of its receipt by the Company.

In most controversies of this kind there is a point where misunderstanding begins, to which may be attributed much of the divergence of view which follows. This misunderstanding is often never discovered, or if it is, matters have gone so far, and so much bitterness has been awakened, that pride prevents a rectification of the error and an amicable settlement. Happily, there was to be no such lamentable outcome to this controversy, which, though stoutly maintained on both sides for some time, yet, when all the facts were disclosed, was seen to be rather a misunderstanding of motives and terms, than a real difference of opinion upon essential points. The Commissioner, in his annual report of 1890, which contains his account of the controversy after a settlement had been reached, refers to a correspondence had by the Company with his predecessor concerning the anti-rebate law, to the defiance of that law by some of the Company's agents from other States, and to the statement of one of its managers that a policy would be devised to evade the law. All these things seemed to the Commissioner parts of a deliberate purpose on the part of the Company. When the Distribution Policy was first issued, in June, 1889, no copy was sent to the Massachusetts Commissioner because, owing to the ill-feeling which had been engendered by the conduct of some of its agents as above noted, the Company did not intend to issue the policy in Massachusetts. When the descriptive lists for the first half of the year were sent to the Commissioner, a copy of the policy and formulas for premiums and reserves were requested and furnished. The Commissioner says: "The policy thus obtained occasioned no surprise, and was recognized as the issue that had been foreshadowed and threatened." After an examination of the policy and its reference to the Attorney-General of the State, he notified the Company to discontinue its issue, as before stated.

The Company replied to the Commissioner, under date of December 31, 1889, recounting its compliance with his requests for information, and claiming that it should have had an opportunity to remove objections before an arbitrary judgment was pronounced and scattered broadcast throughout the country. It also claimed that the letter misrepresented both the policy and the Company. On January 5, 1890, the policy was published in full in both the New York and Boston papers. Shortly afterward the question of its legality under the Massachusetts statute was referred to Hon. John D. Long, ex-Governor of Massachusetts, and Hon. A. E. Pillsbury, of Boston. The actuarial questions involved were submitted to Mr. David Parks Fackler, Consulting Actuary, of New York. These authorities sustained the Company on all points; it also appeared that another New York company, doing business in Massachusetts, had for years issued a policy which was open to the same criticism as the policy in question. The Company then withdrew from the State and petitioned the Legislature for a law authorizing the Supreme Court to pass upon the question. While the matter was before the Insurance Committee a compromise was agreed to between the Commissioner and counsel for the Company, and the latter withdrew its request for legislation.*

---

*Such a law as was asked for by the Company was, however, enacted, and was signed by the Governor on May 20, 1890.

The compromise consisted in a change in the name of the policy to "Combination Term and Life Distribution Policy," and in the addition of twenty-six explanatory words. The premium rates were left unchanged. In the copy of the policy given on the following page, the additional words are in *italic*, and the words which were stricken out are placed in brackets.

While there was thus "peace with honor," between the Company and the Massachusetts Commissioner, there was another phase of the controversy that deserves notice—and that is the use sought to be made of the discussion by the agents of other companies. This will perhaps be best understood by reference to the following extracts from a memorandum statement of the case, which appeared in the Boston "Daily Traveller," of May 20, 1890:

January 10, 1890.—An anonymous letter in the New York "World," attacking the NEW-YORK LIFE, was the subject of a despatch sent out by General Manager Smith of the Associated Press, who asked all papers to take the matter up editorially.

January 25, 1890.—Hon. Charles A. Dana [President of the Association] repudiates the action of Smith, and promises that it shall not occur again.

March 1, 1890.—A two-column paid advertisement appeared in the Boston papers, attacking the NEW-YORK LIFE and its policy, intended for a memorial to the Legislature. The memorial was signed by fifty odd agents of other companies. Between this date and the next several companies withdrew from the remonstrance, claiming to have been deceived by the man who originated it.

Agents of other companies seem to have been deeply interested in the controversy, and, as the Commissioner's objections to the original policy form continued to be circulated long after the revised form had received his approval, it is fair to presume that they were not pleased with the outcome.

At the November meeting of the Trustees a letter was read from Mr. Edward N. Gibbs, one of their number, and now Treasurer of the Company, giving an account of a recent trip to Europe. Regarding the business and agencies of the Company there, Mr. Gibbs said: "I cannot close my letter without allusion to the gentlemen connected with the Company whom I met on the other side; every one of them is evidence of the discriminating care with which they have been chosen for their

No. 000,000. (SPECIMEN COPY.) *$20,000.*

THE NEW-YORK LIFE INSURANCE COMPANY,

BY THIS POLICY OF INSURANCE,

AGE, *40.*

ANNUAL PREMIUM, *$712.00.*

IN CONSIDERATION of the agreements, statements, representations and warranties submitted to its Officers at the Home Office, in the City of New York, in the written Application for this Policy, which are hereby referred to and made a part of this Contract, and in further consideration of the sum of Nine hundred and ninety-four Dollars and —— Cents, to them in hand paid, at the Office of the Company, in the City of New York (being the [first] premium *for two years' term insurance*), and of the annual [premium] *payment* of Seven hundred and twelve Dollars and —— Cents (*being the life premium*), to be paid at said Office on or before the Thirteenth day of December, in every year during the continuance of this Policy, commencing on the Thirteenth day of December, 1891,

NOTICE.—In consideration of the stipulations in case of lapse specified in the Policy, the provisions of Chap. 347, of the laws of 1879, of the State of New York, have been waived in the application for this Policy.

DOTH INSURE the life of John Doe, of ——, in the County of ——, State of ——, (hereinafter called the insured), in the amount of Twenty thousand Dollars, commencing on the Thirteenth day of December, 1889, at noon.

AND THE SAID COMPANY DOTH HEREBY PROMISE AND AGREE to pay the amount of the said Insurance, at its Office in the City of New York, to Mary,, wife of the insured; or, in the event of her prior death, to the insured's Executors, Administrators or Assigns, upon receipt and approval of proofs, as hereinafter required, of the death, during the continuance of this Policy, of the said insured, deducting therefrom all indebtedness to the Company, together with any balance of the year's premium remaining unpaid.

THIS POLICY is issued and accepted upon the following express Conditions and Agreements:

First: If this Policy shall become a claim by death after having been in force two full years, the Company will not contest its payment on account of the incorrectness of any statement in the application, or in the accompanying declarations to the Medical Examiner (except in case of fraud), provided, however, that if the age of the insured is understated the amount of insurance payable shall be such proportion of the amount of the Policy as the premium paid bears to the required premium at the true age.

Second: That if the premiums are not paid, as hereinafter provided, on or before the days when due, then this Policy shall become void, and all payments previously made shall remain the property of the Company, except that if this Policy shall lapse or become forfeited for the non-payment of any premium, after there have been paid thereon three full premiums as above specified (*that is to say, the premiums for four years of insurance*), a paid-up Policy will be issued, on demand made within six months after such lapse with surrender of this Policy, under the same conditions as this Policy, except as to payment of premiums, but without participation in profits—and without Mortuary Dividend—for such an amount as the net Reserve on this Policy at the time of lapse, computed by the American Table of Mortality and interest at four and one-half per cent., after deducting all indebtedness to the Company, will purchase as a single premium at the present published rates of the Company, at the age of the insured at the time of lapse; and all right to any other paid-up Policy or surrender value, provided for by the statute of any State or country, is hereby waived.

EXAMINED,

Combination Term and Life.

[Ordinary Life.]

—

Distribution Policy.

—

Mortuary Dividend.

—

Third: That the provisions, requirements and benefits, printed or written by the Company, upon the next page of this Policy, are a part of this Contract, as fully as if they were recited at length over the signatures hereto affixed.

IN WITNESS WHEREOF, the said NEW-YORK LIFE INSURANCE COMPANY has, by its President and Vice-President or Actuary, signed and delivered this Contract, this Thirteenth day of December, one thousand eight hundred and eighty-nine.

positions, and each of them is fitted to stand for the Company with credit in their respective localities. Without doubt the NEW-YORK LIFE leads all American companies in the confidence of the European public, as it should, for reasons we need not look far to discover. The loyalty of all its men whom I saw, to the Company and its executive officers, was a matter of personal pleasure."

At the request of the officers of the Company Mr. Gibbs visited Budapest, in order that he might advise the Board, after a personal examination of the city and the business of the Company in Hungary, upon the subject of erecting an office building there. He recommended that the matter have "favorable consideration." The subject was accordingly referred to the Finance Committee with full power. Land was acquired in 1891 and work upon the building was finished in October, 1894. When the building was opened, in 1894, Mr. Gibbs was present, and made an address upon Life Insurance in the United States, and the condition and methods of the NEW-YORK LIFE.

In no year of the Company's history has it paid so many death-claims illustrating the benefits of Life Insurance in a variety of circumstances and the value of the special features of its own policies, as in 1890. There were forty-two claims paid for $20,000 or upwards, the aggregate amount thereunder being $1,271,641. Among the well-known names in this list were Viscount Cantelupe, of England, John H. Draper, the famous auctioneer, of New York, James Montieth, the geographer, Adam Forepaugh, the showman, Joseph G. Ditman and F. B. Gowan, of Philadelphia. Others who were insured for smaller amounts, whose names are familiar to many, are Amzi S. Dodd, founder of Dodd's Express, Thomas Cornell, owner of the Cornell Steamboat Co., William H. Wells, editor of "Insurance News," Professor R. H. Mather, of Amherst College, General Clinton B. Fisk, General W. W. Belknap, Captain Ebenezer Morgan, and Rev. Dr. Reuben Jeffery. Mr. Gowan was a well-known railroad man, and shot himself through the head with a pistol. There seems to have been no doubt that it was intentional—but, whether he was "sane or insane," who shall say? Happily the NEW-YORK LIFE'S policies do not raise the question. Mr. Gowan insured five years before; he had violated no condition of his policy; he was dead; that was enough; the Company paid $74,267 on his life within four weeks of his death. Mr. Ditman was a well-known Philadelphia banker, and mysteriously disappeared. His horse and buggy were found in Fairmount Park, and several days later his body was recovered from the Schuylkill River. The question was widely mooted whether or not he was in his right mind or whether or not the drowning was accidental. Again the Company's policies did not raise the question; he was dead; and the Company paid his executors $57,415.85 under three policies. The executors wrote: "We cannot too highly commend the prompt and satisfactory manner in which this payment has been made, your Company being the first to make settlement of the insurance on the life of the deceased. The proofs reached your New York Office on Saturday, February eighth, and check was drawn on Monday, February tenth."*

Experience is the best teacher, and results under the Company's policies are the best answers to objections to Life Insurance. "Suppose I live long," says the objector: the Company answers with twenty-nine policies paid in 1890, each of which had been in force over thirty-five years, and the average return after protection for a whole active life-time, was $125 for each $100 paid out. "There is no hurry, I am in good health," says the laggard: the Company shows one hundred and fifty-three policies which became death-claims within less than twelve months after the insured were examined and found "in good health." The regularity with which these men died was something startling to the uninsured, and something re-assuring to those who put faith in the law of mortality; thirty-seven died in the first quarter-year, thirty-six in the second, thirty-nine in the third, and forty-one in the fourth. "My wife does not believe in insurance," says the man who is willing to hide behind his wife's skirts: the Company shows a letter from a widow in California,

---

* This should not be interpreted to mean that the Company does not make careful examination of death-claims; but it is easier to do this at once, when a death is reported, than after the claim is made and a considerable time has elapsed.

which says, "My husband was insured, much against my wish, on April 19, 1890, and received his policy only five days before his death." There is nothing about "blood-money," it is "love-money" now, and the letter overflows with thankfulness. "The insured gets no dividend under a Tontine policy unless he lives a long time," says the anti-Tontine agent: the Company shows a list of two hundred and sixteen policies which became claims by death during 1890, and which returned either half or all the premiums paid during the dividend period in which they matured, in addition to the face of the policies.

One fèature of the Company's Tontines already noted is, the month's grace in the payment of premiums (now granted under all its policies); this feature saved the $10,000 policy of Mr. Isaac M. Jordan, of Cincinnati, from forfeiture when there was no opportunity for re-instatement. Mr. Jordan's premium fell due November fourth, and remained unpaid; December third he fell down an elevator shaft and was instantly killed. General and Senator John M. Palmer, of Illinois, settled a matured Tontine in August of this year, and wrote to the Company's managers at Springfield concerning it: "No other Ordinary Life Policy is so advantageous or profitable as this, and the results are such as prove the judicious and efficient management of the great Company you represent." Mr. James R. Nairn, of Burlington, Iowa, being then 66 years of age, wrote concerning his maturing Tontine: "This is the second policy I have carried to maturity in the NEW-YORK LIFE, and I can heartily recommend the Company and its plans to any one wishing reliable indemnity and a good investment of funds." The significance of a few seconds of time was illustrated in the death-claim of Mr. Edward P. Johnson, who, with his wife and infant son, were killed in the railroad accident on the Old Colony Railroad at Quincy, Mass., August 19, 1890. It was necessary to decide who died last, in order to know whose estate the claim was payable to. Dr. J. H. Gilbert, of Quincy, who had charge, as medical examiner, of the examination into the disaster, gave his opinion under oath, that the parents were crushed by the accident and killed instantly, while the child, being killed by steam, "survived his parents for several seconds, at least." The policy was therefore paid to the administrator of the child. One more claim, which does such honor to human nature and so shames the man who wishes to put off insuring his life as long as possible, must find record and remembrance here. On November 29, 1889, a gentleman, aged 33, made application to the Company for a policy payable, in case of his death, to a lady whose relation to him was put down in the application as "*fiancée.*" He died in the spring of 1890, being yet unmarried, and his policy was paid in April.

1891. On June 12, 1891, there was published in the New York "Times" an account of the defalcation of Mr. Julio Merzbacher, one of the firm of Sanchez & Merzbacher, Managers of the Company's Spanish-American Department, which defalcation had occurred in the latter part of 1890. It was announced, on the authority of the officers of the Company, that Mr. Sanchez had assumed the amount of the indebtedness and that the Company would lose nothing, being amply secured by the interest of the firm in the business of the department. The next day the amount of the defalcation was announced by the same authority to be $372,000. President Beers was at this time in Europe, and Mr. Sanchez was on his way to Barcelona, Spain, where the new head-quarters of the department were about to be established. These things were made matters of suspicion by the daily press, and soon many wild stories were afloat. Other defalcations were alleged, which, it was stated, would, with that of Mr. Merzbacher, exceed a million dollars. Reference was also made to the charges made by the cashier in 1887. The newspapers were soon in full cry after the Company, and every one who had a grudge or a grievance was allowed opportunity to tell his story, to the Company's disparagement.* In view of the public excitement thus created, the Finance Committee met on June sixteenth and

*Since the first publication last week of the Merzbacher defalcation, every daily paper in the city has had reporters detailed to work up in sensational form every item of either news or gossip they could obtain. There have not been lacking men in the life insurance business who were glad to furnish vague rumors and stale gossip regarding the Managers of the NEW-YORK LIFE INSURANCE COMPANY, and who chuckled with delight when they saw the importance given to such gossip by the daily papers.—*The Spectator, June 18, 1891.*

voted that, they were satisfied there would be no loss to the Company by reason of the defalcation, and in order that the public might be equally satisfied, that the Superintendent of the Insurance Department be invited to make a thorough examination of the Company. This request was communicated to the Superintendent on the same day, who promptly announced his compliance, and the examination was begun on June twenty-second. On June eighteenth the Committee published a statement to the effect that the net deficiency in the accounts of the Spanish-American Department had been charged as a disbursement prior to December 31, 1890, and that the Company's report of that date was correct.

On June nineteenth a full statement was laid before the Trustees, which, in substance, was as follows: The business of the Spanish-American Department had grown very rapidly under the management of Messrs. Sanchez & Merzbacher, and in 1891 the total amount of premiums passing through their hands was about $2,750,000. In view of the large extent of territory covered by the department, and the lack of means of rapid communication, half a million dollars in premiums in transit and in course of collection was considered to be within reasonable limits. It appeared, however, that during the absence of Mr. Sanchez from the head-quarters of the department in New York, Mr. Merzbacher had used the funds of the Company in speculation. This was discovered by Mr. Sanchez on his return, to whom Mr. Merzbacher made a full confession, and turned over such property as he had, amounting to about $47,000.* The renewal interest of the firm in the business was more than sufficient to cover the deficit to the Company, and Mr. Sanchez—a man of ample fortune—at once assumed the indebtedness (as he was bound to do under his contract) and took entire charge of the business. The amount was immediately charged in the accounts of the Company to the expense account and to agency balances, and did not appear as assets or surplus in the annual report of the Company for the year 1890. Upon these representations the Trustees approved the action of the Committee, and

* The actual amount as ascertained by the Superintendent's investigation, was $52,412.35.

passed resolutions declaring their undiminished confidence in the Officers of the Company and in its financial condition, and welcoming the fullest and most searching investigation by the authorities of the State. President Beers cabled from Europe his cordial approval of the action of the Company in inviting investigation.

The action of the Officers and Trustees had thus been prompt and decisive, and the whole matter was now in the hands of the authorities for investigation. The public press, with a few exceptions, recognized the fact that all had been done that could be done by the Company, and suspended judgment until the facts should be officially ascertained. To re-assure policy-holders, and to show the public that, judged by the severest test—results,—the Company had enjoyed more than an average degree of prosperity during Mr. Beers' Presidency, a circular was issued in December reviewing the business of the NEW-YORK LIFE in comparison with the two other largest companies, and with all the remaining companies combined.*

---

*A FIVE YEARS' REVIEW.

COMPILED FROM THE REPORTS OF THE NEW YORK INSURANCE DEPARTMENT.

How shall one ascertain whether a life insurance company is well-managed or not? Manifestly, by the *results* obtained. But what shall be our standard of comparison? We consider a man tall or short, heavy or light, according as he compares with other men. *Results, therefore, considered in themselves, and considered in comparison with the results attained by other companies*, must be our guide in determining whether a life company has been well, or ill, managed. As in judging of the character of a man, or of a mountain, we need to see them from several points of view; so in judging a life company, results should be looked at from several different standpoints in order to get a true estimate of them.

We propose to apply these tests to the NEW-YORK LIFE INSURANCE COMPANY, during a period of five years ending December 31, 1890. In order to make our comparisons as fair, and as significant, as possible, we propose to make them (1) between the NEW-YORK LIFE and the two other companies which are nearest to it in size and in the kind and amount of business done; and (2) between the NEW-YORK LIFE and all other companies doing business in New York State, except the two already indicated.

The two companies with which comparisons will be made singly are the Equitable and the Mutual Life. These two companies, with the NEW-YORK LIFE, have more assets, and more insurance on their books, and have done more business during the last five years,—than all the other companies combined. Their methods of business are also more nearly alike. All issue policies, for the most part, upon deferred dividend plans, and have done so during the whole period in question. They have also made greater efforts for new business than other companies—efforts which, as we shall see, have been amply rewarded.

We have divided the comparisons to be made into groups according to subject matter. The first relates to

Meanwhile, in order to enable the agency force to meet wild rumors and unfounded criticism, a system of weekly bulletins, giving the encouraging features of the situation, and urging the agents to renewed activity, was inaugurated by Mr. George W. Perkins, Inspector of Agencies at Chicago. These bulletins did more than to defend the Company, they gave valuable helps and hints to the solicitor and awakened his enthusiasm in his work. The publicity given to the Company's affairs made an opportunity which was used to press home the substantial results of forty-five years' work, and the duty of every man to insure his life.

The year which was thus closed had been one of the most remarkable and trying in the Company's history. Yet, notwithstanding these adverse conditions, the new insurance issued, less the amount "not taken" during the year was $113,529,918, as compared with $126,681,901 during the previous year. It was a splendid tribute, not only to the loyalty and energy of the agency force, but to the confidence of the public in the strength of the Company and in the integrity of its management.

INSURANCE.

ITEMS OF BUSINESS COMPARED.	NEW-YORK LIFE.	EQUITABLE.	MUTUAL LIFE.	ALL OTHER CO'S COMBINED.
1.—Insurance in Force Dec. 31, 1885	$259,674,500	$357,338,246	$368,952,337	$1,037,552,405
2.—New Insurance Paid for, 1886–1890*....	503,900,650	634,782,458	452,686,792	1,147,545,179
Ratio of New Insurance to Amount in Force December 31, 1885	194.1 Per Cent.	177.6 Per Cent.	122.7 Per Cent.	110.6 Per Cent.
3.—Total of Old and New Insurance	$763,575,150	$992,120,704	$821,639,129	$2,185,097,584
4.—Insurance in Force Dec. 31, 1890	569,338,726	720,662,473	638,041,180	1,614,913,372
Ratio of Insurance in Force Dec. 31, 1890, to above Total	74.56 Per Cent.	72.64 Per Cent.	77.65 Per Cent.	73.91 Per Cent.
5.—Gain in Insurance in Force, in Five Years, 1886–1890....................	$309,664,226 119.3 Per Ct.	$363,324,227 101.7 Per Ct.	$269,088,843 72.9 Per Ct.	$577,360,967 55.6 Per Ct.
Ratio of Amount Gained to Amount of New Insurance Paid for	61.45 Per Cent.	57.24 Per Cent.	59.44 Per Cent.	50.31 Per Cent.

* Does not include policies "not taken."

The significance of these comparisons is obvious. The companies had certain amounts of insurance on their books at the beginning of the period; they secured other amounts; the natural inquiry is—

1. What relation does the new business bear to the old? Business helps to make business, and a company with $100,000,000 of insurance on its books can write new business much more easily than a company with only $10,000,000.

2. Having had certain amounts of insurance and having obtained certain other amounts,—what has become of it? How much of it has been retained?—what proportion of both old and new business

1892. WITH the beginning of the new year the Company announced that its first twenty-year Tontines were maturing with the following results: Ordinary Life Policies, if surrendered for their cash value, were returning from thirteen to forty-eight per cent. in excess of their cash cost; Twenty-year Endowment Policies were returning from fifty-two to fifty-nine per cent. in excess of their cash cost; and Limited-Payment Life Policies were returning from thirty-five to one hundred and thirty-four per cent. of their cash cost. The dividends on Limited-Payment Life Policies, if continued, were from sixty-one, to one hundred and fifty-nine, per cent. of all premiums that had been paid.

The report of the Superintendent, embodying the results of his examination which had occupied six months, was furnished to the news-

---

is now on the books? If a company's business has been poor in quality—if it has been put on the books simply to make a show—the ratio of present business to both old and new business will show it.

3. Having had certain amounts of insurance and gained other amounts,—what relation exists betweeen the amounts gained and the amounts formerly held?—in short, how rapidly are the companies growing?

4. A certain amount of new business having been put on the books and a certain gain made of the insurance in force,—what relation does the gain bear to the new business? What proportion of the new business has been retained after all losses have been made good?

These ratios are not specious; they are founded on the logical relations of the various items, and they establish beyond question the superior character and relative volume of the new business of the NEW-YORK LIFE.

ASSETS.

ITEMS OF BUSINESS COMPARED.	NEW-YORK LIFE.	EQUITABLE.	MUTUAL LIFE.	ALL OTHER CO'S COMBINED.
1.—Admitted Assets December 31, 1885....	$66,515,406	$65,547,594	$108,431,779	$283,169,899
2.—Income in Five Years, 1886–1890.......	125,607,602	135,503,531	136,570,831	352,570,966
3.—Total to be accounted for..............	$192,123,008	$201,051,125	$245,002,610	$635,740,865
4.—Admitted Assets December 31, 1890....	115,093,966	116,887,786	146,494,180	374,752,827
Ratio of Assets December 31, 1890, to above Total........................	59.91 Per Cent.	58.14 Per Cent.	59.79 Per Cent.	58.95 Per Cent.
5.—Gain in Admitted Assets, in Five Years, 1886–1890....................	$48,578,560 73.0 Per Ct.	$51,340,192 78.3 Per Cent.	$38,062,401 35.1 Per Ct.	$91,582,928 32.3 Per Ct.
Per Cent. of Income Added to Assets, in Five Years, 1886–1890............	38.68 Per Cent.	37.89 Per Cent.	27.87 Per Cent.	25.98 Per Cent.
6.—Paid Policy-holders, including Death-Claims, in Five Years, 1886–1890....	$53,536,177	$55,383,105	$74,158,886	$186,053,811
Per Cent. of Income Paid Policy-holders, including Death-Claims, 1886–1890	42.62 Per Cent.	40.87 Per Cent.	54.30 Per Cent.	52.77 Per Cent.
Per Cent. of Income Paid Policy-holders and Added to Assets.............	81.30 Per Cent.	78.76 Per Cent.	82.17 Per Cent.	78.75 Per Cent.

papers on January 22, 1892, and to the Company about noon of the next day. It criticised the agency management; the publication of two books for advertising purposes; the purchase and sale of securities through the firm of Loomis L. White & Co.—Mr. White being a Trustee of the Company; the payment of money to suppress the publication of articles attacking the Company; and the Company's real-estate investments.* Reductions were made in the book values of the Company's property as given in its annual report last preceding, as follows:

On real estate owned, ...	$1,612,060.61
On other securities, ...	243,636.99
Total reductions, ...	$1,855,697.60

Here substantially the same method is followed. The companies are made to account for what they had five years ago and what they have since received. What per cent. of both have they now on hand? and what per cent. of their five years' income did they pay to policy-holders or accumulate for their benefit? These are fair questions, and the fact that the ratios are so nearly equal in many cases precludes the supposition that they are accidental. Their significance for the NEW-YORK LIFE lies in the fact that it accounts for its income, as either paid to policy-holders or accumulated for them, at such a high ratio, while at the same time having the highest ratios as regards insurance.

DEATH-CLAIMS.

ITEMS OF BUSINESS COMPARED.	NEW-YORK LIFE.	EQUITABLE.	MUTUAL LIFE.	ALL OTHER CO'S COMBINED.
1.—Death-Claims Paid, 1886–1890	$22,217,857	$31,210,487	$36,012,767	$105,902,566
2.—Total Amount at Risk, One Year	1,993,304,164	2,614,041,811	2,372,746,257	6,406,318,995
Annual Death-Claims per $1,000 of Insurance at Risk	$11.15 Per $1,000.	$11.94 Per $1,000.	$15.18 Per $1,000.	$16.53 Per $1,000.
3.—Total Premiums Received for Insurance, 1886–1890	$96,893,277	$109,752,256	$101,295,717	$266,249,393
Ratio of Death-Claims Paid to Insurance Premiums	22.93 Per Cent.	28.44 Per Cent.	35.56 Per Cent.	39.78 Per Cent.
4.—Total Income, 1886–1890	$125,607,602	$135,503,531	$136,570,831	$352,570,966
Ratio of Death-Claims Paid to Total Income, 1886–1890	17.69 Per Cent.	23.03 Per Cent.	26.37 Per Cent.	30.04 Per Cent.

It is a credit to a life company to pay all the death-claims it has, provided, of course, that they are not fraudulent, but *it may have too many* to be a credit to its management. It is no small commendation of the NEW-YORK LIFE that, although doing business in countries where the death-rate is higher than in the United States, and where an extra premium is charged, nevertheless its ratios of death-claims to the three most closely related items are so low. To make the comparison fair, as between the NEW-YORK LIFE and companies doing no tropical business, the extra premiums received on this business should be deducted from death-claims paid.

*As these criticisms are referred to more fully in Mr. Beers' reply, they are not dwelt upon at length here.

Increased valuations were allowed as follows:

On real estate, ...	$344,722.18
On other securities sold, ...	84,843.22
Total increase, ...	$429,565.40
Total net reductions, ...	$1,426,132.20

The assets of the Company were given as of June 30, 1890, after these re-adjustments, at $120,710,690.64, and the surplus at $14,708,-675.83.

EXPENSES.

ITEMS OF BUSINESS COMPARED.	NEW-YORK LIFE.	EQUITABLE.	MUTUAL LIFE.	ALL OTHER CO'S COMBINED.
1.—Actual Expenses and Taxes, 1886–1890..	$24,326,978	$26,093,442	$25,359,548	$75,380,471
Ratio of Actual Expenses and Taxes to Total Income, 1886–1890..........	19.37 Per Cent.	19.25 Per Cent.	18.57 Per Cent.	21.38 Per Cent.
2.—Actual Expenses and Death-Claims combined, 1886–1890................	$46,544,835	$57,303,929	$61,372,315	$181,283,037
Ratio of Actual Expenses and Death-Claims combined, to Total Income ..	37.06 Per Cent.	42.28 Per Cent.	44.94 Per Cent.	51.42 Per Cent.

Having seen that the NEW-YORK LIFE's ratios of new insurance are higher, and its ratios of death-claims lower, than others', we might fairly expect it to "give odds" on expense ratios, but here too, upon the whole, the Company stands at the head. A large proportion of new business naturally causes (1) a high expense ratio, and (2) a low death-loss ratio. By combining the two, we get an average that shows how much one offsets the other. The NEW-YORK LIFE has a larger proportion of its income left after making these necessary payments, than its competitors, as above.

SURPLUS AND DIVIDENDS.

ITEMS OF BUSINESS COMPARED.	NEW-YORK LIFE.	EQUITABLE.	MUTUAL LIFE.	ALL OTHER CO'S COMBINED.
1.—Dividends to Policy-holders, in Five Years, 1886–1890....................	$11,323,726	$9,705,029	$12,557,737	$37,032,437
2.—Increase in 4% Surplus................	*5,269,871	*8,659,113	*2,926,858	(*)
3.—Total Profits Earned..................	16,593,597	18,364,142	15,484,595	(*)
4.—Insurance Premiums Received..........	96,893,277	109,752,256	101,295,717	266,249,393
Ratio of Dividends Paid to Insurance Premiums Received.................	11.69 Per Cent.	8.84 Per Cent.	12.40 Per Cent.	13.91 Per Cent.
Ratio of Total Profits Earned to Insurance Premiums Received.........	17.13 Per Cent.	16.74 Per Cent.	15.29 Per Cent.	(*)
Average Annual Dividend to $1,000 Insurance in force over one year	$6.16 Per $1,000.	$3.99 Per $1,000.	$5.61 Per $1,000.	$6.05 Per $1,000.
Average Annual Surplus Earned to $1,000 Ins. in force over one year....	$9.03 Per $1,000.	$7.55 Per $1,000.	$6.92 Per $1,000.	(*)

* Massachusetts valuation, Actuaries' Table of Mortality with four per cent. interest in 1885, and New York valuation, same standard, for 1890. As not all companies doing business in New York did business in Massachusetts in 1885, the increase in four per cent. surplus for all cannot be ascertained.

On the day following the publication of the report, the Company published a card in the daily papers, saying, "The severe language of the criticisms is not justified by the facts as found," and announcing that the report would be submitted to the Trustees the next day. It was so submitted, and a Committee of five members of the Board was appointed to consider what action should be taken. Messrs. William L. Strong (now Mayor of New York City), C. C. Baldwin, John Claflin, Walter H. Lewis and Edward N. Gibbs, were the Committee. The Board adjourned until February first, at which time the Committee asked for further time, and it was voted that they be requested to report on February fourth; on the fourth a second adjournment was had to February eighth. At the meeting of February first the President spoke of the bitterness and personal character of the attack upon himself, as well as upon the Trustees, that had been carried on for so many months, and said he felt the Trustees should be no longer subjected to such attacks on his account. He felt no doubt as to the final result, either on his own account or that of the Company, and of his complete vindication, and that the grand results of a life-time of hard and earnest and honest work upon his part would be fully approved by the

---

The sources of surplus are (1) a death-rate lower than the table-rate, (2) an interest-rate higher than that established by law as necessary to solvency (now 4 per cent.), (3) an expense-rate lower than the allowance made in the premium for expenses, and (4) miscellaneous profits, such as lapses, and gains on securities.

Dividends are paid from surplus, but the amount of dividends paid during any given period will be significant only when considered in connection with the amount of surplus gained (or lost) during the same period. The amount of surplus paid out in dividends, plus the amount gained, will show the actual amount earned by the Company.

The higher dividend ratio of the companies which do, for the most part, an annual dividend business, is accounted for by the fact that they have paid out larger proportions of their surplus earned, but as no insurance reports show the surplus of all these companies in 1885 and in 1890 on the same basis, their actual surplus earnings, with corresponding ratios, cannot be shown.

A Crucial Test.

The ratios of surplus earned sum up and show the significance of all the others. The death-rate, the expense-rate, the interest-rate, the lapse-rate, and every other rate that grows out of the character and amount of business done and affects its profitableness, enter into the rate of surplus earned. This rate combines all the others and shows the final net result of all.

The favorable ratios of the New-York Life in so many of the previous comparisons justified the expectation that the final result would show the superior character of the New-York Life's business and management, *as a whole*. That expectation is not disappointed, and this comparative study of the business of all the life companies is commended to our members and to intending insurers.

calm and final judgment of all interested. He offered for the attention of the Board numerous letters and telegrams from agents and leading policy-holders in all parts of the country, urging him to stand fast and maintain the warfare to the end, and assuring him of their earnest support. He said the report of the Superintendent had fully vindicated his own personal integrity, and he proposed to issue a statement reviewing its conclusions on certain other points.

On February second Mr. Beers issued an address to the policy-holders of the Company, replying to some of the severer criticisms contained in the Superintendent's report.* This was published in the

---

* The following extracts from Mr. Beers' letter of February second cover the points upon which exceptions were taken to the Superintendent's report:

The Department's criticisms cover several phases of management, especially investments in real estate and agency work. The criticisms of real estate matters call attention to losses which may be divided into losses actual, which I admit, and losses theoretical, which arise from difference of opinion. I admit certain losses, which I will point out specifically, with the attendant circumstances, and I raise the question of difference of opinion as to the remainder.

PLAZA HOTEL.

The report alleges a loss on this property of $283,994. The Superintendent of Insurance uses this language in connection: "In property of this character and of such great value, the opinions of real estate experts of equal ability and integrity often differ, and other able and conscientious appraisers might value this property at higher figures, and even beyond its cost." The gentleman who, by direction of the Superintendent of Insurance, valued this property at $2,500,000, is a man eminently qualified to give an opinion on such a question. But it is also a fact that another gentleman of equal ability and character, within a few weeks, testified before the Supreme Court of the State of New York that, in his judgment, the property at the present time is worth $3,000,000. From your point of view, then, is it not fair to conclude that the alleged loss may after all exist only as a matter of opinion? But the case will bear one more comment. This property is as finely located as any on Manhattan Island for hotel purposes, and perhaps as finely as any hotel property in the United States. It is in the line of increasing values and, in my judgment, will ultimately yield the Company a large return on the original investment.

[NOTE.—These estimates of the value of this property have been confirmed by offers since received by the Company.—J. M. H.]

HOME OFFICE BUILDING.

The report alleges a loss on this property of $364,295. Its book value is $1,914,295, and it enters the Superintendent's report at $1,550,000. To illustrate again how opinions vary as to the value of real estate, let us make a parallel between this and property of a similar character in New York, and draw a conclusion. Take the value placed upon our home office building for the purposes of taxation, and place it beside the same value of the Equitable Life Assurance Society's home office building. The official valuation for purposes of taxation of our home office building is $1,050,000; of the Equitable home office building, $3,800,000. A statement of the figures at which each property was entered in the assets of its respective company December 31, 1890, is as follows: The home office building of the NEW-YORK LIFE, $1,914,000; home office of the Equitable, $15,140,000. The Department's estimate of the value of our property is approximately eighty per cent., while the assessor's figures for the purpose of taxation are a little more than fifty per cent. of its book value. As the gentleman who appraised principal journals of the country on February third. When the Trustees assembled on February eighth Mr. Beers presented his resignation.* It was laid on the table until the reading of the report of the Committee. This report was in substance as follows: There was nothing in the report of the Superintendent which showed corrupt or dishonest use of the Company's funds for the private gain of any officer of the Company. Its financial condition, its enormous increase in assets and business showed that, to produce such results the management must have been, upon the whole, intelligent and honest. The business of the Company had, however, outgrown the methods and checks then in use;

---

our home office building has never made an appraisal of the value of the Equitable's home office building, we can hardly draw a conclusion from that basis, but figuring from the value placed upon it by the assessor, its total value would be approximately $7,600,000, if the book value of our home office were accepted at par.

I cite these figures as strongly bringing out the truth of my suggestion concerning opinions as to real estate values. Every one is familiar with the eminent success of the Equitable Life Assurance Society, and no one would be so absurdly unjust to that company as to allege a loss on this one parcel of real estate of $7,500,000, or indeed any loss at all, from the policy-holder's view. Therefore is it not worthy of your consideration that in this case, as in the matter of the Plaza Hotel, the loss alleged is, after all, perhaps a matter of opinion? In fact, I could cite you good authority on real estate values in New York who will place our home office building to-day at a valuation in excess of its cost. There are many reasons why this estimate would be conservative. In the first place, the real estate was purchased in 1869 and is exceptionally well located. Any one who knows anything about the history of real estate values in New York for twenty years will agree that there has been during that period a heavy advance in this and all property similarly situated. The building has not been allowed to deteriorate in any particular, and it would seem that our statement of actual cost, $1,914,000, was a very conservative figure.

HOLBROOK HALL, NOW CALLED THE YOSEMITE.

On this item a loss has been made. Briefly, the facts are these: In 1882 we made a loan on this property when in course of construction, and after the man to whom the loan had been made had spent not only his own means (a considerable sum), but the money loaned him as well, he failed, and we were obliged to foreclose. The cost of this property to us after foreclosing was very little more than the amount of the loan. The work of completing the structure was then placed in the hands of an eminent constructing engineer. He supplemented his own knowledge by employing an architect, and the build-

---

*NEW YORK, Feb. 8, 1892.

To the BOARD OF TRUSTEES OF THE NEW-YORK LIFE INSURANCE COMPANY.

Gentlemen: As you all know, I have nothing at heart but the continued welfare and prosperity of this Company, to which I have devoted the best years of my life. I have no personal ends to serve, but at my advanced age and in my present state of health, I require relief from the very onerous labors of the Presidency, and but for the long-continued and persistent assaults upon the Company, which have been chiefly directed against me personally, I should long ago have asked you to lighten my labors. I also recognize the fact that such assaults, however unjust, may in the end prove detrimental to the Company's interest. I therefore hereby tender my resignation of the office of President, to take effect Wednesday, February 10, 1892. Yours truly,

WILLIAM H. BEERS, *President.*

and the Committee recommended (1) a division of duties of the executive officers, by the appointment of an Auditor who should report direct to the Trustees; (2) the adoption of a By-Law that no salaried employé of the Company, other than the President and Vice-President, should be eligible as a member of the Board of Trustees; (3) that a committee of five be appointed to make nominations to fill vacancies in the Board; (4) that the committees be reörganized and the work of the Board distributed among them; (5) that a committee be appointed to revise the By-Laws so as to carry out these recommendations, and to add to the efficiency of the Board. The Committee further stated that, as the Presi-

---

ing was finished. It was filled with a desirable class of tenants, and would have paid a fair return on its cost but for two errors, which could not have been foreseen and which do not justly subject the Finance Committee to the charge of making a bad investment of money. In carrying out a theory of fire-proof construction the architect made the same error precisely that the architect of Vice-President Morton's hotel, "The Shoreham," at Washington, made, and both buildings had to be reconstructed for substantially the same reason. The mistake of the architect in each case was in creating such a condition that dry-rot speedily destroyed the timbers, and the buildings had to be vacated at once. It was then discovered that, in addition, the foundations of Holbrook Hall, put in by the man who first obtained the loan, were insecure, and as a final result the whole structure had to come down. It was then rebuilt under the supervision of McKim, Mead & White, on the most approved lines, and there is not a finer structure of its class in this country to-day. The absolute loss to us, therefore, was approximately the cost of the first building. This we charged off, and we entered the property in our annual statement at the cost of the present building and ground. The figures, $729,066, the appraiser of the Insurance Department refused to accept; $480,000 was named instead, and entered in the Insurance Department's findings. It is proper to add that on our present basis of rental this property will yield, when fully rented, a net income of six and a half per cent. on the value placed upon it by the Insurance Department, and would yield a little more than four per cent. on our valuation, $729,066.

THE PARIS PROPERTY.

This property was purchased some years ago under the supervision of the Chairman of our Finance Committee, who was on the ground at the time. His investigations as to the value of the property were most searching, and the purchase was made with all due care. That the rental value of the property has since depreciated is true, and that there is an apparent loss is true; but if the Superintendent had not only secured an appraisal of the value of the property as it now stands, but also had investigated the value of the property when it was purchased, he could have fully satisfied his duty as an examiner, and at the same time could have given you a satisfactory reason for the original price paid. But no such investigation was made. And as his findings seem to do us an injustice, not only as above cited, but also in the value placed upon the property now, the matter will bear a word more in explanation.

It was brought to my notice during the Superintendent's investigation that the figures supplied by the Department of Taxation of the French Government, on his request, represented values fixed solely for its particular purposes. Our manager at Paris with great difficulty succeeded in getting the *Crédit Foncier*, the largest institution of its kind in France, and a society the reputation of which is well-known throughout Europe, to have a valuation made of our property. This valuation was made with the greatest care by two of its most competent and experienced Inspectors, and their findings, properly attested, were submitted to the Superintendent of Insurance. He preferred, however, inasmuch as we could not procure in the limited time at our disposal an admission from the French Government that its dent had notified them of his intention to retire from the active direction of the Company at this meeting, they recommended that he be employed thereafter, in an advisory capacity, at an annual salary of $25,000, during the remainder of his life. Mr. Appleton presented resolutions accepting Mr. Beers' resignation, commending his services to the Company and authorizing his employment as recommended by the special Committee, but at an annual salary of $37,500. The resolutions were adopted unanimously, except as to the increase of Mr. Beers' compensation; on this point the Committee adhered to their former views. The special Committee was continued until February tenth, and a motion was adopted that on that date the Board proceed to vote for President.

---

figures represented taxable value only, to reject the figures offered in this way. The estimate of the Inspectors exceeds the figures of the French Government by $163,000, and their estimate of its prospective value, based on improvements certain to be made by the city of Paris, exceeds the figures adopted by the Superintendent by $393,600.

Our Western Buildings.

The report of the Superintendent of Insurance values the office buildings recently erected by us in Minneapolis, St. Paul, Kansas City and Omaha at their cost to the Company, but as his opinion of the wisdom of the investment seems to be uncertain, as this language indicates: "There is no immediate prospect that they (the buildings) will prove as profitable as the investments of life insurance companies should," I desire to offer a word in that connection. There are two reasons why the immediate income from these properties is smaller than we may fairly expect to receive in the future. First, the buildings were begun under normal conditions, but were completed in the midst of a period of business depression in the four cities mentioned, and, accordingly, we have had fewer tenants and lower rents than we may reasonably expect hereafter. Second, the buildings were located with a view to future development of their respective cities. Any one who has observed the rapid growth of the West will appreciate the necessity of considering the future, even more than the present, in the location of an office building. Present revenue was, therefore, not so much of a consideration as that the building should be so located that the future may tend constantly to increase, and not to decrease, the rent-producing power and value of the properties. You will understand, of course, that investments of this character are valuable, because the element of risk in re-investment is practically eliminated. The money expended in this way is a fixed item for a very long period of years. The full wisdom or folly of such a transaction is developed only by time. You will be interested to know, however, that one of these buildings is already yielding us a fair return on the money invested, and I am further advised by competent authority that since the date of our purchase of the real estate on which these buildings are situated there has been a net appreciation in its selling value of $500,000, as shown by appraisals made at the close of 1890, and by purchase of adjoining property since made by other people. In entering these properties on our books, and in submitting our estimate of their value to the Superintendent, which he accepted, we did not take this evident increase into account. As evidence that the erection of this chain of Western buildings was well considered, I point you to the fact that the investment was entered upon after discussion and approval by the Board of Trustees. It is my theory that it is only fair to the members of a company like this, the nature of whose business makes large accumulations of money necessary, that the money to be invested should go, as far as is practicable, to those sections of the country whence it emanates. In this case, a part of the money received was invested amongst the people who paid it.

The Board met on February tenth, adopted the report of the special Committee upon the re-organization of the Company, and heard a further report from the same Committee upon a nomination for President. The Committee had determined to recommend some one who was thoroughly conversant with the business of life insurance, and after considering several names, had sought a conference with Hon. John A. McCall, in whom they found certain requisites that would make him more useful as President of the Company than any other man in the world could possibly be. His whole business life had been devoted to Life Insurance, first in the Insurance Department and afterward as an officer of the Equitable

---

The only theory on which these buildings can be rated as bad, or even doubtful, investments, is one which discredits the future growth of the Western States. The report notices that "As advertisements of the Company, they (the buildings) no doubt have a considerable value." This is eminently true. The territory in which these buildings serve especially to advertise the Company includes the States of Minnesota, North and South Dakota, Montana, Iowa, Nebraska, Kansas, Missouri, Texas, and Indian Territory. The people of these States have constant business and social intercourse with one or more of the cities in which the buildings have been placed. The buildings have therefore become widely known, for, as the Superintendent's report says, "each of them forms one of the attractions of the city in which it is located."

The influence of these buildings upon the Company's business is extremely important. In 1886, the year before the buildings were begun, the aggregate new insurance written by the Company in the territory in question was $8,047,200. This aggregate has steadily increased until, for the year 1891, it amounted to $28,869,950, which is the largest business that was secured in that field during that year by any life insurance company. And not only was the quantity of the business remarkable, but its quality was such as to make it most desirable in every way. Without the buildings, it is safe to say that such results could not have been obtained.

AGENCY MANAGEMENT.

Under the head of Agency Management, the Superintendent of Insurance says that "Funds of the Company to the extent of hundreds of thousands of dollars have been advanced to these agents, without interest and upon insufficient security." To persons unfamiliar with the life insurance business, this statement would seem to indicate the worst possible management of our Agency Department; the facts ought, therefore, to be fully explained. The general system upon which advances have been made to agents by this Company and by other life companies, may be illustrated as follows (the figures used being merely illustrations and not the terms of any actual existing contract): The Company, we will say, enters into a contract with Brown, who is the general agent or manager for a State, that he shall receive a commission of twenty-five per cent. of the first year's premium on all policies placed by him, and a renewal commission of five per cent. on each renewal premium paid on such policies. Brown, of course, finds it necessary to employ Jones and others as sub-agents, and he ordinarily pays them the twenty-five per cent. commission allowed him by the Company on first year's premiums. Brown relies upon his renewal commissions for his own compensation, but while he continues in active service he is frequently allowed to draw a fixed amount against commissions for his living expenses, such amount being regulated by the circumstances of the case.

As competition increases, Brown finds that in order to retain sub-agent Jones he will be obliged to pay more than twenty-five per cent. commission. To do this, Brown is obliged to make a new arrangement with the Company. Instead of increasing Brown's first year's commission, the Company agrees to advance to him a sum equal to two renewals (or ten per cent.) on business secured by Jones,

John A. McCall

PRESIDENT NEW-YORK LIFE INSURANCE COMPANY, FEBRUARY 12, 1892—

Life Assurance Society; he had made two or three examinations of the Company; he understood its methods and accounts; and his views were conservative. His relations to the two other great companies were friendly, and he would be able to harmonize animosities resulting from competition, and so effect a saving of expenses in the conduct of the business. They had asked Mr. McCall for authority to present his name, and he had consented, provided he was not made a competitor with any other candidate. The Board then adjourned until February twelfth.

The Board met on the twelfth and immediately proceeded to ballot for President, and Mr. McCall was unanimously elected. A committee

---

and to hold all of Brown's future renewal commissions under the contract as security for the advance. Brown is now able to pay Jones thirty-five per cent. commission, and so retain his services. But at the end of the year, Brown is apparently in debt to the Company in an amount equal to ten per cent. of all first year premiums secured by Jones, and the larger the business the larger the apparent debt. This will continue until such time as the old business kept on the books greatly exceeds the amount of new business annually done. In a rapidly increasing business, this result will not be reached for several years, but, if the total amount paid to Brown has not exceeded what the business was actually worth, the time will come when the commissions accruing under his contract will exceed the total cost of the year's business. Brown's business from this time forth will require a less expenditure on the part of the Company in proportion to its volume than heretofore, and his so-called indebtedness as it appears under his contract will disappear more rapidly than it accumulated, at which time Brown will realize the profit for which he has worked.

You will notice that this so-called debt does not represent money which Brown has squandered, or retained for his own uses. He has simply used the money to carry on the Company's business. If it should ever happen that Brown's renewal commissions fail to cancel the debt, the business has simply cost the Company what it cost Brown, and the Company has taken good care that the total amount of commissions and advance received by Brown should never be a sum greater than the new business secured by him was worth. The Company having already paid for this business in large part, will have a lower expense ratio to this extent in the future, and its surplus will be correspondingly increased.

L. C. Vanuxem & Co.

The Superintendent criticises the agency of Messrs. L. C. Vanuxem & Co., at Philadelphia, Pa., and alleges a debt to the Company on account of what he terms "extravagant allowances," of several hundred thousand dollars. Referring to the illustration above of the method on which a general agent's business is conducted, and the manner in which an apparent debt might be contracted, when I state that from 1887 to 1891, inclusive, this firm wrote business aggregating one hundred and thirty-two million dollars, a clear explanation is afforded you of how, under the above practice, a large debt might appear to exist. In this particular agency, the advance contemplated in our illustration took on various forms under various contracts (which, however, were always subject to our approval); against the commissions earned and to be earned the members of this firm drew advances for living expenses, as before referred to, and advances on account were made to some sub-agents, but at no time has the amount of money advanced to L. C. Vanuxem & Co. exceeded the value of their entire business. Under this system of organization it has been possible for a single firm to handle a large territory, and by creating a renewal interest (in this case of very large proportions) we have avoided frequent changes in general agents, and have largely escaped the danger of having our business carried to other companies by an agent whose interest in any given policy ceased with the first year of its existence. In this way Messrs. L. C. Vanuxem & Co. have done for years a larger business than the entire new business of several was appointed to wait on the new President and escort him to the room. He was welcomed by the Vice-President and by the counsel of the Company. Mr. McCall said, in accepting the office of President, he meant to be a NEW-YORK LIFE man with all which that implied. His personal relations with those he had left were, however, very dear, and there could be no change in his respect for them. Mr. Beers had always been his personal friend and he thought none the less of him now; the NEW-YORK LIFE was indebted to him for its great progress. Some changes would be inevitable, and he had a proposition to make for which he asked the support of the Trustees. "The agents of this Company," he continued,

---

of the smaller life insurance companies, and the largest business of any single agency in the United States. It has been done at a not unreasonable expense, and the cost of its procurement has been included each year in the disbursements of the Company. The whole theory of this organization, and the purpose of the advance, is first, to produce a large business, and second, to create an incentive for the general agent or manager to procure business at the lowest possible cost, in order that, after a period of years, he may begin to realize a return commensurate with the work done. As the cost of the business is charged off each year, it becomes necessary to keep with the manager a blotter, or sub-ledger, and the items are all brought forward from time to time. Of course, this, under the illustration, would show for an office doing twenty millions of new business in a year, and for a series of years, a large apparent debt, and the Superintendent of Insurance, instead of viewing the business as we have done, as simply business paid for, decided to go into this sub-ledger and spread before you the apparent debt.

It is of first importance that you understand clearly that this money is not due from L. C. Vanuxem & Co. in the ordinary acceptance of the word "debt." It is due under the terms of their contract at such times as the commissions earned on the business done will liquidate the money advanced from time to time for the conduct of the business. It has not been squandered by them, nor retained by them. It has not benefited them personally, and never can, until, as stated, the earnings of their business have liquidated all moneys drawn for every purpose under the contract, including advances and agency expenses of every kind. And here let me call your attention to an extremely important fact, which applies to all discussion of agency matters by the Superintendent, and which he forgot to mention, namely, that these advances, in every case, were charged to expenses in the Company's books when the advances were made, and that the Company has never counted them as a part of its assets or surplus. The Superintendent, therefore, instead of unearthing, with great difficulty, something the Company desired to conceal, as he states, practically sets up an arbitrary standard of what he thought our business ought to cost in any given year, and charged up as a debt the difference between his opinion and ours. It would be scarcely less unjust to the Company had he alleged, in any given year, that the aggregate amount paid for the procurement of the business of that year was one or two millions too large, and in his report had set this up as a sum due from the men to whom it was paid. Right here I desire to state, and I state it with all due respect for the opinion of the official with whose conclusions I differ, that in matters of this character the conclusions of men who have had thirty years' experience in this business, as to the propriety of paying a given sum for a given volume of business (they alone being conversant with all the surrounding circumstances and contingencies), are as likely to be correct, and in the interests of policy-holders, as the opinion of a gentleman who, while eminently qualified for the duties of his office, cannot be credited with special knowledge in the particular interests now under discussion.

[NOTE.—At the present date, October 10, 1895, such progress has been made in the liquidation of the advances made to this firm that there is no longer any doubt but that the accruing commissions "are the most marvelous set of men I ever saw. Throughout this struggle these men have stood by you in the most wonderful way. They come here now impressed with the fact that I am from a rival company. I wish to take some action that will remove the feeling on this account from their minds. The attachment of the agents to Mr. Beers has been the success of this Company, and for the future success of the Company I wish to bring the agents to feel the same attachment for me. There is one of these men of pre-eminent ability and worth, whom I wish to bring to this office and make one of the officers of the Company. This is Mr. George W. Perkins, and I want to make him my right-hand man in the

---

on their business will cancel all advances and leave a handsome surplus, in addition to the amounts drawn for "living expenses."—J. M. H.]

SPANISH-AMERICAN DEPARTMENT.

The Superintendent naturally treats at some length the affairs of the Spanish-American Department. The invitation extended to him by our Board of Trustees to examine the condition of this Company was called out chiefly by an incorrect and misleading statement relative to an alleged defalcation by one of its managers, for which the Company, it was stated, alone must suffer. I shall refer principally in the matters discussed by the Superintendent under this head, to this central, and to you most important, question. It is a fact that Mr. J. Merzbacher, one of the managers, at that time, of the Spanish-American Department, became a defaulter for a large amount. The statement as originally published, that Mr. Merzbacher defaulted direct to the Company, was an error. Under the contract which we had with the two managers of the Spanish-American Department, each became responsible for the actions of both, and Mr. Sanchez, the other general manager at that time, and the manager of the Spanish-American Department at the present time, accepted under the terms of his contract full responsibility for the Merzbacher shortage. This shortage consisted of two parts; a direct theft by Mr. Merzbacher from Mr. Sanchez of $419,822.92, and $119,059.10, which was an over-payment by Mr. Merzbacher to the former general manager of the Spanish-American Department. Since the date on which the accounts were made up and the shortage definitely determined, the item of $119,059.10 has been considerably reduced on the books of the Company by accrued renewal commissions, retained by Mr. Sanchez and by him turned over to the Company in cash. The larger item, representing the money appropriated for his personal use by Mr. Merzbacher, has been reduced since December 31, 1890, by $166,671.89, leaving a balance due January 1, 1892, of $253,151.03. The actual net profits for the year 1891 to this Department have not yet been fully determined, but its balance sheet shows that they will not fall short of $100,000. This leaves the balance due the Company on this account on this date a sum but little in excess of $150,000, for which the Company also holds abundant security.

The Superintendent closes his review of the Spanish-American Department with these words: "From the foregoing facts, we must conclude that Sanchez and Merzbacher were treated with a degree of liberality inconsistent with the best interests of the Company." That conclusion is not correct. The Department has always been eminently successful, and its business has been obtained at a normal cost.

[NOTE.—Mr. Sanchez agreed to make good the deficiency caused by Mr. Merzbacher's defalcation, on or before December 31, 1892; he paid over the last dollar of it on May 30, 1892, anticipating the final date by seven months.—J. M. H.]

MR. LOOMIS L. WHITE.

The Superintendent of Insurance discusses at some length the relations which have existed for about sixteen years between the NEW-YORK LIFE INSURANCE COMPANY and Mr. Loomis L. White, agency business. I would like the assurance of the Trustees that they will support me in this action."

The Trustees gave their informal approval of the President's proposal, and upon the adjournment of the Board he asked them to meet, with him, the principal agents and managers of the Company who were assembled in another room of the building. To this assemblage he spoke as follows:

MEMBERS OF THE BOARD OF TRUSTEES, AGENTS, AND MANAGERS:

We are on the threshold of a new administration. That fact does not necessarily imply great and radical changes in the workings of this magnificent Company, but whenever it shall appear to me, intrusted with the management and responsible for its results, that it is wise to depart from the road over which we have been travelling, I shall not be slow to ask your co-operation in making a new path. This is neither the time nor place for references to the causes that make me your presiding officer. I would speak of the future.

We are called together as the representatives of a purely mutual Company, and in that capacity we cannot be personal except as a directing force. We are bound in

---

a member of the Board of Trustees and of its Finance Committee; and two questions are raised. First, as to whether or not a firm, a member of which was a member of the Company's Board of Trustees and of its Finance Committee, could act for it as brokers, without having the opinions of such Trustee as to the value of securities colored by the probable commission which the firm would receive on such transactions; second, whether or not the Company had the right to purchase securities through such a firm of brokers.

The first question may be briefly disposed of without discussion by a simple statement of the results.

In the years covered by Mr. White's connection with the NEW-YORK LIFE INSURANCE COMPANY, about $65,000,000 of securities have been purchased by the Company's Finance Committee, a considerable proportion of them through the firm of which Mr. White is a member, Messrs. Loomis L. White & Co., and on the thirtieth of June last the Superintendent, after valuing these securities at a time of depression, found them worth to the Company something more than $3,000,000 above the cost value at which they are carried on the Company's books. Such a result is the best answer to all questions as to the wisdom of the Finance Committee's action, and, in so far as Mr. White's action influenced it, is an evidence of the value to the Company of this connection. The second question is one on which opinions of counsel differ.

I have now reviewed with you the graver criticisms contained in the Superintendent's report. I shall stop here. I realize that there are other criticisms which I have not referred to, and I do not deem it necessary to do so. I have tried to present to you fairly the facts concerning those of most importance, and I believe I have shown you that, while there have been errors in the management of this Company, there has been no betrayal of trust. A full criticism of errors, with an equally full statement of management deserving commendation, would have been only fair to you and perfectly satisfactory to me, however severe those criticisms might have been; but the Superintendent of Insurance, who was invited to examine the condition of this Company, while properly criticising whatever he deemed criticisable, omitted to state the other side of the case, and in addition, unfortunately, so stated his criticisms as to make it probable that you may have misunderstood them and overrated their importance. I desire to reiterate my disclaimer of infallibility, and repeat the message sent from Europe last summer, honor to exert ourselves solely and absolutely in the interests of the policy-holders. Let there be no mistake about that conception of our duty. So far as in me lies, that shall be the controlling motive of my administration. I am conscious of the need of your support. It may be that in the recommendations that I shall from time to time present for your consideration, a discussion of them will show that some are crude or unwise to adopt. In such cases—few, I trust, in number—you will never find me so set in my opinion that I cannot be convinced that my judgment is not always the best. On the other hand, if there is any of our number that believes that there is no opportunity for changes and improvements, he owes it to the others that he shall not remain to hamper and retard our work. I am sincerely of the opinion that I will have the support and assistance of each and every Trustee. If not, I shall not hesitate to make the issue. I stand here unpledged to any man or set of men in the slightest particular. No person, high or low, has exacted, nor would he receive it if asked, any pledge of place, power, or emolument under my administration.

So much for my platform. We are members of a vast organization, the power for good in which is not solely in its great amount of resources or its surplus of fifteen millions of dollars. Since its organization, in 1845, it has dispensed to policy-holders about $160,000,000. No mind, however gigantic, can conceive or fancy the good that has been accomplished by the payment of that amount. We have a membership of 175,000 scattered all over the world. To them this Company is as important in the consideration of protection to their families as is their own ability to shield them in time of need. Is it to be wondered at, then, that there are watchful eyes on our guardian-

---

that "in business of our magnitude mistakes are inevitable, and we compare favorably with others, but my integrity of purpose cannot be shaken. General net results are the touch-stones in every business."

We need not go far to find confirmation of this. Errors have been made, perhaps, in the management of every company doing business, but as there are some of common notoriety, I may refer to them without seeming to attack the companies themselves. In addition, I will say that to the best of my knowledge and belief, all of these cases are natural experiences incident to the fact that no one is infallible. The Connecticut Mutual Life Insurance Co. lost outright $440,000 through the defalcation of its financial correspondent at Indianapolis in 1888. The Mutual Benefit Life Insurance Co., a company eminently conservative in all things, lost about the same amount on Elizabeth, N. J., bonds. It is a well-known fact that the Equitable Life Assurance Society marked off in 1889 and 1890 almost $1,000,000 on real estate, and that it carries nearly $2,000,000 in its published statement of assets and surplus as "agency balances," "commuted commissions," etc., which is practically another form of expressing what the Superintendent calls "debt" in the case of L. C. Vanuxem & Co. In the report of the Department examination of the Mutual Life Insurance Company, made in 1880, it was stated that $989,701.43 had been charged off to profit and loss on account of its office buildings. After naming these cases (and others might be referred to) we have simply recited a list of average errors, which, in proportion to the interests at stake, represent less loss than the experience of any business of which I have knowledge, and with which the management of the NEW-YORK LIFE INSURANCE COMPANY invites comparison.

In conclusion, let me say: When my official relations with the NEW-YORK LIFE INSURANCE COMPANY began, twenty-nine years ago, its assets, after eighteen years of existence, were less than two and one-half million dollars, and its surplus less than two hundred thousand dollars; its history since, its officially determined assets, June thirtieth last, of one hundred and twenty million dollars, its fifteen millions surplus, and its annual income of over thirty million dollars, I submit to your impartial judgment as the achievements of my associates and myself during the administration of our trust. I remain,

Yours faithfully,

WILLIAM H. BEERS, *President.*

ship, or that a failure to meet, to the utmost, every demand for a rigorous performance of duty will be visited by condemnation? We must act together in their interests. No diversion from that rule will prevail.

A word to the men who gather the funds that we hold in trust. I refer to the agents and managers who are joined in this meeting at my solicitation. I doubt not that the Trustees understand our responsibility to them. They, above all others, are vitally interested in honest management. To me it is marvellous, when we consider the unparalleled trouble through which the Company has passed, that they have been able to accomplish so much. Just think of it! $150,000,000 of new business in a year, when during one-half the time they were devoted, perforce, to a defence of the Company. No other set of men would be equal to it. They have the admiration and respect of the profession everywhere.

Nay, more than that. We must show our appreciation of it in no uncertain way. I propose, and would ask you to support me at the earliest possible moment in its adoption, to select from their number as one of the Vice-Presidents of this Company a man who is conspicuous among them all for ability and integrity, in whose territory during 1891 his agency placed on the Company's books $46,000,000 in new business, and when the year closed he had no money in his possession that he was not entitled to by his work and contract. No announcement that will emanate from us of changes in our official staff will meet with a heartier response from the men who bear the heat and sustain the trials of the business than that of the election of Mr. George W. Perkins, of Chicago, as a Vice-President.

A word, and I will close. In answering a congratulatory telegram from my friend, the Superintendent of the Insurance Department of this State, the warning of Burke in his reflections on the French Revolution recurred to my mind with striking emphasis: "All persons possessing any portion of power ought to be strongly and awfully impressed with an idea that they act in trust to the one great Master, Author, and Founder of society."

The new President took office with the hearty approval and sincere good wishes of all interested in the Company's welfare and in the progress of Life Insurance. All his previous training had fitted him for the high position to which he had been called. Born in Albany in 1849; educated in her public schools, which rank with the best in the country; from the age of seventeen he had been conversant with the business of insurance, first in a general agency, and afterward for sixteen years in the Insurance Department, where he rose by the force of his own ability and industry from the position of clerk to that of head of the Department.* He was

* In an interview with Mr. McCall, published in the "Morning Press" of February 11, 1892, he made this statement concerning one feature of his early career. "When I first entered the insurance business at Albany, I determined to become familiar with all the old records of insurance cases in the office. I used to work nights at this. Whatever success I have had in the business dates from those extra hours I put in."

Deputy Superintendent and Chief Examiner for the Department during the period when so many rotten companies were exposed and their officers punished upon the evidence which his examinations furnished. He had gained the confidence of every honest manager and incurred the displeasure of others by his fearless exposures of official malfeasance, and under his superintendency the New York Department became the terror of evil-doers and the sure support and defence of those who did well. During the six years preceding his election as President of the NEW-YORK LIFE Mr. McCall had been the Comptroller of the Equitable Life Assurance Society, where he had had opportunity to observe the practical working of a great company and to apply, so far as they were applicable to the business of his department, the conservative rules which he had advocated as the representative of the State, charged with the protection of the best interests of policy-holders and companies alike.

On February twenty-fourth, Mr. McCall issued the following address to policy-holders :

TO THE POLICY-HOLDERS OF THE NEW-YORK LIFE INSURANCE COMPANY:

On the twelfth instant I was unanimously chosen by your Board of Trustees to the position of chief executive officer of this Company. I take the earliest opportunity to address you personally, in order to give in a few words my conception of the task I have undertaken, of my responsibility to you, and of your responsibility to me.

First of all, I believe in a frequent and full accounting, on the part of the officers in charge of such a company as this, to its constituent members. "Even-handed justice" should actuate the administration of every public, or semi-public, institution, and it should be absolutely dominant in the affairs of a mutual life insurance company. There should be no privileges, no favors, no discriminations in such a company. To this idea I am fully pledged. I adopt the thought of Lincoln, and shall aim to conduct an administration "of the policy-holders, by the policy-holders, and for the policy-holders." I accept the power of administration, delegated by you through the Board of Trustees, with full recognition of whence that power emanates, and to whom an accounting must finally be made.

I have accepted the Presidency of the NEW-YORK LIFE under almost ideal circumstances. I am not pledged to any man, or body of men, and in this dedication of my undivided effort to your service, lies the only promise I have made which can affect your interests. Moreover, the recent examination of the Company has given both policy-holders and myself a complete knowledge of its affairs, showing not only its strong financial condition, but also enabling us to judge intelligently as to the results of certain methods, and to apply the proper remedy wherever one is needed.

The Presidency of this great Company, as has been said, may well be considered as constituting "the greatest business opportunity of the age." But that expression, while it stirs the pulse, does not satisfy us. It is not "a business opportunity" in the ordinary acceptance of those words; it is that, but it is vastly more. This Company is not a philanthropic organization, but it is, in the highest sense, a beneficent organization, and from the conduct of its affairs we must eliminate a great deal that is accepted as good business methods, but which aim at personal, and not at general, benefits.

Life Insurance has worked a wonderful change in the minds and characters of men within ten years. Its spirit and purposes have been so closely in sympathy with all that elevates society, that its increasing prominence during that time may be taken as an index of the growth of prudence, unselfishness and better living amongst the people generally.

But it seems to me that the larger opportunity won by the phenomenal growth of Life Insurance has been, in some degree, lost sight of by managers who have done most to achieve it. The effort to secure a large business, and thus increase the benefits of Life Insurance, has gradually become an effort to secure the ***largest*** business, without that regard for the highest interests of all, which should be the controlling motive in a business of this character. I wish to say unequivocally, that while this Company ought, from the nature of the case, to write a very large business, I have no ambition to achieve mere bigness. I shall not depart from what seems to me the line of wisdom and of perfect safety, merely to write a few millions more than some other company. If there was ever any virtue in mere volume of new business, of assets, and of surplus, surely this Company is already richly dowered, and we can afford hereafter to take what seems to be a wider view, conscious that there are better ambitions for the future, however good this may have been in its time.

I do not mean by this to imply that the day of large achievement is over. By no means. Life Insurance is only beginning to touch the homes and lives of the people. Its horizon is still expanding. We have only begun to realize how much of a factor it is to become in the economy of that better civilization into which we are daily growing. I would have its growth in harmony with the great principles upon which it is founded, and with the noble ends it is designed to serve.

This opens a field of thought into which I cannot now enter, but it serves to emphasize to you the sense of overwhelming responsibility that rests upon me. If we view the Company as it is to-day, we are compelled to admit that, while men have frequently been called to accept similar trusts, no man was ever called to accept a ***greater*** trust of this character. If we view it as it promises to become under capable, honest and wise guidance, we must be mutually impressed with the immeasurable possibilities for good which lie in the opportunity before us.

If there is any one feeling predominant in my thoughts at this time, it is that of humility—of my utter inability, unaided, to make the most of the Company's future. Beyond a dedication of my own efforts, I place your cordial sympathy and support; and above both I recognize the designs of an overruling Providence, which seems to have given us the conduct of what should become a most powerful factor in the amelioration of human life.

I can say but little more at this time. As rapidly as is consistent with safety, and to such extent as my judgment dictates, I shall from time to time make such changes in

Henry Tuck, Vice-Prest.
A·H·Welch, 2nd Vice-Prest
Geo·W·Perkins, 3rd. Vice-Prest
Rufus W·Weeks, Actuary.

the methods of conducting the business of this Company as may be necessary to make it conform to the principles herein set forth. But I particularly desire to have it understood that I invite from all policy-holders the fullest and freest intercourse with this office and myself that the demands of such a business will permit. And, in so far as due regard for the rights of all will allow, I shall be pleased to see that matters in interest in each particular case have prompt and careful consideration.

Your obedient servant,

JOHN A. MCCALL, *President.*

The Company's annual report for 1891 was submitted to the Trustees on February 24, 1892. It was too soon after the new President came into power to make the report entirely in accordance with his views, but some changes were significant. The amount reported as new premiums did not include any sums paid as dividends in reversion, nor the reserve values of old policies exchanged for paid-up insurance; these items were given separately in disbursements, and in one sum by itself in income. Payments to policy-holders were given in detail—there was no lumping together of such unrelated items as death-losses and endowments. The conservatism of the report was noticeable; over nine hundred thousand dollars, in addition to the reductions recommended by the Superintendent's report, was charged off in reduction of the book value of office buildings, and the reserve for annuitants was increased nearly a million dollars in excess of the requirements of the State.

At this meeting of the Trustees, in accordance with the recommendation of the President, Mr. George W. Perkins was elected Third Vice-President, and Mr. Charles C. Whitney was elected Secretary. Mr. Perkins' recent achievements in Life Insurance have already been referred to by Mr. McCall; his first experience was in the office of Curran & Perkins, General Agents of the Company at Chicago, in 1877; he was afterward Cashier of the Company's Cleveland Agency, and in 1887 entered the field as a solicitor. Two years later he was made Inspector of Agencies for the Western Department. Mr. Whitney entered the Company's office in 1876 as private secretary to President Beers, having previously been Manager of the Western Union Telegraph Office at Indianapolis, Ind., and Assistant Secretary of the Franklin Life Insurance Company of Indianapolis.

Prompt and energetic measures were taken to bring the agency force into sympathy and touch with the purposes and methods of the new management. On March first Hon. D. P. Kingsley was appointed Assistant Superintendent of Agencies. Mr. Kingsley had been the Company's Associate Manager at Boston since January, 1889, and was previously Auditor and *ex-officio* Superintendent of Insurance for the State of Colorado. On March ninth and tenth a Convention of representative agents of the Western Department assembled in Chicago, in accordance with a programme arranged in the previous October. This Convention was attended by President McCall, who used the opportunity to outline his future policy and to point out the encouraging features of the situation in reference to the Company. The following extracts indicate the general scope and spirit of the President's address:

I came to Chicago in a very busy time, at some inconvenience, but with great willingness, to pay my tribute of respect to the first division of the agency corps. You were entitled by your record in the late contest to the front of the line, and you held the position before and after it. You did not stop to inquire the strength of the opposition, but the place where it could be found, and at no period did you show that you were ready to succumb or change your front. Peace brought honor and recognition of your services. The action of the Board of Trustees in selecting your leader as one of the Company's Vice-Presidents has brought me more comfort and the Company greater credit than aught else that has occurred during my brief administration. * * * *

Now that the trouble has passed away, what are the lessons of the conflict? The principal one is that the policy-holders' interests are paramount to all others. No administration of such a trust as ours is, no matter how powerful or well-intrenched we may believe ourselves to be, will be successful if the confidence of our members is withheld. An indifferent acquiescence is of no avail. They must be made to feel that they have as much interest in their Company's progress and welfare as any of the officers or agents. That interest can only be secured by their belief in the honesty and fair dealing of the managers. In bringing this result about power must concur with prudence to beget faith, and wealth with honor to produce respect. Given the support of our members under the conditions stated, we can defy the machinations of any opposition, no matter from whence it springs. So much as a preface.

No other business has been subjected to the same trials as Life Insurance. No other financial interest founded on public confidence could have withstood the assaults that have been made, and prospered as it has. I do not refer, of course, entirely to the attack made on the NEW-YORK LIFE. I have in mind the history of the business, which has been an open book for a third of a century. There is much to marvel at in that record. Through the experimental period of 1859 to 1869, down through the time of mushroom organizations, when an inflated currency created its like in fictitious organizations, no other class of corporations suffered so much odium from failures and mismanagement as that which we stand here to-night, not to defend, but to eulogize. The record of the companies that stood these tests has no parallel. No other business could have prospered under like circumstances or maintained its position in the business world. The honor belongs to those who have kept the faith by energy and integrity, and who compelled in others respect for them and their companies.

* * * * * * * * * * * *

I want right here to read from an address made by a Trustee of this Company to its newly-elected President:

"Unwilling as you seemed to be from the first to assume the high responsibilities of this office and enter upon the discharge of its duties, you have at length yielded to our united request; and now I ask that I may be permitted to say in behalf of this Board, that they look to you with great confidence for a united devotion of time, talents and industry to this work. You have important interests in your hands. We have placed in your immediate keeping the sacred interests of this institution. The widow and the fatherless will look to you for a faithful account of your stewardship, and in a measure the honor of your Board of Trustees is under your protection. In all these respects we look to you for such results as will reflect credit on all concerned."

You will probably be surprised when I say that the address from which I have quoted was made before I was born, namely, on May 15, 1847, to the second President of the Company, Aaron M. Merchant. What was said forty-five years ago is true at this time, and not a word that I have read could not be uttered with equal truth to-day, and with far more importance, considering the magnitude of the Company as it now stands.

As a token of the loyalty of the agents to the new administration, they placed in the hands of the President applications for over four million dollars of insurance which had been written during the preceding ten days (and nights), and upon a large part of which the first premium had been paid with the application.

The re-organization of the Board of Trustees proceeded on the lines recommended by the special Committee on February fourth. Messrs. Collins, Martin and Actuary Weeks, being in the employ of the Company, resigned as Trustees on February twelfth; Mr. Weeks was elected Secretary of the Board on the same date. The vacancies thus created in the Board were filled on March ninth by the election of Messrs. William C. Whitney, Edmund D. Randolph and Woodbury Langdon; on the same date Hon. Charles S. Fairchild was elected in place of Mr. Alexander Studwell, deceased. In place of Mr. Loomis L. White, resigned, the Board elected, on March twenty-third, Mr. A. G. Paine. On April thirteenth Hon. Hiram R. Steele was elected a Trustee *vice* Mr. John N. Stearns, resigned, and Hon. Wm. R. Grace was elected *vice* Mr. Beers, whose term of office then expired.

At a meeting held on March twenty-third the Trustees adopted the new By-Laws recommended by the Committee on revision. The revised By-Laws created the office of Comptroller, and to this office the Board elected Hon. Hugh S. Thompson. Mr. Thompson, when elected, was a member of the United States, Civil Service Commission, having previously been Superintendent of Education, and Governor, of the State of South Carolina, and Assistant Secretary of the Treasury, of the United States. A re-organization of the Home Office force was effected, which did not involve a change of duties so much as a recognition of service rendered, by giving corresponding rank and authority. Mr. H. C. Richardson, who had been in the Actuary's Department since 1869, was made Assistant Actuary on February twenty-fourth. Mr. Dwight Burdge, who had been in charge of the death-claims since the death of President Franklin, was made Superintendent of the Department of Policy-Claims; and Mr. H. P. Stamford, who had been for several years chief accountant, was made Supervisory Accountant. Mr. James A. Brown, formerly of the Equitable Life Assurance Society, was appointed Auditor, March twenty-second. Later in the year other changes in, and additions to, the official staff were made. The office of Treasurer was created, August twenty-second, and Mr. Edward N. Gibbs, who had been a Trustee since 1889, was elected to the position.

Meanwhile the work of encouraging and directing the field force suffered no abatement. A weekly "Bulletin" was established at the Home Office and issued under the supervision of the Agency Department. The recent troubles of the Company were turned to its advantage. The searching examination by the Insurance Department was everywhere quoted as evidence that people knew all about the NEW-YORK LIFE, and that it had endured the severest tests to which a company could be subjected. With respect to the agents' work, large results were not so much emphasized as constant results; every agent was urged to become "a

Chas. C. Whitney, Secretary
Edward N. Gibbs, Treasurer.
Hugh S. Thompson, Comptroller.
A. Huntington, Medical Director.

steady producer," and to work as many hours in a day and as many days in a week in soliciting insurance as he would in any other business. In order to encourage steady work, frequent competitions were arranged under which agents who obtained one or more applications per week for a certain number of weeks in succession, were rewarded with some token of honor; sometimes it was a small sum of money, sometimes a blue ribbon, sometimes it was honorable mention in the weekly "Bulletin." The habit of persistent work thus secured and the enthusiasm thus awakened soon became powerful factors in the production of business.

While the re-organization and encouragement of the agency force was in progress, the Company suffered the loss of one of its most valued managers. Mr. J. Fisher Smith, for over seventeen years its efficient Manager for Great Britain and Ireland, died on April thirtieth. He was succeeded by Mr. John A. Ferguson, who had been previously General Agent for Wisconsin, and, during the five years immediately preceding his appointment, Agency Director of the Mountain Department, embracing the States of Colorado and Wyoming, and the Territories of New Mexico and Utah.

On May thirtieth a Convention of representative Canadian agents was held in Montreal, at which President McCall was present and delivered an address. He dwelt upon the evils of misrepresentation, and of rebates, and indicated that there was no place among agents of the Company for those who could not sell life insurance upon its merits and at the full table rate. The following extracts indicate the drift of his discourse upon these points:

> You can do more by truthful representations to place the business on a higher plane than all the Officers and Trustees combined. It is mainly, if not solely, by your efforts that the insurance is procured; and if, for the sake of a temporary advantage, you cause the contract to be entered upon by deception and misrepresentation, the injury is not confined to the disappointed policy-holder. Almost as bad, in many of its effects upon the business at large, is the offer to share your commissions, or in the language of the day, to rebate them. * * * It has been flippantly said in excuse that, a man can do as he pleases with his own, and that is about the only argument that has been advanced for the miserable and disgraceful system that robs a whole class of men of their just dues. It is the precursor of more evils in the management of the business than all else besides. The ruinous and extravagant contracts and the bonus allotments,

that are now so thoroughly and properly condemned, are the fruit thereof, and are directly traceable to it.

The ridiculous efforts for supremacy, indicating an absence of intelligence and integrity, find in misrepresentations and in rebates their most efficient allies. In establishing rules for our own guidance, let the avoidance of both these evils be the fundamental principle. If we observe such a course and write but one-half the amount that we could otherwise obtain, take my word for it, the Company, its management and its agents will have a better standing in the community than if by rebating and misrepresenting it had exceeded the highest anticipations of the most "progressive manager."

I trust that I have made plain some of the motives that will control my administration. We are not concerned about those who thrive on coaxing. He who is not with us shall not be of us, and on that issue we are prepared to be combative. * * *

We have an agency corps that has been tried in war and that has shown no disloyalty. Its members did not desert when the banner trailed. I believe that the enunciation of our course for the future will discover no laggards in their ranks; and if it does, their intention to remain in the rear cannot be too soon proclaimed. We have no room for doubters or idlers. They may find shelter in other tents than ours, and if they seek it there will be no remonstrance or whining about their departure.

Let us then proceed to the tasks that have been assigned us, with a feeling of earnestness and devotion. In behalf of the Executive Officers and the Board of Trustees I pledge that your efforts will be sustained at the Home Office, by affording you every opportunity to transact an honorable and conservative business. The days of extravagant commissions, bonuses, and guarantees have passed away, so far as the NEW-YORK LIFE is concerned. * * * We will seek by liberal treatment, in the terms and in the construction of policy contracts, to win our way in the esteem of our members. In policy contracts, and in all matters pertaining thereto, the policy-holders will be given the preference. Ours is a Mutual Company, and the advantages in its operations belong to the membership. The skillful and technical verbiage that confiscates reserves, and forfeits "non-forfeitable" policies, will be missing from future contracts, and thus fortified, the close of the year will find us unassailed and unassailable.

From the time of Mr. Beers' resignation, in February, there had been occasional protests on the part of policy-holders against the contract then made for his employment in an advisory capacity during the remainder of life. As the authority of the Trustees to make such a contract was also questioned, Mr. Hornblower represented to the Trustees on June eighth that an agreed state of facts had been made between counsel for Mr. Beers and counsel for the Company, for submission to the General Term of the Supreme Court of the State, for a decision as to the validity of the contract. This action was approved by the Trustees, and the Court decided (in November) that the contract was void. As there was a possibility that this decision might be overruled by the Court of Appeals, a compromise was agreed to under which, until the agreement should be terminated by one of the parties thereto, Mr. Beers was to receive an annual salary of one-half the amount granted under the contract. This was continued until his death, which took place on November 16, 1893.

With this adjustment of Mr. Beers' contract, the last stumbling-block was removed from the pathway of the new management, which could now devote its whole attention to the work of building up the Company. The closing sentence of the new President's Montreal address was an intimation of one of the measures already resolved upon. On June eleventh the Company made the following announcement:

> The NEW-YORK LIFE INSURANCE COMPANY, which, in 1860, originated and introduced the first Non-forfeitable Policy, now makes another ***radical departure*** in favor of the insured. Life insurance is safe or possible only on the principle that life is more precious than money; but no life company has heretofore fully accepted this principle. The NEW-YORK LIFE, believing from its experience that the time has come when this principle should be fully accepted, now announces that, the physical conditions, habits, etc., of an applicant being satisfactory, it will insure him without future limitations. The Company's new contract, the Accumulation Policy, contains no restrictions whatever respecting occupation, residence, travel, habits of life, or manner of death. The only condition of the policy is that the premiums be paid as agreed. If the insured pays the premiums, the Company will pay the policy.

The new policy thus announced retained all the desirable features of the Non-forfeiting Free Tontine Policy, but differed from it (1) in removing all restrictions upon the insured; (2) in making the non-forfeiture provisions self-acting, so that the paid-up value of the policy cannot be lost by neglect; (3) in allowing loans on the policy for specified amounts, at stated times after five years, at five per cent. interest; and (4) in making the policy incontestable for any cause after one year provided the premiums are duly paid. The first policy with the new conditions and privileges was issued June seventeenth, upon the life of one of the Trustees of the Company. A *fac-simile*, slightly reduced, will be found following page 304.

The issue of the Accumulation Policy marks an era, not only in the history of the NEW-YORK LIFE, but in the history of American Life Insurance. The controversy over the restrictions which should be placed upon the insured had been a long one, although the first life policy of which there is any record was without restrictions.* The early policies in this country contained restrictions with respect to occupation, residence, travel, suicide, dueling, violations of law, and the use of intoxicants and narcotics, and more or less of these have been continued until the present time. There was much more occasion for these restrictions fifty years ago than now, because of the ruder condition of society, the less attention paid to hygienic conditions, and the lack of statistics respecting mortality under given conditions. The history of Life Insurance has shown a constant tendency to relax and eliminate the conditions which were formerly considered necessary for safety. The NEW-YORK LIFE eliminated the suicide clause from its policies in 1850, and when the Accumulation Policy was issued nearly every American company had either relaxed its former conditions on this subject or omitted them altogether. With respect to other restrictions, progress had been made in spots, so to speak; that is to say, there was no restriction which some company had not eliminated, as no longer of value, yet every company still retained some of the old-time barriers to absolute insurance. The situation had become absurd; it remained for the NEW-YORK LIFE to end it.

The other new features of the Accumulation Policy were not new in an absolute sense, but they had never before been combined in a single policy on so favorable terms. The non-forfeiture provisions adopted provide that, in case of default in the payment of any premium after the policy has been in force three years, the insurance will be extended, without request,† for its full amount during a period shown by a table in the

---

* The first life insurance policy on record is the one issued at Florence, Italy, in the year 1610, in favor of Giovanni Ballesta on the life of Ser Brother Ferdinand, for the sum of three thousand scudi, the term extending from the August Festival at Piacenza of that year to the Feast of Epiphany in 1611, the premium being 3¾ per cent. of the amount underwritten. The policy was written in mediæval Latin. The old Florentine policy marks the limit of historical life insurance as a transaction. The policy is incontestable and indisputable. It is agreed in the event of the death of Ser Ferdinand the assurers shall make full payment. It covers natural or accidental death. It gives free residence and travel anywhere in the world, by land or water; it is good at issue, and the claim is to be payable three days after the notice of death.—*Insurance Record* (*London*).

† The Massachusetts Insurance Commissioner, in his report of 1895, after referring to the legislation had and attempted in his own State on the subject of non-forfeiture and to the very general practice of other-State companies in requiring notification and surrender of their policies in order to secure

DOTH PROMISE AND AGREE

Age, 42 — to pay *Ten Thousand* Dollars at its Office in the City of New York, to *the insured's* Executors, Administrators or Assigns, immediately upon receipt and approval of proofs of the death during the continuance of this Policy of *Henry C. Mortimer* of *New York* in the County of *New York*, State of *New York* (herein called the insured).

Quarter Annual Premium, $111.80

This Contract is made in Consideration of the written application for this Policy, and of the agreements, statements and warranties thereof, which are hereby made a part of this Contract, and in further consideration of the sum of *one hundred and eleven* Dollars and *eighty* Cents, to be paid in advance, and of the payment of a like sum on the *first* day of *September, December, March and June* in every year thereafter during the continuance of this Policy, until *Twenty* full years' premiums shall have been paid.

[TO FOLLOW PAGE 304.]

INCONTESTABILITY. After this Policy shall have been in force one full year, if it shall become a claim by death, the Company will not contest its payment, provided the conditions of the Policy as to payment of premiums have been observed.

Examined, [signature]

The benefits and provisions placed by the Company on the next page are a part of this Contract, as fully as if recited over the signatures hereto affixed.

In Witness Whereof, the said **NEW-YORK LIFE INSURANCE COMPANY** has, by its duly authorized Officers, signed and delivered this Contract, this *seventeenth* day of *June* one thousand eight hundred and ninety-two.

Limited-Payment Life.

Accumulation.

92-175.

Chas. C. Whitney Secretary. *John A. McCall* President.

policy. On the other hand, if ordinary paid-up insurance is desired, it may be obtained on request within six months, and the amount of such paid-up insurance is likewise shown by a table in the policy. Similar conditions are contained in the policies of some other companies, but nearly always with the condition that, in case of death within a certain time after the insurance is extended, the regular annual premiums will be deducted with interest. That is to say, if you live, the reserve value of your policy is eaten up in paying for term insurance; but if you die, your insurance is not term insurance at all, you must pay regular rates for your protection.

The loan feature of the Accumulation Policy was the first fruits under the new "Insurance Law" of 1892, which allows life companies organized under the laws of this State to loan money upon the security of their own policies. Life companies declare that their policies are representatives of value, good collateral security for a loan, &c., and yet, strange to say, some of them will not loan their own funds on their own paper, and in this State they had no authority to do so until the passage of the law above mentioned. Now that New York companies have such authority, some of them refuse to use it—refuse to accommodate their own members on the plea that it is not a good thing for the policy-holder to borrow money on his policy. The insured under such policies is, therefore, often compelled either to surrender his policy at a loss, or to borrow of those who are ready to take advantage of his necessities.

In order that the new policy might have the widest possible publicity at once, the following proposition was made: Every agent who secured ten applications for at least $1,000 each, on ten different lives, prior to August fifteenth, was to receive a beautifully engraved certificate, certify-

---

any benefit from their non-forfeiture provisions, says: "The Commissioner very strongly urges the introduction of a provision of law which shall apply to all companies, making, in case of lapse after two or three annual payments, the feature of extended insurance or a paid-up policy automatic. The holder of such a policy has confessedly contributed a certain amount of his premiums to the reserve. This belongs absolutely and unqualifiedly to such policy-holder, and his right to a use of the same in some form ought not to be permitted for one moment to depend on any action or notification on his part. * * * * Some self-acting principle in regard to the reserve ought to be enforced upon every company." *Massachusetts Report*, 1895, page vi.

ing to his "zealous and intelligent service in introducing to the public the Accumulation Policy." Every agent who secured twenty applications during the same period was to receive, in addition to the certificate, a handsome NEW-YORK LIFE badge. The names of both classes were to form a "Roll of Honor." These prizes were of no great value, but they stimulated every agent to do his best in order to secure the recognition and honor which it was the aim of the management to accord to every faithful worker. A *fac-simile* of the certificate, reduced about one-third, is given on opposite page. The "Roll of Honor," as finally published, contained three hundred and forty-one names, two hundred and twenty-eight men having won certificates and one hundred and thirteen having won both certificates and badges.

As soon as the terms of the Accumulation Policy were made known, inquiries began to pour into the Home Office, asking if its privileges would be extended to other policy-holders. The Company replied publicly, in order to save a burdensome correspondence, that the NEW-YORK LIFE was "a mutual Company, with no privileges to any policy-holder not accorded to every other holding a policy in the same class or of similar character." It therefore announced that it would "extend all the benefits of the Accumulation Policy to existing Non-Forfeiting Free Tontine Policies"—these being the only contracts under which the same premium was paid for the same risk. All other policies which had been in force five years were made free as regards occupation, residence and travel.

In pursuance of a purpose to inspect personally the workings of the Company in its most important fields, President McCall sailed for Europe on August twenty-fourth. The Agency Department at once set to work to make the next two months memorable in the history of the Company. It was arranged to have thirty-five men come to New York to welcome the President home in November, and the selection of names was made upon the following plan: The agents were divided into four classes, according to their previous achievements. From each of the first three classes the five men were to be invited who wrote and settled the most

Certificate of Merit and Appreciation

This Certificate is Granted to

W. Edgar Reeve

BY THE

Officers of the NEW YORK LIFE INSURANCE COMPANY in acknowledgement

Accumulation Policy

between the 13th day of June and the 15th day of

In Testimony Whereof, the Signatures of the Officers and the Seal of the Company have been hereunto affixed this first day of

President

Vice President

Vice President

Vice President

new business between September first and October twenty-ninth; from the fourth class, which included all not in the first three, were to be invited the five men who wrote and settled the largest number of applications, and the five men who wrote and settled the largest amounts of new business. When the record was made up it was found that the winners had written and settled over six millions of new business in sixty days. Mr. Gilbert A. Smith, of Sioux City, Iowa, then Manager for Iowa, northern Nebraska and South Dakota, now Manager of the Western Department, headed the list with a score of $1,768,000 of settled business. Two men in one class tied, and both were invited; and Mr. Wm. L. Hill, Manager for Missouri and Texas, was invited in recognition of his service to the whole agency force in the preparation of a very helpful circular setting forth the merits of the Accumulation Policy.

The "Surprise Party," as it was called, came off during the week beginning November seventh. While considerable time was given to sight-seeing, the opportunity was improved to visit the various departments of the Home Office and become familiar with the manner in which the business of the Company is transacted; and one day was given up to a "Big Talk" on "How we got here," in which each guest gave helpful hints from his own experience. At the banquet with which the "Surprise Party" ended, on November eleventh, the President gave a brief description of his European trip and set forth some features of the ideal management toward which he was striving. He said, in part:

We have in Europe a very large business. It has been honestly and carefully administered—since the death of Mr. Homans, by Mr. W. E. Ingersoll. Accompanied by him I visited our agencies in Switzerland, Italy, Hungary, Austria, Germany, Holland and Belgium. In Paris and Berlin I met the representatives of France, Denmark, Sweden, Norway, Turkey and Spain, so that before my departure for home I had the great gratification of taking by the hand every manager of importance in Europe, and of hearing from his own lips the history of his agency and the prospect in his territory. Never was a company represented by better managers. All of them are men of high standing in their own country, with a sense of honor that was very refreshing to observe and which made me proud indeed. Other managers may do more business than some of our men, but no other company has men of higher motive or cleaner records. This without exception. With pardonable pride I make this statement, and the satisfaction afforded me in doing so I know will be shared by you all. I parted from them fully conscious that by no act of theirs would blame be brought to the Company's doors.*

* * * * * * * * * * * * *

The last nine months form no unimportant part of the almost half a century that makes up the Company's corporate life. But one ambition possesses me, and that is, that we shall continue to the end in furthering all that is commendable in management, and in discarding the methods that bring contumely. Our house is set upon a hill to-day. Let us keep the approaches to it inviting and free from pitfalls. We have been given in official language a certificate of regenerated birth, and it behooves you and me, and all of us, that by no act of ours shall the record be tarnished. We are all equally interested that the magnificent position we hold shall be maintained, and we should never be tempted, by an ill-judged expediency, to depart from the course where honor leads. Each one here, in his own way, can do something for the common good of all in jealously guarding, by word and action, the Company's fair name. Example is better than all else.

The Company is now, and will be hereafter, known as the one which is not dependent on any one man for its prosperity and success. I intend, so long as I am intrusted with direction and power, to make room at the top for those whose zeal and probity are conspicuous. No plan or program that argues well for the Company's good will be lightly thought of because it did not have its origin with me, and merit and intelligence will move on apace within our ranks. Years will count in counsel, but not in action, and there is no place in all our ranks that is not open to the aspiration of the lowliest lad in our employ who serves and learns.

The "President's Trophy," presented to Mr. Smith, was a handsome gold watch and chain, the insignia of the Company being in relief upon the case.† Mr. Smith's reply showed the spirit in which he had labored. He said, in part:

I long ago learned, or thought I learned, the lesson of the value of time in this business, but when I sat down about September first to figure out what my time must be worth in the next two months, if I did what I decided I must do, I was convinced that my own ideas were not anywhere near correct. I accordingly put everything aside but life insurance; I thought of nothing else; I talked nothing else. If my man who

---

*In his report to the Trustees on the foreign business of the Company the President said, if the question of doing business in foreign countries had come to him as an original proposition he might not have favored it, but in view of our present organization abroad it was wise to continue our foreign business, and that he hoped so to stimulate it by some changes to be made in the conduct of it that there would be a very large increase in it with little or no increase in expense. As regards the condition and working of the Company so far as he had seen it, the President said that, while the late President had his faults, as all men have, he felt no hesitation in saying that should his own connection with the Company be as long continued as that of Mr. Beers, he should be more than satisfied if no more serious faults could be found in his record than he had found in that of his predecessor.

† The President also presented to each agent a scarf-pin showing the figures "35" set with diamonds.

has charge of my farms wanted to see me, I was not visible; if any one wanted to talk politics I tried to get him off of that subject, or looked for another man. I didn't read a daily paper for sixty days, and confined the little reading I did to life insurance literature. My plan was to write an application every day before 7.30 in the morning; if I failed I counted my chances so much less for that day, and the later in the day the less the chance. I sent a good many telegrams and a great many letters to secure appointments at that hour, and, as a rule, my business was written early in the day. I wrote $2,100,000 in applications in this way, in September and October, reporting the premiums on over $1,700,000 of it. * * * * * * * *

During the time I was writing this business I got another view of this truth which would apply perhaps as well to other professions as to ours, and which made such an impression on my mind that I wish to speak of it here. I met a man in middle life who had, perhaps, used his opportunities as well as the average man does, and who, when he suddenly learned that it was only a question of a few days when the light would fail—when he would become totally blind—felt that he had squandered and wasted the best gifts that nature had bestowed upon him. He found himself suddenly with only a few hours in which to make good years of neglect—not neglect by the ordinary standard, but neglect by the standard with which he was suddenly compelled to measure himself. He talked to me until it seemed as though I could go out into the street and preach from this text to the whole world. The old proverb, "Physician heal thyself," applies, it seems to me, with particular force to life insurance soliciting. Our standard arguments are based on the duty of insuring; on the dangers of delay; on the responsibilities of life; yet the men we talk to are not, as a rule, as dilatory as we are ourselves. They don't neglect as many opportunities and they don't miss such abundant success, simply because they are not in a line of work where possibilities are so numerous.

As the year 1892 drew near its end the Company's books showed it to be the banner year of its history for new business; the year had opened with clouds of doubt and uncertainty, it was coming to a close under brighter skies than ever before. The Company had the confidence of the public; it was never so well organized, and the field force was never so enthusiastic as now. It was natural that the management should indulge in retrospect, and voice the general sentiment of gratitude and joy. With the last "Bulletin" for the year there went to every agent an autograph "Christmas Greeting" from the President of the Company. [See next page.]

In summing up the triumphs of the year the management gave first place to "The Discovery of the Principle of Steady Production." It was said: "At the beginning of 1892, the NEW-YORK LIFE had in the United States and Canada only about twenty men who had at any time

A Christmas Greeting.

PRESIDENT'S OFFICE,
346 BROADWAY.

N.Y. Dec 25th 1892

A Merry Christmas

[A]ccept my cordial wishes for a very Merry Christmas. [I] know of no men who have a better right to feel merry [a]nd to make merry on this glorious Christmas day of 1892 [th]an the representatives of the "Old Reliable" Last year [y]ou sat down to your Christmas dinner in doubt [a]nd uncertainty but you kept a brave front through [i]t all and to day you will enjoy your feast as [c]onquerors. You will sit down with the consciousness [t]hat the past year has been your most succesful [o]ne and therefore the most succesful for your Company [Y]ou will sit down knowing that the future instead [o]f holding doubts and fears, holds still greater possibilities [f]or you. You will sit down with the satisfaction of [d]uty done, feeling that your labors have made bright [m]any a hearth, that otherwise might be a picture [o]f desolation You will rise up with a heart-full of [t]hankfulness, with a fixed determination that next [C]hristmas will find you still more prosperous, your [C]ompany still at the head, and our Accumulation Policy [t]he bright light of uncounted homes that to day have [n]ever heard of it. Will you not?

Yours Truly

John A. McCall
President

written so much as one application a week for six consecutive weeks. At the beginning of 1893 we find on our books about seven hundred men who have written business for eight and ten weeks consecutively during the year, and more than seventy men have written business every week straight through the year. You discovered during the year 1892 a principle in Life Insurance which will become as important as some well-known discoveries are in the world of science. It did wonderful things in 1892; it will do still more wonderful things in 1893. The most remarkable thing of all is its effect on the individual man. It elevates his work; it dignifies his profession; and it is creating an *esprit de corps* in our ranks which strengthens our lines like the elbow-touch on the field of battle."

No time was wasted, however, in congratulations. All who held the Company's commission had been called on early in December to show that they were "alive," by writing at least two applications for at least $1,000 each during the month; and this was made a condition of entrance into a ten weeks' competition which was to begin with the new year. When the month ended, twelve hundred and nine men had thus qualified; it was a token of the greater work to be accomplished in 1893.

1893. The Company's books were closed for the year 1892 on December thirty-first, and the accounts made up as they stood on that date, without waiting for belated returns.* The annual report was submitted to the Trustees on January 14, 1893, and the certificate of the Superintendent of Insurance, certifying to the Company's assets and sur-

* The Superintendent of the Missouri Insurance Department in his report for 1892 thus commented on the contrary custom: "The Statutes (Sections 5839, 5846, 5869, 5890 and 5892) specifically require that the companies asking for authority to transact insurance business in this State, shall file annual statements of their condition and affairs on the 31st day of December, 'on the first day of January, or within thirty days thereafter.' Many of them, in fact some of the largest and some having complicated accounts, do file their statements within the stated limit of time. But others, and some small ones, with comparatively brief and simple reports to make, are in default from thirty to sixty days, to the annoyance of the clerical force and disorder of the business of this Department. It is not a compliance with the law which fixes December 31st, or the last business day of the calendar year, as the day on which the condition of a company is to be ascertained and its affairs to be reported to this office, to permit books to be kept open and accounts to be made up afterwards, so as to show a possibly more favorable condition of things on the statutory day of closing. * * * * *
If books are kept open for the purpose of making any better or different showing than an actual transcript, made just after the office is closed on December 31st, would show, then the practice becomes a fraudulent one.

plus, was dated January nineteenth. The report was made according to the methods advocated by President McCall when he was Superintendent of the Insurance Department. In order to understand just what the change signified, it is necessary to refer to the old method which, as a State official, he had criticised. Under this method—which is still in use by most companies—when a dividend was declared it was immediately entered in the journal as paid to policy-holders, and received back again as a single premium in payment of reversionary additions (paid-up insurance) to the policies. If all policy-holders used their dividends in this manner, these entries would represent the actual facts; but as it is optional with annual dividend policy-holders in most companies to receive their dividends either in cash or in reversionary additions, whenever a dividend was paid in cash, another journal entry must be made to the effect that, the paid-up insurance purchased by the dividend when declared had been sold to the company for cash and the cash paid for surrendered insurance. To the extent in which dividends were taken in cash they appeared twice in disbursements—once as paid in dividends and once as paid for surrendered insurance; and in receipts they appeared as a first premium. By the new method the report showed the final result without any circumlocution or fictitious increase of income or disbursements. Dividends are entered in receipts and disbursements exactly as used, and no part of them is included in first premiums.*

Under the old method, when a running policy was exchanged for a paid-up policy, journal entries showed the original policy sold for its reserve value, this amount paid to the policy-holder, and again received

---

*The report contained the following note on Income: "The income reported represents cash paid to the Company, and nothing else. There are no items of journal entries where dividends are fictitiously treated as premiums to buy additional insurance, and there is no addition to the income by calling the reserve on surrendered policies the premium for new (paid-up) insurance."

The Massachusetts Insurance Commissioner, in his report of 1895, while criticising "marking up real estate values through income," says: "As if the income account had not been sufficiently imposed upon and stultified by making it an omnibus for masses of hypothetical new 'cash' premiums in the shape of 'dividends declared and applied to payment for reversionary additions,' 'lapsed reserves used to purchase paid-up insurance,' etc.; in each case the money simply taken from one pocket (in the mind of the book-keeper) and put into the other, without the least pretence of an outgo or income as between the money drawer and the outside of the office."—*Mass. Report, 1895, pages viii. and ix.*

from him as a first premium on the paid-up policy. Here again both receipts and disbursements were increased without a dollar changing hands. The policy account was also swelled by like entries, the old policy being placed in "terminations" as "insurance surrendered," and the paid-up policy counted as "new insurance issued." Under the new method the only entry necessary is "old policies decreased," by the amount of the difference between the old policy and the new. There is just enough basis of fact in the old method to save it from being false, but not enough to prevent it from making a deceptive showing. The object of classifying premiums is because new premiums on new risks require a much larger expenditure in commissions, while dividends and the reserve values of policies exchanged for paid-up insurance cause no expenditure to agents whatever. The old method, therefore, by an apparent increase in new premiums, payments to policy-holders, and new insurance, provides the basis for deceptive ratios of expenses to both income and insurance.

The Company's report also contained this note on assets and surplus:

> The assets of this Company are advertised at the sums allowed by the Insurance Department, and do not include any items disallowed by the laws of the State or the ruling of the Department. If at any time the commissions of agents are purchased or commuted, or advances are made to agents, such purchases and advances are at once charged as an expense and are not called an asset. The surplus published in the documents and advertisements of the Company agrees with the surplus shown by the Superintendent's report.

This method of treating money paid to agents had always been followed by the NEW-YORK LIFE, and the contrary was thus criticised by Superintendent Barnes in his report for 1866:

> Such advances do not, in the opinion of the Superintendent, constitute actual assets or legal investments under the statute, and all attempts to throw expenses already incurred and paid upon future years are irregular, deceptive and dangerous. Such payments should be returned only under the head of expenditures. Our statute does not allow any loans or advances to agents except upon the regular bond and mortgage or stock securities.

Carlyle says of the father of Frederick the Great that, "he went about strangling imbroglios of coiled nonsense" and "turning deceptions inside out"; that in transacting the business of the Government he had "daylight introduced into the very bottom of the business, fair and square observed as the rule of it, and the shortest road adopted for doing it." The result was, according to Carlyle, "Fact made to stand firm on its feet, with the world rocks under it, looking free to all the winds and all the stars." Something of this sort President McCall did in the matter of report-making; and while his action gave the "ratio-maker" new opportunities for comparisons unfavorable to the NEW-YORK LIFE, it so commended itself to insurance officials that the Massachusetts Commissioner required all reports for the next year to show just how the income account was made up, and the Annual Convention of Insurance Commissioners and Superintendents, held in 1894, adopted a new blank making the same requirement.

When the Company erected the Home Office building in 1868–70, it acquired about one-half of the block bounded by Broadway, Leonard Street, Elm Street and Catharine Lane. Subsequently, as other parts of the plot came into the market, they were purchased by the Company, until the whole block was secured. In order to give a Broadway frontage to the whole property and thus make it as valuable as possible, it was determined, early in 1893, to build a twelve-story building on the rear of the lot, connecting with the present structure in a way that would make it an extension of the latter. A Building Committee was appointed, February seventh, consisting of William L. Strong, C. C. Baldwin, Augustus G. Paine, Woodbury Langdon and Richard Müser, with the Second Vice-President and Treasurer as advisory members, and the Auditor as Secretary. Mr. S. D. Hatch was selected as the architect, and the building was under his supervision until his death, in August, 1894, when it was placed in charge of McKim, Meade and White, who were the architects of two of the Company's office buildings in the West. The building is already well advanced, and will probably be ready for occupancy early in the spring of 1896. The offices of the Company will occupy about five floors and the remainder will be for rental. The old building will be rebuilt to correspond with the new, and the completed structure will be 60′ x 395′ 7″ x 84′ 4″ x 396′ 4″ and open to the light and air on all sides.*

During the year President McCall visited all the agency departments of the Company in the United States east of the Rocky Mountains, and in his addresses to agents special emphasis was laid upon the value (1) of the recent examination, (2) of the new features of the Accumulation Policy, and (3) of the new method of making the annual report. The following extract is made from his address at Chicago on April seventeenth:

We have filed with every official in every State or Territory of the Union complete schedules of all our investments in detail. Every piece of real estate owned or on which we hold a mortgage has been listed by town, city, county and state, and the book and page of record stated by letter and number. The dimensions of the land and buildings, the street numbers of the property and the amount of insurance held as collateral, are all exhibited, item by item, so that every official can readily verify the valuations of the property, no matter where located, without great effort. We own eleven office buildings and ninety-seven pieces of foreclosed property. They are placed in our report at the appraised value of the Insurance Superintendent—$12,531,016.75—and not at their cost value. Our mortgages amount to $24,236,785.51, and at the date of our statement there was but $9,000 interest thereon due and unpaid. Our United States and other stocks and bonds were valued at $86,680,177, and in but three cases out of several hundred different kinds of securities was there default in the payment of either interest or dividend. A complete schedule of every stock or bond owned, with the cost, par and market value, was made a part of our statement. The same also as to our collateral loans on stocks and bonds. The interest on every loan was paid in full, and the values

---

* In October, 1895, a large number of agents and managers were called to the Home Office to consider plans for a NEW-YORK LIFE Agents' Association. The President's address before this body contained the following suggestive references to the original building, and also to a further change in the manner of making the annual report, which will appear in the statement of the Company's business of 1895:

"This is the first opportunity I have had of greeting so many of our men under our own roof. The agents of the Company who, at one time or another, either here or elsewhere, numerous though they are, that I have not had the pleasure of meeting are few in number. This will probably be the last gathering of agents within these walls. Time and energy—and more of the latter than the former—have made it necessary for us to have more commodious quarters, and the safe guarding of $160,000,000 in assets calls for more protection than this building affords. And yet, it seems but a short time ago that this structure was erected, for its praises as a model building are seemingly within our hearing. In 1869, when the building was constructed, it doubtless appeared to those in charge that they had builded for all time and to meet all demands. If you will permit me to review the growth of the Company since then it will be seen that no foresight then could have outlined the needs of the Company in the next quarter of a century now at an end. Twenty-five years ago the insured numbered 33,000, and the total of their policies was $102,000,000. The assets were $13,500,000, and the income $6,000,000. Compare these with the 277,000 policy-holders now constituting our membership and with $813,000,000 representing the sum insured; with assets of $162,000,000, and income of $36,500,000. Whose is the of the securities—$5,059,690—exceeded the loans thereon by $1,200,000. In short, if any policy-holder or agent is doubtful about any item of our securities, he can have a duplicate of the official report by asking for it, as we have had many hundreds of them printed for circulation among our managers and insurance journals—an innovation that has met with much commendation.

In closing, permit me to respond to a question that was asked me to-day by one of our prominent agents. He said: "Mr. President, you have given us (1) an honest statement, without regard to any injury we may suffer by unfair comparisons with reports not made up on the same basis; (2) the Accumulation Policy, which is the most liberal to the insured that was ever issued; and (3) an Official Certificate of the Insurance Superintendent, showing that our advertised assets and surplus do not differ in amount from the same items as reported under oath to him. Now, what more can we expect from you that is equally helpful to our work?"

Well, I can but promise that we shall continue on the lines laid down herein. It will be of no moment to us if our truthful report is measured to our temporary disadvantage against inflated income or decimated expenses, or if our strength is compared with decoy assets, stunted liabilities and paper surplus. We shall not be tempted from holding to the right course by the angles and short cuts that look immensely pleasing, but which are in reality pitfalls for the unwary. No! to my mind there is much more to be gained by insurance officials in reforming the methods of making their reports than in endeavoring to make progress by the use of "book-keeping figures" and fictitious ratios, that are remarkable only because they are misleading.

We shall endeavor to study the insurance situation as we find it in our own experience, but we will not be negligent of the fact that we can also learn from others. When we can add to the comfort and advantage of those who have entrusted the custody of their funds to us, by adopting methods which are fruitful in bringing such conditions about, we will not be lax, even though the suggestion of the improvement had not its origin with ourselves. In other words, all that makes or stands for fair treatment of policy-holders we shall strive to originate, but if others are the discoverers of desirable

---

vision that beholds what the next twenty-five years has in store for us. If I had prophetic capacity I would picture my friend, the Third Vice-President, standing in my position in the halls that will replace these, surrounded by the then silver-haired, his adjutants of to-day, as he with 'ghoulish glee' tells how insignificant are the figures that now fill us with awe compared with the returns of his administration.

"How easily all this leads up to the subject-matter of your gathering, namely, your own identification with the Company for all time to come. I sincerely believe that of all the companies, our own is generally regarded to-day as possessing more agents beyond temptation of leaving than any other. I can understand how at times the offers of other institutions are hard to resist, and that your remuneration by us is not by any means the largest that prevails. Will you also allow me to add that our day for 'fireworks' has passed. I believe you are all imbued with the idea that economy and conservatism are to-day of more importance to the Company's future than aught else. It is for you to aid in carrying out the platform. The organization of your 'Nylic Association' must be productive of great good. Every tie that binds the agent to the Company in good fellowship and for their common welfare makes rebating and eighty per cent. brokerage impossible. We have led lately in the reforms that are so well-nigh universally approved. We have not come in with the mourners as a death-bed penitent.

"There is still work to do, and when I review the efforts of the past four years I say frankly that the announcement I made formally on June first of this year that, hereafter only paid-for business would be published in our advertisements and Department Reports, gives me more comfort than any other of our proclamations. Its effect on your work has been extremely good, as our books show, while the im-

changes we will not put out our lights and sit in the gloom while the procession advances.

The European agencies of the Company were visited early in the year by the Third Vice-President and the Actuary. At the close of a tour of inspection and instruction on the continent, a convention of the Company's representatives in Great Britain and Ireland was held in London, on May eighth and ninth. A convention is said to be peculiarly an American institution, but, judging from the able papers read, and the discussions had at this gathering, the insurance convention bears transplanting remarkably well. From the addresses made at the convention, the following extracts will be found of interest.

From Mr. Perkins' address:

I am sure no one realizes more keenly than President McCall the possibilities there are for the NEW-YORK LIFE in the future. Whatever Mr. McCall may be; whether he prove to be a remarkable General in the securing of new business; or whatever his record may be in comparison with others, there is one thing we know—whatever policy it may be necessary for the NEW-YORK LIFE to pursue, that policy will be, first of all, to protect the interests of policy-holders. You will not go wrong at all if you state, without the slightest hesitation at any time, that whatever the NEW-YORK LIFE does will be on an honest basis.

From Mr. Weeks' address:

I could not respond with any enthusiasm to this sentiment of "Success to our European Business," except that I feel that we do not hurt any one else by our own

---

pression on others of our sincerity in the maintaining of needed reforms has added to our already enviable reputation on this and the other side of the Atlantic. In my conferences with the several Executive Officers we have considered the effect of this change. It will appear at the end of the year as though our business had fallen off, because our statement for 1894 showed in force all policies issued during the year, less cancellations, whether said policies were paid for or not. About forty millions in insurance was thus carried over. The 1895 statement will not contain a policy or a figure in assets, income or outstanding insurance that does not represent contracts on which the Company itself has received the cash. All policies not paid for to the Company will be regarded as not issued and will not be claimed, advertised or found in the Company's report.

"So that you may understand this fully, I want to impress on you that a policy not paid for to the Company will not even be published as an issued policy. The only business that we shall advertise as written in 1895 will be that for which we have the cash in our Home Office. I am thus emphatic, as you may be called on to explain our position. You will not have to defend it; it is self-defending when explained, and mark me, every other company will be compelled by public opinion to do in this case what they have done so often of late—*follow our example.*

"The action lately taken by the Massachusetts Insurance Commissioner is so recently in your minds that I need not go into the details. The combined work of our Third Vice-President and of the Third Vice-President of the Equitable in bringing about the agreement so generally signed, is deserving of great praise. [An agreement to discharge any agent convicted of rebating, and not to employ agents success. In former times it has been the idea among men that the only kind of success which was worth having was that taken from some one else, and to stand with your foot on your prostrate enemy was thought to be a most glorious triumph; but I think the world is reaching a little higher point in that respect, and that really the time is coming—it is almost here—when men of generous natures would not care to have any success that depends on the failure or the suffering of other men. We may feel quite certain that the success of a great mutual life insurance company does not injure any one; it is beneficial and only beneficial to all whom it touches, and that is an encouraging feeling for us all to have. It is very often the case that a man, in the occupation in which he has been led to spend his life, does not feel sure that his work is a benefit in every respect. I want to say that one in this business ought not to have that feeling, as from first to last our work is good, and nothing but good. We feel that we are only upon the threshold of the vast possibilities of life insurance; that it has a great and magnificent work to do for the world, hardly guessed at as yet, and the field being so undeveloped, the success of one company does not hinder the success of others, it rather stirs the ground for them. The competition of life insurance companies is not like competition in trade or commerce. Or, take the matter of stock speculation—there, if one man makes money it is only because another man loses it. That is not the case in life insurance, we are glad to say. Of course, there are individual instances where one company wins the case and another company loses it; but taken in the aggregate, success in one company does not involve loss of business in another. * * * *

Of course, ours is a great Company, and, incidentally, we are proud of it; but, gentlemen, let us not care so much about its being one of the largest companies in the world, but let us be proud rather of its exact and fine adaptation to the ends for which it exists. Let us be proud particularly that it is an absolutely sound and secure Company; that it will carry out all its promises in the future as it has done in the past.

---

discharged by other companies for rebating.] Our position in the premises was neither new nor uncertain, and in answering promptly and energetically the call of Major Merrill, the Company's previous utterances and action were forcibly ratified.

"Just before I came into the room, the Third Vice-President outlined to me in a brief way the proposition that you have discussed this morning, which carries with it a desire on your part to have at this office an Agents' Representative—one who, if there are delays in the issuing of, or reporting on, new policies, would be able at once by reason of his location at the Home Office to appeal immediately to those in charge of the several bureaus for a facilitation of your work. I am willing, within reason, to oblige the agents of the Company, and I do not think unfavorably of this proposition, but I want a little time to turn it over in my mind. Before you leave the city, you shall have my decision in the matter. (Applause.) Please remember that even if this concession is granted, there will still continue to be complaints—there must be—because the Company is managed by human beings, and consequently you cannot have things absolutely perfect. You have the privilege of complaining, with the assurance that you will be listened to by those in authority. Now, this morning I received a letter advising me of the death of a person on whose life a large risk had lately been declined by us—a risk that the agent thought ought to have been accepted because other companies did not turn it down. In mentioning the matter to-day to the Manager of the Southern Department, in whose territory the agent was located, he laughingly replied: 'There are a number of other such cases where we thought the Home Office was wrong, but where you proved to be right.' I cite this case to prove that the agents' judgment about the taking of risks is somewhat apt to be a prejudiced one.

"And now, in bidding you to be at home and at your ease among us, be assured that in all your discussions, and in all that relates to you and your business with us, I have an abiding interest."

And let us all join in the endeavor to attain better and better methods of meeting the exact needs of the community, and of bringing the community to share in the benefits we provide.

Among the educational features of the Columbian Exposition of 1893 were the world-famous Congresses for the discussion of all manner of subjects by the greatest living authorities in every department of human knowledge. The NEW-YORK LIFE'S contribution to these discussions was an address by President McCall before the Life and Accident Insurance Congress, on the "History of American Life Insurance," delivered on the evening of June twenty-third. The speaker traced the growth of the system from the organization of what is now the Presbyterian Ministers' Fund, in 1759, to the magnificent proportions it has since achieved. Referring to the features calling for special mention during the period 1881 to 1892, he dwelt upon these three: the great increase of the business, the rise of industrial insurance, and the greater liberality of the policy contract. Upon the latter point, he said:

The ease with which claims might be disputed under the old policy contract has already been referred to, but during the past twelve years there has been a general disposition among the companies to liberalize the conditions of the contract and to construe it liberally when it became a claim. The clauses of the policy under which contests usually arise are those warranting the answers of the insured in his application to be full, complete and true, and those relating to residence and travel, occupation, habits of life and manner of death. In 1879 the Equitable adopted an "incontestable clause" providing that after three years its policies would not be contested for incorrect answers given in the application. The feature was soon taken up by other companies, its application enlarged, and the period of contestability shortened. It is impossible to follow the practice of different companies upon the various points mentioned—it must suffice to state in a general way what the present practice is, from which it will be seen that the goal of complete and immediate protection under life policies is not far off.

Four companies issue policies that are incontestable for any cause after one year; eighteen companies make the period of probation two years; seven companies make it three years; while others still require the warrantees of the insured to run with the policy. As to residence and travel—seven companies place no restrictions upon either; three companies limit the insured for one year only; seventeen companies limit the insured for two years only; three limit the insured for three years only. As to military service—five companies make no restrictions; seven make restrictions for two years only. Others agree to take such risks at an extra premium to be charged against the policy; others still agree to pay the reserve as a cash surrender value in such cases. As to occupation other than military service—three companies make no restrictions;

hree make restrictions for one year only; seventeen for two years only; two for three ears only. With respect to duels and other violations of law—seventeen companies nake no restrictions; three companies make no restrictions after one year; five companies make no restrictions after two years; four companies make none after three ears. Six companies issue policies without any reference to suicide; in eighteen companies suicide does not invalidate the policy after two years; in six companies the claim s good if the policy has been three years in force. Restrictions as to narcotics and ntoxicants have been eliminated from the policies of most companies. One company ssues policies with no other condition than the payment of premiums, and with no estrictions whatever.

Life Insurance is safe or possible only on the supposition that, to the average man fe is more precious than money—that the insured has a greater interest in his own life han the company has—and that he may be trusted to take care of it. Doubtless men night live longer than they do—but life insurance is based upon actual, and not upon deal, conditions. Its reason of being is that there are risks which the individual cannot afely bear, but which the company, as an aggregation of individuals, may safely underake in consideration of certain sums of money paid. The company is free to decline ny risk offered; but when it accepts a man's money it should take his risk also, without edging and without whining. The history of Life Insurance has shown that its foes re those of its own household. Mortality tables have never betrayed it—managers ave. As it casts the beam out of its own eye it sees more clearly and acts more visely.*

Meanwhile the agency force in the United States and Canada was preparing for a "Columbian Convention," the action of which was destined to have a far-reaching effect upon an evil practice with which underwriters' associations and insurance officials had long grappled in vain.

---

* Life Insurance yesterday observed its festival and contributed to the success of the World's Fair y holding a congress at Chicago, the chief feature of which was an address by our former townsman, he Hon. John A. McCall, President of the NEW-YORK LIFE INSURANCE COMPANY. Mr. McCall 'as peculiarly qualified for the honor bestowed upon him of making the presentation to the country of he facts which constitute Life Insurance's exhibit. All his life he has been identified with it in posiions which have given him the most comprehensive views of the subject, and his present honorable ost places him at the head of the business in this country. Mr. McCall is familiar with Life Insurance rom the point of view of government and from the point of view of the insurance companies; has seen s evil days as well as the days of its prosperity, its mismanagement, and its development into one of he most secure and conservative forms of investment in the world.

The address is not only a splendid demonstration of the capacity, trustworthiness and enterprise hown in the management of the companies; it also discloses the provident character and prosperity of he American people, and it is this second phase of it which renders the address one of the exhibits which the whole country understands, in which it takes pride, and which it is eager to show to the ations of the world. The great palaces of the companies are but one material form of Life Insurance. The humble homes of workingmen and women to be found in every village and town in the land, created nd preserved through this instrumentality by the prudent, self-sacrificing father, husband or son, even nore truly show what Life Insurance is to American life. Mr. McCall is to be congratulated upon an ddress which has set forth so admirably in all its phases so important a feature of our national growth. —*Editorial in Albany Argus, June 24, 1893.*

Representatives to the Convention were selected on substantially the same basis as to the "Surprise Party" of 1892, by so classifying the agency force that men competed with their equals as business getters in the past.* The competition extended from April third to June tenth, and the number invited was about one hundred and thirty, together with twenty-two General Agents and Managers. It was the most thoroughly representative body of men ever assembled under the auspices of the Company, and was intended so to be, in order that the action taken might represent the best thought of the agency corps, and so be made the standard for all. While valuable discussions were had upon other topics, the chief interest in the Convention centered in its action on the question of rebates. After long and earnest discussion the subject was referred to a committee consisting of Messrs. D. P. Kingsley, Superintendent of Agencies; Robert E. Whitney, Manager, Seaboard Department; Gilbert A. Smith, Manager, Western Department; Alex. G. Hawes, Manager, Pacific Coast; Livingston Mims, Manager, Southern Department; J. G. Morgan, Manager, Winnipeg; Daniel Boone, State Agent, Missouri. The next day the committee presented a report condemning the practice, requesting President McCall to exercise every power at his command to exterminate it among the Company's agency force, and pledging the Convention individually and collectively to his support in so doing. The report was adopted by the Convention unanimously.

The President, in reply, said, in part:

It has been said that language was made to conceal thought. That cannot be said of this preamble and these resolutions, and I want to emphasize my own position regarding them in no uncertain way. * * I doubt not, from the unanimous rising vote which was given in affirmation of the resolutions, that every man is as sincere about the principle involved as is your President. And let there be no mistake about this, for come what may, the NEW-YORK LIFE will issue its policies and will expect its agents to deliver its contracts without the payment of a single penny of rebate. I know that in all controversies there are many sides, and there may be differing opinions, but not con-

---

*Four prizes were offered; they were won by the following named gentlemen, on records of the amounts of settled business given: H. H. Kerr, Chicago, $1,064,000; R. M. Kerr, Chicago, $602,000, E. S. Smith, Iowa, $383,000; J. C. Stock, Pennsylvania, $206,000. A fourth prize was awarded to the family of Major Hamp Boon, of Texas, who wrote a very large amount of business, but died before the opening of the Convention.

radictory ones; and I know that many of us here have certain views and that they have . right to be heard, whether or not they seem to be in consonance or in harmony with hose of the majority; and I promise due and full respect to everything that may be ffered as to when this condition of affairs shall be brought about; but let me say, the ooner it can be done the better it will be for all of us.

On the evening of July fourteenth President McCall gave a dinner o the members of the Convention and others, in the Banquet Hall of the New York State Building, on the Exposition grounds. The address of he President on this occasion referred to the Company's purpose in the everal conventions that had been held, reviewed the work since his election, and restated the principles upon which the Company would be nanaged in the future. He said, in part:

Let us review together the work we have accomplished, and cast a horoscope of what is before us. The year 1892 had many peculiar features. It was quite doubtful f the reaction we had hoped for would be at all manifest at the end; and, speaking vith the knowledge of the judgment of leaders in the business not connected with us, it vas a mooted question whether the Company would quite recover from the blows which t had received both from without and within. The superior financial position it was ound to hold after all these attacks proved both its own inherent strength and the trength of the system of which it is a conspicuous representative. With the advantage f demonstrated financial soundness, any proposition that involved our sitting at the gate n lamentation over the past was not to be considered for a moment. So we offered urselves, not in shackles, but in an armor that defied attack from any source. There vas consternation in the very suggestion that we were really alive in any sense, and we vere warned to the confines of restful spirits; but, ungracious though it seemed, we vere bent on a pernicious activity altogether unseemly and unbecoming in a corpse that ad been duly and deeply interred. When, within three weeks after the closing of the ear, our Annual Report appeared, complete in every particular, approved and endorsed n writing as to every item by the Superintendent, who, less than twelve months before, ad stood as our accuser, then every one of us, proud of the old Company in spite of its difficulties, knew that the day of rejoicing in all its fullness was at hand. We had hrown aside all the old methods that had done and are, unfortunately, still doing so nuch to bring contumely on the administration of the business. Our reported income vas cash receipts, not book-keeping devices to make a large divisor to diminish the atio of expenses to income. Our books were not kept open for two months or more to add to the receipts for the self-same reason. Our statement of assets was not inflated y disallowed items, thus differing from the Insurance Department reports by millions f dollars. Our advertisements of the Company's condition did not contain one dollar disallowed or disapproved by the experts of the Insurance Department. And yet, regardless of whatever untruthful and, of course, unfair comparisons that might be made, ve did not hesitate boldly to inaugurate the rule of showing all our transactions in the most open manner, giving every policy-holder full knowledge of our condition, on the day fixed by the law of the State for making our annual statement.

Let me say here, and now, that there will be no divergence hereafter from the principles thus laid down, and permit me also to prophesy that the example we have set in this respect will be followed by others. There is more room for reform in this matter of making annual reports without padding them than in all the rebate and limitation-of-business propositions that are offered for discussion. It is well known that the expenses of procuring business are altogether too high. But so long as State insurance officials (1) permit reports to be filed that bear no relation to the date; (2) admit items of income that are in no sense receipts; and (3) allow in the category of assets commuted commissions, agents' balances and other items that are really disbursements in the profit and loss account, so long high commissions and rebate practices will continue. If every company was compelled to report every item in its proper place, and was punished for advertising assets and surplus that exist only in imagination, then the reforms that are so loudly demanded would follow. There is a greater opportunity for the betterment of the business by bringing about a change in the methods of making reports than in any other particular, and I am better satisfied that we have chosen to lead in this than I would have been had we been compelled to follow an example set first by others, or to yield reluctant obedience to a legal mandate. * * * *

Our own statements are now, and will hereafter be, truthful. We will not deceive ourselves or others by padded reports of income or skeleton expense accounts. Our advertised assets and surplus will not shrink in the washing, nor differ by millions of dollars when compared with our sworn statements. We will call disbursements by the right name as expenditures, and not parade them as "etcetera" in assets. Our reserve will be based on net premiums with interest at four per cent. per annum, and we will have no recourse to, or use for, a law that makes the yard-stick of our liabilities the wavering measure of our necessities.

The President also indicated that the suppression of rebates was a necessary part of his policy in the management of the Company. On this point, he said: "In conclusion, let me say a word with respect to putting into force and effect the resolutions of our Convention on the subject of rebates. You have delegated to me the duty of saying when this reform shall be made obligatory upon all agents of the Company; but I assume that, so far as your personal example and influence are concerned, the reform will begin at once. I know that with many of you it has scarcely had an existence, and the personal and public testimony of the most successful of our agents that rebates are unnecessary to the writing of a large business will have a most helpful influence on others, and so render my task in dealing with persistent rebaters comparatively easy. Thus working together, we shall not fail to realize the high ideal which we have inscribed upon our banners—'No sham statements; no shady subterfuges; no rebates; no rebaters; one policy; one price.'"

"The sooner it can be done, the better it will be for all of us." These were the significant words with which President McCall accepted the resolutions of the Convention on the subject of rebate. Sixteen days later—on July twenty-ninth—the following circular-letter was sent to each agent by the President, in the Agents' "Bulletin":

My Dear Sir: You have been advised through these columns of the resolutions unanimously adopted at Chicago, on the thirteenth inst., under which our agents have referred to me the question of "Rebate" and have asked me to take any necessary steps to eliminate this practice from our ranks.

I do not need to recite to you the evils which result from it. The resolutions already referred to do this sufficiently. And, as I have yet to meet the first man who does not agree that the results of rebating are altogether to be deplored, I take it that such is your opinion. If you happen to live in a State where legislation has been had on this subject, I am sure you have been observing the law, and in so far, this letter does not apply to you. But, be that as it may, I want to say to you, together with all NEW-YORK LIFE field men, that ***henceforth Rebate in any form must cease.***

If anything can be added to the language of the resolutions referred to, it would be this: Rebate is a manifest inequity to some one, since agents representing the same company offer the same policy at different prices. This touches (first) the policy-holder and the principles of mutuality upon which our Company is built; and (second) it interests you in that you are forced, either directly or indirectly, into a conflict within your own household.

Rebate defeats its own purpose, since it does not bring you in the end the thing you seek, even though you may be indifferent to the question of equity. Therefore, Rebating is: first, Unlawful; second, Inequitable; third, Unnecessary.

On the first point I do not need to dwell. On the second, I can only say that you have certain advantages which more than offset any condition you may meet. You have (first) a Company which the world knows all about; which has been tried and not found wanting; which has been indorsed as none of its competitors have been. You have (second) a policy which has more benefits and fewer conditions, at the same price, than the policies offered against it.

To the objection that these advantages (which no insurance man denies) will not always bring you the business against the methods which may be employed by competitors, I can only say (conceding the truth of this, because, unfortunately, it is true) you must let some business go. It will take considerable moral courage to lose a risk, or a number of risks; but if you do it once, standing squarely on the doctrine that your goods are not offered at what you can get, but at what they are worth, you will probably never have to do it a second time, and you may never lose a single risk.

There is something in courage which appeals even to the man who is looking only for a discount, and with the average citizen a frank, direct business statement will always prevail. By adhering to this, you will be constantly moving into a better stratum of society, securing a more intelligent and desirable class of applicants, and thereby not only putting money into your pocket, but materially advancing the general interests of the Company itself.

I am not writing this letter to tell you at this time of any particular penalty to be enforced if you should give a rebate. I am sure I shall never need to write any of our representatives in that way. I believe in the loyalty of our men and their willingness to carry out, without flinching, the Company's wishes in this behalf; but for the benefit of any who may be weak, or who do not respond to these sentiments, I will say: I trust you just as our forefathers trusted in God at Bunker Hill—they did not, at the same time, neglect to keep their powder dry.

While this is a general letter, it is also directly personal, and I, therefore, ask every field man to address me at once, acknowledging its receipt and expressing frankly his position. These letters in reply will be filed as a part of the Company's records on this subject.

With renewed assurances of my interest in each man personally; with earnest thanks for the cordial support you have hitherto extended in the reforms undertaken by the NEW-YORK LIFE, and the firm belief that you will join in eradicating this great evil, I remain, Yours truly,

JOHN A. MCCALL, *President.*

Responses from the field indicated that the new rule thus promulgated was accepted in good faith by the agency force; but a rule never is fully appreciated until it is enforced against an offender. The occasion soon came which was to show whether or not the Company was in earnest in forbidding the giving of rebates. In a publication of the Mutual Life Insurance Company, of October eleventh, appeared a letter from a NEW-YORK LIFE agent (Mr. C. M. Ward), saying he was "a rebater pure and simple, not only on business principle but from religious belief," and citing the parable of the unjust steward as authority for his faith and practice. It was rather an unfortunate reference, seeing the original rebater "had wasted his lord's goods," and was put out of his stewardship. The latter fate also befell Mr. Ward. With a promptness and decision that left no doubt as to the course the President intended to pursue with persistent rebaters, Mr. Ward was notified that he could no longer represent the Company.*

---

*EXECUTIVE DEPARTMENT OF THE NEW-YORK LIFE INSURANCE CO.

John A. McCall, President.

346 and 348 Broadway, New York, October 14, 1893.

C. M. WARD, Esq., General Agent, 115 Broadway, New York City.

My Dear Sir: I have, to-day, read your lately published letter stating your adherence to, and belief in, the system of rebating. The management's views and your own are widely different; and, of course, you cannot continue to represent the Company. I regret that we are at variance, (1) because you have been a most successful agent, as your record of over $1,000,000 in new business written during

The summer of 1893 will long be remembered as the occasion of a financial crisis of an unusual kind. The Baring Brothers' failure, in 1890, had caused a large amount of American securities to be sent home for sale and remittance, and the decline in the price of silver had induced the fear that the United States might not be able to continue the redemption of its demand obligations in gold. The result was a heavy decline in the price of all securities, a decline in bank deposits (between December 9, 1892 and October 3, 1893) of three hundred and thirteen million dollars, and a decline in loans and discounts of three hundred and twenty-three millions. During June and July, 1893, the situation was described as a "currency famine." Over three hundred million dollars in Clearing-House certificates were issued by the associated banks of New York, Philadelphia, Boston, Baltimore and Pittsburgh between June twenty-first and August eleventh. The value of Life Insurance and of the NEW-YORK LIFE'S contracts were aptly illustrated by the operations of the three months, July, August and September. The following cash payments were made: For death-claims, $2,120,690; for endowments, $296,399; for dividends, $328,055; for annuities, $367,341; for purchased policies, $582,979;—total in three months, $3,695,464. The death-claims numbered over five hundred and fifty, and averaged nearly four thousand dollars each. The dividends were cash dividends on actual settlements of maturing Tontine policies, annual dividend and other policies, and not reversionary additions to policies. Purchased policies were only those surrendered for cash—not those exchanged for paid-up policies. There was altogether over one and one-half million dollars paid on the policies of living men. These figures—large as they are—do not tell half the

---

1893 to date conclusively shows; and (2) because our personal relations have been to me, at least, extremely pleasant. But, like yourself, I must be consistent, even though it deprives us of your valuable aid. It may be that there are others in our ranks holding your views, who are more timid and less boastful in making them known. Permit me, for their benefit, to make this a "Bulletin" letter, in order that I may advise such agents, if we have any, that yours is by far the manliest course to follow, as it enables us to relieve our ranks of those who are not in accord with the views expressed in the Columbian Convention and elsewhere by nine-tenths of our agents, and publicly and promptly ratified by the executive officers of the Company.

Yours truly,

JOHN A. MCCALL, *President.*

story of the helpfulness of the provisions of the NEW-YORK LIFE'S policies during these memorable three months. The Company's renewal premiums were about twenty million dollars per year; about one-fourth of this amount fell due in these three months—and upon most of it there was a month's grace. Policy-holders were thus allowed a loan to the amount of their premiums, at five per cent., without the asking. Add to this nearly one million dollars loaned on Free Tontine policies over five years in force, and we have a grand aggregate of about nine million dollars at the disposal of NEW-YORK LIFE policy-holders during the months of July, August and September.

Early in the year application was made to the authorities of the Columbian Exposition for space for an Exhibit of the Company, which was put in place in the Manufacturers and Liberal Arts Building early in May. The following description of the exhibit is from a circular of the time:

This exhibit sets forth and illustrates the theoretical, historical and practical aspects of Life Insurance, as follows:

(1) The Need and the Basis of Life Insurance; (2) The Application of the Theory of Life Insurance by Level Premiums; (3) The Growth of Life Insurance in the United States, 1845–1892; (4) The Growth of the NEW-YORK LIFE INSURANCE COMPANY, 1845–1892; (5) The Development of the Life Insurance Contract; (6) An Object Lesson in Gold Values.

This is done by means of figures, diagrams and policy contracts, in the following manner:

1. *The Need and the Basis of Life Insurance*—(See illustration on page 331). This Need and Basis are found in the Mortality Table. The Need of Insurance is shown by the regularity with which men of every age die, notwithstanding good previous health, long-lived ancestry and favorable surroundings. The safe Basis of Life Insurance is shown by the survival of a practically definite percentage of the living at each age. The Risk of Death and the Probability of Life, and the corresponding Cost of Insurance and Loss in case of Death, are illustrated by age-lines of equal length divided into two parts by different colors, one color representing the Risk of Death, the other the Probability of Life, from age 35 to age 99. This Exhibit is called "The Equation of Life Insurance," and the equations and deductions drawn from the diagram are as follows: (*a*) Risk of Death equals Cost of Insurance; (*b*) Probability of Life Equals Loss in case of Death; (*c*) When the Risk of Death is Small the Loss in case of Death is Large; (*d*) Life Insurance discounts Probability and gives Certainty.

2. *Application of the Theory of Life Insurance by Level Premiums*—(See illustration on page 332). The diagram and accompanying table show that a certain amount,

General View of Columbian Exhibit.

known as the "Net Annual Premium," is exactly sufficient, with four per cent. interest on accumulations, to pay all death-claims, according to the Actuaries' Table of Mortality, and that Large Accumulations are necessary. The table begins with 82,581 persons aged 35, who are supposed to be insured for $1,000 each. Each pays the Net Premium (usually $19.87, sometimes a little more and sometimes a little less, to avoid the long decimal .8666427 +) in advance; and interest is computed on accumulations at 4 per cent. per annum. One thousand dollars is deducted at the end of each year for each death, according to the Actuaries' Table of Mortality—the legal table for the valuation of policies in the State of New York. This process is continued until the table shows the death of the last man and the payment of his claim—when nothing remains. The number 82,581 is chosen because that is the number surviving at age 35 in the Mortality Table used. The different columns of figures show (1) Premiums, (2) Interest, (3) Total Income, (4) Death-Claims, and (5) Reserve Fund, for each year. The latter amount is that which the law of the State of New York requires a company to have on hand for like policies.

The diagram illustrates the progress of the table by lines and spaces. Space from left to right represents years; space from the bottom upward represents amount of money. There are lines for Premiums, for Total Income, for Death-Claims, and for Reserve Fund, and these all meet at zero at age 99, having shown in their course the income and disbursements of each year and the amount of the Reserve Fund at the end of each year. Although the largest amount required for Death-Claims in any single year is only $2,362,000, the Reserve Fund at one time reaches the sum of $22,732,417.23—or nearly ten times as much, yet it is all required to pay the claims of all. If there were lapses and each lapsing member received his share of the Reserve Fund, either in cash or paid-up insurance, the result would be the same. No allowance is made in the table or diagram for expenses.

3. *Growth of Life Insurance in the United States, as shown by Income and Disbursements, 1845–1892*—(See illustration on page 336). This is illustrated by a diagram based upon the figures of companies doing business in New York State. Each year's business is represented by a column of colors. (In the illustrations and description the original references to colors are retained.) The scale of amounts was necessarily determined by the height to which the columns could go, and one millimetre (about $\frac{1}{25}$ of an inch) represents $200,000. Sources of income are shown on the left hand side of the yearly columns—premiums blue (bottom), interest green (top). Disposition of Income is shown on the right hand side of the yearly columns—Payments to Policy-holders red (bottom), Expenses and Taxes purple (middle), Income Accumulated yellow (top). The diagram brings out forcibly the rapid growth of the business after the adoption of Non-forfeitable Policies in 1860, the decline which followed the financial crisis of 1873, and the rapid growth which again took place after the resumption of specie payments in 1879. In 1845 four companies had Income $220,361, Assets $283,383, Insurance $7,811,544. In 1892 thirty-one companies report Income $223,024,998, Assets $903,-734,537.04, Surplus $114,012,912.64, Insurance in force $4,199,444,397.*

4. *Growth of the New-York Life Insurance Company, as shown by Income and Disbursements, 1845–1892*—(See illustration on page 337). In this exhibit the same

* Industrial insurance not included.

THE EQUATION OF LIFE INSURANCE.

RISK OF DEATH = COST OF INSURANCE. PROBABILITY OF LIFE = LOSS IN CASE OF DEATH.

WHEN RISK OF DEATH IS SMALL, LOSS IN CASE OF DEATH IS LARGE.

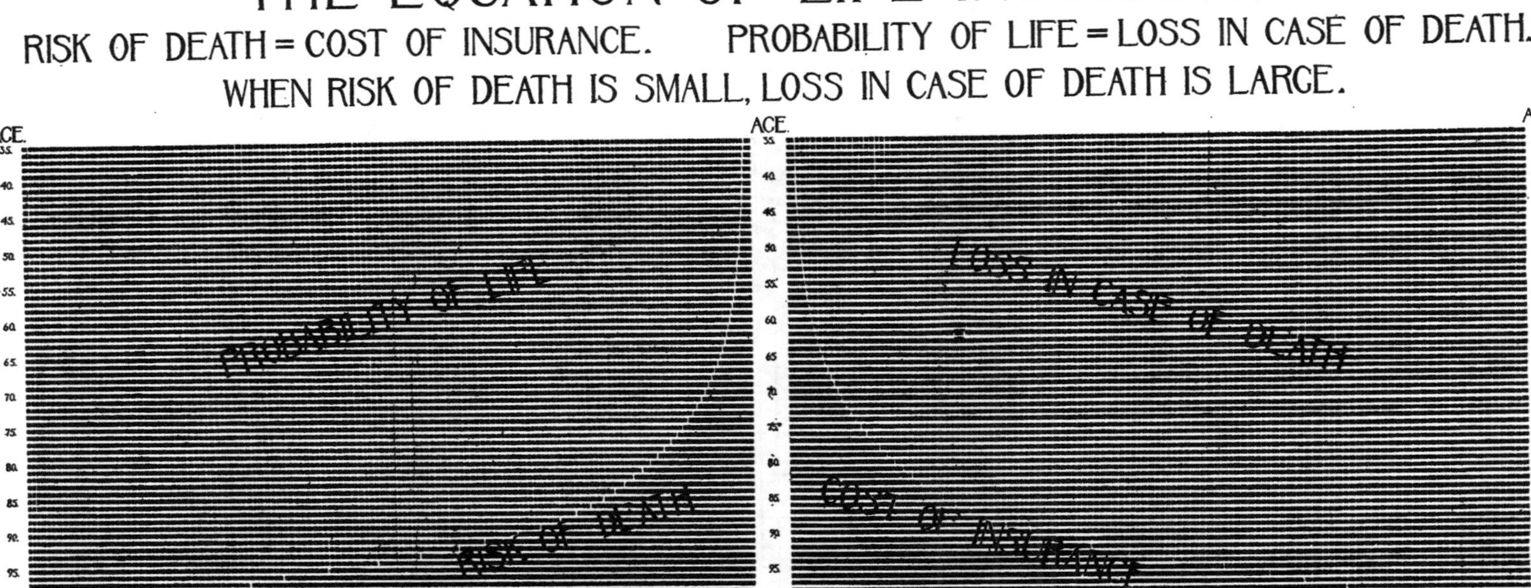

LIFE INSURANCE DISCOUNTS PROBABILITY AND GIVES CERTAINTY.

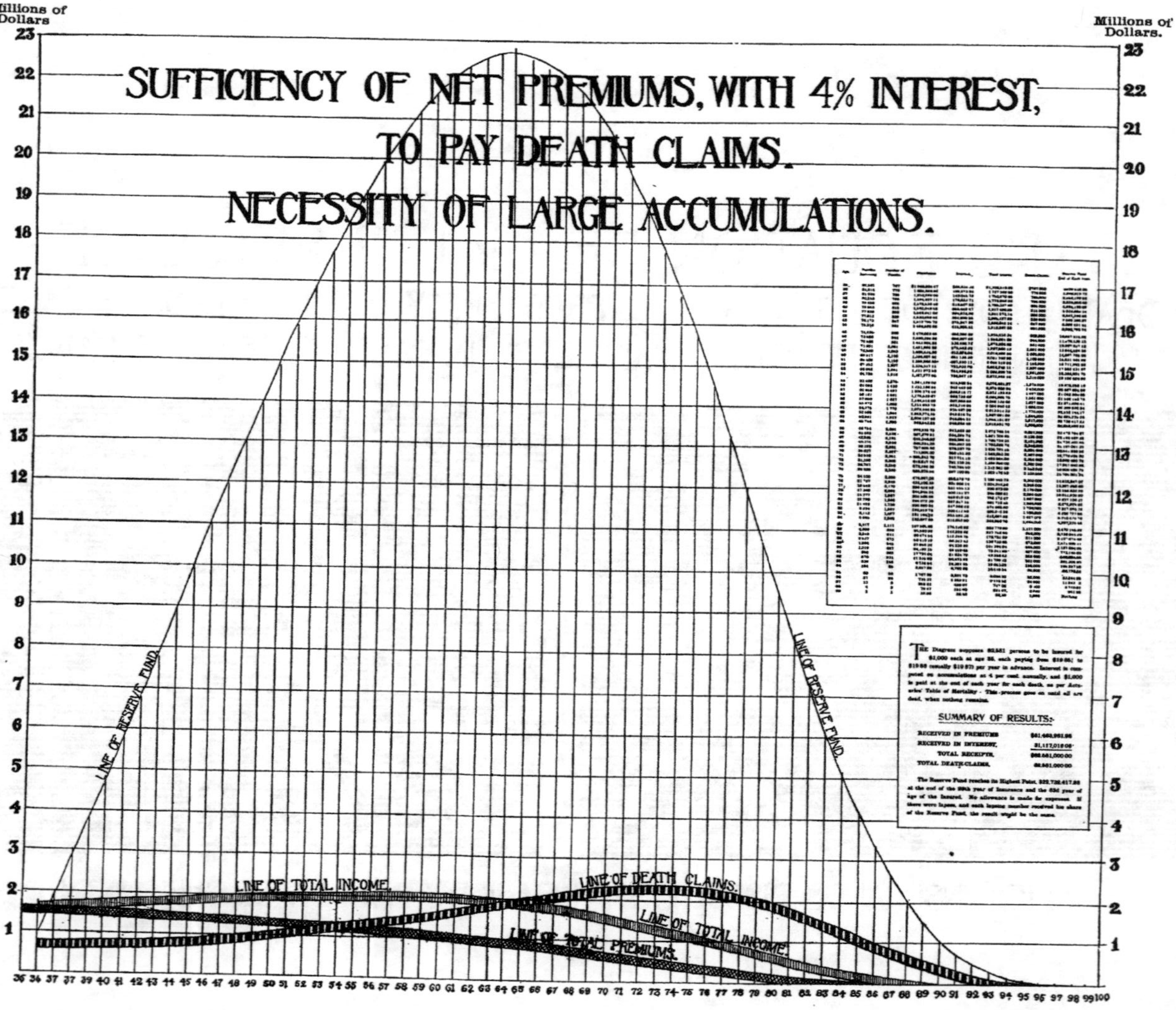
Millions of Dollars
Millions of Dollars.
SUFFICIENCY OF NET PREMIUMS, WITH 4% INTEREST,
TO PAY DEATH CLAIMS.
NECESSITY OF LARGE ACCUMULATIONS.
LINE OF RESERVE FUND.
LINE OF RESERVE FUND.
LINE OF TOTAL INCOME.
LINE OF DEATH CLAIMS.
LINE OF TOTAL INCOME.
LINE OF TOTAL PREMIUMS.
SUMMARY OF RESULTS:-
RECEIVED IN PREMIUMS
RECEIVED IN INTEREST,
TOTAL RECEIPTS,
TOTAL DEATH-CLAIMS,

TABLE OF EXHIBIT SHOWN ON PAGE 332.

Age.	Number Surviving.	Number of Deaths.	Premiums.	Interest.	Total Income.	Death-Claims.	Reserve Fund End of Each Year.
35	82,581	767	$1,640,884.47	$65,635.38	$1,706,519.85	$767,000	$939,519.85
36	81,814	776	1,624,826.04	102,573.84	1,727,399.88	776,000	1,890,919.73
37	81,038	785	1,610,225.06	140,045.79	1,750,270.85	785,000	2,856,190.58
38	80,253	795	1,594,627.11	178,032.71	1,772,659.82	795,000	3,833,850.40
39	79,458	805	1,578,830.46	216,507.23	1,795,337.69	805,000	4,824,188.09
40	78,653	815	1,562,048.58	255,449.47	1,817,498.05	815,000	5,826,686.14
41	77,838	826	1,546,641.06	294,933.08	1,841,574.14	826,000	6,842,260.28
42	77,012	839	1,530,228.44	334,899.55	1,865,127.99	839,000	7,868,388.27
43	76,173	857	1,512,795.78	375,247.36	1,888,043.14	857,000	8,899,431.41
44	75,316	881	1,496,528.92	415,838.41	1,912,367.33	881,000	9,930,798.74
45	74,435	909	1,479,023.45	456,392.89	1,935,416.34	909,000	10,957,215.08
46	73,526	944	1,460,226.36	496,697.66	1,956,924.02	944,000	11,970,139.10
47	72,582	981	1,442,204.34	536,493.74	1,978,698.08	981,000	12,967,837.18
48	71,601	1,021	1,421,995.86	575,593.32	1,997,589.18	1,021,000	13,944,426.36
49	70,580	1,063	1,402,424.60	613,874.04	2,016,298.64	1,063,000	14,897,725.00
50	69,517	1,108	1,380,607.62	651,133.30	2,031,740.92	1,108,000	15,821,465.92
51	68,409	1,156	1,359,286.83	687,230.11	2,046,516.94	1,156,000	16,711,982.86
52	67,253	1,207	1,336,317.11	721,932.00	2,058,249.11	1,207,000	17,563,231.97
53	66,046	1,261	1,311,673.56	754,996.22	2,066,669.78	1,261,000	18,368,901.75
54	64,785	1,316	1,287,277.95	786,247.19	2,073,525.14	1,316,000	19,126,426.89
55	63,469	1,375	1,261,129.03	815,502.24	2,076,631.27	1,375,000	19,828,058.16
56	62,094	1,436	1,233,186.84	842,449.80	2,075,636.64	1,436,000	20,467,694.80
57	60,658	1,497	1,205,274.46	866,918.77	2,072,193.23	1,497,000	21,042,888.03
58	59,161	1,561	1,175,529.07	888,736.68	2,064,265.75	1,561,000	21,546,153.78
59	57,600	1,627	1,144,512.00	907,626.63	2,052,138.63	1,627,000	21,971,292.41
60	55,973	1,698	1,111,623.78	923,316.65	2,034,940.43	1,698,000	22,308,232.84
61	54,275	1,770	1,078,444.25	935,467.08	2,013,911.33	1,770,000	22,552,144.17
62	52,505	1,844	1,043,274.35	943,816.74	1,987,091.09	1,844,000	22,695,235.26
63	50,661	1,917	1,006,127.46	948,054.51	1,954,181.97	1,917,000	22,732,417.23
64	48,744	1,990	968,543.28	948,038.42	1,916,581.70	1,990,000	22,658,998.93
65	46,754	2,061	929,235.75	943,529.39	1,872,765.14	2,061,000	22,470,764.07
66	44,693	2,128	887,379.51	934,325.74	1,821,705.25	2,128,000	22,164,469.32
67	42,565	2,191	845,340.90	920,392.41	1,765,733.31	2,191,000	21,739,202.63
68	40,374	2,246	802,231.38	901,657.36	1,703,888.74	2,246,000	21,197,091.37
69	38,128	2,291	757,603.36	878,187.79	1,635,791.15	2,291,000	20,541,882.52
70	35,837	2,327	711,902.00	850,151.38	1,562,053.38	2,327,000	19,776,935.90
71	33,510	2,351	665,843.70	817,711.18	1,483,554.88	2,351,000	18,909,490.78
72	31,159	2,362	618,817.74	781,132.34	1,399,950.08	2,362,000	17,947,440.86
73	28,797	2,358	572,196.39	740,785.50	1,312,981.89	2,358,000	16,902,422.75
74	26,439	2,339	525,078.54	697,100.05	1,222,178.59	2,339,000	15,785,601.34
75	24,100	2,303	478,867.00	650,578.73	1,129,445.73	2,303,000	14,612,047.07
76	21,797	2,249	433,106.39	601,806.14	1,034,912.53	2,249,000	13,397,959.60
77	19,548	2,179	388,418.56	551,455.13	939,873.69	2,179,000	12,158,833.29
78	17,369	2,092	344,948.34	500,151.27	845,099.61	2,092,000	10,911,932.90
79	15,277	1,987	303,553.99	448,619.48	752,173.47	1,987,000	9,677,106.37
80	13,290	1,866	264,072.30	397,647.15	661,719.45	1,866,000	8,472,825.82
81	11,424	1,730	226,880.64	347,988.26	574,868.90	1,730,000	7,317,694.72
82	9,694	1,582	192,619.78	300,412.58	493,032.36	1,582,000	6,228,727.08
83	8,112	1,427	161,104.32	255,593.36	416,697.68	1,427,000	5,218,424.76
84	6,685	1,268	132,897.80	214,052.90	346,950.70	1,268.000	4,297,375.46
85	5,417	1,111	107,581.62	176,198.28	283,779.90	1,111,000	3,470,155.36
86	4,306	958	85,560.22	142,228.62	227,788.84	958,000	2,739,944.20
87	3,348	811	66,474.54	112,256.75	178,731.29	811,000	2,107,675.49
88	2,537	673	50,410.19	86,323.43	136,733.62	673,000	1,571,409.11
89	1,864	545	37,056.32	64,338.62	101,394.94	545,000	1,127,804.05
90	1,319	427	26,182.15	46,159.45	72,341.60	427,000	773,145.65
91	892	322	17,724.04	31,634.79	49,358.83	322,000	500,504.48
92	570	231	11,325.90	20,473.22	31,799.12	231,000	301,303.60
93	339	155	6,732.54	12,321.45	19,053.99	155,000	165,357.59
94	184	95	3,657.92	6,760.62	10,418.54	95,000	80,776.13
95	89	52	1,767.09	3,301.73	5,068.82	52,000	33,844.95
96	37	24	735.37	1,383.21	2,118.58	24,000	11,963.53
97	13	9	258.21	488.87	747.08	9,000	3,710.61
98	4	3	79.47	151.60	231.07	3,000	941.68
99	1	1	19.86	38.46	58.32	1,000	Nothing

plan is followed as in the preceding diagram, except that the same perpendicular space represents only one-seventh as much money. A comparison of the two, therefore, shows how nearly the NEW-YORK LIFE has done one-seventh of all the business. It will be noted also that the NEW-YORK LIFE'S business continued about stationary after 1873, instead of falling off, as was the case with the business as a whole. The condition of the NEW-YORK LIFE at January 1, 1893, by the report of the Superintendent of the New York Insurance Department, was—Assets $137,499,198.99, Surplus $16,804,948.10, Insurance in force $689,248,629.

5. *Development of the Life Insurance Contract.* The Increase in Benefits and the Decrease in Restrictions, under the policy contract, are illustrated by four policies issued at different dates by the NEW-YORK LIFE INSURANCE COMPANY, with a statement of the Benefits and Restrictions of each.

(1) See pages 340–341. The first policy shown is Policy No. 2, issued April 17, 1845—the first policy in force in the Company. This policy promised but one benefit—the insurance payable at death. On the other hand, it was liable to become null and void and of no value by reason of no less than nine different acts or omissions of the insured.

(2) See pages 344–345. The second policy shown is Policy No. 14,415, issued August 13, 1860, which was the first Non-forfeitable Policy issued by any company doing a general business. The issue of this policy marked an era in Life Insurance. This policy also omitted the suicide clause, but retained numerous restrictions as to residence, travel, habits of life and manner of death.

(3) See pages 348–349. The third policy shown is Policy No. 217,822, issued January 27, 1886. This was a Limited-Endowment Policy, on the Tontine plan, and provided for insurance during twenty years and a definite cash value at the end of this period, if the insured survived. It was non-forfeitable after three years' premiums had been paid, the insurance being extended for the full amount of the policy as long as the reserve thereon would carry it. It also allowed one month's grace in payment of premiums, and contained no restrictions upon residence or travel after two years. In case the policy became null and void by reason of the death of the insured while engaged in certain hazardous occupations named, the reserve value was paid.

(4) See pages 352–353. The fourth policy shown is Policy No. 458,967, issued June 17, 1892, and was the first "Accumulation Policy"—a policy without any restrictions whatever, and with but one condition, namely, the payment of premiums. This policy provides for insurance during a period of twenty years, and six options in settlement at the end of the period, when the insured may either continue the insurance, accept the cash value of the policy, or take part or all of its value in an annuity. The policy allows a month's grace in the payment of premiums, re-instatement within six months after default, if the insured is in good health, and cash loans on the policy at five per cent. interest after it has been five years in force. It is non-forfeitable after three years' premiums have been paid, either extended insurance or ordinary paid-up insurance being granted, the first without request—so that its paid-up value cannot be lost by neglect.

6. *An Object Lesson in Gold Values*—(See illustration on page 329). As a means of attracting attention and of giving some idea of the immense resources of the NEW-

YORK LIFE, a Pyramid and Globe show the bulk of pure gold required to equal the assets of the Company. The Pyramid is 7 feet square at the base, 10 feet in height (above the pedestal), and 4 feet 5½ inches across one side of the top. The Globe is of the same diameter as the last-named measurement. Both Pyramid and Globe are covered with gold-leaf, two colors being used on the latter to represent land and water. The Globe revolves once every twenty-four hours. The meridian of Chicago is indicated by a line from pole to pole, and upon the upper band which surrounds the Globe at the latitude of Chicago the hours of the day and night are marked, so that the meridian shows Chicago time.

The weight of $137,499,198.99 in pure gold would be 228 tons, 104 pounds, 3,400 grains. It would make one hundred good loads for a two-horse team over an ordinary road. The Manufacturers' Building is 787 x 1,687 feet, inclosing 30½ acres. Reduced to square inches it is 191,184,336. The NEW-YORK LIFE'S assets would therefore suffice to lay a gold dollar on seven out of every ten square inches of the main floor of this immense building. Such is the provision the Company has made for discharging its obligations to upwards of two hundred thousand policy-holders.

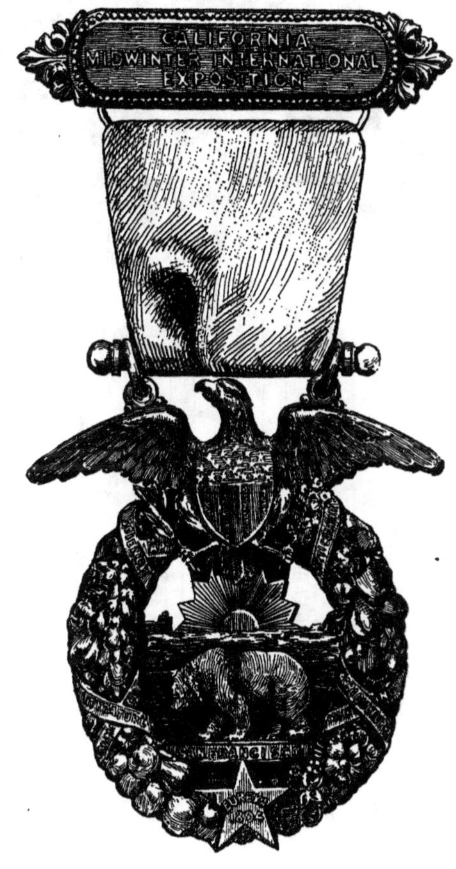

For this Exhibit the Company was awarded a Medal and Diploma, and the designer was awarded a Diploma of Honorable Mention by the Board of Lady Managers. At the close of the Exposition the Exhibit was sent to the San Francisco Midwinter Exposition, where it was awarded a Gold Medal and Diplòma. The Chairman of the Committee of Awards of the Columbian Exposition, Hon. John Boyd Thacher, in notifying the Company of the award, said: "The award consists of a Medal with the name of the NEW-YORK LIFE INSURANCE COMPANY upon it, and the Medal is accompanied by a Diploma on which are duly inscribed the reasons for granting

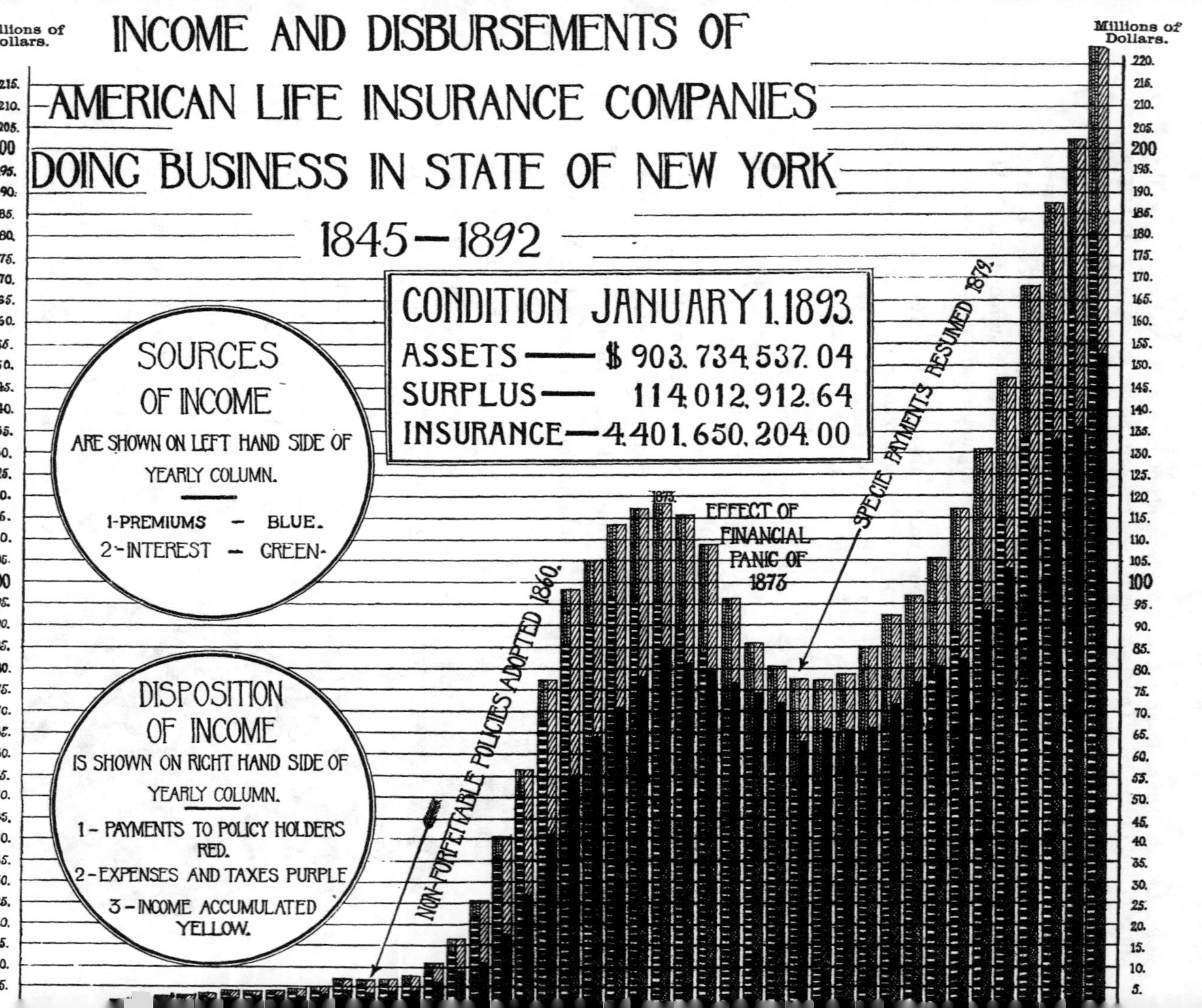

INCOME AND DISBURSEMENTS OF
AMERICAN LIFE INSURANCE COMPANIES
DOING BUSINESS IN STATE OF NEW YORK
1845—1892
Millions of Dollars.
CONDITION JANUARY 1.1893.
ASSETS —— $ 903. 734. 537. 04
SURPLUS —— 114. 012. 912. 64
INSURANCE — 4.401. 650. 204. 00
SOURCES OF INCOME
ARE SHOWN ON LEFT HAND SIDE OF YEARLY COLUMN.
1-PREMIUMS - BLUE.
2-INTEREST - GREEN.
DISPOSITION OF INCOME
IS SHOWN ON RIGHT HAND SIDE OF YEARLY COLUMN.
1 - PAYMENTS TO POLICY HOLDERS RED.
2 - EXPENSES AND TAXES PURPLE
3 - INCOME ACCUMULATED YELLOW.
NON-FORFEITABLE POLICIES ADOPTED 1860.
1873.
EFFECT OF FINANCIAL PANIC OF 1873
SPECIE PAYMENTS RESUMED 1879.

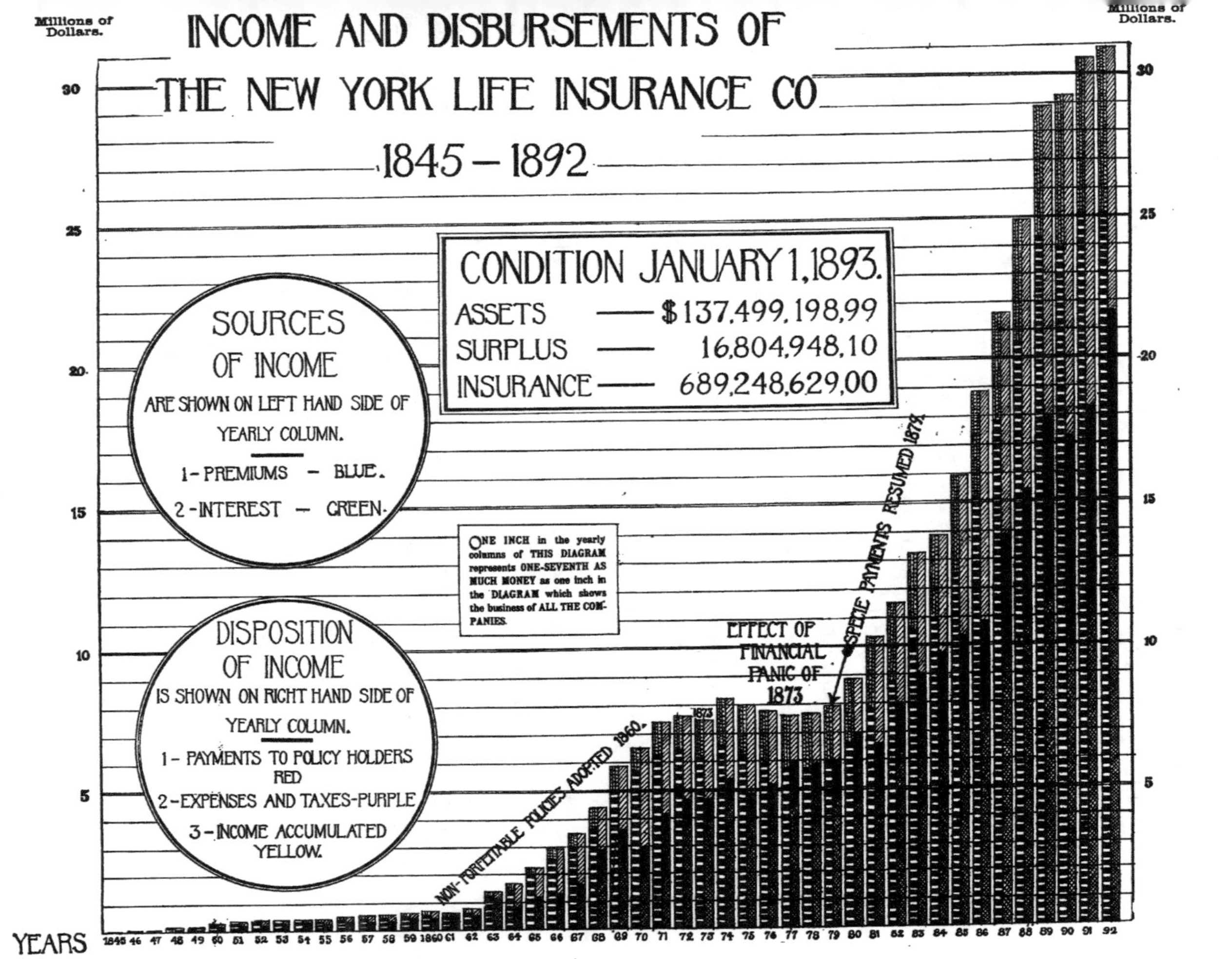

[See Explanation of Color References, page 330.]

the same, signed by the judges and proper authorities. Congratulating you upon the magnificent exhibit you made, I remain," etc. By direction of Congress the work of preparing and delivering the Medals and Diplomas was intrusted to the Secretary of the Treasury; but the unfortunate controversy over the design of the Medal has caused such a delay in the delivery of both these tokens as to render them practically valueless for the purposes for which they were bestowed.

The field work of the year closed with a three months' competition between the Western Department and the Central-Eastern-Southern Department. The dividing line was the western boundaries of Ohio, Kentucky, Tennessee, Arkansas and Louisiana. A purse of $10,000 was made up by managers, agents and the Company, to be presented to the subdivision of the winning department which should contribute most to the victory. The score was remarkably close; the East secured the more business, but the West made the better settlements and so won the prize —a result which completely reversed some popular opinions concerning confidence and cash.

While this contest was at its height, the man who had for so many years been the architect of the Company's fortunes lay a-dying. Mr. Beers had a very severe illness in 1890, and was never a well man thereafter. He was a man capable of an immense amount of work, and he did not spare himself. The Company, under his management, outgrew its methods of business, but he still kept the reins of every department in his own hands. When he succeeded to the Presidency, Mr. O'Dell, for fourteen years the Superintendent of Agencies, resigned; no successor was appointed; thenceforth the President was the director of the agency force, as well as the administrative head of the Company. He had borne up under the attacks of enemies with unfaltering courage, and was both surprised and pained that, on the showing of facts developed by the investigation of the Insurance Department, he should be so harshly judged. He resigned because continuance in office under the circumstances would only injure the institution to which he had devoted his life; and when he could no longer work as of old, life had lost its keenest zest and its chief reward. His last days and the character of his work were thus described by the "Insurance Age" for November, 1893:

The closing months of his life were peculiarly sad. He knew that his days were numbered. One day in early September he rather pressed his physician for a change of treatment, as the results were not satisfactory to him. "I have done for you, Mr. Beers, all that medical skill can do," said his friend-doctor, sadly. "I do not like what you say, doctor," queried the patient, looking searchingly into the physician's face. "The great nerve-centre has been attacked," was the response. Mr. Beers understood the great significance of the few words, withdrew almost in silence, walked home, never again leaving his house in life, dying two months later, November sixteenth, of nervous prostration. He was seventy years old—but until the last year or so, with the vitality and bearing of a healthy man of fifty-five. He was not only one of the ablest insurance presidents that America has produced, but he was a financier of unsurpassed skill; for it must be remembered that of the NEW-YORK LIFE'S $127,000,000, not a $1,000 investment could be made without the approval of Mr. Beers. Again, when it is recalled that his direct management extended over the whole range of the Company's affairs, the herculean task marked out and successfully accomplished must command for Mr. Beers' life-work the admiration of competitors, of co-workers, and of the business and financial world.

Announcement of his death was made by President McCall in a "Special Bulletin," as follows:

NEW YORK, November 16, 1893.

TO THE MANAGERS AND AGENTS OF THE NEW-YORK LIFE INSURANCE COMPANY.

The late President of this Company, Mr. William H. Beers, departed this life this morning, after an illness of several months, during which time he was a patient sufferer. To the Executive Staff and the Agency Corps, naught that I can say will do more than to emphasize their oft-expressed opinions of his valuable services and the unremitting attention he gave to the administration of the Company's affairs. He was by inclination and choice an active official, and no detail of management, however insignificant, escaped his notice. He understood the business of life insurance in all its ramifications, and he was the peer of the best manager in the selection and control of men, and in his conclusions as to their value and efficiency.

He had qualities of mind that commanded the respect of other life insurance officials, and the Company—under his guidance solely—reached and maintained its magnificent position as one of the leading financial institutions of the world. The credit for its great success is his, and his alone. Nothing less could be truthfully said of him; nothing less should be accounted the record of his life. His place in the history of Life Insurance will be well-defined, and the mature and unbiased judgment of the historian will accord to him a foremost position in intelligent, efficient and successful leadership.

My own acquaintance with Mr. Beers dates back for nearly a quarter of a century, and while there was no association that involved personal intimacy, yet it was often a great pleasure to me, as a State official, to discuss with him the progress, methods and

The First Policy in Force

IN THE

NAUTILUS INSURANCE COMPANY,

NAME CHANGED TO

New-York Life Insurance Co.

APRIL 5, 1849.

POLICY NO. 2. ISSUED APRIL 17, 1845.

THE ONLY BENEFIT Provided under this Policy was the INSURANCE PAYABLE AT DEATH.

THE POLICY BECAME NULL AND VOID AND ALL PAYMENTS THEREON WERE FORFEITED TO THE COMPANY from any of the following causes:

1. Any untrue statement in the application;
2. The non-payment of any premium;
3. Death upon the high seas;
4. Death by the insured's own hand;
5. Death in consequence of a duel;
6. Death by the hands of Justice;
7. Death in the known violation of any law of the United States, or of any State or Province wherein residence and travel was permitted;
8. Residence or travel south of the southern boundaries of Virginia and Kentucky, between July 1st and November 1st, or at any time beyond the settled limits of the United States and the British Provinces of Canada, Nova Scotia and New Brunswick;
9. Military or naval service, the militia not in actual service excepted.

THE NAUTILUS (MUTUAL LIFE) INSURANCE COMPANY OF NEW YORK,

This Policy of Insurance WITNESSETH,

ANNUAL PREMIUM
$200 50/100

SUM INSURED.
$5000

That THE NAUTILUS (MUTUAL LIFE) INSURANCE COMPANY OF NEW YORK, in consideration of the sum of Two Hundred dollars and fifty cents, to them in hand paid by Sarah Maria Freeman — wife of Pliny Freeman and of the annual premium, of two hundred dollars and fifty cents, to be paid on or before the Seventeenth day of April in every year during the continuance of this Policy, **Do Assure** the Life of Pliny Freeman of the city of New York in the County of New York State of New York for the sole use of the said Sarah Maria Freeman in the amount of Five Thousand dollars, for the term of his natural life

And the said Company do hereby **Promise and Agree**, to and with the said assured, her executors, administrators, and assigns, well and truly to pay, or cause to be paid, the said sum insured, to the said assured, her executors, administrators, or assigns, for her sole use, within sixty days after due notice, and proof of the death of the said Pliny Freeman — And in case of the death of the said Sarah Maria Freeman before the decease of the said Pliny Freeman — the amount of the said insurance shall be payable after her death to her children, for their use, or to their guardian, if under age, within sixty days after due notice and proof of the death of the said Pliny Freeman as aforesaid

Provided always, and it is hereby declared to be the true intent and meaning of this Policy, and the same is accepted by the assured upon these express conditions, that in case the said Pliny Freeman shall die upon the seas, or shall, without the consent of this Company previously obtained, and endorsed upon this Policy, pass beyond the settled limits of the United States, (excepting into the settled limits of the British Provinces of the two Canadas, Nova-Scotia, or New-Brunswick,) or shall, without such previous consent thus endorsed, visit those parts of the United States, which lie south of the southern boundaries of the States of Virginia and Kentucky, between the first of July and the first of November, or shall, without such previous consent thus endorsed, enter into any military or naval service whatsoever, (the militia not in actual service excepted) or in case he shall die by his own hand, in, or in consequence of a duel, or by the hands of justice, or in the known violation of any law of these States, or of the United States, or of the said Provinces, this Policy shall be void, null, and of no effect

And it is also Understood and Agreed, to be the true intent and meaning hereof, that if the declaration made by the said Sarah Maria Freeman and bearing date the fifteenth day of April 1845 and upon the faith of which this agreement is made, shall be found in any respect untrue, then, and in such case, this Policy shall be null and void or in case the said Sarah Maria Freeman shall not pay the said annual premiums on or before the several days herein before mentioned for the payment thereof, then and in every such case, the said Company shall not be liable to the payment of the sum insured, or any part thereof and this Policy shall cease and determine.

And it is further agreed, that in every case where this Policy shall cease, or become or be null or void, all previous Payments made thereon shall be forfeited to the said Company

N B If Assigned, notice to be given the Company.

In Witness whereof, the said **Nautilus (Mutual Life) Insurance Company of New York,** have, by their President and Secretary and Actuary, signed and delivered this Contract, this Seventeenth day of April one thousand eight hundred and forty-five

Jas. De Ogden President

Lewis Benton Secretary

Pliny Freeman Actuary

regulation of the business of Life Insurance. He was competent, from his intelligent observation and commanding position, to be a good adviser, and I recall, as I write, the perspicacity and wisdom of his views in many conferences thus sought by me.

Mr. Beers had reached and passed the age allotted to man, and yet his sprightliness and activity of thought were characteristics that robbed his years of time's usual accompaniments. His kindly face and gentle tone will be often in our memories, and the mounded earth that marks his resting-place will be moistened by the tears of many to whom he was endeared. To his sorrowing relatives only the consolation of the Great Lord and Master will avail. The assurance of sympathetic friends will not be wanting, nor will the place of his sepulture be neglected by them.

JOHN A. MCCALL, *President.*

Mr. Beers' death was announced to the Board of Trustees, at a special meeting held November twentieth, by the President, who closed his remarks by reading the "Special Bulletin" already quoted. Mr. Gibbs addressed the Board in substance as follows: "In many particulars the business of Life Insurance differs from all others; in one it is unique, viz., it has a literature of its own. In the history of Life Insurance literature, I think the 'Bulletin' of the President announcing the death of the late ex-President William H. Beers, in simple dignity and truthfulness of statement, has no parallel; and while it touches our hearts and voices our sentiments, it presents such a just estimate of what Mr. Beers accomplished while at the head of this Company, that it should find a place in connection with our action here, in the permanent records of the Company." Mr. Gibbs moved that the memorial "Bulletin" be spread upon the records of the Board, and the motion was unanimously adopted. Resolutions presented by Mr. Appleton, recognizing Mr. Beers' ability and zeal, and the energy and efficiency with which he had labored in the service of the Company, were also adopted. Hon. Hiram R. Steele, who was unable to be present, wrote: "It seems to me no better tribute could be paid to the memory of Mr. Beers than the simple statement that, the NEW-YORK LIFE INSURANCE COMPANY achieved its high position, becoming the wonder and admiration of the world, under Mr. Beers' management, and that he died a comparatively poor man."

By the law of 1884 (Chapter 341) the Superintendent of Insurance was required to make annual valuations of policies of companies doing business in the State according to the Actuaries' Table of Mortality with four per cent. interest.* This valuation had been accepted by the insurance officials of all other States, except Massachusetts, which has always kept its own policy registers. The Legislature of 1893, however, enacted that the valuation might be made "according to the table of mortality adopted as its standard of valuation by the company for which such valuation is made; provided, that in every case the standard of valuation made or accepted by him in determining the liabilities of a company shall be stated in his annual report." No reason was ever publicly given why such a law should be enacted. It could only be of advantage to a company which wished to make a more favorable showing than was possible under the old law. It introduced a varying, instead of a uniform, standard, and made each company a law unto itself.

The mischievous nature of the new statute was soon manifest. Before any company had made a valuation under it, the Superintendent of the Missouri Insurance Department sent letters to all the New York companies, under date of November 21, 1893, requiring a schedule of all policies in force on December thirty-first, proximo, to be furnished him for the purpose of making a valuation of the same according to the old standard. For this the laws of Missouri required the companies to pay ten dollars per million of insurance or fraction thereof, and three cents per thousand dollars of reserve on annuity policies. This meant the payment by the companies of about fifty thousand dollars to the Missouri Department alone, with about forty other States and Territories yet to hear from. "This valuation," the Superintendent wrote, "is ordered because of the abandonment by the New York Legislature of a strictly uniform standard of reserve upon the basis of the Actuaries' Table of Mortality with four per cent. interest, which elements are the standard of reserve in this State; and the rule will be continued from year to year until that basis is restored in that State or is abandoned in this."

President McCall at once conferred with the officers of other New York companies, suggesting that all notify the New York Superintendent

* The law went into effect December 31, 1887.

The First Non-Forfeitable Policy

EVER ISSUED.

POLICY NO. 14,415. ISSUED AUGUST 13, 1860.

THE BENEFITS Provided under this Policy were:

1. **THE INSURANCE PAYABLE AT DEATH.**

2. **A PAID-UP POLICY** for a proportional part of the Insurance in case the payment of premiums was discontinued after two annual premiums had been paid.

THE POLICY BECAME NULL AND VOID AND ALL PAYMENTS THEREON WERE FORFEITED to the Company from any of the following causes:

1. Untrue statements in the application;

2 Death from intoxicating drink or opium;

3. Death in consequence of a duel;

4. Death by the hands of Justice;

5. Death in known violation of any law of the United States, or of any State or Province wherein residence or travel was permitted;

6. Residence or Travel south of the southern boundary of Virginia and Kentucky, between July 1st and November 1st, or, at any time, beyond the settled limits of the United States east of the Rocky Mountains, or the settled limits of the British Provinces of Canada, Nova Scotia and New Brunswick;

7. Military or naval service, the militia not in actual service excepted.

[SEE NOTE, PAGE 62]

THE NEW YORK LIFE INSURANCE COMPANY.

This Policy of Insurance

WITNESSETH, THAT

THE NEW YORK LIFE INSURANCE COMPANY,

ANNUAL PREMIUM. $ 54 47 for ten years

Age 45 years

SUM INSURED. $ 1,000 #

Premium payable
Aug 13 1860 $54. 47
" 1861 – 54 47
" 1862 – 54 47
" 1863 – 54 47
" 1864 – 54 47
" 1865 – 54 47
" 1866 – 54 47
" 1867 – 54 47
" 1868 – 54 47
" 1869 – 54 47

in consideration of the sum of Fifty four dollars and forty seven cents to them in hand paid by Julia H. Sigourney wife of William Harrison Sigourney and of the annual premium for nine of Fifty four dollars and forty seven cents, to be paid on the Thirteenth day of August in of the years 1861, 1862, 1863, 1864, 1865, 1866, 1867, 1868, 1869 ~~in every year during the continuance of this Policy~~, **Do Assure** the Life of William H. Sigourney Post Master of Watertown in the County of Jefferson State of New York for the sole use of the said Julia H. Sigourney in the amount of One thousand dollars for the term of his Natural Life commencing on the Thirteenth day of August 1860 at noon

And the said Company do hereby **Promise and Agree**, to and with the said assured, his executors, administrators and assigns, well and truly to pay, or cause to be paid, the said sum insured, to the said Julia H. Sigourney or her legal representatives, within sixty days after due notice and proof of the death of the said William H. Sigourney

And in case of the death of the said Julia H. Sigourney before the decease of the said William H. Sigourney the amount of the said insurance shall be payable after her death to her children, for their use, or to their guardian, if under age, within sixty days after due notice and proof of the death of the aforesaid William H. Sigourney as aforesaid, ~~deducting therefrom all Notes for Premiums on this Policy unpaid at that time.~~ — Without profits.

Provided always, and it is hereby declared to be the true intent and meaning of this Policy, and the same is accepted by the assured upon these express conditions, that in case the said William H. Sigourney shall, without the consent of this Company previously obtained, and endorsed upon this Policy, pass beyond the settled limits of the United States that lie east of the Rocky Mountains, (excepting into the settled limits of the British Provinces of the two Canadas, Nova Scotia, or New-Brunswick,) or shall, without such previous consent thus endorsed, visit or reside in those parts of the United States which lie south of the southern boundaries of the States of Virginia and Kentucky, between the first of July and the first of November, or shall, without such previous consent thus endorsed, enter into any military or naval service whatever, (the militia not in actual service excepted,) or in case he shall die in, or in consequence of a duel, or by the hands of justice, or in the known violation of any law of the United States, or of any state or country, or in case his death shall be caused by intoxicating drink or opium, this Policy shall be null and void.

And it is also Understood and Agreed, to be the true intent and meaning hereof, that if the declaration made by the said Julia H. Sigourney and bearing date the Sixth day of August 1860 and upon the faith of which this agreement is made, shall be found in any respect untrue, then and in such case, this Policy shall be null and void: or in case the said Julia H. Sigourney shall not pay the said premiums on or before the several days herein before mentioned for the payment thereof, then and in every such case, the said Company shall not be liable to the payment of the sum insured, or any part thereof, and this Policy shall cease and determine.

N. B. If Assigned, notice to be given the Company.

In Witness whereof, the said NEW YORK LIFE INSURANCE COMPANY, have, by their President and Actuary, signed and delivered this Contract, this Thirteenth day of August one thousand eight hundred and sixty —

Morris Franklin, President

Pliny Freeman, Actuary

All Receipts for Premiums paid at Agencies are to be signed by the President or Actuary.

[illegible] the insurance we can exchange the policy for a new one for the full value thereof, without further payment.

of their adoption of the former standard of valuation. A statement to that effect was drawn up, signed by all the companies, and forwarded to Albany on November twenty-eighth. To this the Superintendent replied, under date of December second, that the declaration of the companies had been filed in the Department, and would be recognized and enforced accordingly. He further said: "The certificates of valuation on such basis, issued from this Department, should now be accepted in other States requiring the standard you have adopted, with the same faith and credit with which similar certificates have hitherto been received." Copies of these documents having been laid before the Missouri Superintendent, he withdrew his request for schedules of policies, and accepted the valuation of the New York Department, as usual.

A report of this action of the New York companies was made to the Board of Trustees on December thirteenth. At the same meeting the Board approved a proposition to insure the members of the Mutual Benefit Life Insurance Company, of Pennsylvania, upon the payment by said company in cash or acceptable securities of the sum of $394,909, that being the net premium for carrying the risks under new contracts to be issued by the NEW-YORK LIFE. The contracts thus taken over numbered 689, insuring $1,930,700, with annual premiums amounting to $47,599.64.

The general results of the year's work were thus announced to the Company's representatives, by the President, in the "Bulletin" of December thirtieth:

> This issue of the most unique publication in Life Insurance, closes the year 1893; and I am proud to take advantage of it as a medium to announce to the loyal and faithful field representatives of the NEW-YORK LIFE that, within the twelve months of 1893, they have had issued to them, on *bona fide* applications, the enormous aggregate of two hundred and twenty-three millions of insurance.
>
> These figures will be productive, perhaps, in your minds, of as much amazement as pride, because it certainly would have been, under all the circumstances, an entirely creditable performance had your work equaled in its results that done in 1892. The detailed statement of the Company's condition, which I hope to give to the public on or before the 15th day of January, will show you, I have no doubt, that the Company has made progress by equal steps in every department, and the aggregate will make a record unparalleled in the history of Life Insurance. If I had space, I would like to emphasize

the cordiality of my New Year's Greeting by an enumeration of some of the fearful difficulties which you have met and overcome during the last seven months; difficulties which would have appalled and disheartened weaker men, but through which you have brought your department with most distinguished success. * * * *

It is an inexpressible consolation to me, in carrying out my theory of how the affairs of a great life insurance company should be administered, to receive such constant and repeated assurances of the fact that, where the Company touches the great public, it is healthy, active, honest, determined and successful. I recognize in your work the primary source of the Company's success. Other departments, in their way, are of great importance, but your work ranks first, because without it, the others could not exist.

In these days of destitution and want, it re-enforces our faith in the character of our work to realize that, by as much as men listen to our teachings, by so much human suffering is abated. It gives us moral courage to think again that this Company is not a huge monopoly, sweeping on with resistless power, driving out the weak, crushing out the helpless, piling up vast private fortunes; but, in all things, the exact reverse. It is a great, common purse; a great, beneficent, moral force; moving, "without haste, without rest"; carrying shelter and warmth, providence and plenty into the homes of the people. With such thoughts warming our blood and bracing our courage, we enter the new year. I earnestly urge you to work, to work early; not because I am anxious about how much we may do in 1894, but because by that plan you will best serve yourselves and the people who charge us with the administration of so great a trust.

The Agency Department did not fail to emphasize in this result the further fruit of the principle of steady production, discovered in 1892. In the same issue of the "Bulletin" the Third Vice-President said:

We did not start out, on the first of last January, ambitious to write more business than some one else had previously written, or than some one else might write this year. We *did* start out with the determination to further carry out our ideas of steady production, and with the purpose to insure in the NEW-YORK LIFE as many healthy, well-to-do men as we possibly could. The year has been a most fortunate one in which to test our system of agency organization and our ideas of steady production—for there has been no time within recent years when the United States has suffered from such widespread business depression. To make our Company more deservedly popular, to increase by every honorable means the ability of the agents now representing us (and those who shall in the future cast their lot with us) to do each year a business more remunerative to themselves and more satisfactory to the Company in character and volume, will be the further ambition of the Agency Department.

1894. THE annual report for 1893 was submitted to the Board of Trustees on January 12, 1894, and the certificate of the Superintendent of Insurance certifying to the assets and surplus bore the same date. The report was made in the same manner as that for 1892, and already explained. The two hundred and twenty-three millions of new insurance

The First Non-Forfeiting Tontine

Limited-Endowment Policy.

POLICY NO. 217,822. ISSUED JANUARY 27, 1886.

THE BENEFITS Provided under this Policy were as follows:

1. **THE INSURANCE PAYABLE AT DEATH** if death occurred within Twenty Years; or,

2. **AN ENDOWMENT** for one-half the amount of the Insurance payable at the end of Twenty Years if the insured survived; or,

3. **A PAID-UP POLICY**, or an **ANNUITY FOR LIFE**, in lieu of an Endowment, if the insured survived;

4. **EXTENDED INSURANCE** for the full Amount of the Policy as long as its reserve value would keep it in force as temporary insurance, in case of default in payment of premiums after the Policy had been three years in force;

5. **THE RESERVE VALUE OF THE POLICY IN CASH** in case the Policy became null and void from any of the causes named below, except the first.

THE POLICY BECAME NULL AND VOID AND ALL PREMIUMS PAID THEREON WERE FORFEITED to the Company (except as stated in Benefit No. 5 above) from any of the following causes:

1 Any incomplete or untrue statement in the application;

2. Death by reason of a duel;

3. Death by reason of violation of law;

4. Death by reason of being engaged in the manufacture of gunpowder, dynamite or other explosive substances;

5. Death by reason of being engaged in military or naval service in time of war or insurrection.

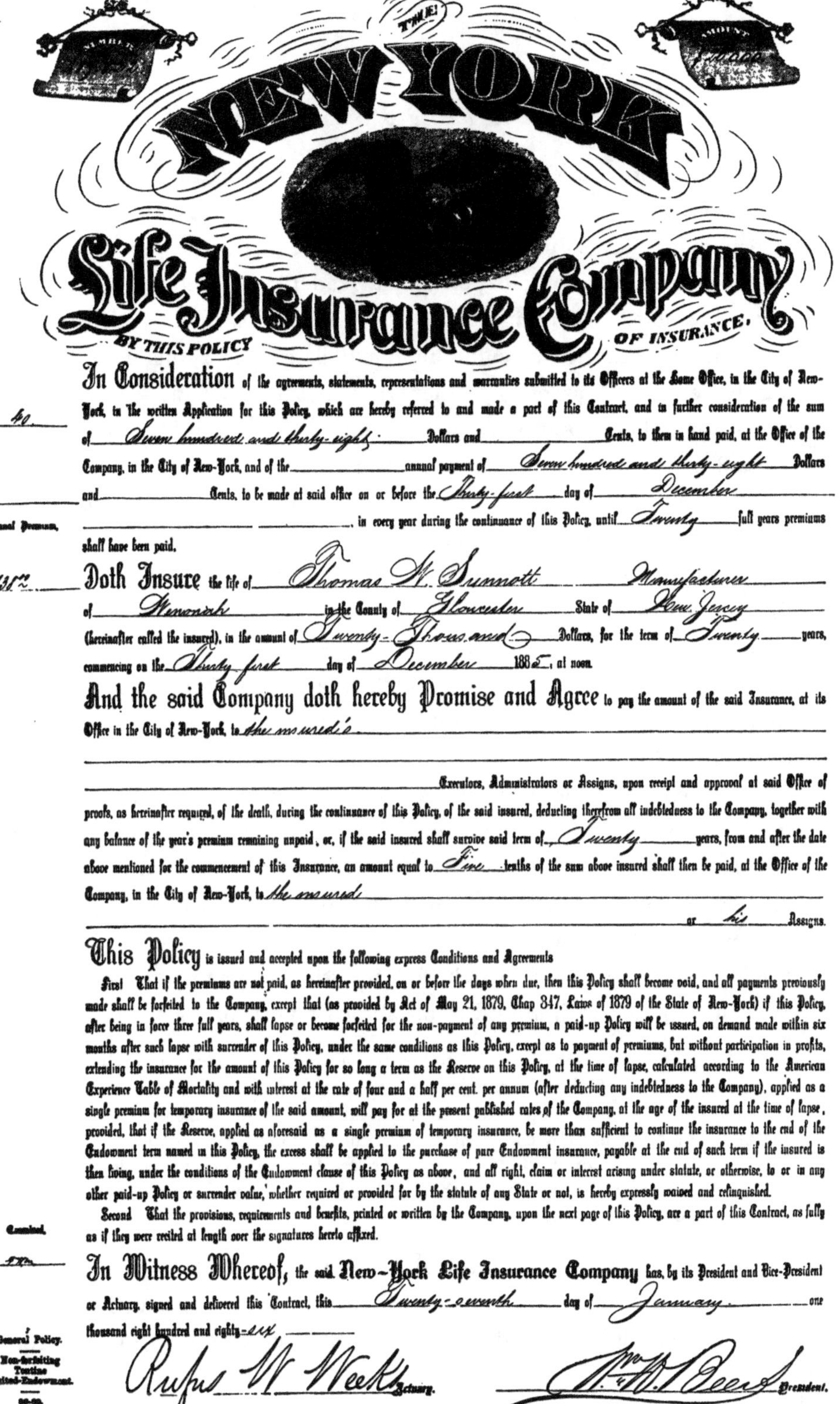

THE NEW YORK Life Insurance Company,

NUMBER

AMOUNT 20,000

BY THIS POLICY OF INSURANCE,

In Consideration of the agreements, statements, representations and warranties submitted to its Officers at the Home Office, in the City of New-York, in the written Application for this Policy, which are hereby referred to and made a part of this Contract, and in further consideration of the sum of *Seven hundred and thirty-eight* Dollars and ——— Cents, to them in hand paid, at the Office of the Company, in the City of New-York, and of the ——— annual payment of *Seven hundred and thirty-eight* Dollars and ——— Cents, to be made at said office on or before the *Thirty-first* day of *December* ———, in every year during the continuance of this Policy, until *Twenty* full years premiums shall have been paid.

40.

Annual Premium.

$738.

Doth Insure the life of *Thomas W. Synnott* *Manufacturer* of *Wenonah* in the County of *Gloucester* State of *New Jersey* (hereinafter called the insured), in the amount of *Twenty-Thousand* Dollars, for the term of *Twenty* years, commencing on the *Thirty first* day of *December* 188*5*, at noon.

And the said Company doth hereby Promise and Agree to pay the amount of the said Insurance, at its Office in the City of New-York, to *the insured's* ——— Executors, Administrators or Assigns, upon receipt and approval at said Office of proofs, as hereinafter required, of the death, during the continuance of this Policy, of the said insured, deducting therefrom all indebtedness to the Company, together with any balance of the year's premium remaining unpaid, or, if the said insured shall survive said term of *Twenty* years, from and after the date above mentioned for the commencement of this Insurance, an amount equal to *Five* tenths of the sum above insured shall then be paid, at the Office of the Company, in the City of New-York, to *the insured* ——— or *his* Assigns.

This Policy is issued and accepted upon the following express Conditions and Agreements

First That if the premiums are not paid, as hereinafter provided, on or before the days when due, then this Policy shall become void, and all payments previously made shall be forfeited to the Company, except that (as provided by Act of May 21, 1879, Chap 347, Laws of 1879 of the State of New-York) if this Policy, after being in force three full years, shall lapse or become forfeited for the non-payment of any premium, a paid-up Policy will be issued, on demand made within six months after such lapse with surrender of this Policy, under the same conditions as this Policy, except as to payment of premiums, but without participation in profits, extending the insurance for the amount of this Policy for so long a term as the Reserve on this Policy, at the time of lapse, calculated according to the American Experience Table of Mortality and with interest at the rate of four and a half per cent. per annum (after deducting any indebtedness to the Company), applied as a single premium for temporary insurance of the said amount, will pay for at the present published rates of the Company, at the age of the insured at the time of lapse, provided, that if the Reserve, applied as aforesaid as a single premium of temporary insurance, be more than sufficient to continue the insurance to the end of the Endowment term named in this Policy, the excess shall be applied to the purchase of pure Endowment insurance, payable at the end of such term if the insured is then living, under the conditions of the Endowment clause of this Policy as above, and all right, claim or interest arising under statute, or otherwise, to or in any other paid-up Policy or surrender value, whether required or provided for by the statute of any State or not, is hereby expressly waived and relinquished.

Second That the provisions, requirements and benefits, printed or written by the Company, upon the next page of this Policy, are a part of this Contract, as fully as if they were recited at length over the signatures hereto affixed.

Examined.

In Witness Whereof, the said **New-York Life Insurance Company** has, by its President and Vice-President or Actuary, signed and delivered this Contract, this *Twenty-seventh* day of *January* one thousand eight hundred and eighty-*six*

Rufus W. Weeks Actuary.

Wm. H. Beers President.

General Policy.

Non-forfeiting Tontine Limited-Endowment.

reported in the President's letter of December thirtieth were new issues on applications received. The additions to old policies by dividends in reversion, actually so used, old policies revived, and the paid-up policies issued in exchange for old policies surrendered, swelled the amount of "new business," according to the Insurance Department forms, to over two hundred and twenty-eight million dollars. The actual new business was larger than that of any other year in the Company's history, and larger than that of any year of any other company in the world. The amount of insurance in force at December thirty-first showed a gain of nearly ninety millions—which also surpassed all previous achievements in this line. The increase in new insurance over the previous year was $54,812,044, and the increase in new premiums was $1,682,698.42; yet the expense ratio was lower. A summary of the report was furnished the agents on January sixteenth, and the full report, as published by the Superintendent of Insurance—with additional information concerning the Company's real estate investments—was published soon after for general distribution.

The results of the year were a complete justification, from a business-getting point of view, of the open methods adopted by the new administration. Unfavorable comparisons with reports made upon different methods might deceive the casual reader, but the Company's agents were well instructed on these points, and in cases of actual competition misleading ratios were no match for the simple truth. Superintendent William Barnes had well said in his annual report for 1867:

> Sunlight is not more conducive to healthy vegetable life than publicity to corporate well-being. * * The American people *will* ask questions, and the more the better for all organizations thoroughly sound and really beneficent at heart. Life Insurance can and should live only by commending itself to the common sense and intuitive judgment of the great body of the people; and those facts which corporate instincts desire to conceal are always detrimental to the public good, and never immaterial when tested by the inexorable, decomposing crucible of Time.

As intimated by the President in his letter of December 30, 1893, the business of the Company moved on "without haste, without rest"; that no time might be spent in boasting of "records," a nine weeks' competition began February fifth, and the condition of entrance was the writing of one or more applications between January first and February third. This time the agents were classified according to the number of applications written during January and during each of the nine weeks thereafter. The number who qualified was fifteen hundred and eleven. Several such competitions were instituted during the year, with small prizes (but large honors) for the winners. Sometimes the prizes were money; sometimes a souvenir of some sort; always recognition, through the weekly "Bulletin," of work done.

All competitions emphasized the principle of steady production, the value of "keeping everlastingly at it," and the necessity of prompt settlements. The "Bulletin" was open to the best thoughts of the most successful and to the complaints of those who failed. The spasmodic worker was brought into contact with the plodder; the hap-hazard worker, with the man of method; the man of sluggish temperament, with the enthusiast. It was "a campaign of education" for the agent, and of resultant victory for the Company. In July and August—when men are apt to think no business can be done—there was a competition for one hundred seats in a Convention, to be held in New York during the first week in September. It was found that life insurance agents are very human; they are moved by many motives—pride in their profession; distinction among their fellow-workers; even the love of battle in a good cause, with honor in defeat and greater honor in victory—all these could be appealed to with good results both to the agents and to the Company.

In pursuance of a settled plan to take the public into his confidence, President McCall, on June first, addressed a letter to the insurance officials of each of the seven States—Massachusetts, Kansas, Ohio, Illinois, Kentucky, Missouri and Texas—inviting them to make a joint examination of the Company as of June thirtieth, instant.*

---

* The letter to the Massachusetts Commissioner was as follows:

Dear Sir: On the 30th of June, 1894, it will be three years since the "special examination" of this Company by the New York State Insurance Department.

Being strong in the belief that great public trusts, such as life insurance companies, should be periodically investigated, at least every three years, as now required of domestic companies by the law

The First "Accumulation Policy"

EVER ISSUED.

POLICY NO. 458,967. ISSUED JUNE 17, 1892.

THE BENEFITS Provided under this Policy are as follows:

1. **THE INSURANCE PAYABLE AT DEATH**;

2 **PAID-UP INSURANCE** in case payment of premiums is discontinued after three years' premiums have been paid—

(a) **POLICY EXTENDED** for its full amount during a period shown therein if no request is made, or

(b) **POLICY ENDORSED AS PAID-UP** for a proportional part of the original amount, as shown therein, if requested within six months;

3 **SIX OPTIONS IN SETTLEMENT** when the Policy has been in force Twenty years. The period may be Ten, Fifteen, or Twenty years, as desired, and the Options include (a) **GUARANTEED CASH VALUE**, (b) **CONTINUED INSURANCE**, (c) **ANNUITY FOR LIFE**, (d, e, f) **COMBINATIONS** of the three foregoing;

4. **ONE MONTH'S GRACE** in payment of premiums;

5. **THE PRIVILEGE OF RE-INSTATEMENT** within six months after default in payment of any premium if the insured is in good health;

6. **CASH LOANS AT FIVE PER CENT.** interest after the Policy has been in force Five or more Years;

7 **NO RESTRICTIONS** of any kind imposed with respect to Occupation, Residence, Travel, Habits of Life or Manner of Death;

8 **THE POLICY INCONTESTABLE** from any cause **AFTER ONE YEAR**, if the premiums are paid as agreed.

DOTH PROMISE AND AGREE

Age. to pay *Ten Thousand* Dollars

at its Office in the City of New York, to *the insured's*

42 Executors, Administrators

or Assigns, immediately upon receipt and approval of proofs of the death during the continuance of this Policy

of *Henry C. Mortimer*

Quarter Annual Premium, of *New York* in the County of *New York* State of *New York*

(herein called the Insured).

$111.80

This Contract is made in Consideration of the written application for this Policy, and of the agreements, statements and warranties thereof, which are hereby made a part of this Contract, and in further consideration of the sum of *one hundred and eleven* Dollars and *eighty* Cents, to be paid in advance, and of the payment of a like sum on the *first* day of *September, December, March and June* in every year thereafter during the continuance of this Policy, until *twenty* full years' premiums shall have been paid.

INCONTESTABILITY. After this Policy shall have been in force one full year, if it shall become a claim by death, the Company will not contest its payment, provided the conditions of the Policy as to payment of premiums have been observed.

Examined *[illegible]*

The benefits and provisions placed by the Company on the next page are a part of this Contract, as fully as if recited over the signatures hereto affixed.

In Witness Whereof, the said **NEW-YORK LIFE INSURANCE COMPANY** has, by its duly authorized Officers, signed and delivered this Contract, this *seventeenth* day of *June* one thousand eight hundred and ninety-two.

Limited-Payment Life.

Accumulation.

92-175.

Chas. C. Whitney Secretary. *John A. McCall* President.

This invitation was accepted by all the officials to whom it was addressed, and the examination was entered upon August first. They called to their assistance three Deputy Commissioners, six Actuaries, two attorneys, three clerks, and five other persons connected with the Actuary's office of the Massachusetts Insurance Department, and spent nearly four months in the examination. Their report bears date November 28, 1894. Referring to the President's request that "the investigation be made as thorough and searching as possible," and that "every item of property, accounts, correspondence and books" was at the command of the investigators, the report said: "In no instance has there appeared, on the part of any one connected with the Company, other than a cordial compliance with the spirit of this suggestion. There has been no shadow of concealment or evasion, but a disposition to place all matters connected with the business of the Company under our inspection."

As regards the Company's methods, the report said:

The several Committees of the Board of Directors meet frequently to count over the Company's assets and compare the vouchers with the expenditures. Payments are made on the authority of the Auditor's requisition and the death-claims are paid upon the approval of the Claim Committee. Agents' contracts are made under the supervision of the Agency Committee. This Committee work seems to be well systemized and thoroughly done.

The Medical Department for examination of risks seems to be well conducted. One branch thereof, the Bureau of Inspection, is used for the purpose of inspecting proposed risks, after medical examination and before issue of policy, for moral hazard. The Bureau has been in existence for two years and employs directly almost twenty men in the larger cities of the United States to inspect the risks. In the smaller places it supplements its work by using mercantile agencies.

---

of your State, and knowing that the New York State Insurance Department is and will be very busy with other insurance companies this year, I invite your department conjointly with those of Kansas, Ohio, Illinois, Kentucky, Missouri and Texas, to make a "special examination" of this Company as of June thirtieth, instant, in such manner and with such expert assistance as you may deem necessary, with the full assurance on my part that I desire the fullest and freest publicity of everything connected with the Company, and for such purposes all books and all transactions are open for your inspection and examination.

I desire at this time to mention that the coming year, 1895, will be the "golden year" of the Company, it having commenced business in 1845, so that it will be undoubtedly satisfactory to our policy-holders, to the public and to the insurance departments, to enter upon the year with a certificate of a "special examination" by seven of our great States. Very truly yours,

JOHN A. McCALL, *President.*

The Company's book-keeping during the past three years has been greatly improved by changing the arrangement and marshalling of items.

An investigation of the Company's contested claims from commencement of business to June 30, 1894, does not show any undue litigation either in amount or character. The refusal to pay in these cases seems based upon a reasonable foundation and desire to protect policy-holders against fraudulent claims. All of the doubtful cases outstanding June 30, 1894, have been examined with much care and nothing found that reflects other than credit upon the present management.

The agency work of the Company at the home department and in the larger offices in other cities has been carefully investigated by a sub-committee. We fully concur in their endorsement of the effective work carried out under the skillful guidance of Third Vice-President George W. Perkins, which has already produced so many desirable results.

The following questions by the Commissioners, and answers (under oath) by the Third Vice-President, form a part of the report:

Q. Are there any private agreements, understandings or conditions, either written or oral, in relation to your various agency contracts, other than clearly stated in the contracts themselves on file at the Home Office, as exhibited to us?

Ans. No.

Q. Our examination shows that it is the Company's practice, in making its Annual Statement, to charge to commission account not only the commissions allowed the agent, as per contract, but any other similar payments, such as advances against renewals, agency loans, commuted or commuting commissions, and every other expenditure of this general character. Why do you do this, since any payment in excess of the rates named in the contract must be made on the theory that it will ultimately be returned to the Company?

Ans. We add these expenditures to the commissions paid as per contract each year, because we hold:

First.—That if a life insurance company, for business reasons, sees fit to pay commissions before they are due, it does not alter the fact that they are commissions, and should be charged up as such when they are paid out; and we hold that the Annual Report to policy-holders should clearly show the total commission expenditures of the preceding year, whether such expenditures were due under the conditions of contracts on file, or were in anticipation of commissions to accrue at a later date, and that any other treatment of them would be misleading to the policy-holders and the public.

Second.—That while some portions of these payments may ultimately return to the Company, they are not assets within the meaning of the law, and cannot in the meantime be used in the payment of death-claims and dividends.

Q. The report of the Agency Committee to the Board of Trustees on the 14th of February, 1894, amongst other things, said:

"From 1882 to 1892, inclusive, the cost of each thousand of business placed on our books was as follows—

1882	$41.82	1886	$37.70	1890	$43.63
1883	39.77	1887	43.00	1891	45.74
1884	40.57	1888	35.55	1892	41.42
1885	39.09	1889	40.02		

Average $41.07

In these years the Company's paid-for business amounted to $905,900,000. The agency expenses for that period were $37,207,000, making an average cost per thousand of $41.07. The paid-for business in 1893 cost the Company $32.20 per thousand. This is $8.87 less than the average of the eleven preceding years."

How do you account for the fact that during the year 1893, on the basis of paid-for business, the cost per thousand to the Company was so much less than in any one of the eleven preceding years?

Ans. The results which you quote from the report of the Agency Committee to the Board of Trustees, covering the year 1893, were achieved by our having done away almost entirely with the old system of general agencies, and establishing in their stead a system of branch offices over which the Company has direct control. Under this system, contracts with nearly all agents are made direct with the Home Office, which has enabled us, *First,* to make more advantageous arrangements, both for the man who actually secures the business and for the Company; *Second,* to save the large profit which has heretofore gone to the middle-man known as General Agent; *Third,* under our present system we have absolute control of all questions of incidental expense, agency loans and guarantees. In the matter of branch office expenses we have improved our book-keeping so as to make a considerable saving in our clerical force. We have done away altogether with the system of hiring agents on salaries, have reduced to a minimum, both in amount and risk, the system of agency advances, and are in continuous and direct touch with every agent and policy-holder.

Q. Do you, either in the field or at the Home Office, adopt plans in the latter part of the calendar year for the purpose of apparently swelling the Company's issues, taking the inevitable risk of having the greater part of such business returned ultimately as not taken?

Ans. No.

The distribution of the Company's business at December 31, 1893, was shown to be as follows:

Countries.	Insurance in Force.		Premiums in 1893.
	Amount.	% of all.	
United States and Canada	$540,136,905	71.26	$20,575,939
Spanish-American Department	93,400,393	12.32	4,353,071
Continent of Europe	91,225,554	12.03	4,046,961
Great Britain and Ireland	17,778,269	2.35	846,702
Australia	7,985,213	1.05	465,957
All other countries	7,525,731	.99	441,732
Totals	$758,052,065	100.00	$30,730,362

The Commissioners did not approve of any company doing business in foreign countries, on account of the "widely varying languages, laws,

FAC-SIMILES OF THE MEDAL AWARDED THE COMPANY FOR ITS EXHIBIT AT THE WORLD'S COLUMBIAN EXHIBITION AT CHICAGO IN 1893.

NOTE.—These illustrations were secured after the printing of the text referring to the award, and in advance of the distribution of the medals.

[TO FOLLOW PAGE 356.]

regulations and methods of business," its distance from the Home Office, and the deposits of funds required.* As regards that of the NEW-YORK LIFE, it was said, "No responsibility for it is imputable to the present management; it is an inheritance pure and simple." * * * "The facts we possess do not show that there has been in this direction any excessive mortality or cost," * * * and "no harm or loss has accrued on its account."

The following question of the Commissioners, and the answer by President McCall, form a part of the report:

Q. We should like to know your views about the conduct of the business generally, and whether, in your opinion, the expenses, including payments to agents, salaries, etc., can be reduced without detriment to the companies and in the interest of policy-holders?

Ans. I have been able to answer your other inquiries by a brief response, but the scope of the last question is so extensive that I crave your indulgence in making a longer reply.

At the outset, permit me to say that I believe the expenses of the life insurance business, by which I mean all payments other than those to policy-holders, are higher than they should be. There are many causes for this, but the principal one is the lack of co-operation between the companies themselves. A little more wisdom and less pride would solve the problem speedily and satisfactorily. A brief reference to our own position will not be out of place as to what we have done and what we intend to do. After an attack of great bitterness upon the Company's management, lasting through more than six months, supplemented by an unfavorable official report, a change of management occurred in the Company in February, 1892. Its financial condition had been favorably commented upon by the State Superintendent, yet his criticisms, which were circulated everywhere by agents of other companies, had a demoralizing effect. Two courses were open to us. We could permit an agency force of 2,500 men to be tempted away from us by the offers of those who were ready to trade on our supposed weakness; we could remain indifferent to the losses caused our policy-holders by the lapses and forfeitures that had already assumed considerable proportions; and we could see a great Company that had, after nearly half a century of hard work, made an enviable record among the great financial institutions of the world, become dismantled and rendered useless for the future. The alternative was to enter upon the field with renewed activity, saving to ourselves an agency corps that had no superior, pressing home with vigor on every side the advantages of our situation purified as we were by the fire through which the Company had passed, and appealing by liberal treatment of our old and new membership in all

---

* Deposits are required as follows:

Small initial deposit required, but no reserve deposit.—Argentina, government securities; Brazil, any acceptable securities; Bulgaria, any acceptable securities; New Zealand, any acceptable securities; Switzerland, government securities; Victoria, any acceptable securities.

Reserve deposits required.—Canada, any acceptable securities; Germany, government securities; Italy, government securities; Russia, government securities.

their rights for the patronage that has since been accorded to us so largely. The alternative course was adopted, though not without some misgivings, because we were obliged to postpone for the time being so desirable a reform as any considerable reduction of expenses. Yet there is, in my mind, no shadow of doubt that we pursued the proper course.

A word at this point on rebates will not be amiss. I know that it has often been assumed that the only thing necessary to do to put a stop to rebating was to reduce commissions. But for this Company to have reduced commissions in 1892 without some concert of action with others—which was attempted, but could not be secured—would have resulted in the loss of both agents and business. Moreover, the adoption of such a course would have been to disregard the genesis of Rebate as well as existing conditions. Rebate was not caused by high commissions, but high commissions were caused by Rebate. The pressure of managers upon agents for business, and their own desire to make records, caused them to give away a part of their commissions in order to secure applications; then, having got the business and made the record, they claimed commissions that would recompense them for the outlay. It seemed wiser, therefore, to begin at the bottom and build upward, first, by offering a contract that should appeal to every man's sense of justice—a contract that should guarantee, in a form as nearly absolute as possible, the greatest benefits to be obtained under a life policy; second, to insist that this contract be sold at a uniform price; and, third, when the Company should be re-established in public confidence, to reduce commissions to such a point as would secure the most efficient service at the smallest outlay. In accordance with this theory, the Accumulation Policy was issued in June, 1892; rebates were forbidden by the Company in July, 1893, and such progress has been made in the reduction of both commissions and general expenses as is herein pointed out.*

After recounting the achievements of the three years following the examination by the New York Department, which included an increase of over thirty-four million dollars in assets, and an increase of over one hundred and seventy-seven millions of insurance in force, the President said:

The Company has thus been re-established in public favor in no uncertain way. The executive staff has labored unceasingly for the accomplishment of this result. *The officers did not seek, for any reason, to make the actual expenditures for securing the business appear less than they were.* The devices that of late have had public attention held no temptation for us. Every penny spent in obtaining new agents and new risks has been reported as an expense and has had no place as an asset, admitted or otherwise. The income account has been published without padding and the ratios of expenses to receipts are actual, not fictitious—although if we had followed old methods and reported our income and disbursements accordingly, said ratios would have been considerably lower than shown in our own previous statement, or in the present statements of other companies doing so large a proportion of new business. Our assets, lia-

---

*See sworn statement of Third Vice-President, already quoted.

bilities and surplus have been advertised and published in accordance with our sworn reports to the several State Insurance Departments, and we have not attempted by legislation or chicanery to make our indebtedness less, or our resources or surplus more, than they actually were by the most rigid ruling of the most exacting State official. You have had ample opportunity during your investigation of our affairs to know that as fast as old agency contracts expired or could be terminated, large reductions have been made in the rates of commission and brokerage. The same economy will hereafter be shown in all other departments. The Company having been placed where there can be no dispute as to its future or its popularity, the pride awakened by so great a task has ended with its accomplishment.

The management intends in the year now near at hand, which will be memorable as the fiftieth anniversary of the Company's incorporation, to pursue a conservative course in every branch of its operations.

As regards the finances of the Company and its condition June 30, 1894, the Examiners said:

The financial statement shows unquestionably the sound and prosperous condition of the Company; and the management, the public, and especially the policy-holders in whose interest the great trust is conducted, are to be warmly congratulated upon its solidity and security.

The following certificate was given showing the scope of the examination as regards assets and liabilities, and the result reached by the Examiners:

COMMISSIONERS' CERTIFICATE.

NEW YORK CITY, November 28, 1894.

WE, the Insurance Commissioners and Superintendents of the States of Massachusetts, Illinois, Kansas, Kentucky, Missouri, Ohio and Texas, pursuant to the invitation of the President of the Company, dated June 1, 1894, do hereby certify that we have been for the past four months engaged in a thorough and searching official investigation into the affairs of the NEW-YORK LIFE INSURANCE COMPANY of the City of New York.

We further certify that each Stock and Bond owned, each Collateral Loan, each Bond and Mortgage Loan made, the Cash and each Bank Certificate of Deposit, was carefully examined, checked and verified; that the Policy Loans and Premium Notes were examined and checked with the Reserve on each Policy; that Interest and Rents due and accrued, unreported and deferred Premiums, were also verified; that the values of Stocks and Bonds owned, and Real Estate owned, were individually and closely scrutinized and conservatively made; that the title to each piece of property secured, and Bond and Mortgage Loan made since the 1891 New York State Insurance Department Investigation, was examined and found satisfactory. That the Policy Reserve was checked and verified by the Actuaries of our several State Insurance Departments, and that every Policy and its Reserve, on the books of the Company, was checked individually with the Valuation Policy Registers of the Massachusetts Department; that all

Sundry Liabilities were also verified; that each debit and credit entry in the Company's books was checked from the date of the said New York State Investigation; and that as a result, on the most conservative basis of valuation, we found the Company possessed of ASSETS satisfactory to us, amounting to $155,453,428.73 and that, after providing for all possible Liabilities, including $135,058,291.00 for outstanding Policy Reserve, as per the "Combined Experience Table of Mortality," with four per cent. interest, the total of the same amounted to $138,124,363.81.

We further certify that, by the severest test, the NET SURPLUS to policy-holders, after providing for every Liability, and deducting Agents' Balances, was on June 30, 1894, $17,329,064.92.

In Witness Whereof, we have hereunto subscribed our respective names, in the City of New York, the day and year above written.

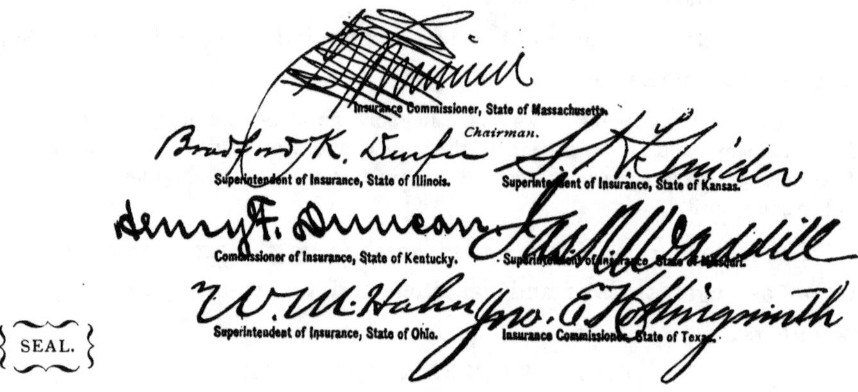

{ SEAL. }

In publishing the general results of this examination in the daily papers the Company gave a complete list of its securities, designating bonds by year of maturity and interest rate, and real estate owned by street and number. Once more agents could say, "the public knows all about the NEW-YORK LIFE, up to date, and there is nothing to cover up, or to be ashamed of."

While this examination was going on the Company lost one of its most efficient administrative officers, in the death of the Auditor, Mr. James A. Brown. His death was announced to the agency force by the President in the "Bulletin" of September twenty-ninth, in the following words:

It is with heartfelt sorrow that I announce the death, on September twenty-fifth, instant, of James A. Brown, the Auditor of this Company. He was my associate for many years in various occupations, and he had endeared himself to me by loyalty of service and untiring devotion in the Company's interests. Nature made him in a rugged mould, and he was a sham-hater by instinct. He served in several public and private trusts, and the marked honesty of purpose that ran through his career will be commended long after his interment, as it was frequently and vigorously during his life on earth.

Mr. Brown was succeeded as Auditor by Mr. John C. Whitney, formerly Chief of the Company's Inspection Department.

During this year the Vice-President, Dr. Henry Tuck, who had formerly been the Chief Medical Director, and Mr. William M. Adams, the Chief of the Policy Department, visited all the chief foreign agencies of the Company in Europe, Australia and the East. They were able to suggest changes of organization and management which have brought these agencies into closer touch with the Home Office, besides effecting a considerable saving in expenses. "Local Insurance Boards" have been established in several countries, by means of which the business of the Company is placed upon a more satisfactory and permanent basis, its prompt dispatch facilitated, and the Home Office is able to act more intelligently, both in the issue of policies and in the payment of claims. Opportunity was also afforded of personal conference with the Medical Referees and Examiners in these countries, and their methods were carefully reviewed and adjusted in harmony with those of the Home Office.

1895. THE announcement made on January third showed over eighty thousand new policies and nearly two hundred millions of new business during the year. The full annual report was submitted to the Board of Trustees on January seventeenth, and the certificate of the Superintendent of Insurance, certifying to the Company's assets and surplus, bore the same date. It went to the agents on the nineteenth. While the new insurance issued was somewhat less than in 1893, the actual new business was greater than that of any other company, the volume of new cash premiums was maintained, and the total income increased over two and one-half million dollars. Again the expense ratio showed a decrease. There were other significant points. The loans secured by pledge of stocks and bonds fell off from $2,428,966.67 to $579,922.00, while those secured by pledge of the Company's policies increased from $2,682,241.39 to $3,205,980.99. The pledge made in the Montreal address of President McCall that, "the NEW-YORK LIFE is a mutual Company and the advantages of its operations belong to the membership," was finding realization in its history. It could no longer be said that the Company, in selling its contracts, proclaimed them the best securities in the world, and then, after large sums had been paid on them, refused to lend a dollar upon their pledge as collateral.

In the Insurance Account, and in Income and Disbursements the report followed the same conservative, solid basis as has already been noted in the report for 1893. Of the total amount reported as "new insurance," under the Insurance Department's forms, 96.3 per cent. was actual new issues on new risks, while of the total amount so reported by the two other largest companies, only 80.2 per cent. was new issues upon new risks. The same difference runs through the figures of income and disbursements—in the NEW-YORK LIFE'S report income is cash or its equivalent actually received, and disbursements is cash or its equivalent actually paid, and these items are not increased by book-keeping entries which swell both accounts on paper without actually adding a dollar to either. As already noted, the new blank adopted by the convention of insurance officials shows exactly how much padding the reports of other companies contain, and, without being invidious, it may be said that the reports of the three other largest companies contain over five million dollars of the items referred to as book-keeping entries, which increase "income" and "payments to policy-holders"—on paper only.

With the new year was begun the use of a new policy form. It differed from that previously in use in being briefer, more specific and more handsome. Every unnecessary word was eliminated, and every obscure clause made plain. A new heading and border were engraved, in order to give fitting form and appearance to a contract that contains the most privileges and benefits of any now in use. The present year being the fiftieth year of the Company's history, this new edition of the Accumulation Policy was called the "Golden Policy." *Fac-similes* of the first and second pages are given following page 364. Page three of the policy contains a copy of the application; it will be seen that the policy-holder has, therefore, in his own possession a complete copy of the contract, in plain English, and that he may know what his rights and privileges are, without dependence upon any rule of the Company and without writing to the Home Office.

Toward the end of January the Company announced a new form of the Accumulation Policy—as respects the manner of its payment in the event of its becoming a claim by death. It was called the "Registered Bond Policy with Bonus Additions." It was an Accumulation Policy, with half premium-return in case of death during the accumulation period, and with a detachable trust clause, under which the Company, by virtue of the powers given it under its charter "to receive and execute trusts," undertakes to invest two-thirds of the face of the policy at three per cent. interest and to pay principal and interest as specified. The method by which the policy-holder avails himself of the Company's services as a trust company, is as follows: When the application is signed, or at any time thereafter, the policy-holder names a payee as beneficiary under the contract. This payee may be changed at any time while the policy is in force by a written communication to the Home Office, or the last nomination may be revoked, and the policy left payable to the estate, or assigned to a beneficiary. In the latter cases the policy is payable at death, in cash, to the estate or to the assignee, like any other policy. If, however, a payee has been named, and the nomination not revoked prior to the death of the insured, the policy is payable as follows: (1) One-third of the face of the policy in cash; (2) one-third in ten Registered Bonds, one of which is due and payable on each anniversary of their issue, during the next ten years, together with interest upon all unpaid bonds at the rate of three per cent. per annum; (3) one-third in one Registered Bond, payable eleven years from date of issue. The Registered Bond Policy is issued at the same premium rate as the Company's Accumulation Policy with return of one-half of all premiums paid (taken at the tabular annual rate) in case of death during the accumulation period, and includes the same premium-return, which is payable in cash with the first third of the face of the policy.

This policy is designed to place the proceeds of a man's insurance in the hands of his family at the time, and in the proportions, which will meet their necessities, and to prevent the loss which so often results from the investment of money by the inexperienced. It extends the protection of insurance through a period of eleven years after the death of the insured. It takes account of the circumstances in which the ordinary family is likely to be placed, and so distributes the proceeds of the policy as to meet their needs. Those needs usually are: (1) a considerable sum in cash—sufficient to pay the expense of beginning the new manner of life which the death of the husband and father makes necessary; (2) a regular income, of something more than the interest on the balance of the policy, during a period of, say ten years; (3) the cash value of what remains, for division among the members of the family, in such manner as time shows to be necessary. A *fac-simile* of the bonds issued under these policies is shown following page 366.

At the meeting of the Trustees on February thirteenth, the President announced that the Company's report for 1894 had been filed with the officials of forty-four States and Territories and accepted by each. At the same meeting was announced the death of Mr. Horace C. Richardson, Associate Actuary of the Company, to whose ability and faithfulness during his twenty-six years' service with the Company, the President paid a fitting tribute. At a meeting held by the employés of the Actuary's Department, Mr. Richardson's character, his services and the lesson of his life were commented upon by the Actuary and by the President, as follows.

By Mr. Rufus W. Weeks, Actuary:

His instinct of social morality was of the feudal type—summed up in the one sentiment of personal loyalty, but expressing itself in four aspects: loyalty to self, loyalty to official superiors, loyalty to equals, loyalty to official inferiors. In every one of these relations he was faithful to his ideal. Respecting himself thoroughly and invariably, he resented any invasion of his personal rights, feeling bound to do so as a matter of self-loyalty; and he always maintained his independence of thought. To the expressed will of his superior officers he rendered a military obedience, at the same time giving them the true service of a candid expression of his own opinion. Among equals he was faithful to every agreement, and responded to friendship with friendship, to affection with his own strong affection. Those under his control he treated in the true feudal spirit—giving them a most hearty protection and guidance in return for the hearty obedience he expected from them. Under the manner of the disciplinarian the heart of the man was always felt.

By Hon. John A. McCall, President:

It is a melancholy satisfaction to be permitted to add a word to the expression of your sympathy and to the remarks of Mr. Weeks. I met Mr. Richardson for the first time about twenty years ago when, in 1874, in the discharge of official duties, I investigated this Company. I had many pleasant memories of him, that were awakened and increased from the date of my inauguration as President, in February, 1892. From this last mentioned date I have seen him almost daily, and whenever he sought an interview it was granted with a certainty on my part that he had something of importance for my consideration, as he had no time for posing. My respect for him increased as each day added to my appreciation of him as a man and an intelligent official. He was large of mind as well as of body, and underlying his seeming brusqueness of manner, he had a spirit as gentle as a woman's and a sympathetic nature that made him the most genial and companionable of men.

There is a lesson in his career that is well worth the consideration of every man who stands before me. He strove to do well in every position to which he was assigned. His success came from the fact that, no matter how insignificant to others was the work he had in hand, to him it was all-significant, and he labored accordingly. He journeyed in his career by the *routes* that each one here is familiar with, and in his footsteps some of you are marching. At times the road appeared to be endless and the obstructions insurmountable, but he faltered not either in expectation or in determination to succeed. In the end he was rewarded by promotion to the high place that his ambition sought and his diligence provided. The possibilities of like accomplishments are for those who labor likewise.

On April third the Company announced that it would thenceforth insure railroad conductors on passenger trains without extra charge; also, that officers of the United States army and navy, and women, would be insured without extra premium, on any form of policy with 20-year accumulation period, and on 15-year Endowment policies with 15-year accumulation period—dividends to these two classes to be adjusted according to the mortality experienced in each class. On June third a further extension of the same principle was announced under the following classification:

Persons who have heretofore been charged an extra premium, and who are now insured in the United States and Canada at the regular rates on the above plan by the

New-York Life, are as follows; (1) United States army and navy officers; (2) members of paid fire departments; (3) railroad engineers, firemen and freight-train conductors; (4) working engineers on steam vessels, harbor pilots and captains of fishing vessels; (5) underground miners of iron, copper, gold and silver; (6) women; (7) the better class of general merchants, store-keepers, and proprietors of hotels and restaurants who also sell wine, spirits and malt liquors by the glass.

Persons in class seven are insured only under 15-Year Endowment policies with 15-year accumulation period; all others either as above, or on other tables with 20-year accumulation period.*

The regular meeting of the Board of Trustees for April, 1895, occurred on the tenth of the month, exactly fifty years from the date of the election of the first Board. To commemorate this event the heads of departments and the oldest employés of the Company were invited to meet the Officers and Trustees at luncheon. Others present were Messrs. Wm. L. Hill, Manager at St. Louis, and David Burke, Chief Agent and Trustee for Canada. The banqueting-room was handsomely decorated for the occasion, a large flower-piece behind the President's table showing the name of the Company and the dates, 1845 and 1895. On the second page of the *menu* appeared the names of the first President and first Trustees, side by side with those of the present time;† while the fourth page con-

* The Company does not insure railroad employés who brake, switch or couple cars; persons engaged in, or connected with, the manufacture of powder or other explosives; telegraph, telephone, or electric light men who climb poles or roofs, or work among live wires; well-diggers, who descend into wells; coal-miners, ordinary laborers, ordinary house servants, ordinary factory operatives, ordinary seamen or fishermen; officers of vessels, who are unacclimated and are going to unhealthy ports, or are engaged on vessels of less than one hundred tons burden; cases where there is an indication that the insurance is desired for speculative purposes, or to cover some temporary extra hazard.

† 1845.

Jas. De Peyster Ogden, Prest.
Wm. H. Aspinwall,
Loring Andrews,
James Brown,
Spencer S. Benedict,
John Cryder,
David A. Comstock,
Edward C. Center,
Henry W. Hicks,
Richard Irvin,
Thos. W. Ludlow,
Schuyler Livingston,
Adam Norrie,
Thomas B. Richards,
Almer Reed,
James Reyburn,
Leonard Suarez,
Edward F. Sanderson,
Robert L. Taylor,
Albert Woodhull,
Prosper M. Wetmore.

1895.

John A. McCall, President.
Wm. H. Appleton,
C. C. Baldwin,
Wm. A. Booth,
Wm. F. Buckley,
John Claflin,
Chas. S. Fairchild,
Edward N. Gibbs,
William R. Grace,
Wm. B. Hornblower,
Woodbury Langdon,
Walter H. Lewis,
Geo. Austin Morrison,
Henry C. Mortimer,
David Nevins,
Augustus G. Paine,
George W. Perkins,
Edmund D. Randolph,
Hiram R. Steele,
Oscar S. Straus,
Wm. L. Strong,
Henry Tuck,
John J. Valentine,
A. H. Welch,
David A. Wells.

NEW YORK LIFE INSURANCE COMPANY

REGISTERED BOND

THE NEW-YORK LIFE INSURANCE CO., AS TRUSTEE,

will pay *Three Thousand Dollars*, to *Mary Doe*

at its Home Office on the *First* day of *January*, 19*06*, upon due presentation and surrender of this Registered Bond, and will meanwhile pay interest thereon annually at the rate of three per cent. (3%) per annum.

This Bond is issued by the Company for value received, under its Policy No. *000,000*, which value the Company holds in trust, but with the right to mingle the same with its General Funds.

Should the above-named payee die before this Bond becomes due, the Company, upon due surrender of this Bond, will pay immediately to the payee's executors or administrators its face amount without discount and with accrued interest then unpaid.

This Bond is registered in the above name upon the books of the Company; it is non-transferable and non-assignable, and payable only to the payee or to the payee's executors or administrators.

In Witness Whereof, the NEW-YORK LIFE INSURANCE COMPANY has caused its corporate seal to be hereunto affixed, and these presents to be signed by its duly authorized officers, at the City of New York, this *First* day of *January*, Eighteen Hundred and Ninety *five*.

Chas. C. Whitney Secretary. *John A. McCall* President.

Presidents Office.
New York Life Insurance Company.
346 & 348 Broadway.

New York, April 3, 1895.

Dear Sir:

The next regular meeting of the Board of Trustees of this Company will occur on the Fiftieth Anniversary of its organization.

It is desired to mark, in a becoming manner, this important epoch in the Company's history, and you are invited to meet the Trustees and Officers at a Luncheon to be given at the Lawyer's Club. 120 Broadway. at two o'clock. P.M. April 10, 1895.

A reply to this invitation will oblige
Yours respectfully,
John A. McCall.
President.

tained the first annual report and a summary of the Company's receipts and expenditures from 1845 to 1895.

Luncheon over, President McCall addressed the assembled company as follows:

Fifty years ago to-day, four men—Caleb S. Woodhull, Wm. V. Brady, Herman W. Childs and Joseph B. Nones—met at No. 3 Nassau Street, in this city, to organize an insurance company. They had a charter which authorized them to do life, fire, marine and inland transportation insurance. They had a little over $50,000 in subscription notes; they had applications for over $300,000 of insurance; but they had not one cent of cash capital, and the money which paid the expenses of organization was borrowed. They elected twenty trustees, and three inspectors to preside at the next annual election, certified their minutes and adjourned. Their names do not occur again in the records of the Company as either trustees or officers. They did their work and went their way unmindful of the influences they had set in operation for the benefit of mankind. Of the board of trustees elected on that day, the gentlemen now before me are the legal successors, and the Company which was then given legal existence, is to-day the possessor of over $162,000,000 in valid securities, and has upon its books the names of 286,000 policy-holders. In view of such a record, whom shall we congratulate—those who laid the foundations, those who built the superstructure by many years of labor, or those who, in the fullness of time, have entered into the labors of all who have gone before them? There is honor enough for all, but upon this day, which marks a half century of our corporate existence, I think it especially behooves us to remember those who gave the Company being, and who guided it through its early years. I propose, therefore, to read in your hearing the names of the first trustees of the Company, and I feel sure that among them the older members of the present board will recognize some whose names were familiar fifty years ago as representative men of the metropolis. [The President at this point read the list as given on page 366.]

Of these men, Spencer S. Benedict, of Sioux City, Iowa, who remained a trustee until 1851, and who, from 1849 to 1851, was Vice-President of the Company, is the only one now living. In response to an invitation to attend this meeting, he expressed great regret at his inability to be present.

The early struggles of the Company have often been recalled, but it may be unknown to those here present that at one time the State Comptroller was advised to prevent it from paying a dividend in 1853, in order to "save it from ruin." Permit me to read the official communication, which is now on file with the Insurance Department at Albany, and which, as I dug it up years ago, when I was connected with the State Government, brought a smile to my lips, as doubtless it will to yours:

"BROOKLYN, December 20, 1852.

"JOHN C. WRIGHT, STATE COMPTROLLER, ALBANY, N. Y.

"*Dear Sir:* I wrote you on the 9th inst., and am at present without any reply. I have, however, in order to prevent the NEW-YORK LIFE INSURANCE COMPANY from declaring another dividend without an examination into their affairs by themselves, sent a copy of the enclosed to each trustee. The Company must be saved, if possible, from ruin. Last year the losses, expenses and dividends amounted to more than their premiums. As soon as I hear from you I will write you more fully.

"Very respectfully, your obedient servant,

EDMUND BLUNT."

Would that the writer of it could be present with us to-day to hear the tale of the giant that was so weak a foundling.

The world into which this new Company was born fifty years ago was a very different world in many aspects from the world of to-day. New York City had a population of less than 400,000. But one steam railroad, the Harlem, entered it. There were but twenty-seven States in the Union, with a total population of about 20,000,000. There were less than 5,000 miles of railroad in the whole country, and the first iron rail was laid in that year. Chicago had about 10,000 inhabitants, San Francisco about 500, Minneapolis, St. Paul and Kansas City a few hundred, Omaha and Denver none. The first telegram had been sent less than a year before, and telephones, electric lights, steam elevators, sleeping cars and typewriting machines had not been thought of. James K. Polk had just been inaugurated President and had announced as the four great measures of his administration the reduction of the tariff, an independent treasury system, a settlement of the Oregon boundary question, and the acquisition of California. Meanwhile, the newspapers were discussing the question whether the annexation of Texas would cause war with Mexico. The expenditures of the United States Government in 1845 were less than $22,000,000. The slave-ship Spitfire was condemned at Boston during the year, and among the first thousand policies written by the Company there were 339 upon the lives of persons of African descent who were held in bondage under the laws of the United States. But I will not continue the subject in illustration of the marvelous changes which fifty years have wrought. I will only add that we have in course of preparation by our Mr. Hudnut, a semi-centennial history of the Company, which we hope to publish soon, and which will show how closely linked the history of the Company has been with that of the country at large, and with what untiring labor and unceasing diligence its prosperity and growth have been promoted through half a century of time.

When the NEW-YORK LIFE was organized there were twelve American companies doing life insurance business, and the new insurance in 1844 was about $3,000,000. Of these twelve companies nine are now in existence, but only four are taking new risks. These four are the Presbyterian Ministers Fund of Philadelphia, the New England Mutual of Boston, the Mutual Life of New York, and the Mutual Benefit of New Jersey. The new business of these companies in 1894 was about ninety times as great as that of all American companies in 1844. Forty-two companies of this country, on January 1, 1895, held $1,000,000,000 of assets. Their premium receipts from date of organization were $2,750,000,000, and they had paid during the same period to policy-holders $1,800,000,000. Colossal, indeed, are the figures that tell this tale, and the results of the great trusts confided to their officers are unparalleled in fable or fact. This Company has contributed nobly to it all, and as we recall the names of its presiding officers, J. De Peyster Ogden, Aaron M. Merchant, Morris Franklin and William H. Beers, we recognize the talent and great ability of each of them in their respective terms of service. Let us not forget them in this hour of rejoicing, and as we think of what they have accomplished, give to their memories a tribute of sorrow and respect.

I will further detain you only to read the first annual statement made in the year 1846, and, for admiring comparison, a summary of the Company's receipts and expenditures from organization to December 31, 1894.

FIRST ANNUAL STATEMENT OF THE

NAUTILUS (MUTUAL LIFE) INSURANCE COMPANY,

APRIL 16, 1846.

Total Amount of Premiums to April 16		*$22,622.71
Charged to Subscribers	$6,057.11	
Settled by Notes	772.60	
Paid in Cash	11,571.20	
In hands of Agents	2,056.58	
Deferred Premiums and Premiums on Policies not yet Delivered,	2,165.22	
		$22,622.71
CASH.		
Received for Premiums as above	$11,571.20	
Received for Interest	32.33	
		$11,603.53
Paid for Re-insurance	$335.79	
Proportion of Charter	341.50	
Office Furniture	116.97	
Books and Stationery	322.72	
Salary	1,500.00	
Physicians' Fees in full	450.00	
Ogden & Lord's written opinions	50.00	
Printing Policies, Circulars, &c	213.50	
Advertising	306.96	
Postage and other small items	263.48	
Agency Expenses, Commissions, &c	1,239.84	
		$5,140.76
Balance		$6,462.77
According to the charter of the Company, the following statement is published:		
There were issued 449 Policies during the year ending April 16, 1846, the Premiums on which amounted to		$22,622.71
Premiums earned during the same period		$10,331.92
Expenses of the Company, viz.:		
Paid for Re-insurances	$335.79	
Paid for Charter, Salary, &c	3,565.13	
Agency Expenses, Commissions, &c	1,239.84	
		5,140.76
Net Profits		$5,191.16

*This amount included $20 received on two fire policies.

RESUME, JANUARY 1, 1895.

RECEIPTS AND EXPENDITURES FROM ORGANIZATION.

Received from policy-holders	$359,451,763.12
Received from all other sources	88,281,236.62
Total	$447,732,999.74
Paid policy-holders	$199,987,073.32
All other payments	85,734,155.49
Total	$285,721,228.81
Balance Assets on hand, December 31, 1894	162,011,770.93
Total	$447,732,999.74

Brief addresses were also made by Messrs. Wm. L. Hill and Wm. B. Hornblower; and letters of regret were read from Superintendent Pierce; from James P. Wallace, of Brooklyn, insured under Policy No. 15, the oldest policy in force; from Major Livingston Mims, of Georgia, Col. Wm. B. Hamilton, of Texas,* both of whom have been connected with the Company since 1868; and from Messrs. Appleton, Booth, and Mayor Strong, members of the present Board of Trustees. The exercises were brought to a close by the reading of the following lines written for the occasion by the compiler of this History:

---

*The following letter, written by Colonel Hamilton to the President of the American Union Life Insurance Company, under date of December 3, 1894, illustrates his feeling toward the NEW-YORK LIFE, after twenty-seven years' service under its banner:

I have read carefully your arguments in favor of your own propositions and, whilst I shall not try to combat them, I must confess that I am "too old a dog to learn new tricks." As I was raised a cotton planter in Louisiana, I followed that employment until slavery was doomed by the late "unpleasantness." In 1868, when I had spent what little was left me by the late war, I was persuaded to try life insurance. The "Old Reliable" NEW-YORK LIFE was my earliest suitor, and I must modestly and blushingly admit that my head, heart and hand have been united to her ever since. It is now second nature with me to serve and love the dear old thing. There are a few things in life that I am not desirous of changing, and flattering temptations would not move me to give up even one of them:

1st.—I am a Presbyterian of the old school, uniting with this church when I was a student in the University of Virginia, in 1851. 2d.—I am a Democrat, "dyed in the wool," born, bred and expect to die one. 3d.—I am a married man, never had but one wife, and pray God every day that my good companion may be spared to comfort and bless me as long as I live. 4th.—I am a recruit of the "Old Reliable" NEW-YORK LIFE. Since May, 1868, it has been my good privilege to labor for her, and to witness her just dealings with all her policy-holders, without regard to location, race, color or previous condition. I glory in her colors, they are "red, white and blue." There may not be many years, or even days, allotted me here, but, having enlisted under Morris Franklin, and renewed my allegiance under William H. Beers, and under the "honest and magnetic" John A. McCall, all three grand men and great leaders, I shall strive, God helping me, to continue to the end—a high private in the ranks, fighting for the care and protection of the widow, the orphan and the aged man.

The New-York Life! The New-York Life!
  For fifty years the widow's shield—
Her foremost champion in the strife—
  Victor on many a bloodless field.
    The tranquil seas of forty-five
      Upbore the tiny "Nautilus";
  With favoring winds and pilots true
  She sailed the main, and while she grew
  The years which held her larger fame
  Bestowed in trust her greater name.

The New-York Life! The New-York Life!
  How fit that one who parries death
And shields the home, the child, the wife,
  Should bear the name and wear the wreath
    Of that great mother city—queen
    Of all Columbia's fair domain!
  Her wealth, her power, her beauty, fame,
    Her throne, rock-based, 'tween waters set—
  Are all betokened by her name—
    But New-York Life is nobler yet.

The New-York Life! The New-York Life!
  Fair shines her record on the page,
When North and South in deadly strife
  Wrought out the problem of the age;
In peace and plenty, storm and stress,
  Still to her mission faithful, true,
To bind up wounds, relieve distress,
  Forget the past, make all things new;
    And thus proclaim the greater good
    Of freedom, justice, brotherhood.

The New-York Life! The New-York Life!
  'Twas hers through all the years to scan
The field with many projects rife,
  And make from all the better plan;—
Outgrown conditions to rescind,
  Put faith for fear and trust for doubt,
To bring the larger freedom in,
  To cast the old restrictions out;
    That in the contract might be set
    The pledge of every benefit.

The New-York Life! The New-York Life!
  What names and memories arise!
What echoes of the toil and strife
  Through which was gained the wished-for prize!

Ogden, Merchant, Freeman, Franklin;
Coleman, Benedict and Kendall;
Benton, Beers, Tuck, Welch and Perkins;
Wilkes and Bogert, Wright and Carney;
Huntington and Weeks and Banta;
Whitney, Thompson, Gibbs, McCall; —
Men of mind and purpose all.

All hail the living and the dead—
Whose hands have wrought, whose minds conceived,
The noble deed, or living thought,
Which want and sorrow has relieved!
Their work shall stand, and coming years
Will show the grandeur of the plan
That nerves the arm and calms the fears
And gives immortal youth to man:
For when the family is safe
The brave man knows nor age nor death.

The President then declared the meeting adjourned; and thus ended, at half past four o'clock, in the afternoon of April 10, 1895, the first half century of the NEW-YORK LIFE INSURANCE COMPANY.

BUSINESS OF THE NEW-YORK LIFE IN 1889 AND IN 1894.

ITEMS.	1889.	1894.
New Insurance Written	$151,119,088	$206,545,392
Income	28,830,123	36,483,314
Paid Policy-holders	12,121,122	15,665,003
Assets	104,415,322	162,011,771
Surplus	15,654,263	20,249,308
Insurance in Force	495,601,970	813,294,160

TOTAL IN FIVE YEARS, 1890–1894.

Total New Insurance Written	$920,808,623
" Income	164,621,448
" Paid Policy-holders	70,649,501
" Increase in Assets	57,596,449
" " " Surplus	4,595,045
" " " Insurance in Force	317,692,190

TABLE SHOWING THE CONDITION OF THE LIFE COMPANIES DOING BUSINESS IN NEW YORK, DECEMBER 31, 1894, THEIR BUSINESS FOR THE YEAR, THE SAME ITEMS FOR THE NEW-YORK LIFE, AND THE NEW-YORK LIFE'S SHARE OF ALL:

ITEMS.	THIRTY-THREE COMPANIES.	NEW-YORK LIFE.	N.-Y. L'S SHARE.
Assets	$1,056,331,683	$162,011,771	15.4
Premium Notes and Loans in Assets	29,474,626	4,231,853	14.4
Surplus	139,740,544	20,249,308	14.5
Liabilities	916,591,139	141,762,463	15.5
Surplus to Liabilities, Per cent.	15.2	14.3	....
Insurance in Force	4,657,583,046	813,294,160	17.5
New Insurance Written	985,520,033	206,545,392	21.0
Total Income	256,624,478	36,483,314	14.2
Premium Notes and Loans in Income	4,062,996	358,367	8.8
Death-Claims Paid	67,910,135	8,228,609	12.1
Death-Claims per $1,000 Insured	14.8	11.5	....
Total Paid Policy-holders	116,054,725	15,665,003	13.5
Expenses and Taxes	61,808,608	8,474,426	13.7
Per cent. to Income	24.1	23.2	....

XII.

RETROSPECT—PROSPECT.

LOOKING back over the half century covering the history of the NEW-YORK LIFE INSURANCE COMPANY, it will be observed that progress has been made chiefly in the application of principles which were as well known fifty years ago as they are to-day. The Actuaries' Table of Mortality—which is now the standard for valuing policies in nearly every State in the Union—was published in 1843. The rate of interest assumed in calculating premiums is the same now, for the most part, as it was in 1845. The premium rates now in use by the NEW-YORK LIFE are slightly lower for ages below forty, and somewhat higher for ages above forty, than the corresponding premiums of the first table used. The necessity of a reserve, or re-insurance fund, has its basis in the level premium, and the companies of fifty years ago made valuations and kept reserve funds. Companies of the present day make valuations more frequently, and on the net, instead of the gross, premiums receivable; but this is only a change in the application of the theory.

The most marked changes have been in the policy contract, and here it has been chiefly a question whether the theory of Life Insurance could be trusted, without making many exceptions. The theory provided for insuring men during their whole life by a uniform annual premium, which should be higher than the current cost at the insuring age, and lower than the current cost at the advanced age which many of the insured were expected to reach. The reserve fund, created by contributions from the early premiums and by interest, was to make up the deficiency of the later years. When a policy was discontinued, its reserve fund was no longer needed for the purpose for which it was accumulated; but it was not the practice of the early companies to return this fund to the discontinuing policy-holder. The theory required it, but various pretexts were found for retaining it:—the company did not agree to do it; the insured had broken his contract; those who discontinued were the best risks, hence the mortality among those remaining would be higher than the average; Life Insurance was yet in its infancy, and no one could tell whether the theory was entirely safe or not, when applied to the particular class of lives insured.

We have seen how, in the United States, the custom gradually obtained of paying a surrender value for discontinued policies, the companies being the judges in each case of what was to be paid; and how this was helped along by the premium note system, under which a policy-holder could always get the amount of his notes for his policy, by simply ceasing to pay either premiums, interest or notes. We have the testimony of Hon. Elizur Wright that the premium note system caused the passage of the Massachusetts non-forfeiture law of May, 1861, in order that all-cash payers might be treated as well as those who paid partly by note. This law—which was anticipated by the NEW-YORK LIFE by about eight months—compelled Massachusetts companies to accept the theory of Life Insurance with respect to the uses of the reserve fund, after making allowance for the element of self-selection against the company. The law wisely made the paid-up insurance good, whether applied for or not, and the NEW-YORK LIFE gave the same construction to its first non-forfeiture clause. The Company's present contract allows a choice in the form of paid-up value, allowing term insurance for the full amount of the policy if no request is made, and ordinary paid-up insurance for a less amount, if requested within six months. In the matter of extended insurance the NEW-YORK LIFE is almost the only company that fully accepts and applies the theory of Life Insurance, by making the purchase of term insurance absolute—nearly all other companies deduct the annual premiums that would have become due under the original policy, in case the insured dies within a specified time after the term insurance begins.

The theory of Life Insurance is applied to the reserve fund by the NEW-YORK LIFE in another way which is not required by any statute, nor allowed by all companies. That fund is in the Company's hands to meet a liability under the policy; therefore, money loaned on the policy, within the amount of the reserve, can never by any possibility be lost to the Company, since a failure to pay principal or interest would relieve the Company of a liability for an equal or greater amount. Loans are therefore made on the security of the Company's policies, within limits specified therein, after they have been in force five years or upwards.

Other points in which the companies of fifty years ago distrusted, and refused to apply, the theory of Life Insurance absolutely, had reference to the death-rate. The mortality tables were based upon the death-rate in certain localities, and under certain conditions. The Actuaries' Table alone was based upon insured lives under various restrictions as to occupation, residence, travel, habits, etc. The United States was a comparatively new country, where men lived under widely varying conditions, and it was a question that only experience could determine whether English mortality tables would prove trustworthy here. The vast areas of unsettled and newly-settled lands; the numerous savage tribes that roamed at will over a large portion of the Northwest; the frequent epidemics of cholera and yellow fever at sea-ports and along the Mississippi River; the lack of good water and of drainage in nearly all our cities;—these conditions certainly furnished ample reasons for caution in those who sought to build up a system of protection based upon longevity. We have seen how the NEW-YORK LIFE dealt with questions of residence, travel and occupation, by a system of extra premiums, until the conditions became so nearly uniform and so well known that inequalities could be adjusted in the distribution of surplus. The question of female risks has been disposed of in the same way, and guess-work has thus been superseded by scientific method.

Other elements of interference with the normal death-rate were supposed to be found in moral characteristics, as shown by the manner of death. The data from which the mortality tables were constructed included deaths from all causes, but in applying the theory of Life Insurance the early companies excluded from its benefits persons who died by reason of violations of law, by suicide, dueling, or the use of intoxicants or opiates. These things doubtless appeared to them dangerous to Life Insurance somewhat in proportion to the moral obliquity attached to them. It seemed like rewarding vice at the expense of virtue to allow the benefits of Life Insurance to the family of a man who did not live as long as possible. Doubtless many persons might live longer than they do, but Life Insurance is based upon actual, and not upon ideal, conditions. Every form of insurance offers, in certain contingencies, much for little, and the first thought of the cautious mind is, will not men take advantage of this principle to defraud the company? But Life Insurance differs from all other insurance in this, that no one can defraud the life company in respect to the point at issue—and live. There is a death-penalty against fraud of this character, and the penalty must be incurred before the fraud can be consummated. But Life Insurance assumes, as one of its fundamental principles, that life is more precious than money—that the insured has a greater interest in his life than the company has, and that he can be trusted to take care of it. If this principle is doubtful, or fails in any considerable degree, then the whole fabric falls.*

The NEW-YORK LIFE'S first policies—like others of the time—made only a partial application of the principles of Life Insurance with respect to causes of death—they were void in case of suicide, death upon the high seas, or in consequence of dueling or the violation of the laws of the United States, or of any State or province. In 1850 the suicide clause, and the clause respecting death upon the high seas, were eliminated, and a clause, making them void in case death were caused by intoxicating drinks or opium, was inserted. In 1885 this latter clause

---

*The reason originally assigned by the Trustees of the NEW-YORK LIFE for eliminating the suicide clause was that, "suicide is usually the result of disease"; and this reason has been powerfully reinforced during the last forty-five years by the consideration that, in many cases, it is impossible to distinguish between suicide, accident and murder. The life companies are under greater obligations not to defraud the family of a policy-holder who is guiltless of wrong in the manner of his death, than they are to prevent the payment of a policy on the life of a deliberate suicide. Statistics which appear to show a larger proportion of suicides under policies without a suicide clause are to be distrusted for this reason: the beneficiaries under such policies have no object in making a doubtful case appear as an accident or a murder, nor has the company any objection to classifying a death according to its apparent cause, whether it chance to be the true one or not.

was omitted from the Company's Five-Year Dividend Policy, and no restrictions were placed upon occupation, residence and travel after the policy had been in force two years. In case of death in consequence of military or naval service in time of war, of dueling, or of the violation of law, the reserve value of the policy was to be paid. Here was a distinct advance—from confiscation of the policy, to a simple refusal to take certain risks. All the new policies issued after 1885 followed the same rule, until 1892, when the Accumulation Policy was issued, without any restrictions whatever. Under this policy the theory of Life Insurance, as respects the risk of death, is fully accepted and applied. The Company claims the right to ascertain, so far as possible, before accepting a risk, whether or not present and prospective physical health, habits, surroundings, occupation and residence are satisfactory; if so, and the policy is issued and paid for, nothing but manifest fraud, discovered and charged within one year, and ultimately demonstrated, can invalidate the insurance if the premiums are duly paid.

The theory of Life Insurance includes the principle of saving and of accumulation. This principle is present in the Whole Life Policy as well as in the Endowment, since there is over-payment of the current cost of insurance in the early years of the policy in order that the burden of full payment may be lightened in the later years. The Endowment Policy, by increasing the element of saving, ends the insurance by paying the accumulations to the insured when they reach a certain amount, or at a specified date. The NEW-YORK LIFE'S policies, beginning with the "Tontine Investment Policy," first issued in 1872, have aimed to make this investment element a practical help and benefit to policy-holders, without abating in any degree the value of the contract as a policy of insurance. An Endowment Policy cannot furnish insurance after a certain period, nor could the old style Life Policy make provision for the old age of the insured; but the NEW-YORK LIFE'S Tontine, and Accumulation, policies, on the whole life tables, make such use of the investment element as to do whichever of these two things time shall show to be most needed. Under these policies the theory of Life Insurance is carried out more fully, and is made to serve more perfectly the ends for which it was designed, than under the old forms of contract.

The Ordinary Life, or Endowment, policy ceases to perform its functions when it becomes due and payable to the beneficiary. It has furnished insurance, and perhaps has accumulated money also; can it be made to do more? The theory of Life Insurance includes the investment and safe keeping of money against a time of need; may not these benefits be extended beyond the time set for the maturity of the policy? If the life company can do some things for the insured better than he can do them for himself, can it not do similar things for the beneficiaries under its policies better than they can do them for themselves? Under its Registered Bond Policy the NEW-YORK LIFE applies the investment principles of Life Insurance to the fund designed for the support of beneficiaries under policies maturing by death. It undertakes to invest two-thirds of the face of the policy, and to pay principal and interest in the manner specified in the contract, and thus secures with greater certainty the ultimate ends for which the insurance was taken. The policy is so completely under the control of the insured during his life-time, and the principles of Life Insurance are so carefully observed after his death, that the ends desired are reached with almost unerring certainty.

If we are to judge the future by the past, progress of Life Insurance must come from new and more perfect applications of its principles, guided by a spirit of liberality—nay, rather of justice—toward the insured. The latter condition is all-important;—change for the sake of change, new features which are devised simply to meet a supposed demand for novelty, will bring no permanent benefits. So also, the company that is only concerned for its own safety, that is always seeking to get the best end of the bargain, will add nothing of value to Life Insurance. The old law of selfishness applies even to corporations, in some degree—he that will save his life—at all hazards—shall lose it.

The theory of Life Insurance has, as its two most prominent elements, taking risks upon human life, and making provision for them by the safekeeping and investment of moneys received. It requires for a safe basis of operations a considerable number of lives and a considerable amount of money, in order to secure the benefits of the law of average. The NEW-YORK LIFE'S policies in force and its money in hand are amply sufficient to secure these benefits in full measure. It has no occasion, therefore, to strive for mere bigness, and the management is free to devote its energies to a study of the best possibilities of Life Insurance within the field already occupied. The question presents itself somewhat in this form: How can men be most completely relieved from the risks which now beset them and their families—mortality risks and financial risks—by the payment of money to a life insurance company?

In considering the risks to be covered, it will be necessary to consider men and things as they are, and not as we may think they ought to be. The perfect life policy must be adapted to the conditions to which it is to be applied. It must be simple as regards the duty of the insured, but comprehensive and flexible as regards the form which the benefit may take. It must foresee contingencies and provide for them, without very much prevision on the part of the insured. His part must consist almost entirely in the payment of money; and for this the company should undertake to do him such service that, within reasonable limits, his family shall not want in case of his premature death, nor he himself come to poverty in case of long life. The benefits offered under the insurance contract must be so clear and unmistakable as to appeal to the ordinary man by their intrinsic merits; there must be no loopholes for the company to escape its due responsibility, and no pitfalls for the unwary policy-holder who trusts himself too implicitly to the solicitor who persuades him to insure.

The theory of Life Insurance is based upon laws which may be mathematically expressed; the practice of it involves moral laws which find expression in fidelity to obligations. These moral laws create alike the duty of the insured and of the insuring company. Life Insurance, in its practical aspects, rests entirely upon the moral obligation which makes it incumbent upon a man to insure his life for the benefit of his dependents; and this benefit can only be fully secured when the moral law underlying the trust created by the policy is faithfully observed by the insurer. Life Insurance will, therefore, find its largest application and its truest success in the development and application of the moral principles which create and underlie the contract. Its past history—while affording admirable illustrations of the value of moral principles applied to economic questions—has not been free from faults incident to all human enterprises; yet the lover of his kind, who looks backward over what has been accomplished, and forward to what seems destined to be achieved, will not fail to invoke a benison upon Life Insurance, nor cease to expect even better things in the future from those nobler impulses of the soul

"That watch to ease the burden of the world."

APPENDIX.

STATISTICAL NOTES.

(SEE TABLES OF INCOME, DISBURSEMENTS, ETC., PAGES 386–8.)

WHEN the NEW-YORK LIFE began business, there were no insurance departments and no fixed methods of making reports. The Company was required by its charter to publish annual reports showing its income, losses, expenses, balance on hand and how the balance was invested. By the law of April 8, 1851, it was required to report to the Comptroller of the State, and the form of the report was fixed by blanks prepared by this officer. The Insurance Department was established by the Act of April 15, 1859, and the form of the report to the Department has since been fixed by the Superintendent. Until 1892 the Company published its report according to its own form, in addition to the report made to the Insurance Department. The Company's form gave the premiums and interest belonging to the year, whether received during the year or afterward; the Department form calls for what is actually received between January first and December thirty-first, no matter what year it belongs to, and credit is given in assets for deferred premiums and accrued and unpaid interest. The Company's form also included in disbursements the amounts paid to other companies for re-insurance; but the Department form required these amounts and the amounts received from re-insuring companies on policies maturing by death, to be deducted from premium income and to be omitted from disbursements, in order to avoid reporting the same amounts twice in the totals of all companies.

The tables which follow have been made in accordance with the present methods of the Company and of the Department, except that re-insurance has not been deducted prior to the establishment of the Insurance Department. A careful examination of the early reports has been made, and a few items have been transferred from one account to another, in accordance with present methods; the items in disbursements will be found, therefore, to differ slightly from those previously published. The first payments on annuity account were rather in the nature of trust fund payments, but were called annuities and are allowed so to stand. The items of "Profit and Loss" have been separated from other items of income and disbursements, in order to show just how the Company's investment account stands at the present time, and to show the actual interest on investments. All the items on the credit side of this account (except the market value of bonds and stocks over book value December 31, 1894, allowed in assets) are profits actually realized on completed transactions; they amount to $2,254,234.46. The items on the debit side belong partly to completed transactions—that is to say, to property bought and sold—and partly to real estate still owned by the Company. The latter is the case with the last and largest item, which represents for the most part* the reduction in the valuation of the Company's office buildings at the time of the Insurance Department's examination in 1891–92. Of this reduction $1,426,132.20 was made by the De-

* The amounts given on both sides of the account are "balances" of gains or losses for the year.

partment, and $919,375.82 by the Trustees of the Company. This money, of course, has not been actually lost; the Company still owns the property, and has, since the examination, refused an offer half a million dollars in excess of the Superintendent's valuation, upon a single parcel; but values have not been marked up because, during a time of business depression, it has been deemed best to keep valuations at a figure which will give a fair rate of income. All losses incurred through agents have been charged in expenses, and the agents' balances at December 31, 1894, have been included in the total of the expense account.

The Income Account shows the following distribution by amounts and percentages:

Premiums for insurance	$337,921,999.37	75.47 per cent.
Considerations for annuities and Trust Fund deposits,	21,529,763.75	4.81 "
Interest, rents, etc.	81,350,741.27	18.17 "
Profit and Loss, Cr.	6,930,495.35	1.55 "
Total	$447,732,999.74	100.00 per cent.

The Disbursement Account shows the following distribution by amounts and percentages:

Death-claims	$86,792,477.67	30.38 per cent.
Endowments	14,696,113.84	5.14 "
Annuities and Trust Fund	15,335,051.30	5.37 "
Policies purchased	37,524,277.12	13.13 "
Dividends	45,639,153.39	15.97 "
Profit and Loss, Dr.	4,311,966.89	1.51 "
Expenses and taxes	81,422,188.60	28.50 "
Total	$285,721,228.81	100.00 per cent.

The total amount paid policy-holders shows the following distribution by amounts and percentages:

Death-claims	$86,792,477.67	43.40 per cent.
Endowments	14,696,113.84	7.35 "
Annuities and Trust Fund	15,335,051.30	7.67 "
Policies purchased	37,524,277.12	18.76 "
Dividends	45,639,153.39	22.82 "
Total	$199,987,073.32	100.00 per cent.

The total Income is accounted for in the following amounts and percentages:

Paid Policy-holders	$199,987,073.32	44.67 per cent.
Expenses and taxes	81,422,188.60	18.19 "
Profit and Loss, Dr.	4,311,966.89	.96 "
Present Assets	162,011,770.93	36.18 "
Total	$447,732,999.74	100.00 per cent.

The dividends paid policy-holders are equal to about thirteen and one-half per cent. of the total premiums received for insurance, and the surplus accumulated is equal to about six per cent. of such premiums; the death-claims paid are about twenty-six per cent., and the endowments about four per cent. of insurance premiums; and the amounts paid for purchased policies are over eleven per cent. of insurance premiums. Insured policy-holders have, therefore, already received nearly fifty-five per cent. of their premiums, and surplus is equal to six per cent. more. There is also to their credit the reserve value of policies now in force held in trust by the Company for their ultimate payment. The total amount received from policy-holders, annuitants and depositors of trust funds is $359,451,763.12; the total amount paid beneficiaries ($199,987,073.32), and that now on hand ($162,011,770.93) are equal to $361,998,844.25; showing that the cost of carrying on the business and of building up so great a Company in so short a time has been less than the use of the policy-holders' money.

The column showing rate of interest on average net assets will be found instructive. During the early years of the Company a considerable portion of its funds were necessarily uninvested, being required as working capital; and where the net assets doubled every year it was impossible to show a normal interest rate. By adding all the intermediate terms to one-half of the first and last, in the column of net assets, we get $1,535,062,548.27 as the total net assets in hand one year; and using this as a divisor of the total interest, gives an average rate of 5.30 per annum.

The first valuation of the Company's policies, according to modern methods, was made in 1852, as explained in the text, when the surplus was found to be $25,313.90, after providing for all liabilities, including $283,539 in dividends outstanding. Prior to that time the method of declaring dividends had been as follows: The premiums earned during the year were calculated according to the time the policies had been in force, and to this amount was added the interest actually received; from this sum was deducted the losses and expenses; the balance was considered net profit for the year, and a large part of it was allotted as dividends and interest on dividends formerly declared. A "contingent fund" had been gradually accumulated, however, and on December 31, 1852, it amounted to $62,445.54. This was exclusive of premiums received but not earned, accrued interest and excess of market values over cost, which swelled the fund to $204,761.23. The transition from the old method to the new was, therefore, comparatively easy.

The Company's valuations antedated any valuations by authority of the State; and after a standard of valuation was adopted by the State, the Company continued to use its own until 1887, although the State standard adopted in 1868 gave it a much larger surplus than its own. This action made the higher reserve standard of the State easy to conform to in 1887. From 1852 to 1859 the Company's valuations were made by the Carlisle Table of Mortality with six per cent. interest; from 1860 to 1886 they were made by the same table, with four per cent. interest for participating policies and five per cent. for non-participating policies; from 1887 the standard has been that of the State, viz., the Actuaries', or Combined Experience Table, with four per cent. interest. Outstanding dividends were placed in liabilities at their full amount, as long as interest was paid on them, viz., until 1861; thereafter they were discounted at four per cent. for the time they were to remain outstanding, according to the plan of redemption adopted. The liabilities and surplus were first given in the Company's published report for 1863. The excess of market values over cost values was first included in surplus in the report for 1866, although it had previously been allowed in the Insurance Department reports.

TOTAL INCOME FROM ALL SOURCES.

YEAR.	INSURANCE PREMIUMS.	ANNUITY CONSIDERATIONS.	INTEREST, RENTS, ETC.	PROFIT AND LOSS, CR.	TRUST FUND.	TOTAL INCOME.
1845	$22,602.71	....	$33.60	....	....	$22,636.31
1846	41,746.41	....	386.09	....	....	42,132.50
1847	69,426.89	....	1,950.27	....	....	71,377.16
1848	144,440.82	....	3,814.21	....	....	148,255.03
1849	120,491.30	....	7,178.67	....	....	127,669.97
1850	256,852.44	....	12,641.86	$3,427.95	....	272,922.25
1851	301,540.63	....	16,805.58	1,902.50	....	320,248.71
1852	323,305.69	$1,998.00	26,398.88	547.50	....	352,250.07
1853	324,494.78	....	41,928.88	....	....	366,423.66
1854	310,609.05	....	38,613.85	....	....	349,222.90
1855	317,239.98	....	55,877.78	....	....	373,117.76
1856	355,238.63	....	55,686.43	1,462.50	....	412,387.56
1857	389,422.47	....	80,331.06	....	....	469,753.53
1858	413,295.88	....	78,991.87	75.00	....	492,362.75
1859	460,136.00	....	90,190.55	150.00	....	550,476.55
1860	478,076.05	....	121,529.98	....	....	599,606.03
1861	434,885.14	4,224.88	99,223.80	....	....	538,333.82
1862	566,828.78	2,087.00	118,334.14	....	....	687,249.92
1863	1,164,980.37	1,245.04	141,644.78	....	....	1,307,870.19
1864	1,345,305.91	3,000.00	171,215.11	72,088.23	....	1,591,609.25
1865	1,926,609.48	3,075.80	229,726.68	22,082 05	....	2,181,494.01
1866	2,546,100.91	3,829.84	320,776.10	38,105.08	....	2,908,811.93
1867	2,974,515.60	3,107.40	439,733.73	49,521.99	....	3,466,878.72
1868	3,618,554.79	6,342.94	540,377.15	217,734.57	....	4,383,009.45
1869	4,971,932.71	11,183.47	674,679.43	192,987.40	....	5,850,783.01
1870	5,609,684.73	48,580.67	798,362.77	17,854.26	....	6,474,482.43
1871	6,182,977.85	38,314.46	1,137,970.66	....	....	7,359,262.97
1872	6,346,632.89	45,101.73	1,200,474.32	2,500.00	....	7,594,708.94
1873	6,028,956.42	73,052.58	1,354,415.18	....	....	7,456,424.18
1874	6,471,965.63	77,062.97	1,633,535.49	....	....	8,182,564.09
1875	5,854,648.11	288,784.09	1,716,284.71	84,645.60	....	7,944,362.51
1876	5,575,734.44	290,302.90	1,863,522.13	....	....	7,729,559.47
1877	5,495,661.69	226,602.40	1,852,120.50	....	....	7,574,384.59
1878	5,286,545.63	403,006.36	1,958,334.55	....	....	7,647,886.54
1879	5,171,223.94	694,015.34	2,021,886.82	....	....	7,887,126.10
1880	5,470,912.37	1,074,548.59	2,076,165.95	202,544.63	....	8,824,171.54
1881	6,130,452.66	1,703,925.47	2,352,739.38	145,827.52	....	10,332,945.03
1882	7,270,869.69	1,460,000.96	2,537,103.92	226,169.23	....	11,494,143.80
1883	8,731,737.31	1,799,202.90	2,657,460.84	19,130.96	....	13,207,532.01
1884	9,900,452.17	1,058,910.67	2,873,389.c2	....	....	13,832,751.86
1885	11,567,452.86	913,395.14	3,089,418.76	334,874.53	....	15,905,141.29
1886	13,979,782.19	1,180,686.32	3,311,290.64	359,998.68	....	18,831,757.83
1887	16,573,911.55	1,252,980.46	3,726,083.46	37,869.45	....	21,590,844.92
1888	19,050,965.60	1,509,643.93	4,236,831.66	73,732.77	....	24,871,173.96
1889	22,572,136.25	1,670,380.75	4,587,605.74	....	....	28,830,122.74
1890	24,716,481.24	1,870,808.80	4,896,411.86	....	....	31,483,701.90
1891	24,952,154.59	1,304,120.81	5,548,727.08	....	$49,192.50	31,854,194.98
1892	24,158,532.41	881,581.52	5,868,163.84	28,313.06	....	30,936,590.83
1893	26,832,430.90	656,226.54	6,241,646.70	108,002.20	25,340.61	33,863,646.95
1894	28,539,665.09	871,721.23	7,037,061.73	12,686.80	22,178.68	36,483,313.53
	$332,350,601.63	$21,433,051.96	$79,945,078.19	$2,254,234.46	$96,711.79	$436,079,678.03
	a. 5,571,397.74	....	*b*. 1,405,663.08	*c*.4,676,260.89	....	....
	$337,921,999.37	$21,433,051.96	$81,350,741.27	$6,930,495.35	$96,711.79	$447,732,999.74*

a. Net amount of Uncollected and Deferred Premiums, December 31, 1894, allowed in Assets.
b, Interest due and accrued, December 31, 1894, allowed in Assets.
c. Market value of Bonds and Stocks over book value, December 31, 1894, allowed in Assets.
* Includes *a*. *b*. *c*.

DISBURSEMENT ACCOUNT.

Year.	Death-Claims.	Endowments.	Annuities.	Trust Fund Paid.	Policies Purchased.
1845	....	....	....	....	....
1846	$6,994.13	....	....	....	....
1847	11,744.28	....	....	....	....
1848	39,949.59	....	....	....	....
1849	53,710.00	....	....	....	....
1850	76,185.62	....	....	....	....
1851	157,054.16	....	....	....	....
1852	106,106.38	....	....	....	....
1853	131,960.02	....	$400.00	....	$9,931.94
1854	173,673.91	....	1,228.13	....	44,153.00
1855	135,726.56	....	....	....	19,242.46
1856	176,558.29	....	....	....	25,376.73
1857	151,403.46	....	....	....	24,115.60
1858	163,218.22	....	....	....	35,239.05
1859	242,045.65	....	107.94	....	27,789.83
1860	204,007.58	....	107.94	....	31,373.90
1861	169,369.39	....	107.94	....	74,659.73
1862	169,297.32	....	955.00	....	50,115.73
1863	295,850.00	....	1,255.58	....	474,881.16
1864	315,200.00	....	2,056.86	....	62,109.93
1865	490,522.03	....	1,893.36	....	43,011.03
1866	480,197.33	....	1,687.94	....	43,997.71
1867	561,921.45	....	4,170.63	....	99,721.86
1868	741,043.22	....	2,662.38	....	133,201.07
1869	758,104.07	....	3,082.64	....	241,807.45
1870	1,278,863.12	....	4,104.06	....	521,603.65
1871	1,318,958.08	$571.44	11,081.18	....	1,105,854.64
1872	1,408,519.87	1,000.00	17,181.47	....	1,481,789.47
1873	1,446,123.04	14,720.00	23,235.35	....	1,508,668.90
1874	1,469,686.04	30,335.72	32,793.98	....	1,539,974.96
1875	1,524,814.83	49,859.24	74,765.91	....	1,111,742.01
1876	1,547,648.42	88,290.50	90,247.56	....	1,107,372.12
1877	1,638,128.39	185,160.12	122,633.73	....	980,911.61
1878	1,687,675.61	673,051.74	158,191.71	....	732,999.60
1879	1,569,854.22	1,015,256.22	194,759.52	....	516,280.61
1880	1,731,721.37	564,579.85	272,727.96	....	377,363.31
1881	2,013,203.32	564,924.96	408,360.13	....	375,063.09
1882	1,955,292.00	427,258.95	509,053.81	....	881,817.87
1883	2,263,092.29	452,229.80	701,214.34	....	869,840.40
1884	2,257,175.79	873,808.50	852,018.52	....	961,871.33
1885	2,999,109.64	741,764.47	899,270.84	....	1,350,460.21
1886	2,757,035.97	559,075.01	921,762.39	....	1,315,117.91
1887	3,916,996.84	444,369.99	967,916.88	....	1,881,704.21
1888	4,412,049.66	1,013,877.12	1,057,386.41	....	2,180,269.06
1889	5,032,466.44	1,219,629.06	1,160,752.95	....	2,240,944.70
1890	6,099,308.11	1,093,725.22	1,274,499.70	....	2,663,563.99
1891	6,087,620.70	1,066,795.11	1,371,634.26	$3,000.00	2,882,100.07
1892	7,896,589.29	1,114,301.99	1,370,130.30	3,000.00	2,202,771.17
1893	8,440,093.46	1,083,445.95	1,407,256.95	4,200.00	2,359,062.13
1894	8,228,608.51	1,418,082.88	1,396,314.48	5,840.57	2,934,401.92
	$86,792,477.67	$14,696,113.84	$15,319,010.73	$16,040.57	$37,524,277.12

SUMMARY OF PROFIT AND LOSS ACCOUNT.

Total Appreciation in Values	$6,930,495.35
Total Reduction in Values	4,311,966.89
Balance Profit	$2,618,528.46

DISBURSEMENT ACCOUNT—*Continued.*

YEAR.	DIVIDENDS.	TOTAL TO POLICY-HOLDERS.	PROFIT AND LOSS, DR.	EXPENSES AND TAXES.	TOTAL DISBURSEMENTS.
1845	....	....	....	$5,140.76	$5,140.76
1846	....	$6,994.13	....	10,431.30	17,425.43
1847	$48.00	11,792.28	....	15,048.07	26,840.35
1848	357.60	40,307.19	....	30,385.68	70,692.87
1849	831.87	54,541.87	....	25,627.17	80,169.04
1850	1,737.20	77,922.82	....	52,046.71	129,969.53
1851	3,450.67	160,504.83	....	57,748.02	218,252.85
1852	7,195.85	113,302.23	....	59,020.02	172,322.25
1853	12,227.30	154,519.26	$230.00	52,443.11	207,192.37
1854	13,606.47	232,661.51	....	46,593.39	279,254.90
1855	20,182.29	175,151.31	....	46,003.88	221,155.19
1856	18,778.37	220,713.39	....	54,972.94	275,686.33
1857	22,332.40	197,851.46	....	64,919.20	262,770.66
1858	29,545.98	228,003.25	3,430.98	71,391.66	302,825.89
1859	32,498.15	302,441.57	3,041.00	87,669.97	393,152.54
1860	38,665.95	274,155.37	4,033.99	92,925.80	371,115.16
1861	124,330.84	368,467.90	6,292.45	95,879.95	470,640.30
1862	99,658.79	320,026.84	....	134,775.11	454,801.95
1863	97,177.93	869,164.67	....	225,734.67	1,094,899.34
1864	93,555.38	472,922.17	....	251,671.37	724,593.54
1865	250,384.14	785,810.56	....	333,680.69	1,119,491.25
1866	282,224.21	808,107.19	....	434,800.33	1,242,907.52
1867	381,958.87	1,047,772.81	....	497,109.11	1,544,881.92
1868	1,225,865.26	2,102,771.93	....	736,359.83	2,839,131.76
1869	1,535,399.11	2,538,393.27	....	1,024,318.34	3,562,711.61
1870	1,058,929.41	2,863,500.24	....	1,055,679.42	3,919,179.66
1871	849,678.43	3,286,143.77	....	854,334.99	4,140,478.76
1872	781,602.60	3,690,093.41	....	907,793.15	4,597,886.56
1873	835,636.43	3,828,383.72	....	820,522.15	4,648,905.87
1874	1,486,630.16	4,559,420.86	....	742,870.20	5,302,291.06
1875	1,369,954.95	4,131,136.94	....	729,623.35	4,860,760.29
1876	1,409,309.04	4,242,867.64	205,539.51	749,696.00	5,198,103.15
1877	1,440,935.75	4,367,769.60	473,142.72	1,032,551.93	5,873,464.25
1878	1,555,674.65	4,807,593.31	97,203.98	936,068.72	5,840 866 01
1879	1,525,339.84	4,821,490.41	135,966.93	1,022,398.28	5,979,855.62
1880	1,553,498.75	4,499,891.24	......	1,217,980.26	5,717,871.50
1881	1,730,268.72	5,091,820.22	....	1,475,695.08	6,567,515.30
1882	2,436,887.08	6,210,309.71	....	1,785,828.23	7,996,137.94
1883	2,413,013.57	6,699,390.40	....	2,231,986.33	8,931,376.73
1884	1,790,081.00	6,734,955.14	469,052.20	2,522,612.25	9,726,619.59
1885	1,691,268.59	7,681,873.75	....	2,639,646.37	10,321,520.12
1886	2,074,238.81	7,627,230.09	....	3,182,977.32	10,810,207.41
1887	2,324,222.87	9,535,210.79	....	4,290,314.08	13,825,524.87
1888	2,309,487.80	10,973,070.05	....	4,416,540.42	15,389,610.47
1889	2,467,328.51	12,121,121.66	....	5,754,828.28	17,875,949.94
1890	2,148,447.00	13,279,544.02	568,525.11	6,682,319.48	20,530,388.61
1891	1,260,340.74	12,671,490.88	2,345,508.02	6,786,599.02	21,803,597.92
1892	1,408,219.58	13,995,012.33	....	7,659,278.43	21,654,290.76
1893	1,744,391.78	15,038,450.27	....	8,386,274.94	23,424,725.21
1894	1,681,754.70	15,665,003.06	....	8,474,426.50	24,139,429.56
	$45,639,153.39	$199,987,073.32	$4,311,966.89	$80,865,542.26	$285,164,582.47
				d. 556,646.34	
				$81,422,188.60	$285,721,228.81 *e.*

d. Agents' balances, December 31, 1894, not allowed in Assets.
e. Includes *d.*

SUMMARY OF RECEIPTS AND DISBURSEMENTS.

Total Receipts	$447,732,999.74
Total Disbursements	285,721,228.81
Balance Assets	$162,011,770.93

INSURANCE, ASSETS, SURPLUS, ETC.

YEAR.	NEW INSURANCE.	INSURANCE IN FORCE.		NET ASSETS.	INTEREST RATE.	SURPLUS. [*Company's Standard.*]
		No. of Policies. (Estimated prior to 1859.)	Amount.			
1845	$929,038	359	$799,000	$17,495.55	%	[See Statistical Notes.]
1846	1,346,828	793	1,846,000	42,202.62	1.28	
1847	1,446,408	1,271	2,831,000	86,739.43	3.03	
1848	2,660,075	2,474	4,722,000	164,301.59	3.04	
1849	1,734,000	2,834	5,552,000	211,802.52	3.82	
1850	3,536,400	3,671	7,816,000	354,755.24	4.46	
1851	3,220,900	4,000	9,492,000	456,751.10	4.14	
1852	2,514,500	4,188	10,325,000	636,678.92	4.83	$25,313.90
1853	1,942,071	3,838	10,510,000	795,910.21	5.85	120,888.08
1854	1,429,961	3,430	10,290,662	865,878.21	4.65	117,082.57
1855	1,467,900	3,426	10,277,101	1,017,840.78	5.93	148,718.23
1856	2,344,010	3,795	11,385,136	1,154,542.01	5.13	135,702.05
1857	2,675,102	4,259	12,778,938	1,361,524.88	6.38	190,898.90
1858	2,382,850	4,326	13,578,478	1,551,061.74	5.42	227,777.41
1859	3,092,525	4,417	15,284,718	1,708,385.75	5.53	193,391.86
1860	3,023,275	4,856	16,388,109	1,936,876.62	6.67	214,981.14
1861	3,264,100	5,125	16,411,259	2,004,570.14	5.03	181,989.11
1862	7,734,645	7,733	22,293,864	2,237,018.11	5.58	109,388.06
1863	11,339,234	9,949	26,194,426	2,449,988.96	6.04	158,137.63
1864	13,147,558	12,920	34,651,300	3,317,004.67	5.94	526,320.66
1865	16,324,888	16,077	45,485,726	4,379,007.43	5.99	590,345.95
1866	22,734,308	20,847	60,433,749	6,044,911.84	6.15	1,070,076.43
1867	22,678,117	23,002	69,406,478	7,966,908.64	6.27	1,642,429.59
1868	30,774,108	28,340	86,733,575	9,510,786.33	6.19	1,689,282.17
1869	34,104,284	33,145	102,132,513	11,798,857.73	6.33	1,670,750.72
1870	27,051,995	37,266	111,355,358	14,354,160.50	6.11	1,152,408.04
1871	24,603,306	38,988	113,154,809	17,572,944.71	7.13	1,488,134.43
1872	27,096,273	41,234	118,622,605	20,569,767.09	6.30	1,642,424.92
1873	26,621,460	43,160	123,672,386	23,377,285.40	6.17	1,742,554.41
1874	21,809,389	43,398	122,835,123	26,257,558.43	6.58	2,184,724.05
1875	21,964,190	44,661	126,132,119	29,341,160.65	6.18	2,807,795.54
1876	20,062,111	45,421	127,748,473	31,872,616.97	6.09	3,144,320.84
1877	20,156,639	45,605	127,901,887	33,573,537.31	5.66	3,456,446.71
1878	15,949,986	45,005	125,232,145	35,380,557.84	5.68	3,852,893.51
1879	17,098,173	45,705	127,417,762	37,287,828.32	5.57	4,491,853.68
1880	22,229,979	48,548	135,726,916	40,394,128.36	5.34	6,047,262.81
1881	32,374,281	53,927	151,760,824	44,159,558.09	5.33	6,881,280.64
1882	41,325,520	60,150	171,415,097	47,657,563.95	5.53	7,040,213.95
1883	52,735,564	69,227	198,746,043	51,933,719.23	5.34	7,238,610.21
1884	61,484,550	78,047	229,382,586	56,039,851.50	5.32	7,004,811.60
1885	68,521,452	86,418	259,674,500	61,623,472.67	5.25	10,188,215.90
1886	85,178,294	97,719	304,373,540	69,645,023.09	5.04	12,256,952.50
1887	106,749,295	113,323	358,935,536	77,410,343.14	5.07	11,846,793.06
1888	125,019,731	129,911	419,886,505	86,891,906.63	5.16	13,549,099.09
1889	151,119,088	150,381	495,601,970	97,846,079.43	4.97	15,654,263.17
1890	159,576,065	173,469	569,338,726	108,799,392.72	4.74	15,069,046.92
1891	152,664,982	193,452	614,824,713	118,849,989.78	4.87	15,141,023.31
1892	173,605,070	224,008	689,248,629	128,132,289.85	4.75	16,804,948.10
1893	228,417,114	253,876	779,156,678	138,571,211.59	4.68	17,025,630.18
1894	206,545,392	277,600	813,294,160	150,915,095.56	4.86	20,249,307.73

FIRST PREMIUM TABLE

USED BY THE

NEW-YORK LIFE INSURANCE COMPANY.

RATES FOR AN INSURANCE OF $100 ON A SINGLE LIFE.

AGE.	Annual Premium for Term of One Year.	Annual Premium for Term of Seven Years.	Annual Premium for Life.	AGE.	Annual Premium for Term of One Year.	Annual Premium for Term of Seven Years.	Annual Premium for Life.	AGE.	Annual Premium for Term of One Year.	Annual Premium for Term of Seven Years.	Annual Premium for Life.
	$	$	$		$	$	$		$	$	$
14	0.72	0.86	1.53	32	1.33	1.46	2.50	50	1.96	2.09	4.60
15	0.77	0.88	1.56	33	1.34	1.48	2.57	51	1.97	2.20	4.75
16	0.84	0.90	1.62	34	1.35	1.50	2.64	52	2.02	2.37	4.90
17	0.86	0.91	1.65	35	1.36	1.53	2.75	53	2.10	2.59	5.24
18	0.89	0.92	1.69	36	1.39	1.57	2.81	54	2.18	2.89	5.49
19	0.90	0.94	1.73	37	1.43	1.63	2.90	55	2.32	3.21	5.78
20	0.91	0.95	1.77	38	1.48	1.70	3.05	56	2.47	3.56	6.05
21	0.92	0.97	1.82	39	1.57	1.76	3.11	57	2.70	4.20	6.27
22	0.94	0.99	1.88	40	1.69	1.83	3.20	58	3.14	4.31	6.50
23	0.97	1.03	1.93	41	1.78	1.88	3.31	59	3.67	4.63	6.75
24	0.99	1.07	1.98	42	1.85	1.89	3.40	60	4.35	4.91	7.00
25	1.00	1.12	2.04	43	1.89	1.92	3.51	61	4.53	5.08	7.25
26	1.07	1.17	2.11	44	1.90	1.94	3.63	62	4.71	5.29	7.55
27	1.12	1.23	2.17	45	1.91	1.96	3.73	63	4.90	5.50	7.85
28	1.20	1.28	2.24	46	1.92	1.98	3.87	64	5.09	5.71	8.15
29	1.28	1.35	2.31	47	1.93	1.99	4.01	65	5.34	5.99	8.55
30	1.31	1.36	2.36	48	1.94	2.02	4.17	66	5.59	6.27	8.95
31	1.32	1.42	2.43	49	1.95	2.04	4.49	67	5.90	6.62	9.45

CLASSIFICATION OF DEATHS.

TABLE SHOWING THE CAUSES OF DEATH, AND THE NUMBER OF DEATHS FROM EACH CAUSE, AMONG PERSONS INSURED IN THE NEW-YORK LIFE INSURANCE COMPANY, 1845–1894.

CAUSES OF DEATH.	Number of Deaths.	CAUSES OF DEATH.	Number of Deaths.
Abscesses (various)	69	Locomotor ataxia	67
Accidents	1,148	Lymphadenitis	1
Addison's disease	6	Lymphangitis	1
Age	1,919	Lupus	1
Alcoholism	62	Malarial fevers	618
Anæmia and leucoythæmia	62	Malignant pustule	1
Apoplexy	1,710	Measles	10
Appendicitis	83	Mumps	3
Asthma	29	Murdered	183
Beri-beri	17	Nasal hæmorrhage	1
Brain disease	715	Necrosis of bone	13
Bright's disease (acute and chronic)	1,219	Obstruction of the bowels	103
Bronchitis (acute and chronic)	205	Oedema of the glottis	18
Cancer	803	Oedema of the lungs	22
Carbuncle	49	Paralysis	287
Cholera	103	Peritonitis	181
Cholera morbus	60	Pleurisy	58
Consumption	3,192	Pneumonia	1,852
Convulsions	7	Purpura hæmorraghica	19
Diabetes	185	Pulmonary apoplexy	235
Diphtheria	45	Pyemia and septicæmia (various causes)	109
Dysentery	276	Rheumatism	130
Embolism	17	Scarlet fever	26
Epilepsy	41	Spinal diseases (various)	93
Erysipelas	152	Smallpox	68
Gangrene	53	Strangulated hernia	29
General debility	48	Suicide	608
Heart diseases (various forms)	1,889	Syphilis	20
Hypertrophy of prostate and cystitis	167	Tetanus	26
Influenza	253	Typhoid fever	1,018
Insanity	210	Typhus fever	41
Insolation	40	Ulcer of the stomach	103
Killed in battle	52	Yellow fever	147
Laryngitis	12		
Liver diseases (various forms)	733	TOTAL	21,723

TRUSTEES OF THE NEW-YORK LIFE INSURANCE CO., 1845–1895.

Name.	Entered.	Ceased.	Remarks.
Andrews, Loring	1845	1848	Died January 22, 1875.
Anthony, Charles L.......	1865	1874	Died May, 1874.
Appleton, William H......	1852	....	Active in 1895.
Aspinwall, William H.	1845	1847	Died January, 1875.
Baldwin, C. C.	1884	....	Active in 1895.
Barton, William...........	1849	1884	Died September, 1884.
Battelle, Lewis F..........	1868	1870	Died March 11, 1870.
Beach, John C..............	1849	1856	Died July 27, 1856.
Beers, William H.	1869	1892	Died November 16, 1893.
Benedict, Spencer S.	1845	1851	Resigned: living in 1895.
Bogert, Cornelius R., M. D.	1870	1877	Died November 11, 1877.
Bogert, Henry K.	1845	1848	Died August 30, 1875.
Bokee, David A.	1848	1859	Died March, 1859.
Booth, William A..........	1863	....	Active in 1895.
Bowers, Henry.............	1866	1891	Died February 12, 1891.
Bristow, Benjamin H.......	1885	1889	Resigned: living in 1895.
Brown, James	1845	1847	Died November 1, 1877.
Buckley, William F........	1887	....	Active in 1895.
Bushnell, Orsamus	1846	1864	Died August 11, 1868.
Bussing, John S.	1847	1864	Died June 1, 1864.
Carman, Richard F.	1846	1846	Died July 13, 1867.
Center, Edward C.	1845	1846	Died November 6, 1860.
Claflin, Horace B.	1868	1885	Died November 14, 1885.
Claflin, John	1885	....	Active in 1895.
Cobb, Sanford	1865	1876	Died May 22, 1876.
Coleman, Robert B.	1846	1849	Died October 31, 1882.
Collins, Robert B..........	1860	1892	Died January 6, 1894.
Comstock, David A........	1845	1847	Died November 26, 1855.
Cryder, John	1845	1847	Died 1868.
Curtiss, Cyrus.............	1849	1852	Died June 25, 1879.
Dart, Russell	1852	1865	Died September 13, 1865.
Dodge, Samuel N.	1848	1849	Died April, 1865.
Dows, David	1856	1885	Died March 30, 1890.
Dusenbury, William C.....	1849	1867	Died February, 1867.
Fairchild, Charles S.	1892	....	Active in 1895.
Fairchild, Robert G.	1850	1852	Died February 9, 1877.
Fisher, Selig S............	1878	1884	Died January, 1884.
Franklin, Morris	1847	1885	Died October 27, 1885.
Freeman, Alfred, M. D.....	1847	1861	Died February 8, 1861.

TRUSTEES — *Continued.*

NAME.	ENTERED.	CEASED.	REMARKS.
FREEMAN, PLINY	1848	1864	Died May, 1879.
FULLER, DUDLEY B.	1863	1868	Died March 18, 1868.
FURMAN, JOHN M.	1875	1884	Died December 11, 1884.
GIBBS, EDWARD N.	1889	....	Active in 1895.
GRACE, WILLIAM R.	1892	....	Active in 1895.
GRANT, RICHARD S.	1880	1887	Declined reëlection.
GREER, GEORGE	1851	1862	Died July 1, 1870.
HARPER, JAMES	1845	1848	Died 1869.
HERRICK, JACOB B.	1847	1851	Died January 2, 1864.
HICKS, HENRY W.	1845	1846	Died September 24, 1867.
HIGGINS, ELIAS S.	1885	1889	Died August 18, 1889.
HONE, PHILIP	1848	1850	Died 1851.
HORNBLOWER, WILLIAM B.	1890	....	Active in 1895.
HOYT, EDWIN	1867	1874	Died May, 1874.
HUTCHINSON, RICHARD J.	1847	1849	Died August 2, 1869.
IRVIN, RICHARD	1845	1847	Died June 27, 1888.
KENDALL, ISAAC C.	1849	1878	Died August 18, 1878.
KING, JAMES G., Jr.	1865	1867	Died June, 1867.
LANGDON, WOODBURY	1892	....	Active in 1895.
LEWIS, WALTER H.	1885	....	Active in 1895.
LINDSLEY, CALEB F.	1846	1849	Died February 28, 1868.
LIVINGSTON, SCHUYLER	1845	1846	Died September, 1863.
LUDLOW, THOMAS W.	1845	1847	Died 1878.
MAIRS, JOHN	1852	1885	Died December 7, 1885.
MARTIN, CHARLES J.	1855	1860	Died 1888.
MARTIN, EDWARD	1867	1892	Resigned: living in 1895.
MERCHANT, AARON M.	1846	1848	Died January 8, 1852.
MCCALL, JOHN A.	1892	....	Active in 1895.
MILLER, DANIEL S.	1849	1877	Died April 9, 1878.
MORRIS, ROBERT H.	1846	1847	Died October 23, 1855.
MORRISON, GEORGE AUSTIN	1894	....	Active in 1895,
MORTIMER, HENRY C.	1889	....	Active in 1895.
MUSER, RICHARD	1885	1893	Died August 10, 1893.
NELSON, HENRY A.	1847	1852	Died December 13, 1861.
NEVINS, DAVID	1894	....	Active in 1895.
NIXON, JOHN M.	1846	1869	Died February 12, 1869.
NORRIE, ADAM	1845	1847	Died June 6, 1882.
OSGOOD, GEORGE A.	1865	1882	Died November 13, 1882.
PAINE, AUGUSTUS G.	1892	....	Active in 1895.
PATRICK, WILLIAM	1852	1863	Died September 8, 1875.

TRUSTEES — *Continued.*

NAME.	ENTERED.	CEASED.	REMARKS.
PAXSON, SAMUEL C.	1847	1852	Died July, 1860.
PERKINS, GEORGE W.	1893	....	Active in 1895.
POTTS, GEORGE H.	1884	1888	Died 1888.
PURDY, RICHARD E.	1846	1849	Died January 14, 1849.
RANDOLPH, EDMUND D.	1892	....	Active in 1895.
READING, RICHARD A.	1846	1848	Died June 7, 1871.
REED, ALMET	1845	1845	Died March 1, 1880.
REYBURN, JAMES	1845	1846	Died 1849.
RICE, JOHN	1852	1856	Died September 10, 1856.
RICHARDS, THOMAS B.	1845	1846	Died April 1, 1848.
ROBERTS, MARSHALL O.	1846	1849	Died September 11, 1880.
ROGERS, JOHN L.	1851	1869	Died December 2, 1869.
SANDERSON, EDWARD F.	1845	1845	Died September 26, 1866.
SEAMAN, HENRY I.	1849	1861	Died May, 1861.
SEYMOUR, JOHN F.	1870	1879	Died July 3, 1879.
SEYMOUR, WILLIAM N.	1847	1851	Died June 5, 1881.
SMULL, THOMAS	1863	1866	Died December, 1866.
STEARNS, JOHN N.	1885	1892	Resigned: died April, 1895.
STEELE, HIRAM R.	1892	....	Active in 1895.
STRAUS, OSCAR S.	1894	....	Active in 1895.
STRONG, WILLIAM L.	1884	....	Active in 1895.
STUDWELL, ALEXANDER	1879	1891	Died October 5, 1891.
SUAREZ, LEONARDO S.	1845	1847	Died 1874.
SUYDAM, HENRY, Jr.	1855	1858	Died April 26, 1858.
TAYLOR, ROBERT L.	1845	1846	Died February 10, 1878.
TUCK, HENRY, M. D.	1878	....	Active in 1895.
VALENTINE, JOHN J.	1894	....	Active in 1895.
VANDERVOORT, PETER H.	1851	1854	Died February 13, 1876.
WADSWORTH, JULIUS	1852	1855	Died May 28, 1887.
WARDWELL, JEREMIAH M.	1847	1851	Died December 20, 1881.
WEEKS, RUFUS W.	1891	1892	Resigned: living in 1895.
WELCH, ARCHIBALD H.	1882	....	Active in 1895.
WELLS, DAVID A.	1894	....	Active in 1895.
WETMORE, PROSPER M.	1845	1847	Died March 18, 1876.
WHITE, LOOMIS L.	1875	1892	Resigned: living in 1895.
WHITNEY, WILLIAM C.	1892	1893	Resigned: living in 1895.
WHITTEMORE, EDWARD A.	1877	1881	Died April 15, 1881.
WILLIAMS, JOHN E.	1858	1868	Died September, 1877.
WOODHULL, ALBERT	1846	1847	Died August 31, 1860.
WRIGHT, CHARLES, M. D.	1877	1883	Died September 2, 1883.

ERRATA.—Page 394. Mr. John N. Stearns, formerly a Trustee of the Company, is not dead. The error arose from the announcement of the death of another well-known gentleman bearing the same name.

[*From "Fisher's National Magazine," June, 1845.*]

THE CURRENCY OF THE UNITED STATES.

By James De Peyster Ogden.

[Note.—This article is printed as an interesting reminiscence of the first President of the Company, and as an illustration of the fact that important questions still remain unsettled that were agitating the public mind fifty years ago. Undreamed of progress has been made in many things, but the currency and tariff questions are still with us. It will be noted that Mr. Ogden's plan of a national currency based on United States bonds was practically that of the present time, without the currency issued directly by the Government, which is considered by many to be at the bottom of our present currency troubles. The number of State banks in 1845 was 707, with a total circulation of $89,608,711. The circulation under State banks reached its highest point in 1857, when it was $214,778,822; then came the great financial crash, and the next year it dropped to $155,208,344.]

A stable currency is an essential element in the prosperity of a country. As a medium of exchange it becomes the representative of all property, and is, therefore, called not only the representative, but the measure as well as the standard of value. When defining the terms "money" and "currency," it is sometimes contended that money can only consist of coined gold and silver, and is not currency; while currency is said to be a contract to pay money; that not being the product of labor, it has no intrinsic value, being merely a representative of value—and both money and currency are alike deemed articles of commerce. These, however, can hardly be called definitions, nor, indeed, are they strictly correct as such. Some nations have nothing but gold and silver as a general medium of exchange. Do not the precious metals then constitute their currency? Bank notes can hardly be called an article of commerce, but gold and silver coin will pay a debt or purchase commodities in any civilized country. Again, it is quite true that bank notes are only a representative of value. Still, a value has been given for them, and value can again be obtained for them, and if they will purchase as much of any commodity as the amount of specie they represent would purchase, they answer the end for which they were designed, and constitute a currency, which in the ordinary acceptation of the term is called money.

The United States have always had a paper currency, issued by banks chartered by the National or State Governments. An ordinance of Congress, during the war of the Revolution, established the Bank of North America in 1781, and after the adoption of the Constitution, the first United States Bank was chartered in February, 1791, and expired in 1811. The second, chartered in 1816, ceased to be the fiscal agent of Government in 1833, and its charter expired in 1836.

Gold and silver alone, however, are a legal tender, and, accordingly, so far as laws can accomplish the object, our paper currency has always been redeemable in specie. There have been, nevertheless, three periods of suspension of specie payments by our banks: two partial, and one general. During the last war the banks throughout the Union, excepting in New England, suspended their payments. During the commercial and financial crisis of 1837 the suspension was general, but the banks in New York resumed payment in 1838; and in 1839, when the large State Bank of Pennsylvania, which had assumed the name of United States Bank, failed for the second time, and the banks South and West accompanied its fall, the banks in New York did not follow its example. All these departures from the specie standard of value took place when no United States Bank was in operation. During nearly forty years of our existence as a nation we had a National Bank acting as the fiscal agent of Government, exercising a controlling influence over the general currency of the country, and maintaining, at all times, the specie standard of value. The friends of such an institution have now no hope of its restoration, its opponents entertain no fear of its finding successful advocates, at the same time it is well to bear in mind that both the great political parties of the country have been at times alike the advocates and opponents of a National Bank. The first bank was passed during the administration of Washington, and was opposed by Mr. Jefferson, and the party of which he was the head. But when in power himself, Mr. Jefferson quietly acquiesced in the opinion that the institution was convenient and useful, and by approving certain laws establishing branches, etc., he even seemed to think that a bank might not be unconstitutional. Still his party refused to renew the charter in 1811. But in 1816 the same party, under Mr. Madison's administration, brought forward and carried the bill establishing the second National Bank, against the opposition of the party that had created the first establishment. We thus find that the political founders of the first bank opposed the establishment of the second, while the opponents of the first became the creators of the last. The late bank was indebted for its fall more to its friends than its foes. It is not impossible that the next institution may owe its existence to those who at present claim to be its enemies, or at least its opponents; opinions may alter, and policy or necessity may produce the change. We have now been ten years without a National Bank or a National Currency.

The first experiment intended to furnish the better currency, was the State bank system, when the various institutions of the respective States became the creators and conservatives of the general currency. During its rapid course the greatest portion of the stock of those States that are now unable to pay their interest, was created, and prices of all commodities, and of everything that represented value, partook of the spirit of the wide-spread inflation.

The better currency, as it was promised to be, was admitted by its authors to have proved a disastrous failure, long after the people, who had suffered from its operation, had come to the same conclusion. An attempt at a still better currency, therefore, became necessary; and as one extreme is sure to beget another, the specie Sub-Treasury system became the next experiment. The idea, however, of making specie alone the currency of the Union, was found to be somewhat too Spartan to find favor with the country, and accordingly the plan was never carried out in the spirit in which it was conceived, for checks and certificates of deposit and bank notes, continued to be employed in its operation, until, having been condemned by the people in 1840, the Act was repealed in 1841. The next and last experiment proposed, was the Exchequer of Mr. Tyler's Cabinet; but the leading feature of Executive control, which gave it the character of a Government Bank of the worst description, destroyed its chance of success with Congress, and the Exchequer hardly found friends enough to usher it into notice. Since the crisis of 1837, more than three hundred millions of State, bank and other stocks, have been stricken out of existence; and now, under altered circumstances, indeed, but with lessened capital, diminished resources, with but the shadow of our former credit abroad, and a want of confidence at home, we are — as we were, when the national deposits were intrusted in 1833 to the State banks — without a system of currency. In almost every State of the Union the banking capital has been seriously impaired; very few, if any, of our Western or South-Western States can be said to have any currency at all. New England being essentially a manufacturing people, has escaped with less loss, and maintained the standard of her currency with less difficulty than any other portion of the Union. New York, however, maintained the integrity of her position, during the trying period of 1839, with equal credit and success, and has since well preserved the character of her currency. The want of a sound and uniform and sufficient currency for the whole country was never greater than at present; but every State is left to its own resources to accomplish, in the best way it can, what we have always been led to consider an object of national concern.

A few of the States have become enamoured of the free banking plan, as it is termed, of our State, requiring bank issues to be based on special security. The security was allowed at first to consist of real estate and all State stocks. It is now confined to stock of our own State, and of the United States. The plan, however, is but another expedient, that may have a conservative tendency for a time, but it is likely to prove fruitful of error hereafter, for, like all expedients of this nature, it is certain to change with circumstances.

During a period of restriction and want of confidence, as at present, the system tends to contract the available means of the banks, by withdrawing so much of their capital. In times of confident speculation and advancing prices, a temptation would be held out to the States to create stocks on which their own banks could issue notes, and they might thus supply the necessities of the States and uphold the general spirit of speculation.

Without concert of action or unity of design, without power to create an union of strength or the means of forming any efficient co-operation, strong in one section of the Union and weak in the other, as unable to afford relief, as unwilling to share responsibility, without the power to regulate the inland or to control the foreign exchanges of the country,—the various local institutions of the different States now constitute the only source of power, not only to furnish a circulating medium, and a representative of value, but to resuscitate and preserve the currency and credit system of our extended republic. We cannot so far forget the maxims of prudence or the lessons of experience, as to suppose that a stable currency can be formed out of such materials as these, nor can we consent to surrender our previous convictions and subscribe to that change of opinion, in reference to the system, hitherto so successful, as to admit the necessity of the "odor of nationality" to-day, and describe it as an "obsolete idea" to-morrow. We believe, on the contrary, with Mr. Madison, who, in 1816, in his message to Congress, said: "But for the interests of the community at large, as well as for the purposes of the Treasury, it is essential that the nation should possess a currency of equal value, credit, and use, wherever it may circulate. The Constitution has intrusted Congress exclusively with the power of creating and regulating a currency of that description."

In the absence, however, of any effort or any intention to change the present system, our attention should be directed to such measures as are likely to accomplish the important objects of affording aid to our credit system, and maintaining the value of our currency.

The system of protection to domestic industry against the efforts of foreign rivalry, whereby to prevent excessive importations, and avoid to any injurious extent an export of specie, arising from an unfavorable state of trade, is among the most effectual means to maintain the stability of the currency. And, on the other hand, an efficient aid from the general Government, in support of State credit, would not only completely restore our national credit, but immediately add a large amount of active and convertible capital to the productive means of the country.

The establishment of manufactures in a country possessing the natural advantages essential to success, tends directly to stimulate industry of the most useful as well as the most productive kind. Science is encouraged to lend its aid to the arts; improvements in machinery tend to abridge labor, and reduce the cost of production. The inventive genius of the country becomes stimulated and rewarded, and we thus facilitate the progress and accelerate the accumulation of wealth. Trade being an exchange of commodities or, as it is usually termed, of equivalents, it is plain that the nation whose labor is so directed as to produce the greatest value exchanges with others to the greatest advantage, and accordingly the country which gives its raw materials in exchange for manufactures labors to a disadvantage; the power of machinery and the complicated works of art being arrayed against the labor of man and the simple operations of nature. The encouragement of manufactures in the United States, by means of protective duties, renders us independent of foreign nations for those supplies required for the consumption of the great bulk of the people, and in this way, aided by the facilities of international communication, each one supplies the other on the cheapest terms, with the various products of their respective industry and skill.

As a general rule, applied to products of general consumption, home competition, when stimulated and encouraged by protection, is certain, in its turn, to protect the consumer against permanent high prices. The agriculturist therefore purchases his goods at little or no greater cost than if they had been made by the poorly fed and cheaply paid labor of Europe; while he sells his surplus produce higher in consequence of the home demand, which but for the employment of manufacturing industry would not have existed, at the same time he finds a steady and a certain market.

Our grain finds no sale in Europe.* Occasional scarcity furnishes only an incidental demand, and should England open her ports to-morrow to the admission of bread-stuffs, at a moderate duty, the Baltic and Black Seas could supply her wants cheaper than we could. It is plain, therefore, that if the agriculturist finds no purchasers abroad he must depend upon the home market for the sale of his produce, and it is equally evident that he can only find purchasers among those who are consumers and not producers, and they can find the means of purchasing what he raises only as manufacturers; and accordingly it follows that, were it not for the home market the agriculturist would be unable to obtain his required supplies of manufactured articles.

The planter of cotton, however, insists that he is injured by a protective tariff. For, as Great Britain requires his cotton, he could obtain directly, in return, her cheap manufactures, were it not for the protection afforded to home industry.

But he forgets that our tariff secures for him another purchaser, while it opens another and a nearer market for his cotton, that increased means beget increased con-

---

*The Walker tariff bill was passed in July, 1846, and went into effect the following December. The British tariff, enacted in March, 1845, removed the duties from cotton and lumber, and the repeal of the "corn laws" in June, 1846, reduced the duty on grain and provided for its entire removal at the end of three years. Schouler says of the Walker tariff: "Great Britain gained no advantage under it for which a full equivalent was not given in return. * * * Hitherto American wheat and grain had been excluded from the ports of every nation in Europe; and of flour, England, in 1844, imported more than twice as much from her American colonies as from the United States."—*Vol. iv., pp. 516–517.*

sumption, while competition ensures a moderate price for the supplies he requires of the manufactured article. If no cotton was manufactured in the United States, there would be an increased supply sent to Great Britain, equal to between one-third and one-fourth of her consumption of American cotton. This additional supply would necessarily reduce the price, while an increased demand from our increasing population would have no tendency to reduce the price of her manufactures in a market of which she would then have entire control. If we estimate the present value of cotton consumed in the United States at twelve millions of dollars, the manufactured product is between three and four times that sum. Here, then, are between two and three additional values beyond the cost of the cotton, retained at home as wages of labor, and interest or profits on capital. And, in order to advance the interests of the industry thus rewarded, and of the capital thus employed, railroads and canals are constructed with a view to extend the markets for the manufactured products, and reduce the cost of transportation on the bulky articles of agricultural products, as well as of the raw material required by the manufacturers. By these means, the interest of all classes is promoted, and capital, seeking employment, becomes distributed through all the varied channels of circulation. It is not easy, therefore, to perceive how the cotton planter would be benefited by having Great Britain as the purchaser of the cotton now consumed in the United States, and the sole source of supply for the cotton goods he might require, for not only would all the advantage be on her side, but he himself would be a serious loser, for by encouraging and rewarding home industry, all parts of the Union, whether furnishing producers of cotton or of grain, or manufacturers, and therefore consumers of each, are equally and mutually benefited. The planter has an additional market and an increased number of consumers; the agriculturist is certain of a sale for his produce. Commerce profits by the increased and accumulating means of the country, augmenting both the imports and the exports, and becomes possessed of new and varied products, with which to prosecute her voyages to distant parts of the world. The capitalist becomes confident in his investment, and industry feels sure of its reward; excessive importations are prevented—the duties remain as a security on our hands, and are not exported in specie, as part of the cost of the imported article; an unfavorable balance of trade is thus avoided, and the means of the people are increased, instead of the country becoming impoverished. But a tariff of incidental or accidental protection, which looks to revenue, and nothing else, which may be high to-day and low to-morrow, as chance or necessity may determine; which is fixed and steady neither in principle nor practice; which is governed by no maxims of public policy, and designed to promote no end or object connected with the public good;—would be certain to depress the industry, destroy the confidence, and blight the prosperity of the country.

We allude not to the present tariff, as a model of perfection. It seems to have been matured and prepared without sufficient reflection or the requisite information; many articles are charged unnecessarily high. Railroad iron, cheap as it was in England, when the tariff was imposed, might have been admitted at a moderate duty for a limited period. A warehousing bill should have been engrafted upon the tariff policy, as a system required by the operation of a protective tariff, and essential to the interests of commerce.* But the principle of protection is what we contend for—it is identified

*The warehousing system was established by the Congress which was in session when this article was printed.

with all interests, and with the prosperity of the whole country, and is absolutely required to maintain the stability of the currency. The necessity of restoring the credit of the non-paying States of the Union, on the ground of private interest and public policy, of individual character and national fame, is among the most urgent and pressing of our wants. One hundred and twenty-three millions of State stock, that appears abroad nearly in the light of the public debt of the United States, is either greatly depreciated or almost without value in the money markets of Europe. When any stock of our paying States now becomes due, it is remitted and not reinvested, while such of them as are salable here gradually find their way to this market for "sale and returns."

There was a time when confidence in our State stocks abounded; for when apprehension was entertained for the financial and political state of Europe, the stocks of this country were looked to as a security beyond the reach of accident or disaster. It was then said, There I can invest, and rest secure. There have I placed a portion of my fortune. There have I secured a part of the property of my wife and children, and there, when I shall have left them, they can look with confidence for principal and interest.

These were once the consoling reflections of many of the capitalists and annuitants of England and the Continent. Such was once the proud and enviable opinion entertained of us and of our country. But during 1836 and a part of 1837, that period of inflation, the States issued their stocks to create banks and construct canals and railroads, the interest on which, since the destruction of bank capital and the suspension of the public works, they are unable to pay; and the principal of which, however honest may be their intentions, however sincere their efforts, we fear they will never be able to discharge in full; for, after the long delay that has occurred, the unaided resources of those States, with the continual increase of debt caused by the accumulation of arrears of interest, will hardly be sufficient to discharge their heavy indebtedness.

Are the States, then, without resources? Is there no common fund from which they could obtain relief? Has the general Government no power or right to apply that fund, or anticipate, by its own credit, the necessary means to pay the interest and secure the principal? It is quite true that the public lands present an available resource, constituting for the future an inexhaustible revenue. It is also true that we have a Federal Government, required by the Constitution to provide for the general welfare. But it is deemed improper to pledge the public lands, although they belong to the States; it is deemed unconstitutional to aid the States, because the Constitution has nowhere, in express terms, authorized the Federal Government to do so.

It is true that just after the adoption of that instrument, the debts of the States were assumed by the general Government. As these debts, however, were incurred for the common defence, during the war of the Revolution, the claim of the States may have been stronger; but the right on the part of the Government under the Constitution is still the same. Then, however, the debts were actually assumed and paid — now the Government is only asked to retain, in its own hands, the security belonging to the States, to exchange its own obligation for that of the States, and pay itself, should the States still prove unable or unwilling to comply with their engagements. If an Act were passed authorizing the issue of three per cent. stock of the United States, by commissioners appointed for the purpose, in exchange for the stock of any State that should appoint commissioners to receive the proceeds of their public works, and of a moderate but certain tax, to be appropriated to the payment of the interest of the debts, pledging also to the general Government their quota of the sales of the public lands, national and State legislation would unite for the public good. The national credit would be granted until the resources of the States should render it unnecessary. The public creditor would be satisfied, the faith of the States would be redeemed, and the credit of the Union restored.

The plan is simple, the means would be effectual, and the result would prove an incalculable blessing, while the existence of the national debt thus created would be known and felt only by the benefits it conferred. Yet no politician is bold enough to bring forward the measure, no senator moves in its favor, no party espouses the cause of the country.

A public writer in France has said: "America could easily replenish the public coffers and pay her debts by submitting to moderate taxation. There are not in her public councils men of sufficient moral courage and patriotic spirit to brave the unpopularity of the true measures, and teach the Democracy its true interests. Therefore is the United States in a condition unworthy a free people."

Yet there are statesmen among us who contend that we require no other system of currency than the one we now possess; that a protective policy is unnecessary; that the indebted States require no aid from the general Government, and if they did, that it would be unconstitutional to grant it. In the meantime it is to be feared that the debts of Texas, with its uncounted and uncertain millions, will be paid out of the public treasury or recognized as a public debt, before that of Illinois or Maryland, part and parcel of ourselves, shall be provided for or cared for, although they have the means, by a pledge of their portion of the public domain, to provide ample security for the final payment of their debts.*

The sentiment of love towards our country, and of pride in her institutions, has its origin in the best feelings of our nature. But it requires to be strengthened by experience, and sanctioned by our understanding. Our early affections, sustained by the consciousness of the diffusion of the benefits and advantages conferred by equal laws and liberal institutions, strike their roots broad and deep, as we become convinced that all feel the influence and share in the blessings of a well-administered Government. An enlightened constituency, whose dearest rights and interests are at stake, are entitled to expect not only good intentions, but a reasonable share of intelligence also, on the part of their representatives in the national councils. But where is our hope, when we find that the prostration of State credit is treated with indifference? That no effort is made to redeem our character, while our name is becoming a by-word and reproach among the nations of the earth? Is there no fear that at last, as a people's confidence is shaken, their attachment may become weakened, when they find that no measure is proposed, none likely to be adopted, to retrieve the sinking honor of the States? Must we become still more and more convinced, by sad and dear bought experience, that this cruel neglect, this willful indifference, has not only prostrated the credit of the nation, and injured the character of the people, but that it must tend inevitably to tarnish the fame and undermine the foundations upon which are to rest the future happiness and prosperity of our country.

---

* Texas was finally paid $10,000,000 to relinquish her claims to territory beyond her present boundaries.

www.ingramcontent.com/pod-product-compliance
Lightning Source LLC
LaVergne TN
LVHW020552110826
845149LV00002B/247